Lecture Notes in Computer Science

T0242861

Lecture Notes in Computer Science

Lecture Notes in Computer Science

Edited by G. Goos and J. Hartmanis

24

Parallel Processing

Proceedings of the Sagamore
Computer Conference, August 20–23, 1974

Edited by Tse-yun Feng

Springer-Verlag
Berlin · Heidelberg · New York 1975

Dr. Tse-yun Feng
Syracuse University
Department of Electrical
and Computer Engineering
Link Hall
Syracuse, NY 13210/USA

Library of Congress Cataloging in Publication Data

Sagamore Computer Conference, 3d, Raquette Lake, N. Y.,
   1974.
   Parallel processing.

   (Lecture notes in computer science ; 24)
   Bibliography: p.
   Includes index.
   1. Parallel processing (Electronic computers)--Con-
gresses. I. Feng, Tse-yun, 1928-   ed. II. Title.
III. Series.
QA76.6.S23 1974   001.6'4   74-34429

AMS Subject Classifications (1970): 00 A10
CR Subject Classifications (1974): 2.2

ISBN 3-540-07135-0 Springer-Verlag Berlin · Heidelberg · New York
ISBN 0-387-07135-0 Springer-Verlag New York · Heidelberg · Berlin

Offsetdruck: Julius Beltz, Hemsbach/Bergstr.

PREFACE

The Sagamore Computer Conference has been held annually for the past three years at the former Vanderbilt summer estate, a 1300-acre preserve surrounding the private Sagamore Lake, in the Central Adirondack Mountains. The first Sagamore Computer Conference was held on August 23 - 25, 1972. The subject of that conference was on "RADCAP (Rome Air Development Center Associative Processor) and Its Applications". About 90 invited participants attended the 2-day conference to hear the 17 technical papers presented. The Conference Proceedings were published and distributed by RADC and Syracuse University, co-sponsors of the Conference. In 1973, the Conference broadened its scope to "Parallel Processing" and issued the Call-for-Papers announcement. Among the submitted papers, 34 were accepted and presented on August 22 - 24, 1973. The 1973 Conference was sponsored by Syracuse University in cooperation with IEEE and ACM. Copies of its Proceedings (IEEE Catalog Number 73 CHO812-8 C) may be available from any one of these institutions.

This year's conference was extended to three days (August 20 - 23, 1974) to provide the participants with more time for individual activities. One new feature added to the conference was the Keynote Address by Col. William Whitaker of the Office of Director of Defense Research and Engineering. We thank Col. Whitaker for his informative remarks. A panel session was organized this year to review the state-of-the-art in parallel processing. We would also like to thank our distinguished panelists: Drs. J. B. Dennis, Robert Downs, David Kuck, Richard Merwin, C. V. Ramamoorthy, and S. S. Yau, for sharing their experience and knowledge with us.

We appreciate the efforts of the authors who submitted papers for consideration. A special acknowledgement is due to the reviewers who evaluated the papers with exceptional attention and punctuality. The success of the Conference is also attributable to the generous assistance we received from the session chairpersons and session organizers. Finally, we would also like to express our appreciation to Diane Sims, Anne Woods, Hazel Laidlaw, Louise Naylor, and Gladys Stith for their administrative assistance and typing help.

The next Sagamore Computer Conference on Parallel Processing is to be held on August 19 - 22, 1975.

Tse-yun Feng
Department of Electrical & Computer Engineering
Syracuse University

TABLE OF CONTENTS

ON A CLASS OF SCHEDULING ALGORITHMS
FOR MULTIPROCESSORS COMPUTING SYSTEMS[a]

N. F. CHEN
Department of Mathematics
C. L. LIU
Department of Computer Science
University of Illinois
Urbana, Illinois 61801

Abstract -- In this paper we study a class of scheduling algorithms for multi-processors computing systems which we call level algorithms. These algorithms are simple and easy to implement. They produce optimal schedules in some cases, and produce close-to-optimal schedules in other cases. Sufficient conditions under which schedules produced by the level algorithms will be optimal are obtained. For the sub-optimal schedules, we are able to compare quantitatively their performance against that of an optimal schedule.

INTRODUCTION

Recent progress in hardware technology and computer architecture has led to the design and construction of computer systems that contain a large number of processors. Because of their capability of executing several tasks simultaneously, the problem of job scheduling in multiprocessor computing systems is of both theoretical and practical interest. Since, for a finite set of tasks, there is only a finite number of possible schedules, the problem of determining a best schedule could in principle be solved by an exhaustive examination of all the possibilities. However, such an exhaustive search will require considerable computation time and will offset the advantage gained by using an optimal schedule. As was proposed by J. Edmonds [2], a scheduling algorithm is considered to be efficient if the number of steps in the algorithm is a polynomial function of the number of tasks to be scheduled. Several authors have designed efficient algorithms to produce schedules which mini-mize the total execution time and thus achieve optimal utilization of the processors [1], [3], [5]. Unfortunately, these algorithms are only applicable to some special cases. As a matter of fact, efficient algorithms that produce optimal schedules are known only for the following cases:

(i) All jobs have equal execution time and the partial ordering over the jobs is such that either every job has at most one successor or every job has at most one predecessor[5].

(ii) All jobs have equal execution time and there are only 2 processors in the computing systems [1], [3].

---

[a] Research supported by NSF GJ-41538.

In view of the difficulty, simple algorithms that produce only sub-optimal schedules are often used in practice. Such a choice becomes even more appealing when the performance, in terms of the <u>total execution time</u>, of these algorithms can be compared quantitatively with that of algorithms producing optimal schedules. Indeed, to study the performance of a class of simple algorithms is the theme of this paper.

DESCRIPTION OF THE SYSTEM

We consider the problem of scheduling a set of jobs on a multiprocessor computing system that has a set of identical processors capable of independent operation on independent jobs. Let $P_1, P_2, \ldots, P_n$ denote the n identical processors in a multi-processor computing system. Let $P = \{J_1, J_2, \ldots, J_r\}$ denote a set of jobs to be executed on the computing system. We assume that the execution of a job occupies one and only one processor. Moreover, since the processors are identical, a job can be executed on any one of the processors. Let $\mu(J_i)$ denote the <u>execution time</u> of task J_i, that is, the amount of time it takes to execute J_i on a processor. There is also a partial ordering < specified over P. It is required that if $J_i < J_j$ then the execution of job J_j cannot begin until the execution of J_i has been completed. (J_i is said to be a <u>predecessor</u> of J_j, and J_j is said to be a <u>successor</u> of J_i. J_j is an immediate successor of J_i if there is no J_k such that $J_i < J_k < J_j$.) Formally, a set of tasks is specified by an ordered triple $(P, \mu, <)$ where μ is a function from P to the reals. A set of jobs can be described by a directed graph such as that in Fig. 2(a). There is a directed arc from the vertex (job) J_i to the vertex (job) J_j if and only if J_j is an immediate successor of J_i.

By <u>scheduling</u> a set of jobs on a multiprocessor computing system we mean to specify for each job J_i the time interval within which it is to be executed and the processor P_k on which execution will take place.[b] (Without loss of generality, we assume that execution of the set begins at t = 0). An explicit way to describe a schedule is a <u>timing diagram</u>, which is also known as the <u>Gantt chart</u>. As an example, the timing diagram of a schedule for the execution of the set of jobs in Fig. 2(a) on a two-processor computing system is shown in Fig. 2(b). In a given schedule, an <u>idle period</u> of a processor is defined to be a time interval within which the processor is not executing a job (while at least one other processor is executing some job). In a schedule, a processor might be left idle for a period of time either because there is no executable job within that time period or because it is an intentional choice. (A job is said to be <u>ready</u> at a certain time instant if the execution of its predecessors have all been completed at that time.) Clearly, it is never necessary nor beneficial in a schedule to leave all processors idle at the same time.

---

[b]Throughout our discussion in this section, we assume that once the execution of a job begins on a processor, it will continue until completion without any interruption.

The total execution time of a schedule is the total time it takes to execute all the jobs according to the schedule. We shall use completion time as the criterion for computing different schedules.

Throughout this paper, the following assumptions are made:

(i)   All jobs have equal execution time, say, unit time.

(ii) All schedules are non-preemptive, meaning that once the execution of a task begins on a processor it will continue until completion.

With these two assumptions it can be easily seen that an optimal schedule can always be found among schedules with no intentional idle periods. That is, a processor is left idle for a certain period of time if and only if no job is ready within that period. Thus we need only be concerned with such schedules. In this case, a scheduling algorithm can be specified by merely giving the rules on how jobs are to be chosen for execution at any instant when one or more processor is free. (Of course, the choice is only among jobs that are executable at that instant.) A simple way to spell out the rule is to assign priorities to the jobs so that jobs with higher priorities will be executed instead of jobs with lower priorities when they are competing for processors. (If two or more processors are available, pick the one with smallest index.) Consequently, we call such algorithms priority-driven scheduling algorithms. The usual practice is to list the jobs in descending order of their priorities from left to right. Such a list is called a priority list. Whenever a processor is free, the priority list is searched from left to right and the first ready job encountered will be executed.

LEVEL AND LEVEL ALGORITHMS

For a given set of jobs and a partial ordering over them, we define the level of a job as follows.

(i)   The level of a job that has no successor is equal to 1.

(ii) The level of a job that has one or more successors is equal to one plus the maximal value of the levels of the successors of the job.

We study in this paper a class of algorithms which we shall call level algorithms. They are priority-driven scheduling algorithms in which a job of a higher level will be assigned higher priority than a job of a lower level. A level schedule is one produced by a level algorithm. Level algorithms are interesting because

(i)   they are simple,

and

(ii) Hu's algorithm [5] and Coffman and Graham's algorithm [1] are both level algorithms.

THE SIMPLE LEVEL ALGORITHMS

We define a __simple level algorithm__ (SLA) as a level algorithm in which the assignment of priorities of jobs within the same level is completely arbitrary. For a given set of jobs, we shall use __h__ to denote the value of the __highest level__ and use N_i, i = 1,...,h to denote the number of jobs at level i. Two jobs are __independent__ if there is no precedence relation between them.

__Theorem 1:__ For an n-processors system, if the partial ordering over the jobs satisfies the condition that the number of independent jobs in the union of the sets of immediate successors of any n jobs is at most n. Then the SLA produces an optimal schedule.

__Remark:__ Theorem 1 is a generalization of Hu's theorem [5]. In his theorem the partial ordering is assumed to be a tree or forest and those partial orderings clearly satisfy the hypothesis of Theorem 1.

Figure 1(a) represents a partial ordering which is not a tree but satisfies the hypothesis of Theorem 1 in the case of 2-processors.

Figure 1(a)

We shall establish 3 lemmas which are needed in the proof of Theorem 1.

__Lemma 1(a):__ Let (P,<) be a set of jobs with unit execution time. A necessary condition for completing the execution of the jobs in time t, where t is an integer, is

$$N_h + N_{h-1} + \ldots + N_i \leq n(t-i+1) \tag{1-1}$$

for i = h, h - 1, ..., 1, where n is the number of processors in the computing system.

__Proof:__ If we are to complete the execution of all jobs at time t, we must complete the execution of all the jobs at levels h, h-1, ..., i by t-i+1. Because if this is not the case, there will be a chain of i jobs to be executed in the remaining i-1 time units, which is an impossibility. Since the computing system can execute at most n(t-i+1) jobs in t-i+1 units of time, the inequalities in (1-1) follow immediately. □

For an arbitrary set of jobs P, there certainly exists a t which satisfies (1-1). Let __t(P)__ be the smallest of all such t's which satisfy (1-1).

The following lemma is trivial.

Lemma 1(b): Under the hypothesis of Theorem 1, m jobs, with $m \leq n$, have at most n independent jobs in the union of their sets of immediate successors.

Lemma 1(c): Under the hypothesis of Theorem 1, if m jobs, with $m \leq n$, $A_1, \ldots, A_m$ have n independent jobs $B_1, \ldots, B_n$ in the union of their sets of immediate successors, then an immediate successor S of any A_i, $i = 1, \ldots, m$, is either (1) some B_j or (2) a successor of some B_j or (3) a predecessor of some B_j, $j = 1, \ldots, n$. Furthermore, if $\{A_1, \ldots, A_m\}$ are executed at time u and $\{B_1, \ldots, B_n\}$ are executed at time u+1 in a certain schedule, then a successor of any A_i, $i = 1, \ldots, m$, is either some B_j or a successor of some B_j, $j = 1, \ldots, n$.

Proof: If S is some B_j, we are done. If $S \notin \{B_1, \ldots, B_n\}$, then $\{B_1, \ldots, B_n, S\}$ is not an independent set by hypothesis of Theorem 1. Hence S either succeeds some B_j or precedes some B_j.

If T is a successor of an A_i, then T is either an immediate successor or the successor of an immediate successor of some A_i. By the argument in the last paragraph T is either some B_j or a successor of some B_j. The added time condition excludes the possibility that T is a predecessor of some B_j. □

Proof of Theorem 1: We shall use the terminologies of Lemma 1(a). Let $t = t(P)$ in (1-1) where P is the set of jobs to be executed which satisfies the hypothesis of the theorem. We shall explicitly construct a schedule that executes all the jobs in time t, and this schedule is the same as the one given by the SLA. Let

$$L = (J_1 J_2 J_3 J_4 \ldots)$$

be the priority list given by SLA. By definition the first N_h jobs are of level h followed by N_{h-1} jobs of level (h-1) and so on.

Suppose we have t columns of boxes indexed from 1 to t and each column contains n boxes indexed from 1 to n. Suppose we regard the jobs as physical objects and we are going to distribute the jobs among the boxes assigning one job to one box according to the following procedure.

(1) Initialize $k = 1$.

(2) Assign J_k to the column with the smallest index which can <u>accommodate</u> J_k (A column can accommodate a job J if that column at that moment contains less than n jobs and all predecessors of J are in columns with smaller index than that of the column) and to the box with the smallest index which is not yet filled.

(3) Increment k, $k = k+1$.

(4) If $k < |P|$, GO TO (2).

(5) STOP.

Thus the jobs are assigned in order of their priorities.

(*)   We <u>claim</u> that after step (2) is executed on J_{k_i} where J_{k_i} is the lowest
priority job of level i, all jobs which have been assigned at this point are in
columns with indices smaller than or equal to (t-i+1), i = h, h-1, ..., 1.

(**)   For i = h, the claim is true by virtue of the inequalities (1-1). Assume it
is true for all i, h $\geq$ i > j. Suppose, for contradiction, that in the process of
assigning jobs of level j we encounter for the first time that a certain job J of
level j cannot be assigned to a column with index smaller than or equal to (t-j+1).
Two possibilities arise. Either each column with index smaller than or equal to
(t-j+1) already contains n jobs or there are some columns in that range which contain
less than n jobs but cannot accommodate J because of some precedence relations. In
view of the inequalities (1-1) only the second possibility could arise. By induction
assumptions jobs of level j+1 or higher are in columns 1 to (t-(j+1)+1) and so column
(t-j+1) is filled with jobs of level j. Let r(< t-j+1) be the largest among indices
of columns preceding column (t-j+1) which are not filled at the time of assigning J.
That is to say all columns succeeding column r up to column (t-j+1) are filled at
this time.

(***)   We assert that each column, s, r < s $\leq$ t-j+1, is a set of independent jobs in
the union of the sets of immediate successors of the jobs in the immediately preceding column. This assertion is clearly true of the column r+1. For, each job in
column r+1 is necessarily a successor of some job in column r (and hence an immediate
successor) otherwise it should have been assigned to column r in Step (2). Assume
the assertion is true up to column s. Let J' be any job in column s+1. Since every
job in columns ranging from r+1 to s is a successor of some job in column r by induction assumption of the assertion, J', too, must be a successor of some job in
column r. Otherwise J' is not a successor of any job in columns from r to s and so
should have been assigned to column r in Step (2). By Lemma 1(c) J' is a successor
of some job in column r+1. Applying Lemma 1(c) repeatedly we arrive at that J' is a
successor of some job in column s and hence an immediate successor. Thus the assertion of paragraph (***) is proved.

Since J cannot be assigned to column r so J is a successor of some job in
columns r to (t-j+1) and hence a successor of some job in column r in any case.
Applying Lemma 1(c) repeatedly, we arrive at that J is a successor of some job in
column (t-k+1). But column (t-j+1) consists of jobs of level j and J is also of
level j and hence must be independent. This contradiction completes the induction
of paragraph (**) and proves the claim in paragraph (*).

Consequently, all jobs are assigned to boxes in columns from 1 to t = t(P).
Corresponding to this assignment is the following job schedule. A job in box i of
column j will be executed on the ith processor at time unit j. It is easily seen
that the above schedule is the same as the priority-driven schedule given by the
priority list L which is produced by SLA.

Since the above schedule completes the execution of all the jobs in time
$t = t(P)$ it is an optimal schedule by Lemma 1(a)   □

Theorem 2: For a 2-processors system,

$$\frac{\omega_{SLA}}{\omega_0} \leq \frac{4}{3}$$

where ω_{SLA} is the total execution time using the schedule produced by a SLA, and ω_0
is the total execution time using an optimal schedule. Furthermore, this bound is
best possible.

The new terms introduced below will be used in the proof of Theorem 2. Another
level algorithm related to SLA will be defined. This algorithm is non-priority-
driven and is defined for a 2-processors system only. We shall denote it by (SLA2)*
and it serves as a vehicle in the proof of Theorem 2.

A job J in (P,<) is a singleton if J is in a level which has only one job,
namely, J. The corresponding level is called a singleton level. It is clear that a
singleton is preceded by all jobs of higher levels. I is compatible with J if I
neither preceded nor succeeds J. I is a companion of J in a schedule if I and J are
executed at the same time on two different processors.

An SLA is defined by giving a priority list $L = (J_1 J_2 J_3 \ldots)$. We shall use L to
define (SLA2)* by the chart in Fig. 2.

(SLA2)* can be described informally as follows: if the system finishes executing a level which is not a singleton-level with Processor 1 executing the last job
of that level then Processor 2 is to be left idle. If that level is a singleton
level then Processor 2 will be looking for a job to execute.

8

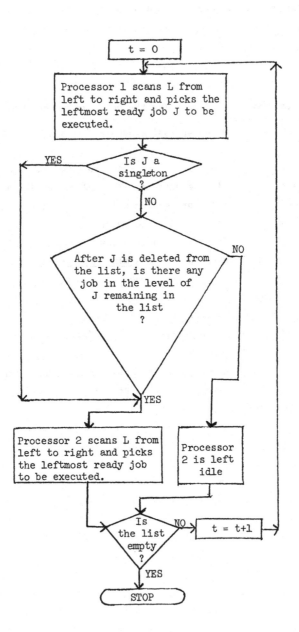

Figure 2

In Fig. 2(a) J_7 and J_{10} are singletons. Level 4 and level 2 are singleton-levels. J_1 and J_6 are compatible. Fig. 2(b) is the schedule produced by (SLA2)* with respect to the list $L = (J_1 J_2 J_3 J_4 J_5 J_6 J_7 J_8 J_9 J_{10} J_{11} J_{12} J_{13})$. J_7 and J_{13} are companions in this schedule. Fig. 2(c) is an optimal schedule for that partial ordering.

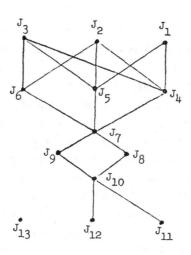

Figure 2(a)

Figure 2(b)

Figure 2(c)

Given a set of job $(P, \prec)$ let ω_{SLA}, $\omega_{(SLA2)*}$, ω_0 be the total execution times using schedules produced by SLA, $(SLA2)*$ and an optimal schedule respectively. The schedule of $(SLA2)*$ is denoted by SCH* and an optimal schedule is abbreciated as OPSCH.

Lemma 2(a):

$$\omega_{SLA} \leq \omega_{(SLA2)*}$$

Proof: Given the set of jobs $(P, <)$ suppose SLA produces the priority list $L = (J_1 J_2 J_3 \ldots)$. Let L' be a sublist of L satisfying (1) Jobs in L' from a subset of the jobs in L. (2) J_k is on the left of J_ℓ in L' if J_k is on the left of J_ℓ in L. (3) If J_k is in L but not in L' then all predecessors of J_k in P are not in L'. (4) L' contains at least a job of each level of $(P, <)$. We claim that the total time executing L' using SLA is less than the total time executing L using $(SLA2)*$. We shall prove this claim by induction on $|P|$ which equals the length of L.

Suppose the top level of P is not a singleton. $(SLA2)*$ takes (say) t time units to complete the top level. According to the definition of $(SLA2)*$, in this t time units $(SLA2)*$ executes no jobs of any lower level. Suppose SLA takes s time units to execute those top level jobs of P which are in L', then $s \leq t$ since $L' \subseteq L$. SLA may or may not have executed another job of a lower level in these s time units. In any case what remains of L' after s time units is a sublist, which satisfies those four conditions, of what remains of L after t time units. By induction on the new length of the latter list the lemma is proved.

Suppose the top level of P is a singleton J_1. Then J_1 is the only top level job in L'. After $(SLA2)*$ assigns J_1 to be executed on Processor 1, the remaining list of L is scanned from left to right to pick the leftmost ready job J_i (if there is any) to be executed on Processor 2. In the case of SLA, Processor 1 executes J_1 and Processor 2 scans the remaining list of L' to pick the leftmost ready job J_k (if there is any). If J_k exists then J_i must exist since $L' \subseteq L$ and $(SLA2)*$ could at least pick J_k or some job to left of J_k. For the same reason J_k is <u>not</u> on the left of J_i. If J_k is on the right of J_i then $J_i \notin L'$ otherwise SLA could pick J_i or some job to left of J_i. In any case what remains of L' after the first time unit is a sublist, which satisfies those four conditions, of what remains of L after the first time unit. Induction on the new length of L completes the proof. In the particular case that $L = L'$ we have Lemma 2(a).

<u>Lemma 2(b)</u>

$$\frac{\omega_{(SLA2)*}}{\omega_0} \leq \frac{4}{3}$$

To prove Lemma 2(b), we need Lemma 2(c).

<u>Lemma 2(c)</u>: Suppose P is executed using the schedule of (SLA2)* (i.e. <u>SCH*</u>) and an optimal schedule (<u>OPSCH</u>) respectively. Let $S_1 < S_2 < S_3 < \ldots < S_n$ be the sequence of singletons in P. Let t_i and r_i be the times at which SCH* and OPSCH start to execute S_i respectively. Let $\underline{L_j(t_i)}$ and $\underline{L_j^*(r_i)}$ be the set of jobs remaining in level j at times t_i and r_i in the respective cases. Let $\underline{k_i}$ be the level of S_i, i = 1,...,n.

Then for i = 1,...,n the following are true.

(1) For each i = 1,...,n, the following k_i-1 inequalities hold

$$|L_1(t_i)| \geq |L_1^*(r_i)|$$
$$|L_1(t_i)| + |L_2(t_i)| \geq |L_1^*(r_i)| + |L_2^*(r_i)|$$

$$\cdot \ \ \cdot \ \ \cdot \ \ \cdot \ \ \cdot \ \ \cdot \ \ \cdot \ \ \cdot \ \ \cdot \ \ \cdot$$

$$|L_1(t_i)| + \ldots + |L_{k_i-1}(t_i)| \geq |L_1^*(r_i)| + \ldots + |L_{k_i-1}^*(r_i)|$$

(2) (1) is true with t_i+1 and r_i+1 replacing t_i and r_i respectively.

(3) If S_i has no companion in SCH*, then S_i has no companion in OPSCH.

<u>Proof of Lemma 2(c)</u>: It could be assumed without loss of generality that OPSCH is priority-driven since an optimal schedule can always be found among priority-driven schedules for unit length jobs.

All jobs on levels higher than level k_1 precede S_1. Each level higher than level k_1 is not a singleton level. So in SCH* no jobs of level lower than or equal to level k_1 are executed before t_1. Hence $L_j(t_1) = L_j$ for j = 1,...,k_1 and $L_{k_1} = \{S_1\}$. Therefore $|L_j(t_1)| \geq |L_j^*(r_1)|$ for j = 1,...,k_1. So (1) of the lemma is established for i = 1. When (SLA2)* executes $L_{k_1} = \{S_1\}$ at t_1 some job J_1 of the highest level below k_1 and compatible with S_1 will be chosen as S_1's companion. If J_1 does not exist then all jobs below level k_1 in P are preceded by S_1 and so S_1 has to be executed alone (without companion) in any schedule. Hence (2) and (3) hold for i = 1 in this case. Suppose J_1 exists. If there is no companion for S_1 in OPSCH then J_1 must have already been executed in OPSCH by time r_1. Again (2) and (3) hold for i = 1. If S_1 has J_1' as its companion in OPSCH, then the level of J_1' is lower than or equal to the level of J_1 since (SLA2)* is a level algorithm. Again (2) and (3) hold for i = 1. Thus Lemma 2(c) holds for i = 1.

Assume the lemma is true for all i < m where m $\leq$ n. By induction hypothesis (1) and (2) are true for i = m-1 and since no jobs below or equal to level k_m are done between $t_{m-1}+1$ and t_m in SCH*, (1) is established for i = m.

Suppose S_m has no companion in OPSCH. This means all jobs which are not yet executed in OPSCH at r_m (and they are necessarily of lower level than S_m) are preceded by S_m. Hence $L_u^*(r_m) = L_u^*(r_m+1) = \text{Suc}(S_m) \cap L_u$ where $\text{Suc}(S_m)$ is the set of successors of S_m in P and u = 1,...,k_m-1. Clearly $L_u(t_m+1) \supseteq \text{Suc}(S_m) \cap L_u$ since

S_m precedes every job of Suc $(S_m) \cap L_u$ and these jobs could not have been executed prior to the execution of S_m. Thus (2) and (3) of lemma is true for $i = m$ in this case.

Suppose S_m has a companion I_m in OPSCH. Since (1) of the lemma for $i = m$ has been established, so the system of inequalities.

$$|L_1(t_m)| \geq |L_1^*(r_m)|$$

(*)

$$|L_1(t_m)| + \ldots + |L_{k_m-1}(t_m)| \geq |L_1^*(r_m)| + \ldots + |L_{k_m-1}^*(r_m)|$$

holds. Either S_m has a job J_m as its companion in SCH* whose level is <u>higher than or equal</u> to that of I_m and we are done with (2) and (3) since the system of inequalities (*) holds then with t_m+1 and r_m+1 replacing t_m and r_m respectively <u>or</u> S_m has a job J_m as its companion whose level is <u>lower</u> than that of I_m <u>or</u> S_m has no companion in SCH*. In the last case again as argued before $L_u(t_m) = \text{Suc}(S_m) \cap L_u$ $u = 1, \ldots, k_m-1$ and hence $|L_u^*(r_m)| \geq |\text{Suc}(S_m) \cap L_u| = |L_u(t_m)|$. Let $I_m \, \varepsilon \, L_v$ for some $v \, \varepsilon \{1, \ldots, k_m-1\}$. Then obviously $L_v^*(r_m) \supsetneq L_v(t_m)$ since I_m is not a successor of S_m. Thus some inequalities of (*) are violated. Hence the only case remains to be considered will be that J_m is of lower level than that of I_m. Let I_m be in L_v and J_m be in L_w. Then $k_m-1 \geq v > w$. Now

$$|L_x^*(r_m)| \geq |L_x(t_m)|$$

for $x = k_m-1, \ldots, v+1$. Otherwise, for some x, $|L_x^*(r_m)| < |L_x(t_m)|$, and since $L_x^*(r_m) \supseteq \text{Suc}(S_m) \cap L_x$ so $L_x(t_m) \supsetneq \text{Suc}(S_m) \cap L_x$, and thus J_m could have been found in some L_x, $x > v$, a contradiction. But $|L_v^*(r_m)| > |L_v(t_m)|$ and so by the inequalities in (*) $|L_y^*(r_m)| < |L_y(t_m)|$ for some $y < v$. Let y be the largest such. Certainly $w \geq y$ otherwise J_m could be picked in L_y. Thus $k_m-1 \geq v > w \geq y$. The only change in the terms of the inequalities (*) by replacing t_m by t_m+1 and r_m by r_m+1 are the following:

$$|L_v^*(r_m+1)| \leq |L_v^*(r_m)| - 1 \quad \text{and} \quad |L_w(t_m+1)| = |L_w(t_m)| - 1 .$$

After making these two changes, it can be easily seen that the first $w-1$ inequalities still hold. If the wth inequality does not hold, then $(k_m-1)^{th}$ one (the last one) will not hold since $|L_x^*(r_m+1)| \geq |L_x(t_m+1)|$ for all $k_m-1 \geq x \geq w \geq y$. This is a contradiction since the last inequality in the new system is obtained from (*) by subtracting 1 from both sides. Thus the new system of inequalities holds. Thus (2) and (3) hold for $i = m$. Induction completes.

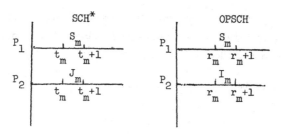

Figure 2(d)

<u>Proof of Lemma 2(b)</u>: In a level schedule we say that t is the <u>start of the execution</u> <u>of a level</u> if Processor 1 in the computing system is, for the first time, executing a job of that level. In Fig. 2(a) and 2(b) (SLA2)* starts to execute level 1 at t = 7 not at t = 4. Dually time t is the <u>end of the execution of a level</u> if all jobs of that level are executed by time t but not prior to t. Figure 2(b) shows (SLA2)* ends executing level 6 at t = 2.

According to the definition of (SLA2)*, SCH* has idle periods only at the end of the execution of a level, <u>and</u> at the start of the execution of that level only an <u>odd</u> number of jobs of that level have not yet been executed.

We now divide idle periods into 3 classes.

First class -- idle periods at the end of a singleton level.

Second class -- idle periods at the end of a level which contains only one un-
                executed job at the start of the execution of that level.

Third class -- idle periods at the end of a level which contains three or more
                unexecuted jobs at the start of the execution of that level.

Let $\phi_1,\ldots,\phi_m$ be the 1st class idle periods in SCH* and let $s_1,\ldots,s_m$ (re-indexing if necessary) be the corresponding singletons. That is to say s_i's do not have companions in SCH*. By lemma 2(b), $s_1,\ldots,s_m$ do not have companion in OPSCH as well. Therefore, $\{s_1,\ldots,s_m\}$ takes m units of time to execute in SCH* as well as in OPSCH. We now turn to compute the time used to execute the jobs in $P-\{s_1,\ldots,s_m\}$.

Let ψ be a second class idle period corresponding to the level which has only one job J at the start of the execution of that level say time t. Since J is not a singleton so there is a job I on the same level of J in the original partial order-ing. I is executed prior to t and must be the companion of some singleton S. Associate ψ with the three jobs J, I, S.

If ψ is a 3rd class idle period then it occurs at the end of the execution of a level with three or more unexecuted jobs at the start of its execution. Associate ψ with these jobs.

So for each idle period ψ of 2nd and 3rd class we can associate ψ with a set S_ψ which has three or more jobs and we further note that $S_{\psi_1} \cap S_{\psi_2} = \phi$ if $\psi_1 \neq \psi_2$.

Let $p = |P|$, $m_1 = p-m$ and n be the total number of 2nd and 3rd class idle periods. SCH* executes $P-\{s_1,\ldots,s_m\}$ in $(m_1+n)/2$ time units. So SCH* executes P in $((m_1+n)/2) + m$ time units. Now

$$(m_1+n)/2 \leq (m_1+m_1/3)/2 = \frac{4}{6}m_1 \qquad \text{and} \qquad \omega_0 \geq (m_1/2) + m.$$

Hence,

$$\frac{\omega_{(SLA)*}}{\omega_0} \leq \frac{\frac{4}{6}m_1+m}{m_1/2+m} \leq \frac{\frac{4}{6}m_1}{\frac{m_1}{2}} = \frac{4}{3} \ . \qquad \square$$

Proof of Theorem 2: By Lemma 2(a) $\omega_{SLA} \leq \omega_{(SLA2)*}$.

Therefore by Lemma 2(b) $\frac{\omega_{SLA}}{\omega_0} \leq \frac{\omega_{(SLA2)*}}{\omega_0} \leq \frac{4}{3}$. The following example (Fig. 2(d) shows

that the bound $\frac{4}{3}$ cannot be improved.

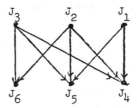

One possible priority list produced by SLA is $L = (J_1 J_2 \ J_3 \ J_4 \ J_5 \ J_6)$. With this list $\omega_{SLA} = 4$. But $L' = (J_3 J_2 J_1 J_4 J_5 J_6)$ gives a schedule which needs 3 time units to complete the jobs and this schedule is clearly optimal. $\qquad \square$

Theorem 3: For a 3-processors system,

$$\frac{\omega_{SLA}}{\omega_0} \leq \frac{3}{2}$$

and this bound is also best possible.

Theorem 3 and all subsequent theorems will not be proved for lack of space. They will appear in a technical report of the Department of Computer Science of the University of Illinois.

THE LEVEL AND COUNT ALGORITHM (LCA)

Suppose jobs of a certain level i have been assigned priorities in some way. Symbolically we write $P_r(J) > P_r(J)$ if J has higher priority than I. We want to assign priorities to the subsets of i in the following way. Let S_1 and S_2 be two distinct subsets of level i. $P_r(S_1) < P_r(S_2)$ if any one of the following is satisfied:

(1) $|S_1| > |S_2|$

(2) $|S_1| = |S_2| = m$ (say). Suppose L_1 and L_2 are the lists of jobs in S_1 and S_2 in descending order of priorities. There exists an n, $0 \leq n \leq m-1$, such that the first n jobs in both lists coincide and the $(n+1)^{th}$ job in L_2 has higher priority than the $(n+1)^{th}$ job in L_1.

Remark: Two jobs or two subsets of a level have the same priority if they are identical.

The <u>level and count</u> (LCA) is a level algorithm (a job of higher level will be assigned higher priority than a job of lower level). LCA will be defined once the priorities of jobs within a level are specified. We shall do this inductively as follows:

(1) Assign priorities to jobs of level 1 arbitrarily.

(2) Assume priorities have been assigned to jobs of level i, for all $1 < i < n$. Let I and J be two jobs of level n. Let $I(i)$ and $J(i)$ be the set of immediate successors of I and J that are in level i respectively, $1 \leq i < n$. Define

$$L(I) = (I(n-1), I(n-2), \ldots, I(1))$$

$$L(J) = (J(n-1), J(n-2), \ldots, J(1)) .$$

We assign a higher priority to I than J if there exists an m, $0 \leq m < n-1$, such that the first m sets of both lists coincide and the $(m+1)^{th}$ set of $L(I)$ has higher priority than the $(m+1)^{th}$ set of $L(J)$. If such an m does not exist then the two lists coincide and we make an arbitrary choice of assignment of priorities between I and J.

<u>Theorem 4</u>: The LCA produces optimal schedules for 2-processors systems.

COFFMAN AND GRAHAM'S ALGORITHM (CGA)

CGA as defined in [1] is a level algorithm which is an optimal algorithm in the case of a 2-processors system. In the case of a 3-processors system we have the following:

<u>Theorem 5</u>: Suppose the partial ordering < over the jobs satisfies the following: Any two jobs of the same level have the same depth (depth is the level of a job in the inverse partial ordering of < i.e. I procedes J iff J precedes I under <). Then

$$\frac{\omega_{CGA}}{\omega_{BLA}} \leq \frac{4}{3}$$

where ω_{CGA} and ω_{BLA} are the total completion times using CGA and a best possible level algorithm respectively, and this bound is the best possible

CONCLUSION

The search for an effective optimal scheduling algorithm is still one of our final goals. But in view of its proven difficulties we have no choice but to settle for simple suboptimal algorithms. While the former task is more noble, the latter is undoubtedly more practical.

REFERENCES

[1] E.G. Coffman, Jr., and R.L. Graham, "Optimal scheduling for two-processor systems," Acta Informatia 2 1972, pp. 200-213.

[2] J. Edmonds, "Paths, trees and flowers," Can. Jour. of Math 17 1965, pp. 449-467.

[3] M. Fujii, T. Kasami, and K. Ninomiya, "Optimal sequencing of two equivalent processors," SIAM Jour. of App. Math 17 No. 3 1969, pp. 784-789.

[4] R.L. Graham, "Bounds on multiprocessing timing anomalies," SIAM Jour. of App. Math 17 No. 2 1969, pp. 416-429.

[5] T.C. Hu, "Parallel sequencing and assembly line problems," Oper. Res. 9 No. 6 1961, pp. 841-848.

SCHEDULING UNIT-TIME TASKS WITH LIMITED RESOURCES [a]

ANDREW CHI-CHIH YAO
Department of Computer Science
University of Illinois
Urbana, Illinois 61801

Abstract -- A set of tasks are to be scheduled on a multiprocessing system
with s resources. Each task takes one unit time to complete, and requires certain
amounts of resources. The schedule is to be consistent with a prescribed partial
order relation on the task , and the total demand for each resource must not exceed
a fixed amount at any instant. In this paper we analyze the worst-case behavior of
several heuristic scheduling algorithms.

Let ω be the time taken for executing all the tasks according to a priority
list, and ω_0 be the time required when scheduled in an optimal way. It is shown
that, independent of the number of processors, $\omega/\omega_0 \leq s\omega_0/2 + 0(s)$ for any list.
When certain heuristic algorithms are used to prepare the list, a significantly improved upper bound can be derived: $\omega/\omega_0 \leq \text{const.} \times s + 0(1)$. Some generalizations
are possible to the case when the "unit-time" restriction is removed.

When the partial order relation is empty, the problem becomes a natural generalization of the bin-packing problem. Tighter bounds for this special situation
are given.

INTRODUCTION

One great advantage offered by the multiprocessing system is the potential decrease in computation time. Because of the sequential constraints that often exist
among the tasks, a good scheduling algorithm is essential for the efficient utilization of parallel processing facilities.

Various aspects of an abstract multiprocessor model have been studied in the
literature [1] - [7]. That model considers a set of tasks $\{T_1, T_2, \ldots, T_r\}$ to be
processed on n identical processors. A partial order < on $\{T_1, \ldots, T_r\}$ is given, and
a function $\mu(T_i)$ which determines the execution time for T_i is specified. In a
schedule a task cannot be executed unless all of its predecessors (in <) have been
completed. Recently Garey and Graham [8] incorporated the idea of "resources" into
this model. Each task requires certain amounts of resources for its execution. A
schedule now has to satisfy the additional constraint that the total demand for each
resource cannot exceed a fixed amount at any instant. It was found [8] that, in
general, the efficiency of a schedule derived according to an arbitrary priority
list is completely unpredictable.

---

[a] Research supported by NSF GJ-41538.

In this paper, we examine an interesting case of the Garey-Graham model in which each task takes unit time to complete. Since efficient methods for finding optimal schedules seem unlikely to exist even without the resource complication [9], it is important to study practical heuristic algorithms. In the present paper, the worst-case behavior of several heuristic algorithms is analyzed. In particular, the total execution time resulting from the use of certain heuristic algorithms is shown to differ from the best possible by no more than a multiplying factor that depends on the number of different resources only.

Some results derived can be generalized to the case when the lengths of execution time for tasks are not the same. This will be briefly discussed in section 10. Even with the "unit-time" restriction, however, this model is of some practical interest in view of its close connection with preemption scheduling [2].

Main results are stated in sections 4 and 5. The proofs are given in sect 6, 7, 8, and 9.

THE MODEL

A system consists of $(n, s, F, <, \vec{R})$ where n and s are positive integers, $F = \{T(1), T(2), \ldots, T(r)\}$ a set of tasks, $<$ a partial order on F, and $\vec{R}$ is a vector function with s components defined on F. We require $0 \leq R_j(T(i)) \leq 1 \; \forall i,j$ where $\vec{R}(T(i)) \equiv (R_1(T(1)), R_2(T(1)), \ldots, R_s(T(1)))$.

(A) A <u>schedule</u> f is a finite sequence of non-empty subsets of tasks $F_1, F_2, \ldots, F$ such that:

(i) $\overset{\omega}{\underset{i=1}{\cup}} F_i = F$ and $F_i \cap F_j = \emptyset \; \forall \; i \neq j$

(ii) if $T(i) < T(j)$, $T(i) \, \epsilon F_k$, $T(j) \, \epsilon F_\ell$ then $k < \ell$

(iii) $|F_k| \leq n \; \forall \; k$

(iv) $\underset{T(i) \, \epsilon F_k}{\sum} R_\ell(T(i)) \leq 1 \; \forall k, \ell$

ω is said to be <u>the running time</u> of schedule f.

(B). <u>Interpretation</u>. n is the number of processors, s the number of resources, $R_j(T(i))$ the amount of resource j demanded by the execution of task i, and F_k is the set of tasks executed simultaneously between time k-1 and k.

(C). <u>List schedule</u>. Given a list (i.e., a permutation of the r tasks), $L = (T(i_1), T(i_2), \ldots, T(i_r))$, a schedule f is generated as follows:

Step (a) Set $i \leftarrow 1$.

Step (b) Let $F_i \leftarrow \emptyset$.

Step (c) If list is empty, stop. Else scan list from the beginning; find the first task $T(i_j)$ such that if we let $F_i \leftarrow F_i \cup \{T(i_j)\}$, all the conditions (ii), (iii) and (iv) of (A) are not violated; set $F_i \leftarrow F_i \cup \{T(i_j)\}$ and delete $T(i_j)$ from the list.

Step (d) If $|F_i| = n$ or no eligible $T(i_j)$ could be found in step (c), then set $i \leftarrow i + 1$ and go to step (b). Otherwise go to (c).

(D). Some useful definitions.

Definition 2.1 m and W are functions defined on F by:

$$m(T(i)) = \max\{R_j(T(i)) \mid 1 \leq j \leq s\}$$

$$W(T(i)) = \sum_{j=1}^{s} R_j(T(i))$$

Definition 2.2 Let A be a set of tasks. $R_j(A)$, $m(A)$, $W(A)$ are defined by:

$$R_j(A) = \sum_{T(i) \in A} R_j(T(i))$$

$$m(A) = \max_j \{R_j(A)\}$$

$$W(A) = \sum_{j=1}^{s} R_j(A)$$

ALGORITHMS TO BE CONSIDERED

The following algorithms are used to generate lists, which in turn produce schedules as was described in section 2.

(A). Arbitrary list. Just form any list.

(B). Level algorithm. This algorithm and its variants have been considered by several authors [2], [5], [6]. First a level function H is defined by:

$H(T(i)) = M$ if the longest chain of tasks that starts with $T(i)$ has length M.

A list L is then defined by the following linear order relation α ($T(i)$ appears before $T(j)$ in L if $T(i) \alpha T(j)$).

(i) $T(i) \alpha T(j)$ if $H(T(i)) > H(T(j))$

(ii) Let $T(i) \alpha T(j)$ if $H(T(i)) = H(T(j))$ and $i < j$.

(C). Resource decreasing algorithm. This is a generalization of the first fit decreasing algorithm used in bin packing problem [7]. A linear order α for L is defined by:

(i) $T(i) \alpha T(j)$ if $m(T(i)) > 1/2$ and $m(T(j)) \leq 1/2$.

(ii) If (i) is not applicable, then $T(i) \alpha T(j)$ if $W(T(i)) > W(T(j))$.

(iii) In (ii), if $W(T(i)) = W(T(j))$, then $T(i) \alpha T(j)$ if $i < j$.

BOUNDS ON THE WORST-CASE BEHAVIOR

We shall discuss the worst-case behavior of algorithms defined in the last section. As explained in section 2, n denotes the number of processors, r the number of tasks, s the number of different resources, and < a partial order on the set of tasks. Let ω_0 be the running time for an optimal schedule (i.e., one which requires minimal running time), and ω_L be the running time associated with list L.

<u>Theorem 4.1</u> If $n \geq r$, then

$$\frac{\omega_L}{\omega_0} \leq \frac{1}{2} s(\omega_0 + 7s) \qquad \text{for any list L} \tag{1}$$

The following theorem states that (1) can be essentially achieved.

<u>Theorem 4.2</u> There exists systems with arbitrary large ω_0 and $n \geq r$ for which

$$\frac{1}{2} s(\omega_0 - 2s) \leq \frac{\omega_L}{\omega_0} \qquad \text{for some list L} \tag{2}$$

When the condition $n \geq r$ is dropped, an upper bound for $\frac{\omega_L}{\omega_0}$ can readily be obtained if we regard "processors" also as a resource. However, a more detailed analysis yields the following stronger result:

<u>Theorem 4.3</u> For any n and any list L,

$$\frac{\omega_L}{\omega_0} \leq \frac{n-1}{2n} s\omega_0 + \frac{7(n-1)}{2n} s + 1 \tag{3}$$

Formulas (2) shows that, unlike in the conventional model where "resources" are not taken into account, the worst-case behavior of ω_L/ω_0 is not bounded by a constant. The following theorems show that this behavior improves drastically if some efforts are made in preparing the list.

<u>Theorem 4.4</u> If a list L is prepared by using level algorithm, then:

$$\frac{\omega_L}{\omega_0} \leq \frac{n-1}{n} (2s+1) + 1 \qquad \text{for arbitrary n} \tag{4}$$

$$\frac{\omega_L}{\omega_0} \leq 2s + 1 \qquad \text{if } r \leq n \tag{5}$$

<u>Theorem 4.5</u> For any given $\varepsilon > 0$, there exists systems with arbitrary large ω_0 such that

$$\frac{17}{10} s - \varepsilon < \frac{\omega_L}{\omega_0} \qquad \begin{array}{l} \text{where L is generated by} \\ \text{level algorithm} \end{array} \tag{6}$$

If the resource decreasing algorithm described in section 3 is used, a still better upper bound exists for ω_L/ω_0.

Theorem 4.6 If a list L is obtained by using resource decreasing algorithm, then:

$$\frac{\omega_L}{\omega_0} \leq \frac{n-1}{n} \left(\frac{7}{4} s+1\right) + 1 \quad \text{for any n} \tag{7}$$

$$\frac{\omega_L}{\omega_0} \leq \frac{7}{4} s + 1 \quad\quad \text{if } r \leq n \tag{8}$$

An asymptotic lower bound is given by:

Theorem 4.7 For any given $\varepsilon > 0$, there exists systems with arbitrary large ω_0 such that

$$\frac{3}{2}s - \varepsilon < \frac{\omega_L}{\omega_0} \quad \text{where L is generated by resource decreasing algorithm} \tag{9}$$

THE SPECIAL CASE IN WHICH < IS EMPTY

An upper bound for ω_L/ω_0 was derived in [8] under the assumption $r \leq n$ for this special case. That bound $\omega_L/\omega_0 \leq s + 1$ is true even when the lengths of execution time for tasks are not the same. The following theorem gives a slightly better asymptotic upper bound when uniform execution is assumed.

Theorem 5.1 If $r \leq n$, and < empty, then for any given $\varepsilon > 0$ and an arbitrary list L,

$$\frac{\omega_L}{\omega_0} \leq s + \frac{17}{20} + \varepsilon \quad\quad \text{if } \omega_0 \text{ is large enough,} \tag{10}$$

The following theorem can be obtained by constructing examples.

Theorem 5.2 For any given $\varepsilon > 0$, then exists systems with > ampty, and arbitrary large ω_0 satisfying

$$s + \frac{7}{10} - \varepsilon < \frac{\omega_L}{\omega_0} \quad\quad \text{for some list L} \tag{11}$$

Theorem 5.3 If < is empty, then for any $\varepsilon > 0$, and any list L,

$$\frac{\omega_L}{\omega_0} \leq \frac{n-1}{n} \left(s + \frac{17}{20}\right) + 1 + \varepsilon \quad\quad \text{for large } \omega_0, \tag{12}$$

(10) (12) may not be the best possible bounds. For example, a stronger statement can be proved for the case s = 2.

Theorem 5.4 If s = 2, $r \leq n$, and < is empty, then for any given $\varepsilon > 0$,

$$\frac{\omega_L}{\omega_0} \lesssim \frac{41}{15} + \epsilon \qquad \text{for large } \omega_0 \qquad\qquad (13)$$

It is interesting to note that the scheduling problem with $s = 1$, $r \leq n$, and $<$ empty is equivalent to the bin-packing problem. The resource demanded by a task corresponds to the weight of an object, and the running time ω corresponds to the number of boxes used in the bin-packing problem. If we extend the concept of weight to an s=dimensional weight-vector, then our problem considered here can be regarded as a bin-packing problem with multi-weight. We shall return to this point in section 9.

PROOF OF THEOREMS 4.1, 4.2, 4.3

(A). Proof of Theorem 4.1. Let f be the schedule generated by list L, and $F_1, F_2, \ldots, F_\omega$ be the sets of tasks corresponding to f as defined in section 2. Several preliminary results are needed to establish the theorem.

Lemma 6.1 For any task $T(j_1)$, there exist a sequence of integers $a_q < a_{q-1} < \ldots < a_2 < a_1$ and a chain of tasks $T(j_q) < T(j_{q-1}) < \ldots < T(j_2) < T(j_1)$ such that

(i) $T(j_\ell) \in F_{a_\ell}$ for $\ell = 1, 2, \ldots, q$.

(ii) $m(T(j_q)) > 1/2$, unless for all $\ell(1 \leq \ell < a_q)$, $m(F_\ell) > 1/2$.

(iii) If $\ell \neq a_i \,\forall i$, and $a_q < \ell < a_1$, then $m(F_\ell) > 1/2$.

Proof. The following procedure generates a sequence of integers $a_1, a_2, \ldots, a_q$ and a chain of tasks $T(j_1), T(j_2), \ldots, T(j_q)$ that satisfy the required conditions.

Step (a) (Initialization) Let a_1 be such that

$$T(j_1) \in F_{a_1} \; ; \; t \leftarrow 1; \; v \leftarrow a_1.$$

Step (b) (Termination condition) If $m(T(j_t)) > 1/2$ or $v = 1$ then stop.

Step (c) (Try to find a $T(j_{t+1}) \in F_{v-1}$ such that $T(j_{t+1}) < T(j_t)$. This is always possible if $m(F_{v-1}) \leq 1/2$, since $T(j_t)$ could not be executed between time $v-2$ and $v-1$.)

If $\exists$ a u such that $T(u) < T(j_t)$ and $T(u) \in F_{v-1}$,

then $v \leftarrow v-1$, $t \leftarrow t+1$, $j_t \leftarrow u$, $a_t \leftarrow v$

else $v \leftarrow v-1$;

Step (d) goto Step (b).

Condition (ii) stated in the lemma is satisfied by the termination condition in Step (b). $\qquad\qquad \square$

Lemma 6.2 For some k, there exist k disjoint chains $C_1, C_2, \ldots, C_k$ of tasks such that the following is true:

Let C_i be given by $T(j_{iq_i}) < T(j_{i,q_i-1}) < \ldots < T(j_{i1})$, then

(i) $\quad m(T(j_{iq_i})) > 1/2 \quad$ for $i = 1, 2, \ldots, k-1$ $\hfill (14)$

(ii) If F_ℓ is such that $F_\ell \cap C_i = \emptyset$ for

$\qquad i = 1, 2, \ldots, k$, then $m(F_\ell) > 1/2$. $\hfill (15)$

Proof. Choose an arbitrary task $T(j_{11}) \in F_\omega$. Find a chain C_1 using the procedure described in the proof of lemma 6.1. Let this chain be $T(j_{1q_1}) < T(j_{1,q_1-1}) < \ldots < T(j_{11})$. Suppose $T(j_{1q_1}) \in F_\ell$. If $m(T(j_{1q_1})) \leq 1/2$ or $\ell = 1$, then stop. Otherwise, choose an arbitrary task $T(j_{21}) \in F_{\ell-1}$. We then construct a new chain C_2 according to the procedure in the proof of Lemma 6.1. Let C_2 be $T(j_{2q_2}) < T(j_{2,q_2-1}) < \ldots < T(j_{21})$. Again we check if $m(T(j_{2q_2})) \leq 1/2$ or $T(j_{2q_2}) \in F_1$, and decide whether to construct C_3. This process is repeated until $m(T(j_{kq_k})) \leq 1/2$ or $T(j_{kq_k}) \in F_1$ where $T(j_{kq_k})$ is the maximum element of the last chain obtained. At this point, k chains $C_1, C_2, \ldots, C_k$ with respective lengths $q_1, q_2, \ldots, q_k$ have been obtained. It is straightforward to verify that they satisfy condition (ii) by using Lemma 6.1. Figure 1 illustrates the result of this process. $\hfill \square$

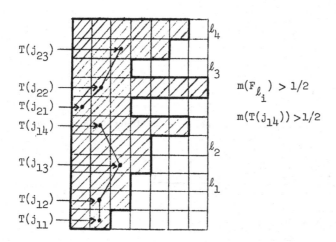

Figure 1

Lemma 6.3 Let $\{j_{ih} | 1 \leq i \leq k, 1 \leq h \leq q_i\}$ be the same as in Lemma 6.2. There exists an integer d $(1 \leq d \leq s)$ and a set of integers $V \subset \{1, 2, \ldots, k-1\}$ such that

(i) $\qquad R_d(T(j_{iq_i})) > 1/2 \quad$ for $i \in V$ $\hfill (16)$

(ii)
$$\sum_{i \in V} q_i + q_k \geq \frac{\sum_{i=1}^{k} q_i}{s} \tag{17}$$

<u>Proof.</u> Define s sets of integers by

$$V_\ell \equiv \{i \mid 1 \leq i \leq k-1, R_\ell(T(j_{iq_i})) > 1/2\} \quad \ell = 1,2,\ldots,s.$$

Since $\cup_\ell V_\ell = \{1,2,\ldots,k-1\}$, we have

$$\sum_{\ell=1}^{s} (\sum_{i \in V_\ell} q_i) \geq \sum_{i=1}^{k-1} q_i$$

Therefore, there exists d such that

$$\sum_{i \in V_d} q_i \geq \frac{1}{s} \sum_{i=1}^{k-1} q_i$$

Let $V \equiv V_d$, we have thus

$$\sum_{i \in V} q_i + q_k \geq \frac{1}{s} \sum_{i=1}^{k-1} q_i + q_k \geq \frac{1}{s} \sum_{i=1}^{k} q_i \qquad \square$$

We are now ready to prove Theorem 4.1. Let

$$G \equiv \{\ell \mid F_\ell \cap (\cup_{i=1}^{k} C_i) = \emptyset\}$$

Obviously

$$\sum_{i=1}^{k} q_i + |G| = \omega \tag{18}$$

Since the total amount of resource available at any instant is s, we have

$$\omega_0 \geq \frac{\sum_i W(T_i)}{s} \geq \frac{\sum_{\ell \in G} W(F_\ell) + \sum_{i=1}^{k-1} W(T(j_{i,q_i}))}{s}$$

$$\geq \frac{\sum_{\ell \in G} m(F_\ell) + \sum_{i=1}^{k-1} m(T(j_{i,q_i}))}{s}$$

By virtue of (14) and (15), we have

$$\omega_0 \geq \frac{\frac{1}{2}|G| + \frac{1}{2}(k-1)}{s}$$

Thus,
$$2s\omega_0 \geq |G| + k-1 \tag{19}$$

Now, according to Lemma 6.3, there exists a set V such that (16) and (17) are true. Let us renumber the chains C_i's ($i \in V$) as $C_1', C_2', \ldots, C_{k_1}'$ where $k_1 \equiv |V|$. Let the length of C_i' be q_i' and let its maximum task be $T(t_i)$. It follows from (17) that

$$\sum_{i=1}^{k_1} q_i' + q_k \geq \frac{1}{s} \sum_{i=1}^{k} q_i \tag{20}$$

Furthermore, no two tasks in the set $\{T(t_i)\,|\,i=1,2,\ldots,k_1\}$ can be executed simultaneously in any schedule since each of them demands more than 1/2 unit of the dth resource. In the optimal schedule, we can assume, without loss of generality, that $T(t_i)$ is done before $T(t_{i+1})$ for $1 \leq i \leq k_1-1$. Using the starting time of $T(t_1)$ as a reference point in time, the last task in chain C_i' cannot be done in less than $q_i' + (i-1)$ time units. Therefore,

$$\omega_0 \geq \max(q_k, q_1', q_2'+1, q_3'+2, \ldots, q_{k_1}' + (k_1-1))$$

$$\geq \frac{1}{k_1+1}(q_k + q_1' + (q_2'+1) + \ldots + (q_{k_1}' + (k_1-1)))$$

$$= \frac{1}{k_1+1}(q_k + \sum_{i=1}^{k_1-1} q_i' + \frac{1}{2}k_1(k_1-1))$$

$$\geq \frac{1}{k_1+1}(\frac{1}{s}\sum_{i=1}^{k} q_i + \frac{1}{2}k_1(k_1-1)) \tag{21}$$

where (20) is used in the last step. (21) can be written as

$$s(k_1+1)\omega_0 \geq \sum_{i=1}^{k} q_i + \frac{1}{2}sk_1(k_1-1) \tag{22}$$

From (18), (19), and (22), it is straightforward to deduce that

$$-\frac{1}{2}sk_1(k_1-1) + s(k_1+1)\omega_0 + 2s\omega_0 \geq \omega + k - 1 \geq \omega \tag{23}$$

(23) can be written as

$$-\frac{1}{2}s(k_1-(\omega_0+\frac{1}{2}))^2 + 3s\omega_0 + \frac{1}{2}s(\omega_0+\frac{1}{2})^2 \geq \omega \tag{24}$$

Now, since ω_0, k_1 are integers, $|k_1-(\omega_0+\frac{1}{2})| \geq 1/2$. Thus (24) implies

$$-\frac{1}{2}s(\frac{1}{2})^2 + 3s\omega_0 + \frac{1}{2}s(\omega_0 + \frac{1}{2})^2 \geq \omega$$

That is,

$$\frac{1}{2}s\omega_0^2 + \frac{7}{2}s\omega_0 \geq \omega \tag{25}$$

This completes the proof of Theorem 4.1.

$\Box$

(B). **Proof of Theorem 4.2.** We need only to exhibit a system with a schedule L such that

$$\frac{\omega_L}{\omega_0} > \frac{1}{2} s\omega_0 - s^2 .$$

Let $F = \{T^{(k)}, T_{j\ell}^{(k)} | 1 \leq k \leq s, 1 \leq j \leq q, 1 \leq \ell \leq j\}$. The partial order $<$ is represented as a precedence graph in Figure 2.

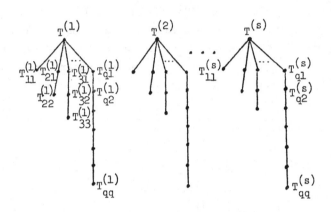

Figure 2

$\vec{R}$ is defined by:

$$\vec{R}(T^{(k)}) = (1,1,\ldots,1) \qquad k = 1,2,\ldots,s$$

$$\vec{R}(T_{i1}^{(k)}) = (0,0,\ldots,0,1 - \frac{\delta}{2^{i-1}},0,\ldots 0)$$

$$k = 1,2,\ldots,s; \; i = 1,2,\ldots,q;$$

$$\vec{R}(T_{ij}^{(k)}) = (0,0,\ldots,0,\frac{\delta}{2^{i-1}}, 0,\ldots,0)$$

$$k = 1,2,\ldots,s; \; i = 1,2,\ldots,q;$$

$$j = 1,2,\ldots,i$$

where δ is a small positive number.

Let $L \equiv L_1 L_2 \ldots L_s$ where, for $k = 1,2,\ldots,s$, $L_k = (T^{(k)}, T_{11}^{(k)}, T_{21}^{(k)} \; T_{22}^{(k)},\ldots,$ $T_{q1}^{(k)}, T_{q2}^{(k)},\ldots,T_{qq}^{(k)})$.

For this list L, only one task is executed at any time. The total execution time is, therefore, equal to $s(1+1+2+3+\ldots+q)$. Thus,

$$\omega_L = s(1 + \frac{1}{2} q(q+1)).$$

On the other hand, the optimal schedule is generated by

$$L_0 \equiv (T^{(1)}, T^{(2)}, \ldots, T^{(s)}) L_1' L_2' \ldots L_s' \text{ where, for each } k,$$

$$L_k' = (T_{q1}^{(k)}, T_{q2}^{(k)}, \ldots, T_{qq}^{(k)}, T_{q-1,1}^{(k)}, T_{q-1,2}^{(k)}, \ldots,$$

$$T_{q-1,q-1}^{(k)}, \ldots, T_{21}^{(k)}, T_{22}^{(k)}, T_{11}^{(k)}) .$$

In this case $\omega_0 = q+s$.

Thus

$$\frac{\omega_L}{\omega_0} = \frac{s(1 + \frac{1}{2} q(q+1))}{q+s} > \frac{1}{2} s\omega_0 - s^2 \qquad \qquad \square$$

(C). <u>Proof of Theorem 4.3</u>. The proof goes essentially the same as the proof for Theorem 4.1. The only difference is that, if $\ell \in G$ where

$$G \equiv \{\ell \mid F_\ell \cap (\bigcup_{i=1}^{k} C_i) = \emptyset\}, \text{ then } \underline{\text{either}} \ m(F_\ell) > 1/2 \ \underline{\text{or}} \ |F_\ell| = n. \text{ Let}$$

$$Q \equiv \{\ell \mid \ell \in G, \ m(F_\ell) > 1/2\}$$

and $Q' \equiv G - Q$.
Then equation (18) is modified to

$$\sum_{i=1}^{k} q_i + |Q| + |Q'| = \omega \tag{26}$$

while equations (19), (22) are unchanged,

$$2s\omega_0 \geq |Q| + k-1 \geq |Q| \tag{27}$$

$$s(k_1+1)\omega_0 \geq \sum_{i=1}^{k} q_i + \frac{1}{2} sk_1 (k_1-1) \tag{28}$$

A new constraint arises from the fact that there are now only n processors. Since there are at least $\sum_{i=1}^{k} q_i + |Q| + n|Q'|$ tasks, we have

$$n\omega_0 \geq \sum_{i=1}^{k} q_i + |Q| + |Q'| \tag{29}$$

Eliminating $|Q|$, $|Q'|$, and $\sum_{i=1}^{k} q_i$ from (26), (27), (28), (29), we obtain

$$\omega \leq \frac{n-1}{n}(-\frac{1}{2}sk_1(k_1-1) + (k_1+1)s\omega_0 + 2s\omega_0) + \omega_0 \tag{30}$$

The following equation can then be obtained from (30) in the same manner that (25) is obtained from (23)

$$\omega \leq \frac{n-1}{n} (\frac{1}{2} s \omega_0^2 + \frac{7}{2} s \omega_0) + \omega_0 \tag{31}$$

PROOF OF THEOREMS 4.4 AND 4.5

(A). <u>Proof of Theorem 4.4</u>. We shall only prove equation (5). The other in-equality, equation (4), can be similarly obtained (cf. the argument used in section 6.(C)).

Consider a schedule generated by the level algorithm. Let ω be the completion time and $F_1, F_2, \ldots, F_\omega$ be defined as in section 2. We introduce a function u defined as follows:

$$u(\ell) \equiv \max_{T(i) \epsilon F_\ell} \{H(T(i))\} \quad \text{for } \ell = 1, 2, \ldots, \omega \tag{32}$$

where H is the level function defined in section 2.

<u>Lemma 7.1</u> $u(\ell) \geq u(\ell+1)$ for $\ell = 1, 2, \ldots, \omega-1$

<u>Proof</u>. Suppose otherwise. Then there exists an ℓ for which $u(\ell) < u(\ell+1)$. Now, let $T(j) \epsilon F_{\ell+1}$ be a task with $H(T(j)) = u(\ell+1)$. Then $H(T(j)) > H(T(i))$ for all $T(i) \epsilon F$. Thus, $T(j)$ must appear before all $T(i) \epsilon F_\ell$ in the list since it is prepared by the level algorithm. Furthermore, there is no $T_i \epsilon F_\ell$ for which $T_i < T_j$. Therefore, T_j should be done no later than any of the task in F_ℓ. This contradicts the assumption that $T_j \epsilon F_{\ell+1}$.   □

<u>Lemma 7.2</u> If $u(\ell) = u(\ell+1)$, then $W(F_\ell) + W(F_{\ell+1}) > 1$.

<u>Proof</u>. Similar to the proof for Lemma 7.1.   □

Now, let $A \equiv \{\ell | u(\ell) = u(\ell+1)\}$, then

$$2 \sum_{i=1}^{\omega} W(F_i) \geq \sum_{\ell \epsilon A} (W(F_\ell) + W(F_{\ell+1})) > |A| \tag{33}$$

Thus,

$$\omega_0 \geq \frac{1}{s} \sum_{i=1}^{\omega} W(F_i) > \frac{1}{2s} |A| \tag{34}$$

On the other hand, according to Lemma 7.1, we have:

$$u(\ell) \geq u(\ell+1) + 1 \quad \text{for } \ell \notin A, 1 \leq \ell \leq \omega-1$$

Therefore,

$$\omega_0 \geq u(1) \geq \omega - |A| \tag{35}$$

(34) and (35) imply $(2s+1)\omega_0 \geq \omega$. This proves the theorem.   □

(B). <u>Proof of Theorem 4.5</u>. Consider a system of tasks with partial order as is shown in Figure 3.

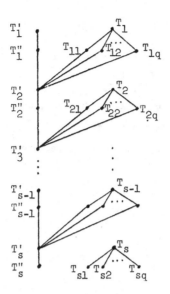

Figure 3

For all $1 \leq i \leq s$, $1 \leq k \leq q$, let

$$\vec{R}(T_i) = (1,1,\ldots,1), \quad \vec{R}(T_i') = \vec{R}(T_i'') = (0,0,\ldots,0)$$

$$R_1(T_{1k}) = R_2(T_{2k}) = \ldots = R_s(T_{sk}) \neq 0$$

$$R_j(T_{ik}) = 0 \quad \text{if} \quad j \neq i$$

The values of $R_i(T_{ik})$ are unspecified at this point.

The list generated by the level algorithm is $L = L_1 L_2 \ldots L_s$ where

$$L_i = (T_i T_i' T_i'' T_{i1} T_{i2} \ldots T_{iq}) \qquad i = 1,2,\ldots,s \ .$$

It is easy to see that T_{i+1} and T_{i+1}' are done <u>after</u> the set of tasks $\{T_{i1}, T_{i2}, \ldots, T_{iq}\}$ is completed, and <u>before</u> the set of tasks $\{T_{i+1,1}, T_{i+1,2}, \ldots, T_{i+1,q}\}$ is started. Therefore,

$$\omega = s + s\omega_1 \tag{36}$$

where ω_1 is the amount of time needed to execute all the tasks in $\{T_{11}, T_{12}, \ldots, T_{1q}\}$ scheduled according to the list L_1.

Now the problem of scheduling $\{T_{11}, T_{12}, \ldots, T_{1q}\}$ is identical to the bin-packing problem [7] since $R_j(T_{1k}) = 0$ for all $j \neq 1$. In fact, we can regard R_1 as the weight function, and the completion time as the number of boxes used in the bin-packing problem (cf. section 9). It is known [7] that we can choose the weight function so that the number of boxes used is $\frac{17}{10} - \epsilon$ times greater than the optimal number needed. Thus, by properly choosing R_1, we have

$$\omega_1 \geq (\frac{17}{10} - \varepsilon)\omega_{10} \tag{37}$$

where ω_{10} is the optimal time needed to finish all tasks in $\{T_{11}, T_{12}, \ldots, T_{1q}\}$ scheduled according to some list $\{T_{1i_1}, T_{1i_2}, \ldots, T_{1i_q}\}$.

Returning to the scheduling of tasks in Figure 3, we form the List $L_0 = (T_1, T_2, \ldots, T_s T_1', \ldots, T_s', T_1'', \ldots, T_s'') L_1' L_2' \ldots L_s'$ where $L_k' = (T_{ki_1}, T_{ki_2}, \ldots T_{ki_q})$. It is clear that tasks in the list $L_1', L_2', \ldots, L_s'$ will be performed in parallel. This leads to

$$\omega_0 \leq s + \omega_{10} \tag{38}$$

A comparison of (36), (37), and (38) shows

$$\frac{\omega}{\omega_0} > \frac{17}{10} s - \varepsilon' \qquad \text{for } \omega_0 \gg s$$

This proves Theorem 4.5. □

PROOFS OF THEOREMS 4.6 AND 4.7

(A). <u>Proof of Theorem 4.6</u>. We shall only prove equation (8). The other equation in Theorem 4.6 can be established similarly.

First we partition the set $\{1, 2, \ldots, \omega\}$ into three parts:

$A \equiv \{k | 1 \leq k \leq \omega, \ \exists \text{ a task } T(i) \ \varepsilon F_k \text{ such that } m(T(i)) > 1/2\}$

$B \equiv \{k | 1 \leq k \leq \omega, \ W(F_k) \geq 2/3\} - A$

$C \equiv \{1, 2, \ldots, \omega\} - A - B$

Next we define s subsets of tasks:

$E_j \equiv \{T(i) | R_j(T(i)) > 1/2\} \qquad j = 1, 2, \ldots, s$.

From the definitions of A and the E_j' s, it follows that $\sum\limits_{j=1}^{s} E_j$ has at least $|A|$ elements. Thus,

$$\sum_{j=1}^{s} | E_j | \geq |A| .$$

Let d, where $1 \leq d \leq s$, be such that $|E_d| = \max\limits_{j} |E_j|\}$. Then $|E_d| \geq \frac{1}{s} |A|$. Since no two tasks in E_d can be executed simultaneously in any schedule, we must have,

$$\omega_0 \geq |E_d| \geq \frac{1}{s} |A| \tag{39}$$

Two more inequalities follow easily from the definitions of A, B, C.

$$\omega_0 \geq \frac{1}{s} (\frac{1}{2}|A| + \frac{2}{3} |B|) \tag{40}$$

$$|A| + |B| + |C| = \omega \tag{41}$$

We need one more inequality. For the moment, let us assume that the following is true.

<u>Claim</u> $\omega_0 \geq |C| \tag{42}$

From the four equations (39), (40), (41), and (42), we can eliminate $|A|$, $|B|$, $|C|$ to obtain

$$(\frac{7}{4} s + 1)\omega_0 \geq \omega \tag{43}$$

which is the formula we want to prove.

The only remaining work now is to prove the validity of the claim, equation (42).

<u>Lemma 8.1</u> Let $\ell \in C$ and $T(i) \in F_\ell$, where $\ell' > \ell$. If for every ℓ'', $\ell < \ell'' < \ell'$, there is no $T(h) \in F_{\ell''}$ satisfying $T(h) < T(i)$, then there must exist a task $T(j) \in F_\ell$ such that $T(j) < T(i)$.

<u>Proof.</u> Suppose otherwise. Then clearly there must be some task in F_ℓ that appears before T_i in the list. We shall prove that this leads to contradictions.

<u>Case (i):</u> There is only one task $T(k)$ in F_ℓ that appears before $T(i)$ in the list. It is clear that $m(T(k)) \leq 1/2$ because $\ell \in C$. Furthermore, since the list is prepared by resource decreasing algorithm, we have $m(T(i)) \leq W(T(i)) \leq W(T(k)) \leq 1/2$. Therefore, $T(i)$ <u>could</u> be done with $T(k)$. Since $T(i)$ has priority over all tasks in F_ℓ other than $T(k)$, $T(i)$ <u>should</u> be done with $T(k)$. This is a contradiction.

<u>Case (ii):</u> There are at least two tasks T_k, T_k' that appear before $T(i)$ in the list. Again we have $W(T(i)) \leq W(T(k)), W(T(i)) \leq W(T(k'))$.

Thus, $W(T(i)) \leq \frac{1}{2}(W(T_k) + W(T_k')) \leq \frac{1}{2} \sum\limits_{T(j) \ F_\ell} W(T(j))$

$$W(T(i)) + \sum\limits_{T(j) \in F_\ell} W(T(j)) \leq \frac{3}{2} \sum\limits_{T(j) \in F_\ell} W(T(j)) < \frac{3}{2} \cdot \frac{2}{3} = 1 \tag{44}$$

where, in the last step, the fact that $\ell \in C$ is used.

Thus, $T(i)$ <u>could</u> be done with all the $T(j)$'s in F_ℓ. This again contradicts the fact that $T(i)$ $F_{\ell'}$. This proves the lemma. □

<u>Lemma 8.2</u> There is a chain $T(j_q) < T(j_{q-1}) < \ldots < T(j_1)$ such that, for any $\ell \in C$, there is a task $T(j_k)$ in the chain such that $T(j_k) \in F_\ell$.

<u>Proof.</u> This chain can easily be constructed "from bottom up" making use of Lemma 8.1. □

An immediate consequence of Lemma 8.2 is that there is a chain of length greater or equal to $|C|$. Thus, $\omega_0 \geq |C|$, which proves the <u>claim</u>, equation (42).

This completes the proof of Theorem 4.6.　　　　　　　　　　　　　　　　□

(B). <u>Proof of Theorem 4.7</u>. We define a system of tasks as follows:

(i)　　　$F = \{T_i, T_i', T_{ij}, T_{ij}' \mid 1 \le i \le s, 1 \le j \le q\}$

(ii)　　The partial order is defined by (see Figure 4):

$$T_i < T_i' < T_j < T_j' \qquad 1 \le i < j \quad \le s$$

$$T_i < T_{ij}, \ T_i' < T_{ij}' \qquad \forall \, i,j$$

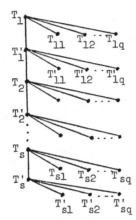

Figure 4

(iii)　$\vec{R}(T_i) = (3\varepsilon, 3\varepsilon, \ldots, 3\varepsilon)$

$$\vec{R}(T_i') = (0, \ldots, 0, \tfrac{1}{2} - \varepsilon + \delta, 0, \ldots, 0)$$

$$1 \le i \le s$$

$$\vec{R}(T_{ij}) = (0, \ldots, 0, \tfrac{1}{2} + \varepsilon, 0, \ldots, 0)$$

$$\vec{R}(T_{ij}') = (0, \ldots, 0, \tfrac{1}{2} - \varepsilon, 0, \ldots, 0)$$

$$1 \le i \le s, \ 1 \le j \le q$$

with q an even number, and $0 < \delta < \varepsilon < 1/8$.

　　Let L be the list generated by the resource decreasing algorithm. Then

$L = L_1 L_2 \ldots L_s (T_1' T_2' \ldots T_s') L_1' L_2' \ldots L_s' (T_1 T_2 \ldots T_s)$ where $L_i = (T_{11}, T_{12} \ldots, T_{12})$ and

$L_i' = (T_{11}', T_{12}', \ldots, T_{iq}')$. For this list, $\omega = s(\tfrac{3q}{2} + 2)$ as can be seen from Figure 5.

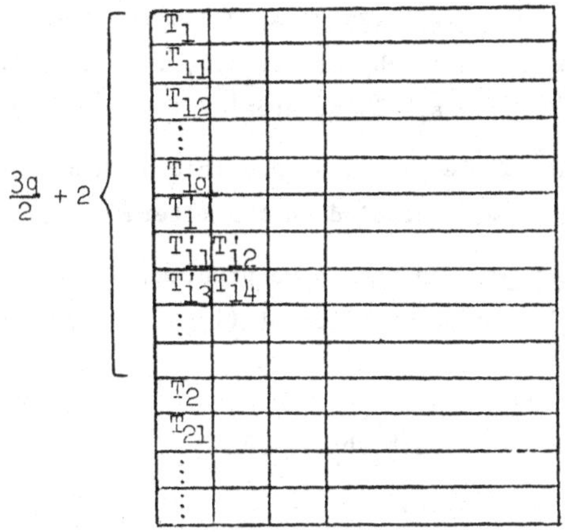

Figure 5

On the other hand, by choosing a proper list, the tasks can all be completed in time $\omega_0 = 2s + q$. (see Figure 6.)

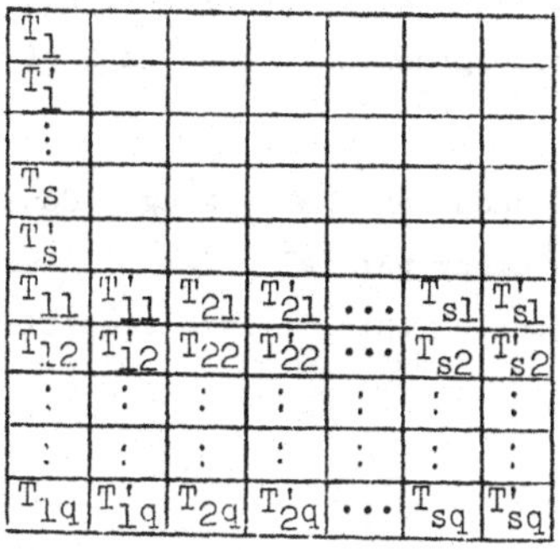

Figure 6

As $q \to \infty$, $\dfrac{\omega}{\omega_0} = \dfrac{s(\frac{3}{2}q+2)}{2s+q} > \dfrac{3}{2}s - \varepsilon_0$ for any fixed $\varepsilon_0 > 0$. $\square$

THE MULTI-WEIGHT PACKING PROBLEM

The proofs for the theorems in section 5 are most conveniently described in the language of a packing problem. In this section we shall define the packing problem and formulate the theorems in section 5 in this new context. The proofs of these theorems will appear in [10].

(A). __The Problem.__ Suppose we have an unlimited supply of boxes of $B_1, B_2, \ldots$ and we want to pack objects $O_1, O_2, \ldots, O_r$ into these boxes. Associated with each object O_j is an s-dimensional __weight vector__ $\vec{a}_j$ whose components are real numbers between 0 and 1. A box B_j can hold objects $\{O_{i_1}, O_{i_2}, \ldots, O_{i_p}\}$ if each component of the sum vector $\vec{a}_{i_1} + \vec{a}_{i_2} + \ldots + \vec{a}_{i_p}$ is no greater than 1. [P] The problem is to pack a given set of objects into as few boxes as possible. When s = 1, this becomes the bin-packing problem which is well-studied in the literature [7].

(B). __First-fit Algorithm__. In the above problem, any __list__ $L = (O_{i_1}, O_{i_2}, \ldots, O_{i_r})$, where $(i_1, i_2, \ldots, i_r)$ is a permutation of $(1, 2, \ldots, r)$, generates a __packing scheme__ as follows:

Step (1): Take a sequence of boxes $B_1, B_2, \ldots, B_r$.

Step (2): Set $\vec{z}(B_i) = 0$ for all i.

Step (3): For $j = 1, 2, \ldots, r$, do the following: Find the least k such that each component of the vector $\vec{z}(B_k) + \vec{a}_{i_j}$ is less than or equal to 1. Set $\vec{z}(B_k) \leftarrow \vec{z}(B_k) + \vec{a}_{i_j}$. And we say that we have "packed" O_{i_j} into box B_k.

We shall use $N_{FF}(L)$ to denote the number of non-empty boxes after the above procedure. N_0 is defined to be the minimum of $N_{FF}(L)$ over all lists L. When s = 1, the first-fit algorithm defined above agrees with the usage of this term in the bin-packing problem.

(C). __Connection Between Scheduling and Packing__. Consider the scheduling of tasks $\{T(1), T(2), \ldots, T(r)\}$ with empty partial order < , resource demand $\vec{R}(T(j))$, and a number of processors $n \geq r$. Let us turn it into a multi-weight packing problem via the following correspondence:

$$T(j) \quad : \quad O_j$$
$$\vec{R}(T(j)) \quad : \quad \vec{a}_j \tag{45}$$

completion time : number of boxes used

Lists: $L' = (T(i_1), \ldots, T(i_r)) : L = (O_{i_1}, \ldots, O_{i_r})$

Given any list $L' = (T(i_1), T(i_2), \ldots, T(i_r))$ we can generate a list schedule for the scheduling problem. This process can be translated via (45) into an algorithm for generating a packing scheme based on list $L = (O_{i_1}, O_{i_2}, \ldots, O_{i_r})$. If we compare this algorithm with the first-fit algorithm, we see that these two algorithms are __not__ the same. However, it is not too difficult to see that the resulting packing __are__ the same. As a result, $\omega'_L = N_{FF}(L)$, and $\omega_0 = N_0$. This allows us to state theorems in section 5 in the following form.

__Theorem 5.1'__ $N_{FF}(L)/N_0 \leq s + 17/20 + \varepsilon$ for large N_0.

__Theorem 5.2'__ There exists situations where $N_{FF}(L)/N_0 > s + 7/10 - \varepsilon$ with arbitrary large N_0

<u>Theorem 5.4'</u> For $s = 2$, $N_{FF}(L)/N_0 \leq 41/15 + \epsilon$ for large N_0.

A slightly modified version of packing problem is needed for Theorem 5.3.

GENERALIZATION TO NON-UNIFORM TASK LENGTHS

When tasks lengths are allowed to be non-uniform, generalizations of our results take the following form: $n \geq r$

Let μ_0 = length of the shortest task

μ_1 = length of the longest task

Then $\omega_L/\mu_0 \leq \frac{1}{2} s \, ((\omega_0/\mu_0)^2 + 7(\omega_0/\mu_0))$ for any list L. Furthermore, let us "pretend" that every task is of length μ_1 and construct a schedule according to level algorithm with every task taking μ_1 amount of time. This schedule can become a schedule for the actual problem since each task really needs no more than μ_1 amount of time. For this schedule $\omega/\omega_0 \leq (2s+1)\mu_1/\mu_0$. In general, this schedule can not be generated by a list.

CONCLUSIONS

We have considered several heuristic list scheduling algorithms in this paper. The bounds obtained on ω_L/ω_0 enable us to make certain conclusions. For example, we learned that a little extra work to prepare the list guarantees a much better efficiency of the multiprocessing system than an arbitrary list. We have also seen that these algorithms do not work as well as they do in the absence of "resource" constraints. If is an intriguing problem to determine the asymptotic behavior of the worst-case behavior here. It is even more interesting if other simple algorithms can be found that make more efficient use of the parallel processing facilities

REFERENCES

[1] R.L. Graham, "Bounds on Multiprocessing Anomalies and Related Packing Algorithms," AFIPS Conf. Proc. 40 (1972), pp. 205-217.

[2] E.G. Coffman, and R.L. Graham, "Optimal Scheduling for two-processor systems," Acta Informatica 1 No. 3 (1972), pp. 200-213.

[[3] M. Fujii, T. Kasami, and K. Ninomiya, "Optimal Sequencing of Two Equivalent Processors," SIAM J. of App. Math. 17 No. 3 (1969), pp. 784-789.

[4] C.L. Liu, Proc. of 13th SWAT conf. (1972), pp. 155-158.

[5] T.C. Hu, "Parallel Scheduling and Assembly Line Problems," Operations Research 9 No. 6 (1961), pp. 841-848.

[6] N.F Chen, and C.L. Liu, "On a Class of Scheduling Algorithms for Multiprocessors Computing Systems, this Proceeding.

[7] M.R. Garey, R.L. Graham, and J.D. Ullman, "Worst-Case Analysis of Memory Allocation Algorithms," Conf. Record of ACM Symposium on Theory of Computing (1972).

[8] M.R. Garey, and R.L. Graham, "Bounds on Scheduling with Limited Resources,"
     4th Symp. on Operating System Principles, Oct. 15-17, 1973.

[9] J.D. Ullman, "Polynomial Complete Scheduling Problems," 4th Symposium on
     Operating System Principles, 1973.

[10] A.C. Yao, "On Scheduling with Limited Resources," to appear.

PROGRAMMABLE RADAR SIGNAL PROCESSING
USING THE RAP

DR. GEORGE R. COURANZ
MARK S. GERHARDT
CHARLES J. YOUNG
Raytheon Company
Equipment Division
Computer Systems Laboratory
Sudbury, Massachusetts

Abstract -- This paper describes the architecture of the Raytheon Associative/ Array Processor (RAP) and its application to real-time radar signal processing. The nature of radar computations is analyzed and parallel processing requirements are characterized. The effects of these requirements upon the design of the RAP are described. Features of the operational RAP system are discussed. Finally, an implementation of a Constant False Alarm Rate (CFAR) Processor is given.

INTRODUCTION

Radar systems design has been undergoing a transition from analog to digital processing. These systems are becoming ever more complex to improve jamming immunity as well as acquisition and tracking performance. First attempts at replacing analog systems with digital equivalents involved design and fabrication of hardwired circuitry. As radar processing algorithms increase in complexity, the effort and development time required to implement a hardwired digital design result in expensive systems which are practically obsolete upon completion. Modification and upgrading of these systems are almost always not cost effective.

A programmable digital computer suitable for real time radar signal processing would provide flexibility and ease of modification of the processing algorithms. Continuously changing system requirements may then be reflected by changes in the processing programs rather than by new hardware. Multiple functions (FFT, CFAR, etc.) could be performed by the same programmable element rather than by separate functional units as previously done, again reducing system cost.

Integration of a programmable processor into a radar system requires that the processor have sufficient throughput capability to handle the workload. Conventional computer timing makes this procedure difficult because the sequential nature of the processor limits its throughput.

Increased throughput rates may be achieved in the following ways:

1. Multiple sequential machines may be configured in a multiprogramming/multiprocessing environment - This leads to a very complex operational structure.

2. Faster execution times - Technology projections do not indicate a major

reduction in this area for sequential processors.

3. Tailor a machine architecture to operate on a large set of data simultaneously - An array processor is a specific implementation of this idea.

An analysis of the structure of radar data and the level of parallelism in the
processing algorithms is the first step in developing the requirements for an array
processor suitable for radar processing applications.

THE RADAR SIGNAL PROCESSING PROBLEM

Radar data is returned for processing in digitized form from the antenna/re-
ceiver subsystem. For systems under consideration, the receiver is coherent and the
resultant data provides in-phase and quadrature components. The conventional approach is to think of the radar signal data as a serial stream of information. The
more detailed processing techniques require data from a number of pulse transmissions
(PRI Strobes). Thus, the data base may be thought of as an array of information,
the individual resolution cell being located by the pulse repetition interval (PRI)
strobe and the range cell, as shown by Figure 1.

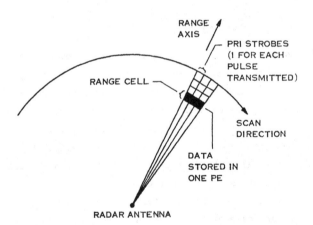

Figure 1. Search Radar Data Organization

Figure 2 is a representative functional diagram depicting the required computational steps involved in reducing the raw radar data into meaningful target update
and display information. After A/D conversion, the data is passed through an input
weighting network to reduce antenna sidelobe effects before entering the buffer
storage.

The buffer storage unit then builds up the block of data upon which computations will be performed. This aggregation into block format may be viewed as a
serial-to-parallel data transformation. Complex time samples are then transformed
to spectral frequency components via a Fast Fourier Transform (FFT). The FFT calculation requires a complete arithmetic capability, including a fast multiply. The

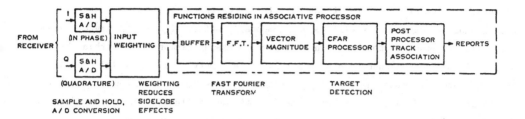

Figure 2. Typical Radar Signal Processor

complex frequency samples are then reduced to magnitudes for further processing.

In a radar with automatic detection, a target is said to be present if the signal amplitude crosses some predetermined threshold. The presence of noisy signals, such as from electronic countermeasures, can cause the number of false alrams to increase to an intolerable extent. If the radar output is being automatically processed by a computer using a constant threshold, an overload can readily occur. Thus, it is important that the receiver present a constant false alarm rate (CFAR) to data processing equipment. CFAR processing involves computation of average background level for the area surrounding each range cell and a determination of which cells contain reports exceeding this level. [1] In the simplest case, this amounts to determining if the signal level within a subelement is significantly larger than the surrounding subelements and should be declared a target. Thus, an associative/parallel processor operating on radar signal data must have capability to easily exchange data between processing elements if the inherent parallelism is to be fully exploited.

Post CFAR processing steps involve higher-level analysis of current track files to provide for tracker updating and countermeasure control as well as emitter identification. These computations require a capability to examine a data base against a target report and to determine which data base entries match the given value within limits. Since much of the post-detection processing consists of sequential data inputs and exact match operations, the capability to input (output) data to (from) specific processing elements of the parallel array easily is desirable. Also, during post-detection operations such as target tracking, Downs [2] has indicated the desirability of the inter-processing element data exchange paths previously mentioned.

It is a basic requirement that the processor have the capability to easily accept large blocks of data for processing with a minimum of program intervention.

The previous paragraphs have described the characteristics of radar signal processing. The array nature of the data indicates that simultaneous computation upon a block of range cells will reduce computation time. Data for a given range cell will be organized to reside in a single Processing Element (PE) within the array. PE's function under global control from a supervisory sequential processor. Large amounts of unprocessed, digitized data must flow into the processor and only highly processed data (i.e., radar targets, ECCM strobe signals, etc.) should exit.

The desirable features of an array processor suitable for radar signal processing are shown below. These features provided the motivation behind the Raytheon Associative/Array Processor (RAP).

1. Ability to store data within each PE.

2. Arithmetic/logic capability within each PE.

3. Inter-PE data transfer - this facilitates CFAR computation using adjacent range cell data.

4. Ability to conduct array search operations. An example would be the search of track records for identification of emitters. The results of a search operation (between limits, exact match, etc.) should be stored in each PE.

5. Ability to select a subset of the array for participation in array operations. A typical case is the subset generated by a between limits search.

6. The capability to easily accept large blocks of data for processing with a minimum of program intervention.

7. Input/output data from a specified PE location.

8. Dynamic array data field management. It is desirable to have data fields of variable lengths and to be able to alter field assignment under program control. This facilitates transitions from one functional task to another to optimize usage of available PE memory bits.

9. Capability of the Processing Unit to handle traditional sequential computer functions including I/O control, program sequencing, and arithmetic/logic operation on data from general purpose registers and/or program memory.

RAYTHEON ASSOCIATIVE PROCESSOR DESIGN

Using these requirements as basic criteria, preliminary study and design efforts were initiated for the development of a general purpose associative/parallel processor. A breadboard unit was completed in 1971 which provided insight into many of the problems of processors of this type. In 1972, the design of the Raytheon Associative Processor (RAP) was initiated. This second generation parallel processor (Figure 3) is a bit serial word parallel processor. The unit shown is configured for aerospace application.

Figure 3. Raytheon Associative/Array Processor (Including an Array of
64 Processing Elements).

Figure 4 is a system block diagram of the RAP. The processor may be subdivided
in four functional areas. (1) The processing element array provides the means for
parallel computation. (2) The array control logic provides data field addressing
and control for the PE array and facilitates read/write operations on selected PE
data fields. (3) A sequential control unit (essentially a microprogrammed, 32-bit
minicomputer) reads instructions from the program memory and executes the prescribed
functions. (4) The Direct Array Access Channel (DAAC) facilitates bulk data transfer
of data to/from the PE array.

Processing Element Structure

The chief distinguishing feature of the AP is the processing element array. The
function of the PE is to perform various arithmetic, logic, and search operations on
data stored in its own private memory. Each PE may be thought of as a bit serial
microprocessor with associative memory capability.

The PE array is organized in modular groups of 32 words (PEs). User needs determine the size of the array up to a maximum of 4096 words. It should be noted
that while each PE has its own individual memory data, all selected PE's perform the
same function at any given time as specified by the control. Present addressing
structure allows storage of 1024 bits per PE.

Figure 5 shows the basic PE structure, consisting of two independent memories
(called the workspace and the bulk memory), a Word Processing Unit (WPU) composed of
a full adder, two one-bit accumulators, a one-bit result register, a TAG (Match)
Register, and the attendant control logic.

The WPU logic is fabricated on a single Large Scale Integration (LSI) chip.
Work is underway to include in a single LSI chip the WPU, data selectors, fast

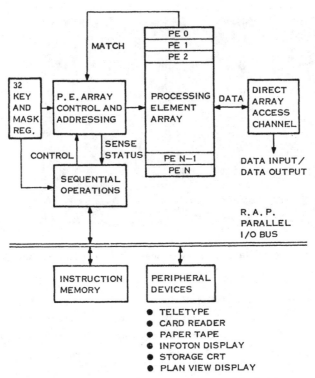

Figure 4. Raytheon Associative/Array Processor Block Diagram

multiply logic, and the inter PE's transfer logic. Conversion to LSI dramatically
decreases the cost of the PE array due to the fact that a relatively large quantity
of the identical part are used to make up the array.

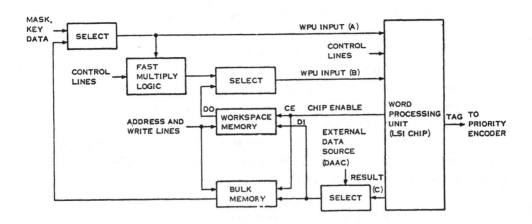

Figure 5. Simplified Block Diagram of One Processing Element

Having two memories permits the simultaneous fetch of both data fields for an arithmetic/logic operation, saving one cycle time. These arguments may be loaded into the accumulators in preparation for arithmetic or logic manipulation. The Result Register (RR) output is available for two possible functions:

. During an arithmetic or logic operation, the result register is written into both PE memories simultaneously as one bit of the answer. This allows the flexibility of reading the answer out of either memory during subsequent array microinstructions.

2. After a search operation, the Tag Register indicates whether or not the PE met the search criterion. The Tag is loaded from the RR.

Four bits of temporary storage are provided to each word for use as a scratchpad. Typical uses are temporary saving of Tag or Carry flip-flops.

DATA FIELD MANAGEMENT

Each PE memory may be pictured as one word of N bits. A data field may be defined as any contiguous subset of the N bit word. A particular bit location may be contained in more than one field.

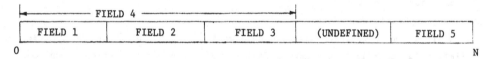

For example, any bit in fields 1, 2 or 3 in this example configuration is also part of Field 4. The user is free to define (in the control unit) the length and position of his data fields so as to best meet his goals. Masking allows selection of noncontiguous bits. In a typical instruction such as Array Subtract, three fields are specified:

$$(\text{FIELD 1}) \text{ MINUS } (\text{FIELD 2}) \rightarrow (\text{FIELD 3})$$

The contents of Field 1 are read from the bulk memory beginning with the least significant bit while at the same time the contents of Field 2 are read from the Workspace. The result from the WPU is then written into Field 3 of both memories. Data is assumed to be in 2s complement form, so if one input field is shorter than the other, sign extension is assumed. Sign extension is automatic if the resultant field is longer than required by the input fields.

SEARCH OPERATIONS

The RAP instruction set includes several array search operations such as the exact match, greater than, less than, maximum, and minimum. At the completion of each of these instructions, the Tag flip-flop of each PE will indicate whether or not its PE met the search criterion. The next instruction in the program sequence might then be a second-level search with only those PEs whose Tag is set participating. Tags may be selectively reset on a priority basis to resolve multiple matches.

MEMORY IMPLEMENTATION

The RAP system user may choose from two PE memory technologies depending on the characteristics of his particular application. One type, most efficient in dealing with array search or I/O operations, uses the Raytheon CMOS CAM.

In 1972 Raytheon, in conjunction with a semiconductor manufacturer, began development of a Content Addressable Memory using CMOS technology. This was undertaken because, after a survey of existing CAM devices, it was found that none could be integrated into a large array in a cost-effective manner. Each exhibited one or more of the following characteristics: low storage capacity, slow operating speed, high power consumption, or complex interface. The goal of the development of a new CMOS device was to provide a more optimum combination of the critical parameters. The important features are as follows:

1. low power - 100 MW
2. 150 nsec match interrogate time
3. 8x8 storage capacity
4. TTL compatible interface

Its 8 bit x 8 word structure permits Read/Write/Exact Match of eight-bit bytes in parallel. This capability increases efficiency of array I/O and search operations by a factor of eight over bit serial processes. During Read/Write functions, the CAM operates in exactly the same way as a Random Access Memory (RAM) would. In addition, on-the-chip logic allows the CAM to perform an exact match search on an eight-bit "key" word supplied by the array control unit. If the contents of the selected CAM byte match the key word exactly, the match output indicates that a successful search has occurred. The match output indicator is also used to "read" data out of the CAM in serial fashion for array arithmetic/logic operations.

The other alternative is to use semiconductor RAMs for the workspace and bulk memories. In this case, all array operations are bit serial, including I/O. The exact match search is accomplished in bit-serial fashion using the WPU logic instead of the internal logic in the CAM device. The RAM-based PE option advantage is its lower cost. If the majority of the program instructions do not involve array search or array I/O (e.g., CAFR, FFT), then the RAM based PE is the more cost-effective choice.

Two inter-PE data transfer channels are available to the user. First, each PE has the capability to transfer data on a bit serial basis to adjacent PEs. This achieves a right or left circular shift across PEs. Using this arrangement, data transfers between a given PE and any other PE may be conducted. As in other processors of this class, [4] [5] each PE contains a Tag Register to control PE participation in the instruction. In the case of transfer instructions, the individual tag registers condition the PE for data acceptance if set. If the Tag Register is not set, the destination location contents are unchanged.

A second data transfer channel implements the "perfect shuffle" interchange as discussed by Stone [6]. One of the basic routines performed by state-of-the-art signal processors is the Fast Fourier Transform. Stone and Pease [7] have indicated the advantages of using the shuffle interconnect in computing transforms in an efficient manner.

The instruction that most often breaks the back of the bit serial processor is multiply. In the case of FFT calculations, the multiply operation largely defines the processing time. The RAP processing element was designed using Booth's multiply algorithm, cutting the execution time by a factor of two relative to the more standard test, shift, and add approach.

Array Control

Three identical Field Definition Memories (FDMs) are employed to store array data field definitions. This allows dynamic programmer redefinitions of fields. Having three equivalent FDMs saves valuable time because the three field definitions required by many instructions are obtained in parallel. Each field is defined by a least significant bit and a most significant bit. These field definitions are referenced by program instructions to specify operand field numbers.

Sequential Control

Non-array operations available within the RAP provide capability similar to that of a 32 bit general purpose minicomputer.

Instructions executed by the RAP may either operate upon array data, register data, or memory data (residing in instruction memory). Combinations of register-register, register-memory and register-array instructions are provided. There are 32 addressable registers in the processor. In non-array usage they represent 32 working registers. For array search operations, they serve as 16 pairs of Key-Mask registers. Array data may be read/written to/from any specified register.

Information transfer within the sequential control unit is facilitated by the use of a 32-bit parallel I/O bus. This same bus also provides an interface medium to external devices and the instruction memory. The bus is a tri-state bidirectional I/O bus and has 16 address lines associated with it.

Instruction Set Formats

The instruction set of the processor is divided into four classes (formats). The formats are summarized below with representative examples given. Table 1 lists example execution times.

Class 0 - Field Definition and Non-Field Reference

OP CODE	MSB OF FIELD	LSB OF FIELD	FIELD NR
31 24	23 15	14 6	5 0

Examples:

Complement Tags (06) - CTG, Arguments: None

Load Field Definition (07) - LFD, Arguments: MSB, LSB, FIELD NUMBER

Class 1 - Memory/Register Logical Action Instructions

OP CODE	T	M	PE ADDR, SHIFT CNT, OR KEY REG NR	FIELD NR
31	24	23 22 21		6 5 0

T bit (23: If the T bit is set, all PEs in the array will take part in the specified operation. If the T bit is not set, only those PEs whose tags are set will participate. M bit (22): If the M bit is set, the bit masks specified by the Mask register will determine those bits which are to take part in the operation. If the M-bit is reset, all bits in the field will participate.

Examples:

Equal to Key (40) (Exact Match)

EQK, Arguments: T, M, Register, Field

Maximum in Set (45)

MAX, Arguments: T, Field

Store to Memory (58)

STM, Arguments T, Register, Field

Read from PE Word (62)

RFW Arguments T, PE Address, Field

(Contents of the specified field and PE are read into key register 0.) The significance of the T-bit is as follows:

T = 1, Effective PE Address is specified within the instruction.

T = 0, Effective PE Address is specified by the Match Address Register.

Logical AND (49)

AND, Arguments: T, Register, Field

Transfer UP (63)

TUP, Arguments: T, COUNT, FIELD

Class 2 - Control and Memory Reference Instructions

OP CODE	I	INST MEM OR BUS ADDR OR SHIFT COUNT	REG NR
31	24 23 22 21		6 5 0

I bits (22-23):

I = 00 Memory Address Field contains the effective address.

I = 10 Memory address field contains a pointer to the effective address (Indirect addressing)

I = 11 Same as I = 10 except that the effective address is incremented by one prior to use.

I = 01 the Match Address Register will be added to the contents of the address field and this sum will be used to reference the Instruction Memory.

Examples:

Jump on Match (85) (Jump if any Tags are set)

JOM, Arguments: I, Memory Address

Load Key Register (89)

LDR, Arguments: I, Mem. Address, Register

Add to Key Register (91)

AKR, Arguments: I, Mem. Address, Register

Class 3 - Arithmetic operations

OP CODE	T			FIELD A	REG NO. OR FIELD B	FIELD C

31   24 23 22 21   18 17   12 11   6 5   0

T bit (23): Same as Class I

Example:

Array Multiply (C2)

MPY, Arguments:T, Field A, Field B, Field C

    (the contents of Field A multiplied by Field B are stored in Field C)

Table 1.   Representative Processing Rates for 16 Bit Operations (times in micro-seconds)

Add Field to Field/Register to Field	$9.25 + \alpha$ [a]
Multiply Field by Field/Field by Register	$101.25 + \alpha$
Exact Match (CAM based PE)	$1.5 + \alpha$
Load Field Definition	$0.75 + \alpha$

Direct Array Access Channel

The Direct Array Access Channel (DAAC) provides for automatic transfer of data into/out of the PE array. The program being executed by the sequential control unit is not slowed by the DAAC process because of the "cycle sharing" technique involved. A typical array microinstruction consists of a read, process, and write cycles. During the process time, the PE memories are idle, as far as the active program is concerned. It is during these process cycles that the DAAC has control of the PE memory addressing for data transfer.

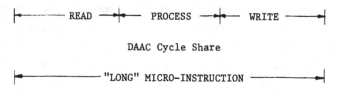

DAAC Cycle Share

There are also "short" micro-instructions consisting of time for only one PE read or one PE write. DAAC cycle sharing is inhibited during short cycles unless the array is not involved in the micro-instruction. Upon completing a block of data (PE Array filled), an interrupt is sent to the RAP control.

A CFAR EXAMPLE

Pre CFAR Processing

Digital processing begins when weighted serial data has filled the required samples into the buffer matrix shown in Fig. 1. Each PRI is subdivided into N range cells with a sample of the video being converted for each cell. Sets of data are generated for M pulse repetition intervals, M being a power of two. These sets of data referred to as a dwell are the basic processing blocks.

In order to develop a dwell of data, digitized video is temporarily stored in a buffer memory. When a number of samples have been gathered, the data is entered into the PE array by way of the DAAC. Since other processing is going on within the array, care must be taken not to overwrite active memory fields within the PE array. Double buffering, i.e., dividing each PE memory into two independent work areas, may be invoked. One section is used for active computation while the other is involved with data setup. The two sections are then functionally interchanged and the process repeated. An interrupt is issued to the processor control unit when dwell data transfer is complete.

The next step in processing the digitized video signal involves taking the discrete Fourier Transform of the dwell. Data has been ordered within the PE array such that all dwell data for a given range interval (2M samples) are stored within the same PE. This data organization allows conventional FFT procedures to be implemented on all range cells in parallel.

After the transform has been completed, the PE array contains a series of M velocity terms in the N range cells. The real and imaginary components are combined to give the magnitude. These magnitudes may be passed through a clutter filter prior to the CFAR process.

Generalized CFAR Process

A typical CFAR process [8] is performed as follows: (reference Figure 6). The greatest spectral magnitude for each range cell is identified. The sum of all remaining spectral components within this range cell is computed. The CFAR threshold is determined by multiplying a CFAR constant by the larger of this sum or a threshold minimum. For target detection, the value of the strongest spectral line is compared with the computed CFAR threshold. Actual aircraft targets will appear in one or two range cells. Thus, the threshold level used for target detection is based on the average signal level surrounding the range gate of interest plus an offset level to be selected for a constant noise false alarm rate. It is within this processing cycle that the inter-PE communication paths are most important.

CFAR Implementation

Figure 6 shows the first step in the chain to develop the average. The data on adjacent range cells are in separate, but adjacent, PEs, as in Figure 7. Therefore, the Transfer UP (TUP) array instruction may be used to move the specified field from each PE into a workspace field in the next higher PE. Similarly, other transfers from additional neighboring range cells may be achieved by further use of the TUP or Transfer Down (TDN) instructions.

The assembly coding for the RAP to perform a typical CFAR process is shown on the following page. The background noise level is computed from the range cell of interest and the four nearest neighbors for spectral components F_6-F_{10}. (It is these components that represent moving targets.)

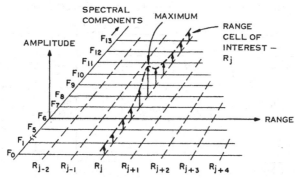

1. FIND GREATEST SPECTRAL MAGNITUDE FOR EACH RANGE CELL.
2. SUM SPECTRAL COMPONENTS LESS THE MAXIMUM $(\Sigma F_i - F_{MAX})$
3. COMBINE SUMS FROM ADJACENT RANGE CELLS $(R_{j-1}, R_{j-2}, R_{j+1}, R_{j+2})$
4. TEST COMBINED SUM AGAINST MINIMUM THRESHOLD.
5. MULTIPLY CFAR CONSTANT TO LARGER OF NO. 4 FOR CFAR THRESHOLD.
6. TARGET DETECTION; MAXIMUM SPECTRAL COMPONENT COMPARED TO CFAR THRESHOLD.

Figure 6. General CFAR Algorithm

The first section of code finds the largest spectral component for each range cell. This value and its component number are stored in fields A1 and A10 of the PE array respectively. Note that these operations are performed upon all range cells simultaneously. Note also the dynamic redefinition of the working field (FB) by use of the LFD instruction.

The second section of code performs the background noise computation and threshold comparison. Each range cell background noise level $(\Sigma F_i - F_{max})$ is evaluated using array add and subtract instructions. Transfer Up (TUP) and ADD as well as Transfer Down (TDN) and ADD are then used to compute background noise level for each range cell across its four nearest neighbors.

This background noise level is then scaled to produce the CFAR threshold. A limit clutter test is then performed to detect receiver saturation. This involves the associative Greater Than Key (GTK) seach instruction. All PEs meeting the search criterion of field FO being greater than the clutter limit (KR3) will have their tags set. The following Store to Memory (STM) will replace the CFAR threshold (field A3) by the clutter limit level (KR2) in only those PEs whose tags were set by the GTK instruction. Multiplication of all PE thresholds by a scale factor (KR4) is then performed and an array subtract computes for each range cell the differences between the largest spectral component and the CFAR threshold. An associative check on the most significant bit (MSB) of this result will result in tag bits being set in those PEs where targets are detected.

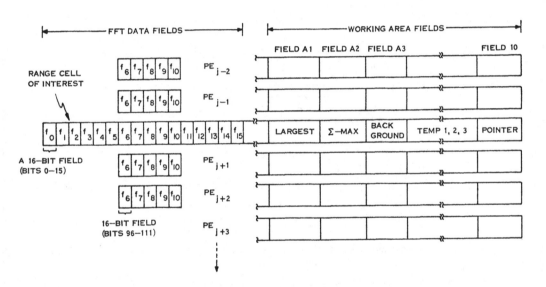

Figure 7. PE Array Field Allocation for CFAR Calculation

At this point, the target reports are read out through the key register in the sequential mode of the processor to be transmitted to users of the data or to be retained in a memory until a target tracking cycle can be entered by the processor. It should be noted that the mass of radar data originally transmitted to the processor has now been reduced to a small number of target reports per dwell. Dependent upon time constraints, the processor may also perform associative target tracking for the radar system, or, if the number of targets is small, the data may be passed on to a system controller.

SAMPLE RAP PROGRAM - CFAR

Register Initialization

        $KR1 \leftarrow 0$

        $KR2 \leftarrow$ Limit Clutter Value

        $KR3 \leftarrow$ Limit Clutter Test Level

        $KR4 \leftarrow$ Multiply Constant (Scale factor)

        $KR5 \leftarrow -4$ (Loop Counter)

        $KR6 \leftarrow 0$ (Index Pointer to LFD List)

        $KR7 \leftarrow 1$ (Initial Max Pointer)

<u>Section 1</u> - Find largest Spectral Component for each range cell

			Comments
	LFD	96, 111, FA	Define Working Field - Initially F6
	ARA	1, FA, KR1, A1	Move FA to A1, initializing maximum component (all PE's)
	STM	1, KR7, A10	Initialize maximum pointer to 6 (All PE's)
MORE	LBS	1, (LIST-1), KR6	Load LFD instruction
	STR	0, $+1, 0	Store to XEQ
	NOP		LFD instructions stored here
	SUB	1, A1, FB TEMP1	Test for a new maximum, if FB > A1, set tag
	TBO	1, MSBTEMP	
	ARA	0, FB, KR1, A1	Move new maximum value to A1 if tag is set
	IMF	0, A10	Update maximum pointer if tag is set
	IKR	KR5	Increment key register 5
	JRN	0, MORE, KR5	Jump to MORE if KRs is negative
	JMP	0, CFAR	Done, maximum spectral component has been found and is stored in A1. A10 contains component number.
LIST	LFD	112, 127, FB	(F7)
	LFD	128, 143, FB	(F8)
	LFD	144, 159, FB	(F9)
	LFD	160, 175, FB	(F10)

<u>Section 2</u> - Calculate CFAR threshold and detect presence of target

CFAR	ADD	1, F6, F7, A2	
	ADD	1, F8, A2, A2	Sum F6 + F7 + F8 + F9 + F10
	ADD	1, F9, A2, A2	
	ADD	1, F10, A2, A2	
	SUB	1, A2, A1, A2	$A2 \leftarrow \sum_{6}^{10} F_i - F_{max}$

ARA	1, A2, KR1, TEMP2	Copy A2 to TEMP2
TUP	1, COUNT = 1, A2	$A2_j \leftarrow A2_{j-1}$
ADD	1, A2, TEMP2, TEMP3	$TEMP3_j \leftarrow (A2_j + A2_{j-1})$
TUP	1, COUNT = 1, TEMP3	$TEMP3_j \leftarrow (A2_{j-1} + A2_{j-2})$
ARA	1, TEMP2, KR1, A2	Copy TEMP2 to A2
TDN	1, COUNT = 1, TEMP2	$A2_j \leftarrow A2_{j+1}$
ADD	1, A2, TEMP2, TEMP2	$TEMP2_j \leftarrow (A2_j + A2_{j+1})$
TDN	1, COUNT = 1, TEMP2	$TEMP2_j \leftarrow (A2_{j+1} + A2_{j+2})$
ADD	1, TEMP2, TEMP3, A3	$A3_j \leftarrow A2_{j-2} + A2_{j-1} + A2_{j+1} + A2_{j+2}$ (Sum of 4 nearest neighbors)
GTK	1, KR3, F0	Limit clutter test, Set tag if F0 > KR3
STM	0, KR2, A3	Replace A3 with clutter limit if tag is set
ARM	1, A3, KR4, A3	Scale CFAR threshold
SUB	1, A3, A1, TEMP4	Subtract - set tag if A1 > A3
TBO	1, MSBTEMP4	i.e., Tags now indicate target detections

CONCLUSIONS

This paper is one example of how an associative/array processor may be employed as programmable signal processors for radar systems. The application of such programmable array processors to new systems reduces risk and increases the flexibility of the system. As technology progresses, the cost of array processors will decrease. Improvement in algorithmic structures suitable for parallel/associative architectures will further motivate the use of parallel processors in real-time radar and ECM/ELINT systems. The authors believe that the RAP, using special LSI devices, is a significant step toward a greater use of array processing techniques.

REFERENCES

[1] M. Bernfeld, Manuscript, "A Comprehensive Refresher in Radar Theory," pp. 3-23.

[2] H.R. Downs, "Aircraft Conflict Detection in an Associative Processor," AFIPS Conference Proceedings, Vol. 42, 1973, AFIPS Press, pp. 177-180.

[3] G.R. Couranz, M.S. Gerhardt, and C.J. Young, "Associative Processor", Internal Raytheon Report ER74-4003, March 1974.

[4] G. Estrin, and R. Fuller, "Algorithms for Content-Addressable Memories," Proc. IEEE Pacific Computer Conf., pp. 118-130, 1963.

[5] K.J. Thurber, and R.O. Berg, "Applications of Associative Processors," Computer Design, November 1971, pp. 103-110.

[6] H. Stone, "Parallel Processing with the Perfect Shuffle," IEEE Trans. on Computers, February 1971, pp. 153-161.

[7] M.C. Pease, "An Adaptation of the Fast Fourier Transform to Parallel Processing," J. ACM, Vol. 15, April 1968, pp. 252-264.

[8] P. Barr, "Study and Documentation of Existing Algorithms for Signal Processing of Radar Returns," Raytheon Memo EM74-0173, 28 February 1974.

ANALYSIS AND DESIGN OF A COST-EFFECTIVE ASSOCIATIVE PROCESSOR FOR WEATHER COMPUTATIONS [a]

WEI-TIH CHENG
Advanced Systems Development Division
International Business Machines
Yorktown Heights, N. Y. 10598

TSE-YUN FENG
Department of Electrical & Computer Engineering
Syracuse University
Syracuse, N. Y. 13210

Abstract-- An associative processor organization with application to weather computations, and specifically, to a two-level atmospheric general circulation model developed by Mintz and Arakawa is used as the application problem to be implemented for system analysis and design. These system parameter changes include the arithmetic-logic capabilities, the number of processing elements, different speeds, structures, and access techniques of the memory, addition of a high speed temporary storage, and the use of an auxiliary storage unit. Pertinent data are calculated for all these systems and a cost-effective system is finally determined after the comparisons of these analysis results are made. This final system is then evaluated and compared with the original system.

I. INTRODUCTION

Since it would be impossible for a system designer to expect a computer system to be cost-effective for all areas of applications, in this study an associative processor organization is selected to solve the weather computation problems. This is because associative processing provides a natural combination of arithmetic-logic and search-retrieval capabilities which is a desired characteristic for many mathematical problems, such as matrix operations, fast Fourier transform, and partial differential equation [1]. The solution of partial differential equations is essentially the basic mathematical tool for weather computations. Among many other weather problems, a two-level atmospheric general circulation model developed by Mintz and Arakawa [2] is chosen as one representative example for demonstrating the suitability of the associative parallel processor for such problems. The essential use of this general circulation model is as an experimental tool for studying the nonlinear behavior of the atmosphere. It is intended to use this model to explore the sensitivity and response of the world's climate to either deliberate or inadvertent modification, through the various settings of the initial and boundary

---

(a)

The work reported here was performed at Syracuse University and was supported by The Air Force Rome Air Development Center under Contract F30602-72-C-0281.

conditions.

II. AN ASSOCIATIVE PROCESSOR ORGANIZATION

In order to make our investigation meaningful an associative processor organization is first assumed. The system consists mainly of five component [3] as shown in Figure 1. It is assumed that there are a total of 1024 PE's in this system. Each PE has a 256-bit associative word divided into four 32-bit fields (A, B, C, D), 16 bits of temporary storage (TS), an M bit, and one bit-serial arithmetic-logic unit. All 1024 M bits form a <u>mask register</u> which is used to activate or deactivate the corresponding PE's. Data words stored in the fields are fetched bis*-sequentially to be processed by the arithmetic-logic unit. The results are stored back to the designated destination.

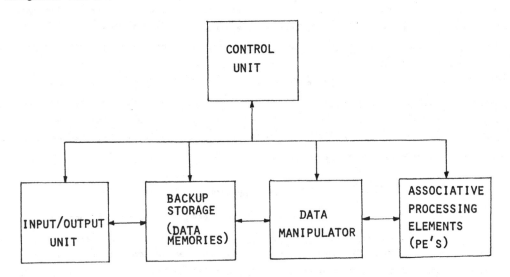

Figure 1. An associative parallel processor organization.

The data words are 32-bit long and represented in two's complement form throughout the system. Floating-point numbers have an 8-bit exponent and a 24-bit mantissa.

III. IMPLEMENTATION OF THE GENERAL CIRCULATION MODEL ON AP

The original program of the Mintz-Arakawa two-level atmospheric general circulation model was written in FORTRAN [2]. It has been translated into parallel processing programs [4]. The whole program is constructed mainly of two components.

---

*All ith bits of a given set of operands from the ith bit slice, or <u>bis</u>, of the set.

The first is the updating of variables in five time-steps by computing their time derivatives without the influence of the source terms. During each time-step the computing procedure is processed twice as required by the backward differencing scheme. We shall designate this computing procedure as PART I program which is executed in a total of ten times during the five time-steps. After the variables have been updated ten times through the five time-steps by PART I program, the effect of the source terms is added to the computation of the time derivatives. The part of program which produces the source terms is designated as PART II program.

PART I and PART II programs are segmented into 18 and 17 subprograms, respectively. These subprograms are executed one at a time in a sequential manner with each program. All these subprograms are used to update the basic variables of the general circulation model [2]. Each variable has a data set of the size of $46 \times 72 = 3312$. Since the capacity of the AP is assumed to be 1024, each of these data sets as well as other generated along the process, will have to be segmented into groups of proper size. For implementation details and other considerations see Reference [4].

IV. OPERATIONAL CHARACTERISTICS AND ANALYSIS OF THE GENERAL CIRCULATION MODEL

A. Operation Counts

Based upon the parallel processing programs we first obtain the operation counts of each subprogram. The distribution of operations is then analyzed.

Table 1 gives the operation counts for OVERALL program which includes the execution of PART I program ten times and the execution of PART II program once over the complete data sets.

B. Operation Distributions

From Table 1 we can see that arithmetic operations take up more than one third of all operations; data transfers among PE's take up more than one fifth; while load and store operations are about 15% and 5%, respectively.

Another type of operation distribution is obtained by calculating the distribution according to the system components involved in the operations. Two major categories of operations are operations involving both the backup storage and PE's and operations involving PE's alone (Table 2). Within each of these two categories of operations some operations require data manipulating functions and others do not. The total involvement of the data manipulator is also given in Table 2.

C. Estimation of Execution Time

The most fundamental operation executed in PE's to perform various arithmetic operations is the addition of two bises. This addition consists of the reading of two bises to be added, execution of the addition and the writing of the resultant

Table 1. Operation Counts and Execution Times of Overall Program

			Number of Operations	Execution Time per Operation (μsec)	Total Execution Time for OVERALL Program (μsec)
ARITHMETIC	Common	$+$	1528	126.7	193903.2
		$\times$	1544	107.2	165516.8
	Field	$+$	8660	136.3	1180358.
		$\times$	4354	207.4	903019.6
		$/$	1496	269.9	403770.4
	$x,/$ by 2^i		1616	2.4	3878.4
LOAD	Pattern	1	3888	20.8	80870.4
		2	696	49.75	34626
		3	1516	49.75	75421
		4	1880	49.75	93530
	One-Bis		292	0.65	189.8
STORE	Pattern	1	1066	27.225	29021.85
		2	292	59.775	17454.3
		3	904	50.95	46058.8
		4	440	59.775	26301
	One-Bis		28	0.85	23.8
TRANSFER	Direct		884	8.0	7072
	Shift		4424	16.1	71226.4
		M	2522	16.1	40604.2
	One-Bis		3504	0.25	876
TEMPORARY STORAGE			1423	27.2	38705.6
LOGIC			650	0.05	32.5
SET MASK			5054	0.10	252.7
MULTIPLICATE			660	28.9	170.4
MULTIPLE WRITE			1136	0.15	2547.2
SEARCH			398	6.4	2878.2
BIT SHIFT		24	468	6.15	670.8
		8	312	2.15	374.4
FIXED-POINT ADD		C	156	2.4	374.4
		F	156	2.4	3438802.15
TOTAL			51947	No. of Operations/sec = 15106	

sum bis into PE's. With the semiconductor type of PE associative memory (PEAM), two bises can be read out simultaneously, one in true form and the other in complement form. Thus a single bis addition takes 300 nsec, with the following timing assumptions for our system.

Operation:	Read PE	Write PE	Execute	Read backup storage	Write backup storage	Set DM control	DM delay
Time(n.sec):	100	150	50	500	750	100	250

Based on the above assumptions, the execution times for various operations and routines can be estimated. And according to the estimated execution time of the various basic operations we can calculate the total execution time for the OVERALL program. These are also given in Table 1. Notice that more than 80% of the total execution time is spent on arithmetic operations. A discussion on how to improve the total performance by speeding up the arithmetic operations will be given in the following section.

The execution time distribution of this system (System 1) according to system components can also be found in Table 2. Table 2 shows that only 13.41% of the total execution time is spent on executing operations involving both the PE's and the backup storage, the rest of the time is on operations executed in PE's alone. The operations which involve the data manipulator take up about 11.5% of the total execution time in processing the general circulation model.

D. Utilization and Efficiency of PE's

We define utilization, u, and efficiency, E, of PE's as follows:

$$u_i = \frac{\text{No. of PE's utilized in operation i}}{\text{Total No. of PE's available}} \qquad (1)$$

$$E = \sum_i u_i \cdot t_i/T = \sum_i u_i \cdot r_i \qquad (2)$$

where t_i is the execution time of the operation i, T is the total execution time of a program and r_i the percentage of t_i with respect to T.

From the parallel processing programs we see that almost all the arithmetic operations involve all the PE's where data are stored. This, however, does not give a 100% utilization. This is because the subprograms are executed four times for four groups of data of each complete data set and the first three groups of data occupy all the $14 \times 72 = 1008$ PE's but the fourth group utilizes only $4 \times 72 = 288$ PE's. Thus an average utilization for arithmetic operations is calculated as follows:

$$u_1 = \frac{1}{4} \times (1008 + 1008 + 1008 + 288) \times \frac{1}{1024}$$

$$= 0.8086$$

Table 2. Operation Counts and Execution Times According
to System Components for OVERALL Program

		Operation		Execution (System 1)		Execution (System 10)	
		Count	%	Time (μs)	%	Time (μs)	%
Backup Storage ⟷ PE's	With DM	5547	10.68%	283470.85	8.24%	51985.30	4.38%
	Without DM	7536	14.51%	177887.45	5.17%	42980.15	3.62%
	TOTAL	13083	25.19%	561358.30	13.41%	94965.45	8.00%
PE's Alone	With DM	6946	13.37%	111830.60	3.25%	111830.60	9.42%
	Without DM	31918	61.44%	2865899.00	83.34%	980005.50	82.58%
	TOTAL	38864	74.81%	2977729.60	86.59%	1091836.10	92.00%
Total DM Involvement		12493	24.05%	495301.45	11.49%	163815.90	13.80%

The load and store operations have four different patterns and each pattern
involves the loading or storing of different subsets of groups of data set. When
different numbers of PE's are being loaded or stored in various patterns of operations, different average utilizations result. Utilizations for transfer operations
can similarly be calculated. Table 3 includes all the utilizations for different
operations.

Now that we have obtained the PE utilizations of the major operations we can
calculate the PE efficiencies for processing PART I, PART II and OVERALL programs
according to Eq. (2). Table 3 also gives the efficiencies of the three programs.

E. Relative Performance Measure

Evidently, the overall performance of the processor for the general circulation model programs cannot rely on the efficiency alone. At least two other important items should also be included in the consideration, these are the total
execution time and the cost of the hardware. But for the moment, we shall concentrate only on the performance aspect of the system.

We now define the performance measure of a given system to be

$$P = \frac{E}{T^{\alpha}} \tag{3}$$

where E is the efficiency of PE's, T is the execution time, and α is a weighting
index of execution time with respect to efficiency. The reason that α is necessary
is that a range of measurements with different degrees of emphasis on execution time
with respect to efficiency can be made. Using the performance measure defined above
we can do some comparative study of the overall performance evaluation of different
systems. To achieve this we define a relative performance measure of System A with
respect to System B, R_{AB}, to be

Table 3. PE Utilizations and Efficiencies

OPERATION	UTILIZATION u_i	PART I t_i/T	PART I $u_i t_i/(T \times 10^{-2})$	PART II t_i/T	PART II $u_i t_i/(T \times 10^{-2})$	OVERALL t_i/T	OVERALL $u_i t_i/(T \times 10^{-2})$
ARITHMETIC	0.8086	0.8031	64.9400	0.9266	74.9200	0.8290	670809
Pattern 1	0.8086	0.0206	1.6670	0.0336	2.7150	0.0235	1.9020
Pattern 2	0.4922	0.0128	0.6300	0.0010	0.0500	0.0101	0.4960
Pattern 3	0.4922	0.0271	1.3340	0.0048	0.2370	0.0219	1.0880
Pattern 4	0.5223	0.0354	1.8480	0	0	0.0272	1.4210
One-Bis	0.8086	0.00005	0.0040	0.00005	0.0040	0.00005	0.0860
STORE	0.8086	0.0083	0.6750	0.0089	0.7170	0.0084	0.6820
Pattern 1	0.4621	0.0063	0.2930	0.0009	0.0420	0.0051	0.2350
Pattern 2	0.5391	0.0170	0.9140	0.0016	0.0840	0.0134	0.7220
Pattern 3	0.4621	0.0099	0.4600	0	0	0.0076	0.3530
Pattern 4	0.8086	0	0	0.00003	0.0020	0.0000	0.
One-Bis	0.8086	0.0016	0.1270	0.0037	0.3000	0.0021	0.
Direct	0.7598	0.0268	2.0360	0.0005	0.0380	0.0207	1.5730
Shift M	0.0130	0.0153	0.0200	0.0002	0.0003	0.0118	0.0150
One-Bis	0.8086	0.0001	0.0100	0.0007	0.0560	0.0003	0.0310
EFFICIENCY $\Sigma u_i t_i/T$		0.7506		0.7919		0.7570	
OPERATION TOTAL $\Sigma t_i/T$		0.9843		0.9826		0.9812	
TOTAL EFFICIENCY $(\Sigma u_i t_i/T)/(\Sigma t_i/T)$		0.7626		0.8059		0.7715	

$$R_{AB} = \frac{P_A}{P_B}$$

$$= \frac{E_A}{E_B} (\frac{T_B}{T_A})^\alpha \qquad\qquad (4)$$

which will be used repeatedly in comparing the relative merits of various systems.

V. SYSTEM VARIATIONS AND PERFORMANCE EVALUATIONS

In the preceding section the programs of the general circulation model were analyzed based upon the assumed AP organization and its capabilities presented in Section II. Now we shall examine how some of the system parameter changes affect the overall performance of the system processing these programs. The alternative systems with the following variations are presented:

1. four-bis-parallel arithmetic-logic capabilities,

2. 2048 PE's,

3. 4096 PE's,

4. new backup storage with slower speed,

5. new backup storage with faster speed,

6. modularized backup storage,

7. backup storage banks with interleaving capability, and

8. addition of a high speed temporary storage (HSTS).

We shall designate the system with the above system parameter changes as Systems 2, 3, ..., and 9, respectively, with the original system as System 1. For each of the alternative systems the following data are calculated for the processing of the general circulation model programs.

1. new execution time and speedup ratio when compared with the original system,

2. new PE utilizations and efficiencies, and

3. relative performance evaluation with respect to the original system.

A. Four-Bis-Parallel Arithmetic-Logic Capabilities

In the following paragraphs we consider a four-bit-parallel arithmetic unit for each PE.

If the four-bis-parallel capability is provided to the system, yet the data transfer rate is not increased accordingly, there cannot be any significant increase in overall processing speed. Therefore, we have to change the data path between PEAM and the arithmetic-logic unit so that four bises of data can be accessed simultaneously. This provision may be realized through the use of four identical associative memories with proper interconnections between them and the arithmetic-logic unit.

The essential hardware requirement for four-bis-parallel add and subtract operations is a four-bis-parallel adder due to their simple iterative read-add(subtract)-write sequence. As for multiplications, not only there are many different algorithms, but also each algorithm requires different hardware setup. Since we are trying to obtain a balance between speed gain and hardware economy in providing four-bis-parallel arithmetic-logic operations, before we finalize the design of the arithmetic and logic unit, we examine some of the multiplication algorithms. Three algorithms are under consideration: direct multiplication scheme used by TI's SIMDA [5], Booth algorithm used in bis-sequential version of the processor, and polynomial algorithm used in Machado's proposed SPEAC system [6].

After examining and comparing these three multiplication algorithms, the polynomial algorithm is chosen due to its speed advantage and less storage requirements.

Based upon the four-bis-parallel capabilities in the arithmetic-logic unit of PE's, a complete set of algorithms for all the necessary arithmetic operations were developed [4]. Using the same timing assumptions as we used for bis-sequential operations we have the estimated execution time for the four-bis-parallel arithmetic operations (Table 4). Table 4 also compares the execution times of bis-sequential and four-bis-parallel arithmetic operations by giving the speedup factors.

Table 4. Execution Time of Floating-Point Arithmetic Operations (μsec)

	Operation	Bis-Sequential	Four-Bis-Parallel	Speedup Factor
Add	Common	126.7	28.85	4.39
	Field	136.3	52.5	2.6
Subtract	Common	126.7	28.85	4.39
	Field	136.3	52.5	2.6
Multiply	Common	107.2	55	1.95
	Field	269.9	95.80	2.82
Divide	Common	253.9	95.60	2.66
	Field	269.9	95.80	2.82

With the new execution times for these various operations, we can calculate the subtotal and total execution times for each individual operations and the entire programs. The first row of Table 5 gives the speedup factors of PART I, PART II, and OVERALL programs when compared with the original system. We can see that the speed for processing the general circulation model on System 2 is more than doubled.

The utilization of PE's for all operations remain unchanged in System 2. The new PE's efficiencies, derived from the new execution time distribution are reduced

Table 5. Speedup Factors

SYSTEM	SPEEDUP FACTOR WITH RESPECT TO SYSTEM 1		
	PART I	PART II	OVERALL
2	2.12	2.66	2.22
3	2.05	2.00	2.04
4	4.26	4.02	4.08
5	0.91	0.95	0.92
6	1.06	1.03	1.05
7	1.04	0.99	1.03
8	1.14	1.05	1.12
9	1.06	1.02	1.05
10	2.86	3.04	2.90

as shown in second row of Table 6. This reduction results from the great decrement in execution time of arithmetic operations which have a high utilization of 0.8086.

Table 6. Comparison of PE Efficiencies

SYSTEM	EFFICIENCY		
	PART I	PART II	OVERALL
1	0.7626	0.8059	0.7715
2	0.7064	0.8008	0.7246
3	0.7757	0.8070	0.7830
4	0.7948	0.8083	0.7981
5	0.7467	0.8042	0.7594
6	0.7704	0.7065	0.7788
7	0.7748	0.8069	0.7825
8	0.7857	0.8078	0.7911
9	0.7722	0.8067	0.7803
10	0.7713	0.8063	0.7632

We can now calculate the relative performance of four-bis-parallel processing with respect to bis-sequential processing. R_{21} in Fig. 2 shows the relative performance between Systems 1 and 2 versus α. It indicates that if the improvement in execution time is more important than in PE efficiency, the four-bis-parallel arith-

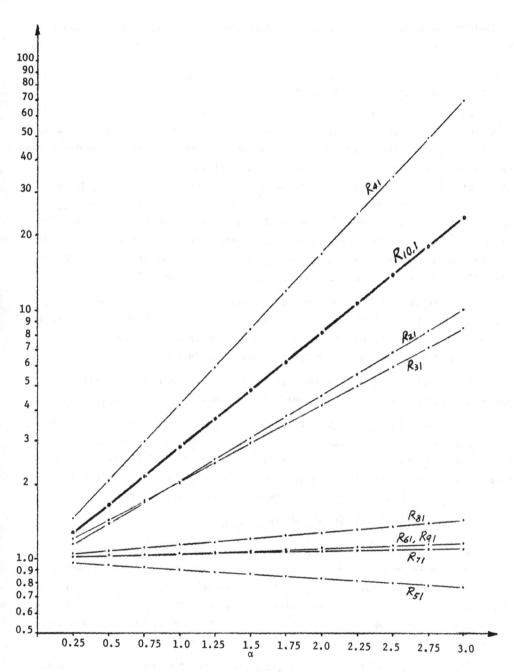

Figure 2. Relative performance evaluation.

metic-logic technique is more effective. Even when α is 1 (the efficiency and the execution time are of equal importance) the relative performance measure has a value of about 2.

B. Change of Number of PE's and Its Effects

We are going to examine some of the effects when the capacity of the associative processor is doubled or quadrupled. We first study the case of the system with 2048 PE's. Along with the expansion of PE's the dimensions of both the backup storage and the data manipulator have to be changed to match the PE's structure. Since the AP capacity is doubled to 2048, we can now finish processing of any complete data set in two iterations instead of four. Data sets are now grouped into two groups. Since the discontinuity between groups of data still exists all the operations concerning patterns 2, 3, and 4 remain unchanged. The average execution time for each of these operations have changed due to the new grouping. Designating this AP with 2048 PE's as System 3 the speedup factors can be found in Table 5.

Utilization of PE's in System 3 has changed also due to change of grouping of the data sets. Load and store operations now take fewer basic operations to achieve. As a result, most of the new utilizations are greater than the original ones. The efficiencies for three programs in System 3 are given in Table 6.

From the efficiencies and execution times of three programs processed by System 1 and System 3 we derive the relative perfomance evaluation, R_{31} (Fig. 2).

System 4 is the system with 4096 PE's and the other units in the system expanded proportionally. The total execution times for all three programs are calculated and compared with those of System 1 (Table 5). The PE efficiencies for System 4 are given in Table 6. A rather high relative performance evaluation of System 4, R_{41}, (Fig. 2) thus results. Its value exceeds 70 as α reaches 3.

C. Change of Backup Storage Speed and Its Effects

The speed of the backup storage we considered for System 1 is 500 nsec for read and 750 nsec for write, without considering the addressing time. We shall in the following analysis change the speed to 1 μsec-read and 1.5 μsec-write for System 5 and to 250 nsec-read and 375 nsec-write for System 6. We shall see how this change of the backup storage speed affects the execution time, PE efficiencies, and overall performance.

The speedup factors for Systems 5 and 6 can be found in Table 5. It is noted that halving the storage speed brings a substantial slowdown in all operations while doubling the speed brings only about 5% speedup.

The PE efficiencies of three programs, PART I, PART II, and OVERALL, processed in System 5 are lower than those in System 1 due to the increase of percentages in load and store operations while the PE efficiencies for System 6 are increased (Table 6). The relative performance evaluations of Systems 5 and 6 are plotted in Fig. 2.

D. Modularization of Backup Storage and Its Effects

In Section III we have mentioned the discontinuity of data sets when they are stored in groups of blocks. The suggested means to solve this problem is the creation of new data sets to speed up the data transfer between the backup storage and PEAM. As a result of using these new data sets a 24% speedup is computed for all the load operations performed in PART I program of the general circulation model.

An alternative way to speed up the loading of Patterns 2, 3, and 4 data sets is to modularize the backup storage. The backup storage has Q modules with equal dimensions. Their vertical dimensions is the same as that of the data manipulator and also the number of PE's. A mask register is associated with each storage module in order to select or "screen" the words to be read out or written into. At most one ith word of all the storage modules can be read out or written into at a time. The words thus read out from any number of modules can then be manipulated to be loaded in a desired format into PEAM. Storing data from the PEAM into the backup storage modules goes through the same procedure in reverse order.

All other operations are executed in exactly the same way as in System 1. The speed comparison between System 1 and this system with the modularized backup storage, designated as System 7, is given in Table 5. The consequent changes in execution-time distributions contribute to slightly increase in PE efficiencies (Table 6). The relative evaluation of System 7 is plotted in Fig. 2.

E. Backup Storage Banks with Interleaving Features and Its Effects

In using an interleaving system to process the general circulation model, we do not change either the data structure or the programs used in System 1. It affects the execution time of load, store, multiplicate and temporary store operations.

The total execution times for this system, System 8, are calculated and compared with those of System 1 (Table 5). From Table 5 we see that the improvement in total execution time in this system with interleaving BSB's is an excellent 12% over System 1, even though the combined execution time of load, store, temporary store, and multiplicate operations take only 13.425% in the original system for the OVERALL program. This speedup is also reflected in the calculation of PE efficiencies. As the data transfer type of operations take less portion of the total execution time to perform, the arithmetic operations which have higher PE utilization now take larger percentage of the total time. This boosts the PE efficiencies (Table 6). The plot of the relative performance evaluation of System 8 with respect to System 1, R_{81}, can be found in Fig. 2.

F. Addition of A High Speed Temporary Storage and Its Effects

Here we present a system with a separate storage unit, a high-apeed temporary storage (HSTS), used to handle the temporary store operations and also used as a buffer between the backup storage (through the data manipulator or bypassing it) and PEAM. The speed of this high-speed temporary storage is compatible to that of the PE.

The comparison of subtotal and total execution times between System 1 and System 9 is given in Table 5. Note that the speed improvement of the OVERALL program in System 9 over System 1 is about 5%, a very significant gain, considering that the number of operations with improved execution time by the use of HSTS is only 12.02% of all the operations.

PE efficiencies are increased in System 9 as compared to System 1 because the execution times in performing load and store operation are reduced (Table 6). The relative performance evaluation of System 9 with respect to System 1, R_{91}, does not have large values as shown in Fig. 2.

G. Storage Requirement and Auxiliary Storage Unit

When every data set is too large in size to be processed at one time as in this weather computation problem with the assumed organization, there are two kinds of processing schemes: the complete data set processing scheme and the complete program processing scheme. The complete data set processing scheme is such a design of program flow that every data set is completely processed by each subprogram before going through the next subprogram. On the other hand, a complete program processing scheme is so designed that a segment (i.e., group) of the data set is processed by the entire program before the next segment of data set is processed. The result of a detailed analysis of all subprograms and their storage requirements for both schemes is summarized in Table 7 .

From Table 7 we see that the sizes of the backup storage required to process the general circulation model are 160K and 79K in the complete data set processing scheme and the complete program processing scheme, respectively, without the use of the temporary storage. When the size of the grid system becomes larger, say, doubled in both horizontal and vertical dimension, the size of the backup storage increases rapidly (277K and 115K) and its access speed may be slowed down considerably. The use of an auxiliary storage unit is thus considered.

An APL simulation program [4] is written to simulate the data transfer activities between the backup storage and the disk. Various sizes of the backup storage are used in the simulation program. From the simulation we see the rapid decrease in the number of roll-in and roll-out operations required as the size of the backup

Table 7. Storage Requirement for the General Circulation Model

PROCESSING STORAGE SCHEME	ONE STORAGE	SEPARATE STORAGE		
	Backup Storage	Backup Storage	Temporary Storage	Total
Complete Data Set Processing Scheme	160K	156K	10K	166K
Complete Program Processing Scheme	79K	75K	10K	85K

storage increases, especially when the size of the backup storage is small. When
the size of the backup storage reaches 43K words, 48 roll-in and 36 roll-out operations are required and they remain constant for larger backup storage sizes. This
total of 84 roll-in and roll-out operations account for the roll-ins and roll-outs
of the twelve residing data sets at the beginning and the end of each updating cycle,
respectively. Thus, if an extra 36K words capacity is added to the backup storage
no roll-in and roll-out operations are necessary. This agrees with the backup
storage requirement for the general circulation model when processed by the complete
program processing scheme, namely, a maximum of 79K words are required for the backup storage without the use of the auxiliary storage unit.

VI. A MORE COST-EFFECTIVE ASSOCIATIVE PROCESSOR SYSTEM

In Section V we have presented eight different systems and showed, in each of
them, how the system parameter change affects the overall performance. However,
each of these system parameter changes was concentrated in only one component of the
entire system. Three of these eight system variations were on the associative processing elements and five on the backup storage. In this section we try to compare
the advantages and disadvantages of these systems and then combine the merits of
these systems in order to arrive at a more cost-effective system than the assumed
system presented in Section II.

A. Comparison of the Cost-Effectiveness of Alternative Systems

1. Associative Processing Elements

Three systems, Systems 2, 3, and 4 mentioned in Section V dealt with altera-
tions of the capability and the number of the associative processing elements in the
system. Among these the four-bis-parallel processing capability affects only the

hardware of PE's leaving the rest of the system intact. But in the cases of the other two alternatives, the sizes of other components in the system change along with the size change of the associative processing elements. A cost analysis on these two alternatives [4] show that System 3, with 2048 PE's, and System 4, with 4096 PE's, have, respectively, a cost of double and quadruple of that of System 1 and the overall cost of System 2 is less than double of that for System 1.

Thus, from the cost analysis and the speedup factors given in Table 5 for Systems 2, 3, and 4, it seems that System 2 is most favorable. Table 6 indicates that the PE efficiencies for Systems 3, and 4 are a little higher than that for System 2 in processing this weather problem, but in applications where the sizes of the data sets being processed are not as large as the capacity of PE's the efficiency will become much smaller. In short, System 2 is relatively more cost-effective.

2. The Backup Storage Unit

There are five variations on the speed, the capability, and the structure of the backup storage unit, resulting in five different systems, Systems 5, 6, 7, 8, and 9. In considering the cost factors of these systems in comparison with System 1, it is apparent that System 5 is the only system which is less costly than System 1 because it has slower speed. System 7 and 8 have basically the same memory modules but with different accessory equipments such as masking control in System 7 and interleaving control in System 8. System 9 has the largest storage requirement in terms of overall storage size. If we process the general circulation model programs in a complete program processing scheme, Systems 5, 6, 7, and 8 would need only a total of 79K words while System 9 would need 75K words of backup storage and 10K words of HSTS (Table 7). With the speed of HSTS compatible to that of the associative memory System 9 evidently is much more costly than the others.

It may be difficult for us to have a more precise cost comparison among these systems without going into implementation details. On the other hand, it may not be necessary for us to have a more precise cost comparison to determine which of these systems is the most cost-effective one. From Tables 5 and 6 we can see that System 8 demonstrates the best performance in execution time in processing the general circulation model and also it improves the PE efficiency from 0.7715 in the original system to 0.7911. It seems that despite the difficulty in having a very precise absolute-cost comparison among Systems 5, 6, 7, 8, and 9, it is reasonable to choose System 8 for the improvement of the backup storage over the original system.

B. Examination of a Cost-Effective System

We shall now examine how the new system, designated as System 10, with the combined improvements from System 2 and System 8, performs in implementing the general circulation model. The operation distribution remains the same as in System 1 since there is no change in programming. The total execution times for PART I,

PART II, and OVERALL program are 92833.94 μsec, 258462.15 μsec, and 1186801.5 μsec, representing speedup ratios over System 1 of 2.86, 3.04, and 2.90, respectively (Table 5).

We may look at the execution time from another point of view. As done in Section IV, total execution times are analyzed according to the utilization of the major components in the system. The associative processing elements are kept busy in all the operations so it has a 100% component utilization. Only 8.00% of the total time is spent on the data transfer operation between PE's and the backup storage, either through the data manipulator or bypassing it (Table 2). Again, the decrease in this figure from that for System 1 is due to a tremendous speedup in data transfers by interleaving the bises when transferred in and out of the backup storage. This low utilization of the backup storage suggests a need for further improvement in component utilization. To achieve this data sets to be processed in the associative processing elements may be stored at different levels of the memory hierarchy originally and can be brought to the unit physically right next to the PE's. The time required in the more complicated data management can be overlapped with the PE processing time. Even some of the data manipulating functions can be performed either before the data sets are actually being loaded into the PEAM or if necessary, after they are outputted from PEAM and before they are stored back into the storage. More sophisticated controls and detection of special features of the instruction sequences should be provided for this more efficient processing technique in order to prevent any type of conflicts among the components.

Table 2 also shows a quite significant increase, about 20%, in the use of the data manipulator when compared with System 1. The new PE efficiencies in processing the three programs of the general circulation model on System 10 are 0.7713, 0.8063, and 0.7632, respectively (Table 6). A slight decrease in efficiency is evident in PART I and OVERALL programs where the percentages of execution time in arithmetic operations (having a high PE utilization of 0.8086) dropped. The relative performance evaluation $R_{10,1}$ of System 10 with respect to System 1 ranges from 1.29 to a very respectable 23.88 as α varies from 0.25 to 3.0 (Fig. 2).

The efficiencies of the backup storage and the data manipulator for Systems 1 and 10 are summarized in Table 8. The efficiencies of System 10 are improved substantially over those of System 1.

C. Further Consideration of a Cost-Effective System

Consider that a disk unit is added to the system and dual control units are provided so that concurrent operation both in the PE's and in the backup storage and the disk unit can be performed. Adding this disk unit has twofold advantages: the utilization of the backup storage is improved and the size of the backup storage can

Table 8. Efficiencies of Backup Storage and Data
Manipulator in System 1 and System 10.

SYSTEM COMPONENT	SYSTEM	PART I	PART II	OVERALL
BACKUP STORAGE	1	0.5972	0.7672	0.6153
	10	0.6104	0.7751	0.6303
DATA MANIPULATOR	1	0.4546	0.4112	0.4539
	10	0.4746	0.4376	0.4743

be reduced. From the result of Section V we have already known the number of roll-in and roll-out operations required for the system with certain size of the backup storage to process the general circulation model program. Our attempt here is to find the optimal size of the backup storage in the most efficient system.

Let us assume that an Alpha Data 16" disk unit is used. It has an average latency time of 16.8 msec and a flow rate of 10^7 bit/sec approximately. It takes about 3.2 msec to perform a roll-in or roll-out operation. The approximate time required to accomplish all the roll-in or roll-out operations is then the number of roll-in and roll-out operations times 20 msec. The optimal size of the backup storage should be such that the roll-in and roll-out operations do not increase the total execution time. That is, the roll-in and roll-out operations should overlap as much as possible with the time when the backup storage is idle. From Table 2 there is about 1120 msec during which period the backup storage is idle. Thus the maximum number of roll-in and roll-out operations is 1120/20 = 56. By checking Fig. 4 we find out that the minimum number of roll-in and roll-out operations is 84 when all 12 residing variables data sets (48K words) are stored on disk and the backup storage has a size of 43K words. If we add extra 12K words to the backup storage for three residing variables and the rest nine remain stored on the disk then the number of roll-in and roll-out operations is exactly 56. Thus, for implementing the general circulation model on such a system with four-bis-parallel capabilities and interleaving backup storage banks, the optimal size of the backup storage is 43K + 12K = 55K, provided that the complete program processing scheme is used.

The reduction of the size of the backup storage from 79K words in a system without a disk unit to 55K words, and about 30% reduction, may not be significant in terms of hardware cost. But when the grid system used in the general circulation model becomes denser, say, the numbers of grid points on the latitudinal and the longitudinal lines are doubled there could be much greater savings in the backup storage.

D. A Cost-Effective Associative Processor Organization

In summarizing the result of the analyses, a final system, is presented here. Figure 3 gives a more detailed diagram of the optimal system. The descriptions of the system components are given below:

1. Control Unit: This unit stores the main programs, executes the instruction sequence, performs some sequential arithmetic operations and controls other components in the system by sending out appropriate control signals to them. Dual control capability must be provided in this unit so that the concurrent operations of data transfer between the backup storage banks and the disk unit, and executing arithmetic, search, or other operations in PE's alone can be successfully achieved. This dual control units supervise all the activities and prevent any conflicts from occurring.

2. Input/Output Unit: A disk unit with an average latency time of 16.8 msec is used as the auxiliary storage unit. Input/Output unit receives the commands from the control unit and performs data transfers between the disk unit and the backup storage without sacrificing the total execution time.

3. Interleaving Backup Storage Banks: There are four backup storage banks, each having a size of 14K words. When reading or writing data bises out of or into the backup storage banks in an interleaving manner the effective read and write times are 150 nsec/bis and 200 nsec/bis, respectively. This provision increases the overall system performance to a quite substantial extent. When the total execution time for processing the general circulation model programs is considered, it has an improvement of about 12%. When PE's are processing some data sets without the use of this component, the backup storage banks can load and unload data sets from and to the disk. This kind of concurrent operation increases the utilization of the system components and thus improves the overall system efficiency.

4. Data Manipulator: In order to have an efficient parallel processor some kind of data manipulating unit must be included in the system otherwise the time spent on preparing data sets to be processed may well offset the time saved by parallel processing. The separate data manipulator provided in this system not only speeds up data preparation but also adds more flexibility to the choice of data source and destination. A very competent set of data manipulating functions are built into this unit to enhance its performance. A total of about 14% of the total execution time is spent on operations involving this data manipulator when the general circulation model is implemented on this system. Shift and multiplicate operations are greatly used in this weather problem.

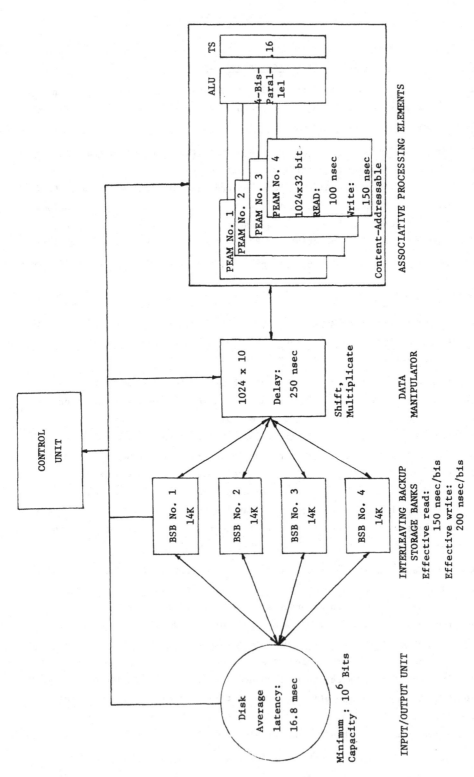

Figure 3. A cost-effective associative processor organization for weather computations.

5. Associative Processing Elements: After the analysis on the execution time speedup ratios it is evident that it is very advantageous to equip the PE's with four-bis-parallel processing capabilities. The overall speed improvement is more than 100% as a result of this change. The processing elements associative memory (PEAM) can be implemented by four smaller PEAM's each with 1K words. The data sets are stored in these PEAM's. One bis of data is accessed from each of the four PEAM's simultaneously to be processed by the arithmetic-logic unit. The read and write time of these PEAM's are 100 nsec/bis or word and 150 nsec/bis or word, respectively. There are 16 bises of TS for temporarily storing mask conditions, results of logic or search operations.

VII CONCLUSIONS

A cost-effective system for weather computations was determined after some comparisons were made among all the system alternatives. The comparisons included the cost factors (in terms of hardware complexity), total execution time, and PE efficiency. It has 1024 PE's equipped with four-bis-parallel processing capabilities and content-addressability, a separate data manipulator, four interleaving backup storage banks, a control unit with dual control capability and a disk unit. The implementation of the general circulation model on this optimal system was then analyzed. This system was again compared against the original system. The total throughput is increased by almost three times. A system efficiency evaluation which included the utilizations and efficiencies of all three major system components, the cost factor, and the total execution time was made for the two systems. There is about 10% increase in system efficiency in the optimal system.

The whole project required very tedious and laborious work of studying thoroughly the particular application problem and its program, rewritting the program into parallel processing program, gathering operational statistics, developing detailed algorithms for arithmetic operation (both bis-sequential and four-bis-parallel), analyzing, evaluating, and comparing system performance, and finally determining an optimal system. The completeness of the original document of the general circulation model facilitated the validity of this undertaking.

REFERENCES

[1] W. T. Cheng and T. Feng, <u>Associative Computations of Some Mathematical Problems</u>, Technical Report, RADC-TR-73-229, Rome Air Development Center, Rome, New York, August 1973, 76 pp.

[2] W. L. Gates, E. S. Batten, A. B. Kahle, and A. B. Nelson, _A Documentation of the Mintz-Arakawa Two-Level Atmospheric General Circulation Model_, R-877-ARPA, December 1971, Rand Corp., 408 pp.

[3] T. Feng, "Data Manipulating Functions in Parallel Processors and Their Implementations", _IEEE Trans. on Computers_, Vol. C-23, March 1974, pp. 309-318.

[4] W. T. Cheng, "A Cost-Effective Associative Processor with Application to Weather Computations," Ph.D. Dissertation, Syracuse University, Syracuse, New York, July, 1974.

[5] SIMDA, _Single Instruction Multiple Data Array Processor Programmer's Manual_, Handbook No. HB55-A72, Texas Instruments, Inc., October 1972.

[6] N. C. Machado, _An Array Processor with A Large Number of Processing Elements_, CAC-25, University of Illinois at Urbana-Champaign, January 1972.

THE IMPLEMENTATION OF APL
ON AN ASSOCIATIVE PROCESSOR

M. J. HARRISON
System Development Division
W. H. HARRISON
Research Division
IBM
Yorktown Heights, N. Y., 10598

Abstract -- This paper describes an implementation of an APL interpreter on a
hypothetical associative array processor. The processor is described along with
those portions of its instruction set which relate to the associative array processing capabilities of the machine. The data representations used in the APL implementation are described, followed by descriptions of several useful service
functions. An algorithm is presented for each APL operator. A general evaluation
of the performance of this implementation is made, followed by a technique for producing detailed performance estimates from trace information. A detailed performance
analysis of each APL operator is provided for this purpose.

HARDWARE ASSOCIATIVE PROCESSOR DESCRIPTION

The following diagram depicts an associative processor appropriate for an implementation of APL.

Associative Processor Organization

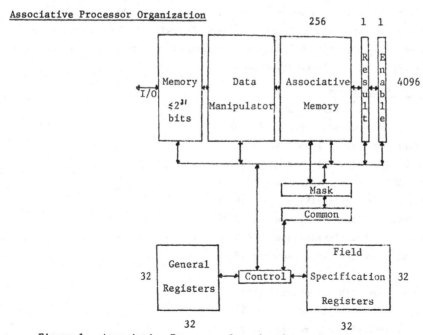

Figure 1: Associative Processor Organization

Associative Processor Number Formats

integer	$m_0\ m_1 \ldots m_{n-1}$ s	field size $n > 1$
float	$e_0\ e_1 \ldots e_{14}$ m m $\ldots m_{n-15}$ s	field size $n \geq 16$
bit string	$b_0\ b_1 \ldots b_n$	field size $n \geq 0$

Associative Processor Instructions

The operands of the machine instructions may be any of the machine components listed below.

Machine Component	Symbol	Operand Width
associative memory field	AM field spec	$0 \leq n \leq 128$
common word field	C field spec	$0 \leq n \leq 128$
mask word field	M field spec	$0 \leq n \leq 128$
field spec register	FSR field spec	$n = 16$
general register	GR register spec	$n = 32$
enable vector	ENABLE	$n = 1$
result vector	RESULT	$n = 1$
constant zeros	0	$0 \leq n \leq 128$
constant ones	1	$0 \leq n \leq 128$
literal	$\{+,-\}$ integer	$0 \leq n \leq 128$

field spec::=fA| fB| ...| fZ| f0| ...| f5
register spec::=a| b| c| ...z| g0| ...| g5

Each operand is a scalar or a vector. Scalars(s) reside in the GR's, FDS's, COMMON, MASK, or the only active AM element. Vectors(v) reside in the AM or are distributed from a scalar. Literals, 0, and 1 are scalars or vectors as needed.

The associative processor instructions are listed below.

Computational Instructions.

FIXADD target(vFIX) source1(vFIX) source2(vFIX)

FIXSUB target(vFIX) source1(vFIX) source2(vFIX)

FIXMUL target(vFIX) source1(vFIX) source2(vFIX)

FIXDIV target(vFIX) source1(vFIX) source2(vFIX)

FIXCMPR $\neq$ target(vBIT) source1(vFIX) source2(vFIX)

FIXCMPR < target(vBIT) source1(vFIX) source2(vFIX)

FIXCMPR $\leq$ target(vBIT) source1(vFIX) source2(vFIX)

FIXCMPR = target(vBIT) source1(vFIX) source2(vFIX)

FIXCMPR $\geq$ target(vBIT) source1(vFIX) source2(vFIX)

FIXCMPR > target(vBIT) source1(vFIX) source2(vFIX)

FLTADD target(vFLT) source1(vFLT) source2(vFLT)

FLTSUB target(vFLT) source1(vFLT) source2(vFLT)

FLTMUL target(vFLT) source1(vFLT) source2(vFLT)

```
FLTDIV target(vFLT) source1(vFLT) source2(vFLT)
FLTCMPR ≠ target(vBIT) source1(vFLT) source2(vFLT)
FLTCMPR < target(vBIT) source1(vFLT) source2(vFLT)
FLTCMPR ≤ target(vBIT) source1(vFLT) source2(vFLT)
FLTCMPR = target(vBIT) source1(vFLT) source2(vFLT)
FLTCMPR ≥ target(vBIT) source1(vFLT) source2(vFLT)
FLTCMPR > target(vBIT) source1(vFLT) source2(vFLT)
AND target(vBIT) source1(vBIT) source2(vBIT)
OR  target(vBIT) source1(vBIT) source2(vBIT)
XOR target(vBIT) source1(vBIT) source2(vBIT)
BITCMPR ≠ target(vBIT) source1(vBIT) source2(vBIT)
BITCMPR < target(vBIT) source1(vBIT) source2(vBIT)
BITCMPR ≤ target(vBIT) source1(vBIT) source2(vBIT)
BITCMPR = target(vBIT) source1(vBIT) source2(vBIT)
BITCMPR ≥ target(vBIT) source1(vBIT) source2(vBIT)
BITCMPR > target(vBIT) source1(vBIT) source2(vBIT)
NOT  target(vBIT) source(vBIT)
MOVE target(vBIT) source(vBIT)
```

The FIXADD, FIXSUB, FIXMUL, and FIXDIV instructions set the RESULT vector to one for each AM element in which an overflow occurs, and to zero otherwise.

Search Instructions.

```
SEARCHMAX
SEARCHMIN
SEARCH≠          comparand(sBIT)
SEARCH<          comparand(sBIT)
SEARCH≤          comparand(sBIT)
SEARCH=          comparand(sBIT)
SEARCH≥          comparand(sBIT)
SEARCH>          comparand(sBIT)
```

Manipulative Instructions.

```
ROTATEUP     target(AM-BIT) source(AM-BIT) regionsize(sFIX) count(sFIX)
ROTATEDOWN   target(AM-BIT) source(AM-BIT) regionsize(sFIX) count(sFIX)
MULTIPLICATEUP   target(AM-BIT) source(AM-BIT) regionsize(sFIX) count(sFIX)
MULTIPLICATEDOWN target(AM-BIT) source(AM-BIT) regionsize(sFIX) count(sFIX)
```

Memory Access Instructions.

```
LOADAM  fieldspec(AM-BIT) firstelementno(sFIX) count(sFIX) address(sFIX)
        multiplier(sFIX)
```

```
STOREAM fieldspec(AM-BIT) firstelementno(sFIX) count(sFIX) address(sFIX)
        multiplier(sFIX)
LOAD  value(sBIT) address(G-BIT) offset(LIT)
STORE value(sBIT) address(G-BIT)offset(LIT)
```

Control Instructions.

```
BRANCH branchtarget(sFIX)
BRANCHIFONES branchtarget(sFIX) teststorage(vBIT)
CALL subroutineaddress(sFIX) arguments
RETURN
BREAKTIE
```

IMPLEMENTATION OF APL ON THE ASSOCIATIVE PROCESSOR

Implementation of the APL Environment.

The data representations, the program management, and the common functions related to the implementation of the APL environment are discussed below.

Data Representations.

Computational Data..

scalars

bit	machine bit string of width 1
character	machine bit string of width 8
integer	machine integer of width 32
float	machine float of width 64

arrays

arrays of scalars are stored in row major order

Program Data.. A program has three components as illustrated in Figure 2: the local variables list, the constant pool, and the statement vector. The local variables is a sequence which contains for each local variable an index into the workspace-wide symbol table. The constant pool contains a sequence of pointers to the descriptors for constant values. The statement vector is a sequence of addresses of the last syllable of each individual statement. A statement is a sequence of syllables each of which is an operator syllable, a constant reference syllable, or a variable reference syllable. An operator syllable contains an encoding of the APL operator. A constant reference syllable contains an index into the constant pool. A variable reference contains an index into the symbol table.

Descriptors.. All APL data are referenced through descriptors. As illustrated in Figure 3, there are three types of descriptors, those which describe scalars, those which describe arrays and those which describe projections onto linear progressions.

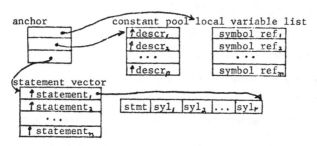

Figure 2: Program Representation

scalar		array		linear progression	
size	use ct.	size	use count	size	use count
type	rank=0	type	rank>0	INTEGER	rank>0
data		pointer to value		LINEARPROGRESSION	
		off to first elem		additive quantity	
32 bits		dimension		dimension	
types:		multiplier		multiplier	
INTEGER		• • •		• • •	
BOOLEAN		dimension		dimension	
FLOAT		multiplier		multiplier	
CHARACTER					
PROGRAM		32 bits		32 bits	

Figure 3: Descriptor Formats

<u>Symbol Table</u>. The symbol table is a sequence of elements each of which has a
256 bit wide symbol and a pointer to the head of its value list. The value list is
a list of pointers to descriptors. An undefined value is represented as a null
descriptor pointer. The head of the list represents the current value of the symbol.

<u>Execution Stack</u>.. Each workspace contains an execution stack which is a se-
quence of entries each of which is a descriptor pointer, an operator, or a program
pointer.

<u>Program Management</u>. Program management has two major areas: text translation
and program interpretation. It is the case, however, that with the exception of
symbol table searches, parallel processors do not significantly apply to these problems. After decoding the operation to be performed, the program interpretation
routine uses an operation dependent routine to compute the rank of the result.
Space is then allocated for the result descriptor. An operation dependent routine
then fills in the descriptor. In the case of the descriptor manipulative operators,
the operation is then complete, otherwise space is allocated to hold the result, and
the main semantic routine for that operator, as described below is entered, passing

it the descriptors for all of its operands.

Common Functions. Six functions are used in the implementation of the APL operators. These are described below.

1. LOAD.S loads a sequence of scalars from the ravelled form of a matrix into successive AM elements.

2. STORE.S stores a sequence of scalars from the AM into the ravelled form of a matrix.

3. LOAD.V treats an n-dimensional matrix as an n-1 dimensional matrix of vectors. It loads the same sequence of scalars from each of a specified sequence of vectors into successive AM elements.

4. STORE.V stores successive AM elements into the same sequence of scalars in each of a specified sequence of vectors. The vectors arise from treating an n-dimensional matrix as an n-1 dimensional matrix of vectors.

5. ALLOCATE allocates storage for the results of an operation.

6. FREE notes the erasure of a reference to a storage area and frees the storage if the reference count becomes zero.

LOAD.S(field mode, field specification, source descriptor, first element number, last element number) The LOAD.S function can be generally realized via a single application of the LOADAM machine instruction. The source is loaded into the appropriate part of the specified field, and the remaining part of the field is set to zeros. If the source is a scalar, it is loaded into COMMON, otherwise it is loaded into the AM using the last multiplier from the descriptor as the multiplier, and the first and last element numbers to determine the count. Whenever the product of an index and the multiplier would be outside the storage area occupied by the matrix, multiple LOADAM instructions may be needed to wrap back into the storage area.

STORE.S(field specification, target descriptor, first element number, last element number) The STORE.S function operates in the same manner as the LOAD.S function except that it uses the STOREAM machine instruction instead of the LOADAM machine instruction.

LOAD.V(field mode, field specification, source descriptor, first element number, last element number, vector dimension, first vector number, last vector number) The LOAD.V function can be generally realized by the iterative application of the LOADAM instruction, with at least one application for each vector to be retreived. The multiplier is the multiplier for the specified vector dimension, and the count is determined from the first and last element number. Wraparound considerations may force the use of more than one LOADAM instruction for each vector.

STORE.V(field specification, target descriptor, first element number, last element number, vector dimension, first vector number, last vector number) The STORE.V function operates in the same manner as the LOAD.V function except that it uses the STOREAM machine instruction instead of the LOADAM machine instruction.

ALLOCATE(size) The ALLOCATE function maintains a table of free storage with some installation specified number of entries no greater than 4096. The table entries have the following field specification:

fA:position 0, length 32, address of a block of free storage
fB:position 32, length 32, size of the block, zero if this entry is unused
fC:position 64, length 32, a temporary space

To allocate storage, the free storage table is loaded into the AM, and a search is made for the nearest value of fB above the specified size plus overhead for the header. If no free storage is found large enough, a compaction algorithm is invoked to cause all free storage to occupy a single block of storage.

FREE(location) The FREE function decrements the use count for the storage block at the specified location. If the count becomes zero, the storage returned must be added to the free storage table (see ALLOCATE). The table is loaded into the AM and examined on fA to see if there is an entry whose starting location succeeds the block being freed. If so, the freed storage is combined with the block described by that entry. Whether or not such combination takes place, fC is computed in the AM by adding fA to fB. A search is then made to see whether an entry has an fC value preceeding the block being freed. If so, the freed block, or the combination arrived at above, is combined with the block corresponding to the matching entry. This may result in one fewer table entry. If neither match described above occurs, a new entry is added to the table. If there is no room in the table for another entry, the compaction algorithm is invoked to cause all free storage to occupy a single block of storage.

Implementation of the APL Operators

APL Operator Table.

The operators utilizing parallel processors are listed below.

1. Scalar Distribution

    Dyadic Operators--Plus, Minus, Times, Divided By, Exponentiation, Maximum, Minimum, Residue, Logarithm, Binomial Coefficient, Circular and Hyperbolic Functions, Less Than, Less Than or Equal To, Equal To, Greater Than Or Equal To, Greater Than, Not Equal To, And, Or, Not Both And, Neither or

    Monadic Operators--Positive Of, Negative Of, Sign Of, Reciprocal Of, To the Power, Ceiling, Floor, Magnitude Of, Natural Logarithm Of, Factorial, 'PI' Times, Random Integer, Not

2.	Reduction	10.	Outer Product
3.	Base	11.	Ravel
4.	Compression	12.	Roll
5.	Expansion	13.	Deal
6.	Grade Up	14.	Rotation
7.	Grade Down	15.	Selection
8.	Index	16.	Concatenate
9.	Inner Product	17.	Membership

The operators not utilizing parallel processors but implemented by redescribing existing data are listed below.

18.	Index Generator	23.	Dimension
19.	Ravel	24.	Reversal
20.	Take	25.	Rotation
21.	Drop	26.	Transposition
22.	Reshape		

Other operators not utilizing parallel processing are listed below.

27.	Representation	29.	Specification
28.	Branch		

This is the operator set defined for APL by S. Pakin, Reference 1.

APL Operator Algorithms.

1. Scalar Distribution

Field Specifications.

fA:position 0, length 64, first source operand value or result value
fB:position 64,length 64, second source operand value

Algorithm Summary. If the entire result fits in the AM, fA is loaded from the first source operand (using LOAD.S), fB is loaded from the second source operand (using LOAD.S) if the operator is dyadic. The operation is performed, and fA is stored into the target (using STORE.S). If the entire result does not fit, it is processed in 4096 element sections.

2. Reduction

Field Specifications.

fA:position   0, length 64, source value
fB:position 64, length 64, alternate source value
fC:position 128, length 64, partial results
fE:position 192, length 1, mask
fF:position 193, length 1, initial mask
fG:position 194, length 1, temporary

Algorithm Summary. Two different algorithms apply depending upon the scalar operator: 1) for +, -, ×, ÷, $\lceil$, $\lfloor$, =, ≠, ∨, ∧, ⩹, ⩺, and 2) for *, ⊛, !, |, ο, <, ≤, >, ≥.

Case 1. If the k-th dimension of the source operand is not greater than 8192, the odd numbered vector elements are loaded into fA, and the even numbered vector elements into fB, padding the evens with a scalar having the value of the operational identity if the vector has an odd number of elements. As many vectors as will fit are loaded into the AM, which is treated as a series of regions, one for each vector. Field fF is initialized to contain ones in all positions except the last position in each region. The operation is performed (see 1. Scalar Distribution-Dyadic), and the result is moved from fA to fC.

If the k-th dimension is larger than 8192, successive blocks of 8192 are loaded into fA and fB, with the entire AM treated as one region. The operation is performed, and the results in fA are combined with fC using the reduction operator unless it is - or ÷ , in which case + or × are used instead.

Each region is then reduced as follows. The values in fC are moved to fA and fF is moved to fE. The following iteration occurs for values of i from 0 to the floor of the logarithm of the region size, inclusive. The entire AM contents in fA is rotated up 2^i positions into fB. Using fF as the enable mask, the reduction operator (or + or × as described above) is applied to fA and fB, leaving its result in fA. Then, in all AM elements, fF is rotated up 2^i positions into fG, and fG is anded with fF to produce a new fF. After all iterations are complete, fA of the first element in each region is stored into the corresponding target element, the next group of vectors are fetched and the whole process repeats until the source is exhausted.

Case 2. The AM is used such that each element processes a different vector of the source operand. The last scalar of each vector is loaded into fB, and its predecessor scalar is loaded into fA. The operation is performed (see 1. Scalar Distribution-Dyadic) leaving its result in fA, which is then moved to fB. This process is repeated, each time loading fA with the predecessor of the scalar of the previous iteration. After all iterations are complete, the results are stored into the target (using STORE.S).

3. Base

Field Specifications.

fA:position 0, length 64, base
fB:position 64, length 64, exponent

Algorithm Summary. A vector of multipliers is constructed from the first source operand, and then the +.× inner product is invoked to complete the operation. If the first source operand is a vector, it is sequentially processed from right to left, beginning with a value of 1 and successively storing the current result and computing the next by multiplication with the current scalar in the vector. If the first source operand is a scalar, it is treated as a base for exponentiation. The linear progression from 1 by 1 is loaded into fB (using LOAD.S), and the first source operand is loaded into COMMON. Exponentiation is performed (see 1. Scalar Distribution-Dyadic), and the resulting fA is stored as the multiplier vector. In either case, the multiplier vector is used as a new first operand, and the inner product routine is invoked.

4. Compression

  Field Specifications.
fA:position 0, length 64, second source operand
fB:position 64, length 64, temporary

  Algorithm Summary. Before applying the compression a series of masks are computed from the first source operand. Each mask $M(i)$ has zeros in positions from the first to that position preceeding by $i-1$ the i-th zero in the first source operand, and ones in the remaining positions. If the AM is at least as large as the k-th dimension of the second source operand, the compression algorithm iterates through each vector of the second source operand which is to be compressed. The vector is loaded (using LOAD.V) into fA. Then the DM is employed iteratively, each time rotating fA upward into fB, from which it is moved under the enable mask $M(i)$ into fA. When all iterations are complete, the result is stored (using STORE.V). The actual algorithm loads as many vectors from the second source operand as will fit in the AM, repeating the $M(i)$ masks with a period the size of each input vector. If even one vector will not fit in the AM, the vectors are broken into frames of length $C(i)$ modulo 4096, where $C(i)$ is 4096 minus the number of zeros in the first $4096i$ bits of the first source operand.

5. Expansion

  Field Specifications.
fA:position 0, length 64, second source operand
fB:position 64, length 64, temporary

  Algorithm Summary. Before applying the expansion, a series of masks are computed from the first source operand. Each mask $M(i)$ has zeros in positions from the first to the i-th zero in the first source operand, and ones in the remaining positions. If the AM is at least as large as the k-th dimension of the target operand , the expansion algorithm iterates through each vector of the second source operand which is to be expanded. The vector is loaded (using LOAD.V) into fA. Then the DM is employed iteratively, each time rotating fA downward into fB, from which it is moved under the enable mask $M(i)$ into fA. When all iterations are complete, the complement of the first source operand is used as the enable mask and the relevent fA's are set to zero or blank. Then the result is stored (using STORE.V). The actual algorithm loads as many vectors from the second source operand as will fit in the AM after expansion, repeating the M(i) masks with a period the size of each result vector. If even one vector will not fit in the AM, the vectors are broken into frames of length C(i) modulo 4096, where C(i) is 4096 minus the number of zeros in the first 4096i bits of the first source operand.

6.   Grade Up

Field Specifications.

fA:position   0, length 64, source value
fB:position   64, length 15, index of value in fA
fC:position   79, length 64, source value
fD:position 143, length 15, index of value in fB
fG:position 158, length 79, temporary field
fH:position 237, length 1, match vector
fI:position 238, length 1, mask vector
fAB: position 0, length 79, value, index pair
fCD: position 79, length 79, value, index pair

Algorithm Summary. The source operand, or 4096 element sections of it, are loaded into the AM. A bitonic sort/merge is then performed using fCB to accomodate shifted results and fG for space to interchange fAB with fCD as needed. If the entire result fits into the AM, the final fB is stored into the target, otherwise a series of 4096 entry temporary spaces are allocated to hold intermediate fAB's. When a sort pass has been made over the entire source, each buffer is assigned one AM entry and the contents of the first buffer element are loaded into fAB of the AM entry. Iteratively, the maximum value of fA is sought, the corresponding fB is stored into the next target element, and the element is reloaded from its buffer.

7.   Grade Down

Field Specifications.

fA:position   0, length 64, source value
fB:position   64, length 15, index of value in fA
fC:position   79, length 64, source value
fD:position 143, length 15, index of value in fB
fG:position 158, length 79, temporary field
fH:position 237, length 1, match vector
fI:position 238, length 1, mask vector
fAB:position 0, length 79, value, index pair
fCD:position 79, length 79, value, index pair

Algorithm Summary. The source operand, or 4096 element sections of it, are loaded into the AM. A bitonic sort/merge is then performed using fCB to accomodate shifted results and fG for space to interchange fAB with fCD as needed. If the entire result fits into the AM, the final fB is stored into the target, otherwise a series of 4096 entry temporary spaces are allocated to hold intermediate fAB's. When a sort pass has been made over the entire source, each buffer is assigned one AM entry and the contents of the first buffer element are loaded into fAB of the AM entry. Iteratively, the minimum value of fA is sought, the corresponding fB is stored into the next target element, and the element is reloaded from its buffer.

8.   Index Of

Field Specifications.
fA:position   0, length 64, new result indexes
fB:position 64, length 15, old result indexes
fC:position 79, length 64, source1 data field (searched vector)
fD:position 143, length 15, searched vector indexes

Algorithm Summary. The first source operand (or successive 4096 element sections of it) is loaded into fC (using LOAD.S) and the corresponding element numbers are loaded into fD. The elements of the second source operand are then processed iteratively) (over i) as follows:

1.   The i-th element of the second source operand is loaded into fC of COMMON.
2.   The AM is searched for equality on fC. If any match is made, the tie breaking match vector (in RESULT) is used as the activity mask and fD is stored into fC of COMMON, else the fail value is set into fC of COMMON.
3.   i is set into fD of COMMON.
4.   The AM is searched for equality on fD. Using the search result as the activity mask, fA is loaded from fC of COMMON.

After the second source operand is processed (or each group of 4096 elements), if this is the first section of the first source operand, fA is stored (using STORE.S) into the target, otherwise, the corresponding target values are loaded into fB of the AM. The minimum operation (see 1. Scalar Distribution-Dyadic) is performed and the resulting A fields are stored into the target.

9.   Inner Product

Field Specifications.
fA:position   0, length 64, source1 data field
fI:position 64, length 31, source row and col indexes
fB:position 95, length 64, source2 data field
fC:position 159, length 64, result data field
fRR:position 223, length 15, result row index
fRC:position 238, length 15, result column index
fT:position 253, length 1, result tag

Algorithm Summary. The algorithm for Inner Product is as described in Ref. 2, pp. 28-34 except that arrays of rank greater than 2 must be treated as arrays of rank 2 by ravelling all dimensions except the last for the first source operand and the first for the second source operand. This can be done by constructing two temporary descriptors for the source operands which treat each of them as at most rank 2 arrays. Arrays of rank 1 are treated by treating them as rank 2 arrays with only one row for the first source operand, or one column for the second source operand. This can also be done by manipulating the descriptor. Addition and multiplication in the referenced algorithm may be replaced by any of the APL scalar dyadic operators (see 1. Scalar Distribution-Dyadic).

10. Outer Product

Field Specifications.

fA:position   0, length 64, source1 or result
fB:position 64, length 64, source2

Algorithm Summary. Let M be the number of elements in the first source operand. Let N be the number of elements in the second source operand. If the AM had sufficient bis-length to hold the entire result, the technique would be to load the second source operand into fB (using LOAD.S) repeating the group M times. The first source operand is loaded (using LOAD.S) into fA but each element is repeated N times into successive locations. The operator is then performed (see 1. Scalar Distribution-dyadic) and the resulting fA is stored (using STORE.S) into the target. The actual algorithm proceeds by performing this process 4096 elements at a time.

11. Ravel

Field Specification.

fA:position 0, length 64, source data field

Algorithm Summary. The elements of the source (or groups of 4096 elements) are loaded in ravel order into fA of the AM (using FETCH.S) and then are stored into the target.

12. Roll

Field Specifications.

fA:position   0, length 64, result
fB:position   64, length 64, source1 data field
fC:position 128, length 64, seed

Algorithm Summary. The seed vector is loaded (using LOAD.S) into fC. The source operand is then loaded (using LOAD.S) into fB. A standard random number algorithm is executed byall parallel processors to produce a floating number between 0 and 1 in fA. fA is then multiplied by fB (see 1. Scalar Distribution-Dyadic Multiply) and the ceiling operation is performed (see 1. Scalar Distribution-

Monadic Ceiling). The resulting fA is then stored (using STORE.S) into the target. When the operation is complete, fC is stored (using STORE.S) back into the seed vector.

13. Deal

Field Specifications.
fA:position   0, length 64, possible values
fB:position   64, length 64, possible values
fC:position 128, length 64, possible values
fD:position 192, length 64, temporary

Each field contains a dealt value as the result vector is being computed.

Algorithm Summary. For this operation, the two source operands are scalars, but the target is a vector whose length is given by the value of the first source operand. If the length of the target is less than 12,288, the AM is loaded with the numbers from 1 to the length of the target, using fA, fB, and fC as needed. The algorithm proceeds by generating a random number from the seed. This number (modulo the number of indexes remaining in the AM) is used to select an index from the AM. This index is stored as the next result and then removed from the AM by rotating the appropriate field of the AM upward into fD and then selectively moving the results into the appropriate field.

If the length of the target exceeds 12,288, the full index vector is laid out in the main storage and randomly chosen disjoint groups of 12,288 or less are moved to the AM after which the above algorithm is used.

14. Rotation

Field Specifications.
fA:position 0, length 64, second source operand
fB:position 64, length 64, result

Algorithm Summary. If the AM is large enough to contain a vector in the k-th dimension, the algorithm proceeds by iteratively loading into fA (using FETCH.V) as many vectors of the second source operand as will fit in the AM, and then rotating them up or down into fB as specified by the value of the first source operand. The contents of fB are then stored in the target (using STORE.V). If the AM is not suf- ficiently large, the rotation is performed by properly ordering the loading from the second source operand and storing into the target.

15. Selection

Field Specifications.
fA:position 0, length 32, a subscript in the AM
fB:position 32, length 32, a multiplier in COMMON
fC:position 64, length 32, a partially compiled displacement in the AM

Algorithm Summary. The parallel processor is used to compute the displacements into the source matrix for copying to the target. If the entire result fits in the AM, the algorithm iterates on the dimensions of the source matrix. For each dimension i, the values of Si are loaded into fA of the AM and duplicated to fill all AM elements involved in the computation, and the multiplier for that dimension is loaded into fB of COMMON. The product of fA and fB is then placed into fA and added to fC to produce a new value in fC. After all dimensions are processed, the algorithm iterates over all the displacements, loading a value into COMMON and then storing it into the target. If the result does not fit, this computation is carried on in sections of 4096 elements.

16. Concatenate

Field Specification.
fA:position 0, length 64, source data field

Algorithm Summary. If the AM is at least as large as the k-th dimension of the target, the concatenation operation iterates through each vector of the target fetching (using FETCH.V) into the AM first the corresponding vector from the first source operand, then from the second source operand and storing (using STORE.V) the concatenated result into the target. The actual algorithm breaks the result into frames of 4096 elements as needed.

17. Membership

Field Specifications.
fA:position 0, length 64, source data field
fB:position 64, length 1, match result bit
fC:position 65, length 1, result bit

Algorithm Summary. The first source operand (or 4096 element sections of it) is loaded into fA of the AM. The second source operand is then processed iteratively. Each element of the second source operand is loaded into fA of COMMON. A search for equality on fA is performed and the result vector is stored into fB of the AM. fB is then or'ed into fC of the AM. After all elements of the second source operand have been processed, fC is stored (using STORE.S) into the target.

18. Index Generator

Algorithm Summary. Index Generator constructs a linear progression descriptor with a multiplier of one and an offset of zero.

19. Ravel

Algorithm Summary. A descriptor is constructed sharing the same underlying values as the second operand but describing a vector with the same multiplier as the last dimension.

20. Take

   Algorithm Summary. If the number of elements to be taken is greater than the k-th dimension the operation is actually an expansion so the expand algorithm is used, otherwise a descriptor is constructed sharing the same underlying values as the second operand but the k-th dimension is reduced to the number of elements to be taken. If the first operand is negative, the offset is augmented by the product of the k-th multiplier and the number of elements not taken.

21. Drop

   Algorithm Summary. A descriptor is constructed sharing the same underlying values as the second operand but the k-th dimension is reduced by the number of elements to be dropped. If the first operand is positive, the offset is augmented by the product of the k-th multiplier and the number of elements dropped.

22. Reshape

   Algorithm Summary. If the second source is disconnected, it is first ravelled (see 11 above). A descriptor is constructed sharing the same underlying values as the second operand but using the dimensions specified by the first operand.

23. Dimension

   Algorithm Summary. A descriptor is constructed using the dimensions part of the source operand as the value and specifying an appropriate length vector as the description.

24. Reversal

   Algorithm Summary. A descriptor is constructed sharing the underlying values of the second operand but the offset is constructed by adding the offset of the source operand to the product of its k-th dimension and k-th multiplier, and the k-th multiplier is constructed by negating the k-th multiplier of the source operand.

25. Rotation

   Algorithm Summary. If k specifies the first dimension of the second source operand, a descriptor is constructed sharing the same underlying values of the second operand, but the offset is constructed by subtracting from the original offset the product of the value of the first source operand the first multiplier of the second source operand.

26. Transposition

   Algorithm Summary. A descriptor is constructed sharing the same underlying values as the second operand but the rank of the descriptor is the maximum value in the first source operand vector. The dimension for the k-th dimension of the result is the minimum of all dimensions corresponding to the value k in the source vector. The multiplier for the k-th dimension is the sum of all multipliers corresponding to the value k in the source yector.

27. Representation

   Algorithm Summary. The representation is computed by iteratively dividing the second source operand by the elements of the first source operand, taken in reverse order, and storing the remainders into the target in reverse order.

28. Branch

   Algorithm Summary. If the source operand is not empty, its first value is set into the next statement number component of the interpreter and causes the current statement to cease being interpreted.

29. Specification

   Algorithm Summary. The current value of the target symbol is freed and replaced by the source whose use count is then incremented by one.

EVALUATION OF THE IMPLEMENTATION OF APL
ON THE ASSOCIATIVE PROCESSOR

   The largest single surprise to the authors was the extent to which APL could benefit from the use of a parallel processor. The programming support can be neatly divided into high and low processing requirement operators, program management, and common functions.

   The high processing requirement operators can be roughly graded into three utilization classes. Operators in the first class keep as many processing elements busy as there are scalars in their arguments. They are the monadic and dyadic distributed operators, Base, Grade Up, Grade Down, Index Of, Inner Product, Outer Product, Roll, Deal, and Membership. Operators in the second class keep as many processing elements busy as needed to process an integral number of vectors in some dimension of one of their operands. They are: Compression, Expansion, and Rotation. Operators in the third class are primarily moving in nature and bendfit only as they can from the parallel processors. Only two of the high processing requirement operators thus failed to benefit from the parallelism, Ravel and Concatenate. They are primarily concerned with moving data. The Selection and Rotation operators also move significant amounts of data, but have additional operations which can be assisted by the parallel processor. Although it is true that if all operands to all the APL operators were, in practice, generally scalars or small vectors, then the parallel processor is generally idle, two observations should be made: first, APL's style of programming leads its users to perform much of their computation in a parallel fashion, and second, the number of processing elements should be set according to some statistical patterns of usage. If most matrices have several hundred elements, perhaps 512 processors is a better choice. Conversely, if most matrices have several tens of thousands of elements, perhaps 32768 elements is a better choice.

The low processing requirement operations are those whose execution time is small and essentially independent of the size of their operands. Most of these operators merely describe existing data from another point of view. Parallel processing does not assist these operators, but in view of their nature, no significant time is spent performing them anyway. These operators are Index Generator, Ravel, Reshape, Take, Drop, Dimension, Reversal, Rotation, Transposition, Branch and Specification.

Program management is a generally serial process which contains certain sub-processes (usually searching or sorting) which benefit from parallel processing. However, the essential system programming nature of program management is to spend all of its time deciding what needs to be done, and invoking some routine to do it. These decision processes are essentially serial.

The common functions of storage management and data transfer between the AM and the MEMORY benefit considerably from parallel processing. The storage management algorithms can be adapted to parallel searching for their manipulation of a free space table. If the interface between the AM and the MEMORY is sufficiently powerful to perform scatter store/gather fetch operations, the loading/storing of the AM can proceed on many elements at once. It does not suffice to have the DM do the scatter/gather operations because: 1) the scalar density is often so low that a 10:1 ratio of fetched to useful data would pertain, and 2) it is desirable to store without having to first fetch the unchanged portions of the target.

In summary, it is the case that a parallel processor such as that described above can be of material assistance to an implementation of APL.

The following more detailed performance analysis is to be interpreted as describing the way in which the performance of the various algorithms depend on the data. In order to evaluate an actual proposed implementation, the various constants must be evaluated according to the detailed coding of the algorithm and timing of the instructions. A trace can then be made from a running APL system. This trace should contain for each executed operator, the descriptors of the operands and results. The trace can then be run against coded versions of the formulae in order to arrive at the performance figures. This analysis is divided into two sections paralleling two sections of the software description. These sections deal with: A) Common Functions, and B) Operators.

Common Functions

The performance of the various common storage functions can be estimated by way of two functions called memoryscalar and memoryvector. These two functions are used to compute the time required by the LOAD.S and STORE.S functions, and by the LOAD.V and STORE.V functions, respectively. Both of these functions rely for their evaluation on a third function called memorytime.

memorytime. The memory is assumed to be divided into independent, interleaved units. The width of each unit in bits is called w, and the number of such units b. The cycle time of a memory unit is called a. The memorytime function takes two arguments, the number of elements to be accessed (called d), and the multiplier which describes the distance between elements (called m). We then have:

mt(d,m)=if m≤bw then a*ceil(md/bw)
       if m≥bw then a*ceil(d/min(b,bw/gcd(m,bw)))

memoryscalar. The memory scalar function takes as its arguments the rank of the matrix from which scalars are to be fetched, called R, the dimensions of this matrix, called D, and the multipliers of the matrix, called M. The definition then is:

ms (R,D,M)=if R is LP then mt(D,M)
       if R=0 then a
       if R>0 then
           if M=the connected multipliers for D
              then mt(N,M[R])
              else N/M[R]*mt(D[R],M[R])

memoryvector. The memory vector function takes as its arguments the rank of the matrix from which vectors are to be fetched, called R, the dimensions of this matrix, called D, the multipliers of the matrix, called M, and the dimension along which the vectors are to be taken, called k. The definition then is:

mv(R,D,M,k)=N/D[k]*mt(D[k],M[k])

numbercycles. The numbercycles function takes as its arguments the total num - ber of elements to be processed, called N and the number of elements in that unit of which several can be placed simultaneously in the AM. The definition then is:

nc(N,D)=ceil(N/(D*floor(S/D)))

Operators

The meaning of various symbols used in the subsequent formulae are defined be- low. In the description of the performance of each operator the lines labelled mem: contain the time required for memory access and the lines labelled op: contain the time required for computation.

<e>:the list containing the element e
e.f:the concatenation of e with f
k←A:remove the kth element from the list A
Ri :rank of operand i or result (R)
Di :dimension list of operand i or result (R)
Mi :multiplier list of operand i or result (R)
Ni :number of scalars in operand i or result (R)
k:for those APL operators with a dimension specifier, k specifies the dimension

ki: various constants which depend on instruction timings.

S: the size of the AM in words

ti:the number of bits for a scalar of the type of operand i or result

1. Distributed Operations

    a. monadic

        mem:$\underline{ms}$(R1,D1,M1)+$\underline{ms}$(R1,D1,MR)

        op:k1*ceil(N1/S)

    b. dyadic

        mem:$\underline{ms}$(R1,D1,M1)+$\underline{ms}$(R2,D2,M2)+$\underline{ms}$(RR,DR,MR)

        op:k1*ceil(max(N1,N2)/S)

2. Reduction

    a. non-cascade

        mem:$\underline{mv}$(R1,D1,M1,k)+$\underline{ms}$(RR,DR,MR)

        op:k1*ceil(log2(D1[k]))*$\underline{nc}$(N1/2,D1[k])

    b. cascade

        mem:D1[k]*$\underline{ms}$(R1-1,k←D1,k←M1)+$\underline{ms}$(RR,DR,MR)

        op:k1*D1[k]*ceil((N1/D1[k])/S)

3. Base

    a. vector

        mem:$\underline{ms}$(1,D1,M1)+2a+$\underline{ms}$(1,D2,M2)

        op:k1*ceil(log2(D2))+k2*N1

    b. scalar

        mem:$\underline{ms}$(LP,D1,1)+$\underline{ms}$(1,D2,M2)

        op:k1*ceil(log2(D2))+k2

4. Compression

    mem:$\underline{ms}$(LP,D1,1)+ceil(N2/D2[k])*

        ($\underline{mv}$(R2,D2,M2)+$\underline{mv}$(RR,DR,MR))

    op:k1*DR[k]*$\underline{nc}$(N2,D2[k])+k2*DR[k]

5. Expansion

    mem:$\underline{ms}$(LP,D1,1)+ceil(N2,D2[k]*

        ($\underline{mv}$(R2,D2,M2)+$\underline{mv}$(RR,DR,MR))

    op:k1*DR[k]*$\underline{nc}$(NR,DR[k])+k2*DR[k]

6,7. Grade Up, Grade Down

    a. source fits in AM

        mem:$\underline{ms}$(R1,D1,M1)+$\underline{ms}$(R1,D1,MR)

        op:k1*log2(N2)

    b. source does not fit in AM

        mem:$\underline{ms}$(R1,D1,M1)+2*N1*a+ceil(N/S)*

            $\underline{ms}$(1,<S>,<t1>)

op:k1*N2/S+k2(N2)

8. Index of

   a. op2 fits in AM

      mem:<u>ms</u>(R1,N1,D1)+N2*a+<u>ms</u>(R2,D2,MR)

      op:k1*N2ceil(N1/S)

   b. op2 does not fit in AM

      mem:<u>ms</u>(R1,N1,D1)+N2*a+<u>ms</u>(R2,D2,MR)+

          2*ceil(N2/S)*<u>ms</u>(1,<S>,<32>)

      op:k1*N2*ceil(N1/S)+k2*ceil(N2/S)

9. Inner Product

   See Ref. 2, pp. 34-40

10. Outer Product

   mem:<u>ms</u>(R1,D1,M1)+<u>ms</u>(R2,D2,M2)+

      <u>ms</u>(R1+R2,D1.D2,MR)

   op:k1*ceil(N1*N2/S)+k2(N1+N2)

11. Ravel

   mem:<u>ms</u>(R1,D1,M1)+<u>ms</u>(R1,D1,MR)

   op:0

12. Roll

   mem:2*<u>ms</u>(1,<S>,<64>)+a+<u>ms</u>(1,DR,<32>)

   op:k1*ceil(DR[1]/S)

13. Deal

   a. result fits in AM

      mem:<u>ms</u>(LP,NR,1)+NR*a

      op:k1*NR

   b. result does not fit in AM

      mem:2*<u>ms</u>(LP,NR,1)+2*NR*a

      op:k1*NR

14. Rotate

   mem:<u>mv</u>(R1,D1,M1,k)+<u>mv</u>(R1,D1,MR,k)

   op:k1*ceil(N1/S)

15. Selection

   mem:nSIGMA(i=1)<u>ms</u>(Ri,Di,Mi)+

      <u>ms</u>(nPI(i=1)Ri,D1.D2. ... .Dn, MR)

   op:k1*ceil((nPI(i=1)Ri)/S)+k2*nSIGMA(i=1)Ri

16. Concatenate

   mem:<u>mv</u>(R1,D1,M1,k)+<u>mv</u>(R2,D2,M2,k)+

      <u>mv</u>(RR,DR,MR,k)

   op:0

17. Membership

   mem:<u>ms</u>(R1,D1,M1)+<u>ms</u>(RR,DR,MR)+

      ceil(N1/S)*N2*a

   op:k1*ceil(N1/S)*N2

REFERENCES

[1] S. Pakin, <u>APL/360 Reference Manual</u>, Science Research Associates, Inc.,
     (1968), 160 pp.

[2] T. Feng, and W. Cheng, "Associative Computation of Some Mathematical Problems,"
     Dept. of Electrical and Computer Engineering, Syracuse University,
     (May, 1974), 76 pp.

A UNIFIED ASSOCIATIVE AND VON-NEUMANN PROCESSOR
EGPP AND EGPP-ARRAY

WOLFGANG HÄNDLER
Universität Erlangen-Nürnberg

In this paper we propose a simple extension to a general purpose processor (GPP), which allows it to be used also as an associative array processor (AAP).

Disregarding input/output in this discussion, we concentrate on the structure of the GPP. Very simple GPP's have registers of the following kind, for example with a 64 bit wordlength.

Accumulator-Register	A
Multiplicand-Register	B
Carry-Register	C
Multiplier-Quotient-Register	D
Auxiliary-Register	E

In contrast an AAP has at least four registers:

Mask-Register	M
1. Operand-bit-Register	X
2. Operand-bit-Register	Y
Comparator-Register	K

A slice containing one bit of each register M, X, and Y is called a Processing Element (PE). Accordingly, typical AAP-operations are composed of micro-operations, where in most cases the i'th bits of the registers C and Y hold the corresponding operand-bits. The mask-register M has to mask some operations and, for example, some writing to the array-memory (as in STARAN).

Unfortunately the contemporary AAP has a considerable drawback in that it needs a connected GPP for operation. To avoid this twofold expenditure we investigate the question whether it is possible to combine both structures, GPP and AAP, in one unique structure. This, indeed, is the case for a structure which we will call an EGPP, the Erlangen version of a General Purpose Processor.

If we think of a GPP with N-bit-wordlength as an AAP with N PE's we have the main idea of the EGPP. We propose to enlarge the set of micro-operations, if necessary, to extend the set of instructions, in order to achieve a satisfactory performance for both GPP and AAP operation modes.

For a first discussion let us assume a number of N=64 PE's, as we have assumed a 64 bit wordlength. We may have to supplement slightly the stock of micro-operations. From these the unified instruction set is chosen and implemented. In doing so we have to cover at least the following AAP-operations, in addition to known GPP-mode operations:

Search or identification operations

Field operations (in most cases dependent on the state of the activity-bit in this column and other criteria)

Extremum-search operations

Greater-than and smaller-than search operations

Resolving multiple responses

Input/Output operations

Insertion of an item into a list (and cancellation)

The data for AAP-mode operations are stored vertically in the primary memory. Assuming a one-address-type, the instructions are stored horizontally in the same memory. They are fetched and interpreted by the program-control in the conventional way.

A "turning chip", which converts vertical data to horizontal data, and vice versa, greatly increases the efficiency of the EGPP.

It is emphasized that the memory of the EGPP is quite conventional, in the sense that it is a Random Access Memory (RAM), addressable as it is in other general purpose computers by numbers from 0 to 2^{n-1}, where n is the number of bits in the address. This address plays the usual role in the GPP-mode of the EGPP computer. In the AAP-mode, on the other hand, this address denotes a bit-slice which can be processed simultaneously (i.e., in parallel). In the applications we have in mind the bit-slice normally contains one bit from each of 64 vertical words. However this entirely different interpretation leads to a different result and makes the memory appear as an associative memory.

In the AAP-mode operation 64 vertical words are processed simultaneously (but one bit-position after the other). The number 64 seems to be a hard restriction, if compared with 256, 512 or up to 8192 as in STARAN. However one can modify the otherwise conventional memory in such a way that, for example, 8 blocks of memory configure a bank of synchronously working interleaved blocks. Alternatively fields containing more than 64 items can be chained so that 64 items at a time are processed in parallel.

The main advantages of the proposed EGPP-computer would be:

1. One EGPP instead of one GPP and a connected AAP. The costs of the EGPP are only slightly higher than those of a contemporary GPP.

2. Full utilization in the EGPP of conventional features of interrupt and multi-programming, also in AAP-mode processing.

3. Full utilization of the memory-space in the EGPP by an arbitrary partition between

   a. GPP-mode programs (horizontal)

   b. GPP-mode data (horizontal)

   c. AAP-mode programs (horizontal)

d. AAP-mode data (to be interpreted vertically).

4. Easy programming in the sense that AAP-mode computation in an EGPP-System does not differ too much from the conventional philosophy of programming in GPP's.

We have described the basic concept of the EGPP processor. We are also planning to connect a number of these processors to an array, which will enable us to compute in any of the modes: ILLIAC IV, STARAN, PRIME, C.mmp.

REFERENCE

[1] Händler, W, Unconventional Computation by Conventional Equipment. Arbeitsberichte des IMMD. 7 (1974), Number 2.

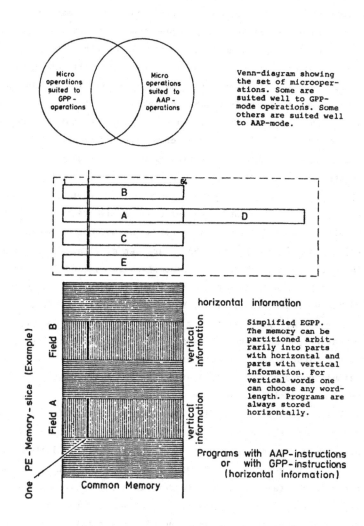

Venn-diagram showing the set of microoperations. Some are suited well to GPP-mode operations. Some others are suited well to AAP-mode.

Simplified EGPP. The memory can be partitioned arbitrarily into parts with horizontal and parts with vertical information. For vertical words one can choose any wordlength. Programs are always stored horizontally.

horizontal information

Programs with AAP-instructions or with GPP-instructions (horizontal information)

DISCRIMINATING CONTENT ADDRESSABLE MEMORIES

CARL H. SMITH and LARRY WITTIE
Department of Computer Science, SUNY/Buffalo
4226 Ridge Lea Road, Amherst, N.Y. 14226

SUMMARY

Computers achieve their generality, in part, from the flexibility of their memories. Sometimes this generality makes frequently used processes overly time consuming. This report describes a special purpose memory to cope with scheduling problems [5]. Recurrent scheduling problems in a large multiprogramming environment include entering a job into the mix, choosing a job from the mix to process, and interrupt handling. This class of problems is characterized by first choosing from a list of potential tasks the ones which currently match the dynamically changing resources of the machine, then making a final selection based on an implied or assigned priority. A content addressable memory is capable of making the first type of selection, but certain modifications are necessary for the memory to discriminate amongst responders based on some priority scheme. A discriminating content addressable memory (DCAM) performs the entire scheduling operation in one memory query.

A DCAM consists of a memory M containing w words M_1, M_2, ..., M_w. Each word is b bits long. M_i^j for $1 \leq i \leq w$, $1 \leq j \leq b$ denotes the jth bit of the ith word. Associated with the memory are a comparand register C and a mask register MSK, each b bits long. A result register R, of w bits, records the outcome of a memory query. Where $R_i = \bigwedge_{k=1}^{b} (((M_i^k = C_k) \wedge MSK_k) \vee -MSK_k)$. All the R_i are set simultaneously and this is referred to as a similar-to search [2]. To accomplish the second discriminating phase of a memory query the DCAM uses a temporary result register, T, containing w bits. Each word has a distinguished field, P, called the priority field. If P is p bits long then $P_i = M_i^{j+1}$, M_i^{j+2}, ... M_i^{j+p} for $1 \leq i \leq w$ and some constant $j \leq b - p$.

The discrimination process takes place in p steps of two stages each. At the kth step (k $\leq$ p) the first stage sets T, where $T_i = R_i \wedge M_i^{j+k}$, for $1 \leq i \leq w$. All the T_i are set simultaneously. The second stage occurs if at least one bit of T is set to true. If this condition is met then R_i is set equal to T_i, for $1 \leq i \leq w$, via a jam transfer. This sequentially modifies the result register without changing the contents of the C and MSK registers and without initiating another memory query. To complete the entire memory query quickly it is essential that the decision to modify R be made quickly. By using a tree of OR gates this can be done in time proportional to $\log_n(w)$, where n is the fan-in. Using standard IC's the entire process can be completed in one microsecond after termination of the similar to search. Since a similar to search can be done in one microsecond [1], the total query time for a DCAM is two microseconds.

What the operation of the DCAM accomplishes in the discrimination phase is to single out the word(s) stored in the memory which responded to the similar to search and contained the largest binary number in the P field. This operation is referred to as maximizing on the P field. Conventional techniques for performing this operation rely on additional logic external to M to manipulate the C and MSK registers using several memory queries to achieve the final result [3]. A DCAM has the additional logic internal to M. Minimizing on the P field is also possible. The necessary modification is to set $T_i = R_i \wedge \neg M_i^{j+p}$, $1 \le i \le w$, in stage two in each of the p steps.

As an example, consider selection of a job from the current mix. A DCAM performs low level scheduling each time a new job takes control of the central processor [4]. Each job in the mix corresponds to a word in M. The word remains in M until the job is completed. Stored in this word are the job's parameters such as field length, time estimate, and priority. A similar to search for job constraints finds all the jobs which may run on the machine based on currently available storage, available tape units, etc. A similar to search for jobs using less than a particular field length can be done by looking for high order zeros in the field length parameter in the corresponding field across all words in the memory. The discrimination phase of a DCAM operation selects the highest priority job fitting the run time constraints, which completes the low level scheduling operation.

In a large multiprogramming environment control of the central processor switches from job to job frequently. The overhead of dynamically choosing which job in the mix is next to seize the processor is currently handled by a software search through a linked list. A DCAM would introduce significant savings. Furthermore a DCAM, shared by several asynchronous processors, would greatly simplify the low level scheduling problem in a highly parallel system.

REFERENCES

[1] C.G. Bell and A. Newell, Computer Structures: Readings and Examples, McGraw-Hill, 1971.

[2] T. Feng, "An Associative Processor", Rome Air Development Center, TR-68-449, 1969.

[3] M.H. Lewin, "Retrieval of Ordered Lists from A Content-Addressed Memory", RCA Review, (1962).

[4] H. Lorin, Parallelism in Hardware and Software: Real and Apparent Concurrency, Prentice-Hall, 1972.

[5] C. Smith, "Discriminating Content Addressable Memories", M.S. Project, SUNY/Buffalo, 1974.

A FUNDAMENTAL THEOREM OF ASYNCHRONOUS
PARALLEL COMPUTATION

ROBERT M. KELLER
Department of Electrical Engineering
Princeton University[a]
Princeton, N.J. 08540

Abstract -- A recurrent phenomenon in models of asynchronous parallel computation is expressed in an abstract model. Many previous models, or special cases thereof, possess three local properties: determinism, commutativity, and persistence, as they are defined here. We show that the possession of these local properties by a system is a sufficient condition for the possession of the global confluence or "Church-Rosser" property. The relation of this property to the "determinacy" of asynchronous systems was suggested in recent work by Rosen. We show that determinacy proofs for many models, and proofs of some other properties of interest, are really corollaries of the main theorem of this paper.

Summary. Numerous models of asynchronous parallel computation have appeared in the literature [1-10,12]. Most of these involve some notion of "determinacy", which means that certain quantities are independent of the order in which basic operations are performed.

This paper presents an abstract model, the "transition system", which is sufficiently general to include most previous models, and yet is quite simple. Its components are simply a set of states (not necessarily finite) and a set of connecting transitions, which may be named, in which case we call it a "named transition system". The local properties of determinism, commutativity, and persistence will be introduced. Similar properties with these names have been presented elsewhere, but we caution the reader that they are similar, but not necessarily precisely the same as those properties here. It will be shown that a system with these local properties also possesses the global property of confluence, also called the Church-Rosser property, as discussed by Rosen [13]. By interpreting "state" in various, sometimes unusual, ways, we exploit this relation in a series of applications. It is hoped that results of this kind will provide some cohesiveness to the diverse area of asynchronous parallel computation.

1. AN ABSTRACT MODEL

The first model we present is so general as to capture almost any notion of asynchronour parallel computation which has been proposed. Formally, we will call this model a "transition system".

[a] Work reported herein was performed while the author was visiting Stanford University, and was sponsored by NSF grant GJ-30126

1.1 <u>Definition</u> A <u>transition system</u> is a pair $(Q, \rightarrow)$, where Q is a set of <u>state</u> names and $\rightarrow$ is a binary relation on Q, called the set of <u>transitions</u>. (We do not restrict Q or $\rightarrow$ to be finite.)

When q, q' are state names, we think of q $\rightarrow$ q' as meaning that there can be an <u>indivisible</u> progression from state q to state q'. In a system which allows "parallelism", for a given state q there may be many states q' such that q $\rightarrow$ q'. Each such state represents the result of one of a number of possible actions, each of which is <u>simultaneously enabled</u> when the system is in state q.

We have not yet said what, in reality, is happening when the action corresponding to a transition occurs. It could be that the action represents a <u>single</u> event, or perhaps several events occurring <u>simultaneously</u>. However it is usually assumed that an action does represent only a single event, and if there is any possibility of simultaneous events occurring, such an occurrence can be represented as a sequence of occurrence of events in some arbitrary order. This assumption will be made in most of what follows, and will be referred to as the <u>arbitration condition</u>. Nevertheless, the machinery required to back up this assumption may be non-trivial in a truly asynchronous system.

The events which correspond to transitions may be represented by assigning <u>names</u> to the transitions. More than one transition may have the same name, and hence represent the same event. The manner in which names are assigned can be of importance in describing the properties of a system, as will be seen.

Another use of names is in the presentation of a system. For example, suppose that the set of states is the set of all pairs of non-negative integers, $\omega \times \omega$. We wish to say that for each two states (x,y) and (x',y'), there is a transition (x,y) $\rightarrow$ (x',y') provided x $\geq$ 1, x' = x - 1, and y' = 2y. As the set of such transitions is infinite, we cannot hope to list them all. But we can present them all at once by the "name"

if x $\geq$ 1 then (x',y') = (x-1,2y)

If the expression above were considered a statement of a program, then this naming would be quite natural, as the change in state corresponds to the execution of the statement.

It will be useful to extend our definition of transition systems as follows:

1.2 <u>Definition</u> A <u>named transition system</u> is a triple $(Q, \rightarrow, \Sigma)$, where $(Q, \rightarrow)$ is a transition system and each transition is assigned a single name in the set Σ.

According to the preceding discussion, a named transition system can be presented, in the case that Σ is finite (or, more generally, recursive), by presenting a binary relation on Q, $\rightarrow_\sigma$, for each σ in Σ. In other words, q $\rightarrow_\sigma$ q' means that there is a transition from q to q' with name σ.

If Δ is any set, let Δ^* denote the set of all finite sequences of elements from Δ, Δ^ω the set of all countably-infinite sequences, and $\hat{\Delta} = \Delta^* \cup \Delta^\omega$. We extend the notation $\rightarrow_\sigma$ to $\rightarrow_x$ for each x ϵ Σ^* in the customary manner. We may also leave the second state unspecified. That is, if $x \in \Sigma^*$ then $q \to_x$ means that $(\exists q' \in Q)$ $q \to_x q'$, and if $x \in \Sigma^\omega$ then $q \to_x$ means that for every finite prefix $y \leq x$ we have $q \to_y$. Finally, $q \overset{*}{\to} q'$ means $(\exists x \in \Sigma^*)$ $q \to_x q'$ and in this case we say that q' is reachable from q. We refer to the set of x such that $q_0 \to_x$, where q_0 is some understood initial state, as the <u>behavior</u> of the system.

1.3 <u>Definition</u> A named transition system $(Q, \to, \Sigma)$ is classified as

(D) <u>deterministic</u>, if $(\forall q, q', q'' \in Q)$ $(\forall \sigma \in \Sigma)$

$$\text{if } q \to_\sigma q' \text{ and } q \to_\sigma q'' \text{ then } q' = q''$$

(C) <u>commutative</u>, if $(\forall q \in Q)$ $(\forall \sigma, \pi \in \Sigma)$

$$\text{if } q \to_{\sigma\pi} \text{ and } q \to_{\pi\sigma}$$
$$\text{then } (\exists q' \in Q) \; q \to_{\sigma\pi} q' \text{ and } q \to_{\pi\sigma} q'$$

(P) <u>persistent</u>, if $(\forall q \in Q)$ $(\forall \sigma, \pi \in \Sigma)$

$$\text{if } \sigma \neq \pi \text{ and } q \to_\sigma \text{ and } \sigma \to_\pi \text{ then } q \to_{\pi\sigma}$$

1.4 <u>Observation</u> Property D implies that for each $x \in \Sigma^*$, $\to_x$ is a partial function. That is, given q, there is at most one q' such that $q \to_x q'$.

1.5 <u>Definition</u> A transition system $(Q, \to)$ is classified as

(F) <u>confluent</u>, if $(\forall q, q', q'' \in Q)$

$$\text{if } q \overset{*}{\to} q' \text{ and } q \overset{*}{\to} q'' \text{ then } (\exists q''' \in Q) \; q' \overset{*}{\to} q''' \text{ and } q'' \overset{*}{\to} q'''$$

(LF) <u>locally</u> <u>confluent</u>, if $(\forall q, q'' \in Q)$

$$\text{if } q \to q' \text{ and } q \to q'', \text{ where } q' \neq q'',$$
$$\text{then } (\exists q''' \in Q) \; q' \to q''' \text{ and } q'' \to q'''$$

Properties D, C, and P clearly depend on the way transitions are named, in addition to the state-transition structure itself. Thus these properties will not necessarily remain invariant under a renaming. In contrast, properties F and LF are independent of names.

Informally, property D says that there can be at most one (but perhaps no) transition leaving a given state with a given name, i.e. that for each $\sigma, \to_\sigma$ is actually a partial function. Property C says that if two transitions can occur in either order from a given state, then there is at least one common resulting state which is independent of the order. (Property C holds vacuously if $\sigma = \pi$.) Property P says that the occurrence of a transition with name π cannot <u>disable</u> the occurrence of a transition σ, if the latter is enabled. That is, the condition "σ is enabled" <u>persists</u> until σ occurs.

Property F says that for any two states reachable from a common state, there is a common state reachable from both. Property F has been called the "Church-Rosser" property [13]. The term "confluent" is borrowed from [11,14].

The classical importance of the Church-Rosser property has been to show that if an "irreducible state" (in our terminology, a state in which no transitions are enabled) is reachable from a given state, then this state is unique. If the irreducible state is thought of as a "normal form" for the state from which it is reachable, then the Church-Rosser property implies that if a state has a normal form at all, then it has a unique one. Some of the applications for this property here will be less traditional.

Of the properties D, C, P, F, and LF, all except F may be considered local, as each depends on sets of states related by the occurrence of two transitions. In some cases, local properties are easier to determine, hence the importance of the results to follow.

1.6 <u>Lemma</u> (D, C, and P) imply LF.

<u>Proof</u> Assume D, C, and P. Suppose that $q \to q'$ and $q \to q''$, where $q' \neq q''$, to show the existence of a q''' as in LF. We have for some $\sigma, \pi \in \Sigma, q \to_\sigma q'$ and $q \to_\pi q''$, where $\sigma \neq \pi$ by D. By P then, $q \to_{\sigma\pi}$ and $q \to_{\pi\sigma}$, and by C, there exists $q''' \in Q$ such that $q \to_{\sigma\pi} q'''$ and $q \to_{\pi\sigma} q'''$. Thus by D, $q' \to_\pi q'''$ and $q'' \to_\sigma q'''$, so LF holds.

1.7 <u>Lemma</u> LF implies F

<u>Proof</u> An informal proof is seen by an argument which "completes the diagram" shown in Figure 1 using LF, to get the diagram in Figure 2. An => in the diagram means $\to \cup =$.

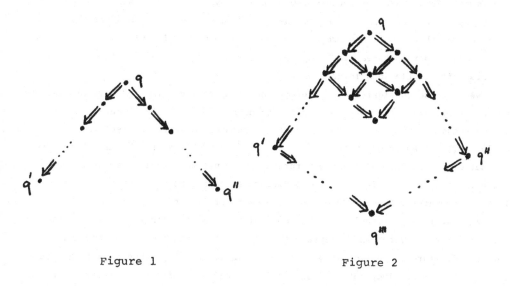

Figure 1   Figure 2

1.8 <u>Theorem</u> (D, C, and P) imply F.

The preceding theorem follows immediately from lemmas 1.6 and 1.7. It is quite simple, yet constitutes the central result in the paper, to be applied in the following sections. Before presenting these applications, one further definition will be presented.

1.9 <u>Definition</u> Given two named transitions systems with the same set of names,

$S^1 = (Q^1, \rightarrow^1, \Sigma)$ and $S^2 = (Q^2, \rightarrow^2, \Sigma)$, we may combine them to form a third system S which we call the coupling of S^1 and S^2. Formally, $S = (Q^1 \times Q^2, \rightarrow, \Sigma)$ where

$$(\forall (q, q'), (q'', q''') \in Q^1 \times Q^2) \; (\forall \sigma \in \Sigma)$$
$$(q, q') \rightarrow_\sigma (q'', q''')$$

$$\text{iff} \qquad q \rightarrow^1_\sigma q'' \text{ and } q' \rightarrow^2_\sigma q'''$$

It is then clear that $(\forall x \in \Sigma^*) \; (q, q') \rightarrow_x (q'', q''')$ iff $q \rightarrow^1_x q''$ and $q' \rightarrow^2_x q'''$.

It is possible to couple two systems which do not have property F to obtain one which does. An instance of such a coupling will be seen in the following section.

2.   FIRST APPLICATION - DETERMINACY OF PARALLEL PROGRAM SCHEMATA

The control of a parallel program schema in the sense of [7] will be considered. Extension of the discussion to schemata in the sense of [5] is also possible, but somewhat more cumbersome. We consider the control aspect of a schema to be a named transition system, where each "terminator" of a particular operation is assigned the same name. This system will therefore be generally non-deterministic. The terms "persistent" and "commutative" as defined in [7] are assumed to hold for the control. We note that these imply the properties with the same name in this paper, provided that no two control states are "congruent". We assume that this is the case in what follows, with little loss in generality.

We may also consider the interpretation or "data manipulating" part of a schema to be a named transition system, again with each terminator of an operation having the same name. A "state" in this case is considered to be the contents of all memory cells. (This transition system may be formally described as the "full schema" over the set of operations [7].) An interpretation is not necessarily commutative, because the order of application of two different operations will matter in general. It is deterministic however, and also vacuously persistent.

When we form the coupling of the control of a schema with its interpretation, we get a transition system which represents the possible computations of the schema under that interpretation (formally, this is Lemma 1.2 of [7]). The resulting system may not be commutative, but will be persistent and deterministic. However, if the conflict-free condition [7] is satisfied by the control, i.e. that concurrently executing operations don't have overlapping range and domain cells, then we have commutativity of the resulting coupled system. This in turn implies that the system is confluent, which means, among other things, that if some computation terminates, then all must terminate and do so with the same value in each memory cell. This is one possible sense of the word "determinate".

If we change the meaning of "state" to include cell-value sequences, rather than simply cell values, then it is not hard to see that the conflict-free condition again implies commutativity, and confluence again results. Confluence is "determinacy" in this case in the sense of [5], or in the E_Ω sense of [7]. If we interpret "state" in a slightly different way, we get E_ρ determinacy in the sense of [7]. Similar results are obtained for the model of Luconi [9].

The conclusion for this section is that Theorem 1.8 may be applied to obtain sufficient conditions for determinacy of parallel program schemata, in several possible senses. This was suggested by Rosen [13] for the first sense of determinacy mentioned above. The analysis has turned out to be less complicated than he indicated.

3. SECOND APPLICATION - DETERMINACY OF QUEUE MODELS

We next introduce a representation which relates and generalizes several previously studied models. Our aim is to reduce results for these models to instances of Theorem 1.8, as in the preceding section.

3.1 **Definition** An operational queue model (OQM) is a named transition system specified by a 5-tuple $(\Delta, \Pi, \Sigma, T, q_o)$ where

    (i) Δ is a set called the **queue domain**

    (ii) Π is an index set for the set of **queues**

    (iii) Σ is a set of **operation names**

    (iv) q_o is an **initial state**,

where the **state set** of the system is $(\Delta^*)^\Pi$, the set of functions from Π into Δ^*. That is, each state specifies an assignment of an element of Δ^* to each queue. Frequently, we will want $\Pi = \{1, 2, \ldots, n\}$ for some n, in which case we write a state as an n-tuple of elements from Δ^*. For general Π, we refer to elements of the state set as Π-tuples. Continuing the definition,

    (v)   with each operation name $\sigma \in \Sigma$ is associated a set T_σ of pairs (U, W) where U, W $\in (\Delta^*)^\Pi$. U is called a test vector and W a replacement vector. To continue the definition, additional notation will be required.

Consider the set $(\Delta^*)^\Pi$ of Π-tuples of elements in Δ^*. We define the product on this set as $\overline{xy} = \overline{z}$, where for each $i \in \Pi$ $z_i = x_i y_i$. We define $\leq$ on this set by $\overline{x} \leq \overline{y}$ iff $(\exists \overline{z} \in (\Delta^*)^\Pi) \ \overline{xz} = \overline{y}$. The extension of product and $\leq$ to allow elements of $(\hat{\Delta})^\Pi$ on the right is also clear.

In an OQM, there is a transition $q \rightarrow_\sigma q'$ iff for some (U, W) $\in T_\sigma$

    (vi) $U \leq q$

and, letting q" be such that $Uq'' = q$.

    (vii) $q''W = q'$

In other words, the sequences corresponding to U are removed from the left ends of the queues and the sequences corresponding to W are appended to the right ends when the transition occurs. The transition is enabled, by definition, when the state is such that this action can meaningfully take place.

It is easy to extend the OQM to one in which the operations themselves have "internal" states, and each T_σ is a function of the state, rather than being constant. We refer to this model as the extended operational queue model, but will not give a formal definition. Moreover, any such model can be represented as an OQM by adding extra queues to hold the internal states of the operations. The statements which follow also apply to the extended version.

3.2 Definition Two elements $\bar{x}, \bar{y} \in (\hat{\Delta})^\Pi$ are called compatible if there exist $\bar{x}'$, $\bar{y}'$ such that $\bar{x} \bar{x}' = \bar{y} \bar{y}'$. Otherwise they are called incompatible.

3.3 Lemma If $x, y \in (\hat{\Delta})^\Pi$ are incompatible, then for any $\bar{z}$, it cannot be the case that both $\bar{x} \le \bar{z}$ and $\bar{y} \le \bar{z}$.

3.4 Lemma A sufficient condition for an operational queue model to be deterministic is that for any $\sigma \in \Sigma$, if (U, W) and (U', W') are in T_σ, then U and U' are incompatible.

Proof The condition of 3.4 in conjunction with 3.3, implies that for any given state at most one of the pairs of T_σ is applicable for any $\sigma \in \Sigma$.

For a given OQM, we say that a queue $p \in \Pi$ is input to an operation σ if there is a pair $(U, W) \in T_\sigma$ such that $U_p \ne \Lambda$, the null element. Similarly, we say that σ is output to p if there is a pair $(U, W) \in T_\sigma$ such that $W_p \ne \Lambda$. The relation of input and output, when viewed as a graph, give us many of the so-called "graph models" of parallel computation.

We say that a queue is input shared if there is more than one operation to which the queue is input, and output shared if there is more than one operation from which the queue is output.

The queueing models of Karp and Miller [6] and Adams [1], are special cases of the present model which are deterministic and in which no queues are input or output shared.

3.5 Observation If an OQM has no input shared queues, then it is persistent.

3.6 Observation If an OQM has no input or output shared queues, then it is commutative.

Both of the above observations result from examining the actions of two different simultaneously-enabled transitions. A formal proof is not felt necessary.

Given an OQM, we can adjoin to its state set additional queues which record every value placed on each queue by each operation. These queues, which we call indicators, are not input to any operations, and each is output from a unique operation. The addition of these queues clearly does not change the behavior of the system, nor the properties D, C, or P (however F and LF may not remain invariant unless, for example, D, C and P held to begin with).

From the preceding observations we then have, due to property F for the augmented system, that every deterministic OQM without shared queues (e.g. [1],[6]) is determinate in the sense that the sequence of values which is placed on each queue is independent of the order in which operations place them there.

It is possible to introduce a recursion discipline into an OQM, as is done in [1], for example. We note that properties D, C, and P might then only hold for certain evaluation rules. A more detailed explanation will appear in a future paper.

Another type of queue model which has appeared will be called a functional queue model (FQM). Instances of FQM's appear in Patil [12] and Kahn [4]. Every OQM without shared queues can be viewed as an FQM, but FQM's are potentially more abstract. The idea here is that each operation is represented as a function from sequences (of queue values) into sequences, representing the transformation of the sequence of values which appear on the input queues during the entire history of the system's operation to those which are produced on the output queues.

The greater abstractness of FQM's has led to the imposition of additional conditions so that meaningful results could be obtained. These conditions are intuitively the ones which are required if one is to be able to convert an FQM to an equivalent extended operational queue model, but carrying out the conversion process in complete detail appears difficult. We only comment here about these additional conditions.

(i) "consistency" [12] or "monotonicity" [4], i.e. that $x \leq y$ implies $F(X) \leq F(Y)$, is analogous to persistence. That is, adding more input cannot disable the production of any output which would have otherwise been produced.

(ii) "dependency" [12] or "continuity" [4] is necessary for an FQM to be realistic, in the sense that it never requires an infinite number of input values to produce an output value. This condition enables us to get the pairs $(U,W) \in (\Delta^*)^{\Pi}$ (rather than from $(\hat{\Delta})^{\Pi}$) required for an OQM.

A further special case of OQM's will be discussed in the following section.

4. THIRD APPLICATION - IMMORTALITY OF VECTOR REPLACEMENT SYSTEMS

A vector replacement system (VRS) [8], or generalized Petri net [3] is an OQM in which the queue domain consists of only one element.

In a VRS, queues are usually referred to as places, and their values, because of the commutativity of concatenation over a one-symbol alphabet, are representable by natural numbers, sometimes called the number of tokens assigned to a place.

4.1 Observation Every vector replacement system is commutative. A vector replacement system with no input-shared queues is also persistent (thus, for example, every "marked graph" [2] is persistent).

The preceding observation follows by observing that if there is only one element in the queue domain, then the order in which elements are added to, or removed from, queues is unimportant.

Vector replacement systems have been used to study control structures of asynchronous systems, including parallel program schemata with counters [5], semaphores [15], generalized semaphores [8], etc.

An interesting decidability question concerning asynchronous systems in general, for which partial answers can be obtained for vector replacement systems, concerns the "immortality" of selected transition definitions.

4.2 <u>Definition</u> Let $(Q, \to, \Sigma)$ be a named transition system. We say that $\sigma \in \Sigma$ is <u>live</u> with respect to $q \in Q$, denoted $L(q, \sigma)$, if $(\exists x \in \Sigma^*)\ q \to_{x\sigma}$. We say that σ is <u>immortal</u> with respect to $q \in Q$, denoted $I(q, \sigma)$, if $(\forall q' \in Q)\ q \to^* q'$ implies $L(q', \sigma)$.

In other words, $I(q, \sigma)$ holds if, no matter what sequence of transitions has occurred, it is still porsible to reach a state in which σ is enabled. We might alternatively say that "σ is not deadlocked" in state q.

Whether or not the predicate I is decidable for an arbitrary VRS is a question which has been open for some time [3,8,15]. L, on the other hand, is known to be decidable [3,8,15]. We now use Theorem 1.8 to show that for persistent vector replacement systems, I is decidable. The proof will make use of the additional concept of "boundedness".

4.3 <u>Definition</u> Let $(Q, \to, \Sigma)$ be a named transition system. We say that $\sigma \in \Sigma$ is <u>bounded</u> with respect to $q \in Q$ if there is a natural number n such that $(\forall x \in \Sigma^*)\ q \to_x$ implies σ occurs at most n times in x. Otherwise we say that σ is <u>unbounded</u> with respect to q and write $U(q, \sigma)$.

4.4 <u>Observation</u> $I(q, \sigma)$ implies $U(q, \sigma)$

4.5 <u>Observation</u> $U(q, \sigma)$ implies $L(q, \sigma)$

It is not difficult to give examples, even when restricted to vector replacement systems, such that the converse implications to the preceding observations fail to hold [8].

As discussed in section 3, we may adjoin additional <u>indicator</u> places which, for vector replacement systems, serve merely to count the number of occurrences of each transition name. The indicator concept, together with the "reachability tree" construction [5,8], can then be used to decide whether a transition in a VRS is bounded. As mentioned above, immortality of a transition with respect to a state q implies that the transition is unbounded with respect to q, but the converse is not generally true. However in the persistent case, the converse does hold, which we will prove using Theorem 1.8.

4.6 <u>Lemma</u> A transition σ is immortal with respect to a state q iff for every q' reachable from q, σ is unbounded with respect to q'.

<u>Proof</u> (=>) Immortality implies unboundedness, as mentioned in observation 4.4. Furthermore, immortality is preserved by the occurrence of any sequence of transitions. Hence unboundedness of immortal transitions is preserved.

(<=) Unboundedness implies liveness, from 4.5.

4.7 <u>Lemma</u> For a named transition system with properties D, C, and P, $U(q, \sigma)$ implies $I(q, \sigma)$.

<u>Proof</u> Assume without loss of generality that the system has an indicator for σ. By Theorem 1.8, the system has property F. Suppose that $U(q, \sigma)$ and that $q \stackrel{*}{\to} q'$. It suffices to show that $L(q', \sigma)$, by Definition 4.2. Let $n = N_\sigma(q')$, the value for the indicator of σ in state q'. We must show that there is a q'' with $q' \stackrel{*}{\to} q''$ and $N_\sigma(q'') > n$. Since $U(q, \sigma)$, there is a q''' such that $q \stackrel{*}{\to} q'''$ and $N_\sigma(q''') > n$. By property F, there is a q'' such that $q' \stackrel{*}{\to} q''$ and $q''' \stackrel{*}{\to} q''$. Clearly $N_\sigma(q'') \geq N_\sigma(q''') > n$, and so this q'' satisfies the desired condition.

5. FOURTH APPLICATION - SPEED-INDEPENDENT SWITCHING THEORY

Muller and Bartky [10] were the first to present results of the type presented here in the context of asynchronous systems. We note that a fundamental theorem in their work can be viewed as an instance of Theorem 1.8.

An asynchronous switching network, as defined in [10], can be viewed as a named transition system. We will restrict ourselves to the two-valued signal case, and define the transition names to be changes on particular lines, either from 0 to 1 or 1 to 0, although other namings are possible. The theory of [10] is unique in that it does permit simultaneous transition names to occur, if they are named as we have suggested. However, many results of [10] assume the "semi-modularity" condition, whcch can be shown to be the same as persistence when we restrict ourselves to occurrences of single transitions at a time. The nature of the states in such systems (n-tuples of 0's and 1's) implies that each system is deterministic and commutative. It follows that, for the persistent case, any parallel change can be decomposed into a sequence of sequential changes with the same resulting state, and for this reason, our theory applies.

By observing that for a persistent system no "pseudo-final" state classes [10] can exist, Theorem 1.8 gives immediately that every persistent (i.e. semi-modular) system is speed-independent in the sense of [10].

CONCLUSION

We have shown that several results for different models of asynchronous parallel computation can be cast into a common abstract model and proved as instances of a single theorem. It is hoped that work of this type will aid in the unification of the theory of such models.

REFERENCES

[1] D. Adams, "A Computation Model with Data Flow Sequencing", Tech. Report CS 117 (Ph.D. dissertation), Computer Science Dept., Stanford Univ. (Dec. 1968).

[2] F. Commoner, A.W. Holt, S. Even, and A. Pnueli, "Marked Directed Graphs", <u>J. Computer and System Sciences</u>, <u>5</u>, 5 (Oct. 1971) pp. 511-523,

[3] M. Hack, "Decision Problems for Petri Nets and Vector Addition Systems", MIT Project MAC, Computation Structures Group Memo 95 (Mar. 1974).

[4] G. Kahn, "A Preliminary Theory for Parallel Programs", IRIA Research Report
No. 6, (Jan. 1973).

[5] R.M. Karp, and R.E. Miller, "Parallel Program Schemata," J. Computer and System
Sciences, 3, 2, (May 1969), pp. 147-195.

[6] R.M. Karp, and R.E. Miller, "Properties of a Model for Parallel Computations:
Determinacy, Termination, and Queuing," SIAM J. Applied Math., 14, 6. (Nov.
1966), pp. 1390-1411.

[7] R.M. Keller, "Parallel Program Schemata and Maximal Parallelism," J. ACM, 20,
3, (July 1973) pp. 514-537 and 20, 4, (Oct. 1973) pp. 696-710.

[8] R.M. Keller, "Vector Replacement Systems: A Formalism for Modeling Asynchronous
Systems," Tech. Rept. 117, Computer Science Laboratory, Princeton University
(Jan. 1974).

[9] F.L. Luconi, "Asynchronous Computational Structures," MIT Project MAC Rept.
MAC-TR-49 (1968).

[10] D.E. Muller and W.S. Bartky, "A Theory of Asynchronous Circuits," Annals of
the Computation Laboratory of Harvard University, 29, Pt. 1, (1959) pp. 204-243.

[11] M.H.A. Newman, "On Theories with a Combinatorial Definition of 'Equivalence'"
Annals of Math., 43, 2, (April 1942), pp. 223-243.

[12] S. Patil, "Closure Properties of Interconnections of Determinate Systems,"
Proc. Project MAC Conference on Concurrent Systems and Parallel Computations,
(June 1970), pp. 107-116.

[13] B. Rosen, "Tree Manipulating Systems and Church-Rosser Theorems", J. ACM 20,
1, (Jan. 1973), pp. 160-187.

[14] R. Sethi, "Theorems of Confluence for Unions of Replacement Systems with Equi-
valences," Tech. Rept. 131, Computer Science Dept., Pennsylvania State University (Oct. 1972).

[15] R.C. Holt, "On Deadlock in Computer Systems," Univ. of Toronto Computer Science
Research Group Rept. CSRG-6, (April 1971).

THE HYPERPLANE METHOD FOR AN ARRAY COMPUTER

LESLIE LAMPORT
Massachusetts Computer Associates, Inc.
Wakefield, Massachusetts 01880

Abstract -- Techniques are described for implementing the hyperplane method for an array computer with a limited form of memory-processor interconnection, such as the Illiac IV. A new pipelined hyperplane method is introduced. It is useful for compiling a convergent iterative computation, if the computation is programmed with a non-deterministic end of loop test.

INTRODUCTION

The hyperplane method of [1] is a compiling technique which translates a nest of DO loops into a form containing explicit parallel operations. However, it may be impossible to execute these operations in parallel on an array computer because of restrictions on how individual processors can reference memory. This paper shows how the hyperplane method can be applied to yield useful parallelism for an array computer such as the Illiac IV.

I assume that the reader is familiar with the description of the hyperplane method given in [1]. Page references such as [p. 83] refer to [1]. They are employed throughout to facilitate the use of concepts from that article.

If a DO loop nest has no missing index variables [pp. 87-88], then it will be shown that the parallelism found by the hyperplane method is easily exploited by an array computer. When the outer loop variable is missing, a technique called the pipelined hyperplane method can be used. This method gives less parallelism than is theoretically possible, but the resulting parallelism can be exploited by an array computer.

It will be shown that an iterative convergent algorithm, when properly coded, can often be translated into a DO nest with a missing outer variable to which the pipelined hyperplane method can be applied. We will see that proper coding of such a computation requires the introduction of a non-deterministic loop terminating procedure. Convergent iterative methods, such as relaxation procedures for solving boundary value problems, are very important numerical analysis tools. (Although direct methods may be faster if nothing is known about the solution, iterative methods are still often better because a good approximation to the solution can be obtained from a previous calculation.) Hence, the pipelined hyperplane method can be an important compiling technique for an array computer.

MEMORY ASSUMPTIONS

I assume that an array computer consists of P individual processors capable of the synchronous parallel execution implied by a DO SIM loop [pp. 89-90]. (A DO CONC loop [p. 84] is considered to be a special form of DO SIM loop.) In general, the P processors will not be able to access simultaneously any arbitrary set of P memory words. Practical considerations will restrict the type of simultaneous memory access permitted by the hardware. This forces some restriction on the form of variable occurrences allowed in a DO SIM loop. For example, the occurrence A(B(I)) could not be allowed in a DO SIM I loop if B is an arbitrary array.

I will assume that memory is composed of P modules, and that the P processors can simultaneously access words $w_0, \ldots, w_{P-1}$ if w_i is the $f(i)$th word of module $i+k \mod P$, where k is independent of i, and f is a function such that $f(0), \ldots, f(P-1)$ are easily computed in parallel. For example, a simple skewed storage scheme [2] for a two-dimensional array A allows simultaneous access to the words $A(0, j), \ldots,$ $A(P-1, j)$ by letting $A(i, j)$ be the $(i+A_0)$th word of memory module $i+j \mod P$. (For convenience, the range of all array subscripts is assumed to begin at 0.) I also assume that a single item of data can be "broadcast" to all processors.

An allocation scheme for storing arrays in such a computer is described in [3]. Using this scheme, a

$$\text{DO } \alpha \text{ SIM FOR ALL } (I^1, \ldots, I^k) \in \mathcal{S}$$

loop can be executed in parallel if the following condition is satisfied, where a loop constant is defined to be any expression which is not a function of the I^j or of any variable generated [p. 85] in the loop body.

SR. For each array variable V occurring in the loop body, there exist integers $i_1, \ldots, i_k$ such that each occurrence of V is of the form $V(e^1, \ldots, e^m)$ and either

(i)   the occurrence is a use [p. 86] and each e^i is a loop constant, or

(ii) for each $\ell = 1, \ldots, k$: $e^{i_\ell} = I^\ell + c^\ell$ for some loop constant c^ℓ.

In the storage scheme of [3], this condition implies that $(i_1, \ldots, i_k)$ is a non-aligned multi-index for V, and that if j is not one of the i_ℓ and some e^j is not a loop constant, then j is part of an aligned multi-index.

As an example, suppose U is a two-dimensional array, f(K) is any arbitrary function of K, and the x_i and y_i are integer constants for $i = 1, \ldots, r$. Then the occurrences $U(f(K)+x_i, K+y_i)$ may all appear in a DO SIM K loop. Rule SR is satisfied with $k = 1$ and $i_1 = 2$. The loop can be implemented by storing $U(i, j)$ in memory module $j \mod P$. In the notation of [3], this is the allocation [#(1), (2)]. Note that the occurrence $U(K, f(K))$ cannot also appear in the loop body.

Variables will also be used whose values are subsets of $\mathbb{Z}^n$ [p. 85]. Such a variable $\mathcal{S}$ is actually implemented with an n-dimensional boolean array S, where

$S(i^1,\ldots,i^n)$ = .TRUE. means that $(i^1,\ldots,i^n) \in \mathcal{S}$. An assignment statement for such a variable is thus an implicit DO SIM loop, which must satisfy SR.

THE SIMPLE HYPERPLANE METHOD

An Example

I will begin with the case of a loop having no missing index variables. Consider the following example loop, which will be used throughout the paper.

Loop 1:

```
DO 99 J = 1, M
DO 99 K = 1, N
U(J,K) = [U(J+1, K) + U(J, K+1) + U(J-1, K) + U(J, K-1)] * .25
99 CONTINUE
```

This is essentially the same as the inner DO J/DO K loop of the example in [pp. 83-85]. It is a simplified version of the inner loop of a relaxation method for solving Laplace's equation with given boundary values.

To apply the hyperplane method to Loop 1, we use the algorithm of [p. 88] to find the mapping $\pi : \mathbb{Z}^2 \to \mathbb{Z}$ defined by $\pi(j, k) = j+k$. With this π we can choose new coordinates $\overline{J}, \overline{K}$ defined by

$$\overline{J} = J + K$$
$$\overline{K} = K$$

and rewrite Loop 1 as follows:

Loop 2:

```
DO 99 J̄ = 2, M+N
DO 99 SIM FOR ALL K̄ ε {k : 1 ≤ k ≤ N and 1 ≤ J̄-k ≤ M}
U(J̄-K̄, K̄) = [U(J̄-K̄+1, K̄) + ... + U(J̄-K̄, K̄-1)] * .25
99 CONTINUE
```

The DO SIM loop of Loop 2 satisfies SR, since all occurrences of U are of the form $U(f(\overline{K})+x, \overline{K}+y)$ for x, y = 0, ± 1. Hence, it can be executed in parallel by an array computer. Assume that the value of U(j, k) is stored in location j of memory module k. Figure 1 illustrates the execution of Loop 2 for the case M = 4, N = 8 < P. For a given value of $\overline{J}$, the DO SIM loop simultaneously generates new values for the elements of U lying along some diagonal line. For $\overline{J}$ = 5 all the circled elements are generated, and for $\overline{J}$ = 6 all the boxed elements are generated.

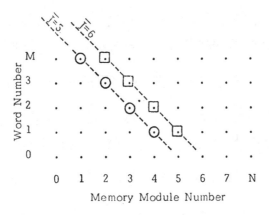

Figure 1.   Execution of Loop 2.

The General Case

The method used to rewrite Loop 2 will now be applied to the following general loop, for $n \geq 2$.

Loop 3:

$$DO \ \alpha \ I^1 = \ell^1, \ u^1$$
$$\vdots$$
$$DO \ \alpha \ I^n = \ell^n, \ u^n$$

| loop body |

α CONTINUE

For convenience, I will assume throughout that the ℓ^i and u^i are loop constants. The generalization to arbitrary DO limits is straight forward and will not be discussed. I also assume that the body of Loop 3 satisfies (A1)–(A5) of [pp. 85, 87].[a]

If Loop 3 has no missing index variables, then it can be handled by essentially the same procedure as Loop 1. Only the slope of the dashed lines in Figure 1 may be different. We first construct the mapping $\pi : \mathbb{Z}^n \to \mathbb{Z}$ [p. 86]. This can be done with the algorithm used in the proof of the Hyperplane Theorem [p. 88]. However, since we are only interested in DO SIM loops rather than the more powerful DO CONC loops, π need only satisfy (S1) [p. 91] rather than (C2) [p. 87]. This allows the following modification to the algorithm. Let $\mathcal{P}_j^+ = \{X \in \mathcal{P}_j : X \in \ <f, g> \text{ for some } f,$ g such that $f \not\to g$ [p.90]$\}$. The a_j are constructed sequentially for $j = n,\ldots,1$ by choosing a_j to be the smallest non-negative integer such that for each $X = (0,\ldots,0,x^j,\ldots,x^n) \in \mathcal{P}_j$, we have $a_j x^j + \ldots + a_n x^n \geq 0$ and $a_j x^j + \ldots + a_n x^n > 0$

---

[a] I will actually assume that (A5) holds for any variable containing some I^i in a subscript position rather than just for generated variables. (A4) and (A5) can be weakened to allow VAR to have additional subscript positions containing arbitrary expressions. Any of these subscript positions containing an expression which is not a loop constant must belong to an aligned multi-index in the allocation for VAR. For simplicity, this generalization has been omitted.

if $X \in \mathscr{P}_j^+$.

If all the a_i are zero, then Loop 3 can be written as a DO SIM $(I^1,\ldots,I^n)$ loop, which satisfies SR because of (A5) and the assumption of no missing index variables. Hence, we may assume that the a_i are not all zero.

The first non-zero a_i which is chosen by the algorithm equals 1. We can therefore choose a j such that $a_j = 1$. For $i = 2,\ldots,n$ we then define

$$\textcircled{i} = \begin{cases} i-1 & \text{if } i \le j \\ i & \text{if } i > j \end{cases},$$

so $\textcircled{i} \ne j$ for all i. Define the mapping J by $J[(I^1,\ldots,I^n)] = (J^1,\ldots,J^n)$, where

$$J^1 = \sum_{i=1}^{n} a_i I^i$$

$$J^i = I^{\textcircled{i}} \text{ for } i \ge 2 \tag{1}$$

This gives the inverse relations

$$I^j = J^1 - \sum_{i=2}^{n} a_{\textcircled{i}} J^i$$

$$I^{\textcircled{i}} = J^i \text{ for } i \ge 2 \tag{1'}$$

so J is a 1-1 correspondence. Loop 3 can then be rewritten as follows.

Loop 4:

$$\text{DO } \alpha \ J^1 = \sum_{i=1}^{n} a_i \ell^i, \ \sum_{i=1}^{n} a_i u^i$$

$$\mathscr{S}_{J^1} = \{ (j^2,\ldots,j^n) : \ell^{\textcircled{i}} \le j^i \le u^{\textcircled{i}} \text{ and } \ell^j \le J^1 - \sum_{i=2}^{n} a_{\textcircled{i}} j^i \le u^j \}$$

$$\text{DO } \alpha \text{ SIM FOR ALL } (J^2,\ldots,J^n) \in \mathscr{S}_{J^1}$$

loop body

α CONTINUE

The loop body of Loop 4 is obtained from that of Loop 3 by using (1') to substitute for $I^1,\ldots,I^n$. Note that "$\mathscr{S}_{J^1}$" is just the name of a single set-valued variable, and is not a subscripted quantity.

The assumption of no missing variables, (A5), and (1') together imply that SR is satisfied by the DO SIM loop of Loop 4. Let A be any variable occurring in the loop body with some subscript which is not a loop constant. Then after permuting the subscript positions, the occurrences of A can be put in the form

$$A(I^1 + c^1,\ldots,I^n + c^n) \tag{2}$$

where the c^i are loop constants. Then A is stored so that $A(i^1,\ldots,i^n)$ is in memory module $g(i^2,\ldots,i^n) \underline{\text{mod}} P$, where g is one of the usual functions for assigning consecutive numbers to the different elements of an $(n-1)$-dimensional array. In the notation of [3], A has allocation $[\#(j), ((2),...,(n))]$. For Loop 2, we chose $j = 1$ and $g(i) = i$.

The Choice of j

There may be several different values of i for which $a_i = 1$, thus permitting several choices for j. In our example, we could also have chosen $j = 2$. Let us now consider the problem of finding the best choice for j.

Let $N^i = u^i - \ell^i + 1$. The sets $\mathcal{S}_{j^1}$ of Loop 4 contain up to $N^{(2)}...N^{(n)}$ elements. This implies that there will be

$$[1 + \sum_{i=1}^{n} a_i(N^i-1)] \lceil (N^{(2)} ... N^{(n)})/P \rceil$$

iterations of the DO SIM loop body in a simple implementation of this loop, where $\lceil x \rceil$ denotes the smallest integer $\geq x$. (Some of these iterations may be for an empty index set, so they could be done quickly by testing for this.) Therefore, we should choose the value for j which minimizes $\lceil (N^2 ... N^n)/P \rceil$. This can always be done by choosing the j for which N^j is smallest.

THE PIPELINED HYPERPLANE METHOD

An Example

Let us now consider the case of a missing outer loop index variable. As an example, enclose Loop 1 in an outer DO I loop to get the following.

Loop 5:
```
DO 99 I = 1, L
DO 99 J = 1, M
DO 99 K = 1, N
U(J, K) = [U(J+1, K) + ...] * .25
99 CONTINUE
```
This is essentially the same as (1) of [p. 83].

As described on [p. 84], the hyperplane method gives a mapping π defined by $\pi(i, j, k) = 2i + j + k$ and new coordinates $\bar{I}, \bar{J}, \bar{K}$ defined by

$$\bar{I} = 2*I + J + K$$

$$\bar{J} = I$$

$$\bar{K} = K.$$

Loop 5 is then rewritten as follows:

Loop 6:
```
DO 99 Ī = 4, 2*L + M + N
```

$$\mathcal{S}_{\bar{I}} = \{(j, k) : 1 \leq j \leq L, 1 \leq k \leq N, \text{ and } 1 \leq \bar{I} - 2*j - k \leq M\}$$

DO 99 SIM FOR ALL $(\bar{J}, \bar{K})$ ε $\mathcal{S}_{\bar{I}}$

$U(\bar{I} - 2*\bar{J} - \bar{K}, \bar{K}) = \ldots$

99 CONTINUE

An examination of the subscript expressions reveals that this DO SIM loop does not satisfy SR. Hence, the parallelism in Loop 6 cannot in general be exploited by an array computer without some bizarre reformating of the array U. Figures 2 and 3 of [p. 85] indicate why this is the case.

With ordinary storage schemes, the DO SIM loop can only be executed in parallel along the $\bar{K}$ coordinate. If U is stored as above, then the entire loop would have to be executed as follows:

DO 99 $\bar{I}$ = 4, 2*L + M + N

DO 99 $\bar{J}$ = 1, L

$\mathcal{S}_{(\bar{I}, \bar{J})}$ = {k: $1 \le k \le N$ and $1 \le \bar{I} - 2*\bar{J} - k \le M$}

DO 99 SIM FOR ALL $\bar{K}$ ε $\mathcal{S}_{(\bar{I}, \bar{J})}$

.
.
.

This requires $L(2L + M + N - 3)$ sequential interations, which is more than the $L(M + N - 1)$ sequential iterations obtained by applying the hyperplane method only to the inner DO J/DO K loop.

However, in applying the hyperplane method to Loop 5 we could have chosen π to be defined by $\pi(i, j, k) = M*i + j + k$, assuming that $M \ge 2$. We then get the new coordinates

$\bar{I} = M*I + J + K$

$\bar{J} = I$

$\bar{K} = K$

and the following rewritten loop.

Loop 7:

DO 99 $\bar{I}$ = M + 2, M*L + M + N

$\mathcal{S}_{\bar{I}}$ = {(j, k) : $1 \le j \le L$, $1 \le k \le N$, and $1 \le \bar{I} - M*j - k \le M$}

DO 99 SIM FOR ALL $(\bar{J}, \bar{K})$ ε $\mathcal{S}_{\bar{I}}$

$U(\bar{I} - M*\bar{J} - \bar{K}, \bar{K}) = \ldots$

99 CONTINUE

Using the same storage scheme for U as before, the circles in Figure 2 indicate the elements of U which are generated in the single execution of the above DO SIM loop for $\bar{I}$ = 14 (assuming $L \ge 3$). Figure 3 shows the same thing for $\bar{I}$ = 15. Observe that all the circled elements in Figure 2 lie in separate memory modules, and the same is true for Figure 3. In fact, all the elements generated by any single execution of the DO SIM loop lie in separate memory modules, so all the generations can be performed simultaneously by an array computer. This fact can be derived from the following observation: for any $\overline{I}$ and $\overline{K}$, there is at most one value of $\overline{J}$ such that $(\overline{J}, \overline{K}) \varepsilon \mathbf{S}_{\overline{I}}$. The values of $\overline{J}$ are the same for all the elements lying on any single dashed line in Figures 2 and 3. (Note that $I = \overline{J}$.)

Comparing Figures 2 and 3 with Figure 1, we see that Loop 7 pipelines with successive iterations of Loop 4. I.e., execution of the loop body for $I = j+1$ begins before execution is completed for $I = j$.[b] Figures 2 and 3 of [p. 85] show that this is also true of Loop 6. However, in Loop 7 the execution for $I = j+1$ is not begun until there is no memory conflict with the execution for $I = j$.

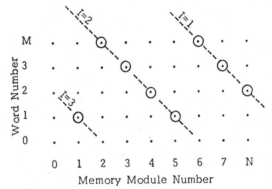

Figure 2. Execution of Loop 7 for $\overline{I} = 14$.

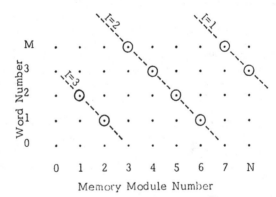

Figure 3. Execution of Loop 7 for $\overline{I} = 15$.

---

[b] This method of executing Loop 5 was discovered by R. Faneuf.

Let us now rewrite Loop 7 so it satisfies SR. Observe that if $(j, k) \in \mathcal{S}_{\overline{I}}$, then j is the largest integer such that $M*j + k \leq \overline{I} - 1$. But this is just $\lfloor(\overline{I}-1-k)/M\rfloor$, where $\lfloor x \rfloor$ denotes the largest integer $\leq x$. With this observation, we can rewrite Loop 7 as follows.

DO 99 $\overline{I}$ = M + 2, M*L + M + N

    DO 9 SIM FOR ALL $\overline{K} \in \{1,\ldots,N\}$

9 $\overline{J}(\overline{K})= \lfloor(\overline{I} - 1 - \overline{K})/M\rfloor$

    $\mathcal{S}_{\overline{I}} = \{k : 1 \leq k \leq N, 1 \leq \overline{J}(k) \leq L$, and $\overline{I} - M \leq M*\overline{J}(k) + k\}$

    DO 99 SIM FOR ALL $\overline{K} \in \mathcal{S}_{\overline{I}}$

    $U(\overline{I} - M*\overline{J}(\overline{K}) - \overline{K}, \overline{K}) = \ldots$

99 CONTINUE

The DO 99 SIM loop is easily seen to satisfy SR.

This loop has M*L + N - 1 sequential iterations, which is (L-1)*(N-1) fewer iterations that are obtained by applying the hyperplane method just to the inner DO J/DO K loop. For L >> 1, this is a speedup by a factor of about (M+N)/M.

In this example, we can interchange the roles of J and K if necessary when choosing new coordinates to guarantee that N≥ M. Hence, the pipelined hyperplane method gives at least twice as much parallel execution as applying the simple hyperplane method to the inner DO J/DO K loop.

If M is not known at compile time, then it may be more convenient to choose a different mapping π. We can define π by $\pi(i, j, k) = \gamma*i + j + k$ for any constant $\gamma \geq M$. The rewriting is then similar to the one given above. If $\gamma > M$, then there will be more space between the diagonal dashed lines in Figures 2 and 3, and fewer than N values will be generated in each execution of the DO SIM loop.

The General Case

The above example is easily generalized to Loop 3 when $n \geq 3$ and I^1 is the only missing index variable. We use the same procedure as before to choose the $a_i \geq 0$ and j with $a_j = 1$, and define the J^i by equations (1).

If j = 1, so $a_1 = 1$, then the rewritten Loop 4 satisfies SR because none of the variables $I^2,\ldots,I^n$ are missing. Since I^1 is a missing variable, we must have $a_1 \neq 0$. We can therefore assume that $a_1 > 1$, so 2 = 1.

The algorithm for choosing the a_i allows us to increase a_1 without changing any of the other a_i. We can therefore choose a_1 to be $\geq u^j - \ell^j + 1$. (We should choose a_1 as small as possible subject to this constraint.) For a fixed value of J^1, this implies that for any given (n-2)-tuple $(j^3,\ldots,j^n)$ there is at most one value of j^2 for which $(j^2,\ldots,j^n) \in \mathcal{S}_{J^1}$ in Loop 4. This value equals

$$\lfloor(J^1 - \ell^j - \sum_{i=3}^{n} a_i j^i)/a_1\rfloor.$$ Loop 4 can therefore be rewritten as follows.

Loop 8:

$$DO \ \alpha \ J^1 = \sum_{i=1}^{n} a_i \ell^i, \ \sum_{i=1}^{n} a_i u^i$$

$$R_{J^1} = \{(j^3,\ldots,j^n) : \ell^{\textcircled{i}} \le j^i \le u^{\textcircled{i}}\}$$

DO β SIM FOR ALL $(J^3,\ldots,J^n) \in R_{J^1}$

$$\beta \ J^2(J^3,\ldots,J^n) = \lfloor (J^1 - \ell^j - \sum_{i=3}^{n} a_{\textcircled{i}} j^i)/a_1 \rfloor$$

$$\mathcal{J}_{J^1} = \{(j^3,\ldots,j^n) \in R_{J^1} : \ell^1 \le J^2(j^3,\ldots,j^n) \le u^1,$$

$$\text{and} \ \ J^1 - a_1 J^2(j^3,\ldots,j^n) - \sum_{i=3}^{n} a_{\textcircled{i}} j^i \le u^j\}$$

DO α SIM FOR ALL $(J^3,\ldots,J^n) \in \mathcal{J}_{J^1}$

| loop body |

α CONTINUE

The body of this DO α SIM loop is obtained from that of Loop 4 by substituting $J^2(J^3,\ldots,J^n)$ for J^2.

Equations (1), the assumption that none of the variables $I^{\textcircled{3}},\ldots,I^{\textcircled{n}}$ are missing, and (A5) together imply that the DO α SIM loop of Loop 8 satisfies SR. With the notation used above in reference to (2), the element $A(i^2,\ldots,i^n)$ is stored in memory module $g(i^{\textcircled{3}},\ldots,i^{\textcircled{n}}) \ \underline{\text{mod}} \ P$. I.e., A has the allocation $[\#(j), (\textcircled{3},\ldots,\textcircled{n})]$.

Execution Time and the Choice of j

The sets R_{J^1} of Loop 8 contain $N^{\textcircled{3}}\ldots N^{\textcircled{n}}$ elements. This implies that there are

$$[1 + \sum_{i=1}^{n} a_i(N^i-1)] \ \lceil (N^{\textcircled{3}} \ldots N^{\textcircled{n}})/P \rceil \tag{3}$$

sequential iterations of the DO SIM loop bodies. Hence, we should choose j to minimize (3). This is not trivial because a_1 depends upon j, since we chose $a_1 \ge N^j$. We must evaluate (3) for each possible choice of j in order to find the best one.

Let us now compare the pipelined and the simple hyperplane methods. Applying the latter to the inner DO $I^2/\ldots/DO \ I^n$ loop of Loop 3 yields a loop requiring

$$N^1[1 + \sum_{i=2}^{n} a_i(N^i-1)] \ \lceil (N^{\textcircled{3}} \ldots N^{\textcircled{n}})/P \rceil \tag{4}$$

sequential iterations of the loop body. Suppose we can choose $a_1 = N^j$. (This will usually be the case if N^j is known at compile time.) Then (4) is always $\ge$ (3), and equality holds only if all the a_i are zero except for $i = 1$ and $i = j$. In this case, the coordinate method [pp. 89-92] would obtain a DO SIM $(I^{(3)}, \ldots, I^{(n)})$ rewriting, so no hyperplane method is needed. Thus, the pipelined hyperplane method will usually yield more parallelism than applying the simple hyperplane method to the inner loops. The reason for this can be seen by comparing Figure 1 with Figures 2 and 3.

PROGRAMMED OUTER LOOPS

Deterministic Loops

Unfortunately, the pipelined hyperplane method described above will seldom be of any use because an example like Loop 5 is unlikely to occur. Instead of using a DO loop to repeat Loop 1 exactly L times, a real program would probably repeat the DO J/DO K loop only until some convergence criterion is met. The following is there-fore a more realistic example.

Loop 9:
```
1 E = 0
    DO 88 J = 1, M
    DO 88 K = 1, N
    T = U(J, K) - [U(J+1, K) + ...] * .25
    IF ( | T | >E) E = | T |
    U(J, K) = U(J, K) - T
88 CONTINUE
    IF (E > MAXERR) GOTO 1
```

The first step is to perform the operations indicated in Section III of [1] to put the DO loop into a more reasonable form. We then rewrite the outer loop as an infinite DO loop to get the following loop. (For convenience, I assume that T is not used elsewhere in the program.)

Loop 10:
```
    DO 88 I = 1, ∞
    DO 77 J = 1, M
    DO 77 K = 1, N
    TT(J, K) = U(J, K) - [ ... ] * .25
    U(J, K) = U(J, K) - TT(J, K)
77 CONTINUE
80 E = MAXIMUM { | TT(j, k)| : 1 ≤ j ≤ M, 1 ≤ k ≤ N}
81 IF (E ≤ MAXERR) GOTO 99
88 CONTINUE
99 CONTINUE
```

The next step is to insert explicit references to the "iteration number" I in all variable occurrences. This yields the following loop, where an asterisk indi-cates a DO SIM over all subscript values. (The non-terminating DO 11 I loop will be dealt with later.)

Loop 11:

```
      UU(0, *, *) = U(*, *)
      DO 11 I = 1, ∞
      UU(I, 0, *)    = U(0, *)
      UU(I, M+1, *)  = U(M+1, *)
      UU(I, *, 0)    = U(*, 0)
      UU(I, *, N+1)  = U(*, N+1)
   11 CONTINUE
      DO 88 I = 1, ∞
      DO 77 J = 1, M
      DO 77 K = 1, N
      TT(I, J, K) = UU(I-1, J, K) -
         [UU(I-1, J+1, K) + UU(I-1, J, K+1) +
         UU(I, J-1, K) + UU(I, J, K-1)] * .25
      UU(I, J, K) = UU(I-1, J, K) - TT(I, J, K)
   77 CONTINUE
   80 E = MAXIMUM { | TT(I, j, k)| : 1 ≤ j ≤ M, 1 ≤ k ≤ N}
   81  IF (E ≤ MAXERR)  GOTO 99
   88 CONTINUE
   99 U(*, *) = UU(I, *, *)
```

If we forget about statements 80 and 81, then we can apply the simple hyper-plane method to the DO I/ DO J/ DO K loop to get new coordinates $\bar{I}$, $\bar{J}$, $\bar{K}$ defined by

$$\bar{I} = \gamma*I + J + K$$

$$\bar{J} = I$$

$$\bar{K} = K$$

for any $\gamma \geq 2$, and the following new loop.

```
      DO 77 Ī = γ + 2, ∞
      S̲ = { (j, k) : 1 ≤ j, 1 ≤ k ≤ N, and 1 ≤ Ī - γ*j - k ≤ M}
       Ī
      DO 77 SIM FOR ALL ( J̄, K̄ ) ε S̲
                                     Ī
      TT(J̄, Ī - γ*J̄ - K̄, K̄) = UU(J̄ - 1...) - ...
      UU(J̄, Ī - γ*J̄ - K̄, K̄) = ...
   77 CONTINUE
```

Consider the γ consecutive executions of the DO SIM loop for $\bar{I} = \gamma*I_s + 2$ through $\bar{I} = \gamma*I_s + \gamma + 1$, for some value of I_s. From (5) we see that they execute the loop body for values of I ranging from $I_s - \mu$ through I_s, where $\mu = (M+N-2)/\gamma$. Hence, these executions begin the execution of the loop body for $I = I_s$ and finish the execution for $I = I_s - \mu$.

There are only $\mu + 1$ active values of I at any one time, so all the I subscripts (the left-most subscripts of TT and UU) can be evaluated modulo $\mu + 1$.

In the above set expression for $\mathcal{S}_I$, we always have $I - \mu \leq j \leq I$. Let $j' = j \bmod (\mu+1)$, so $0 \leq j' \leq \mu$. Then we have $j = j' + (\mu+1) * \lfloor I/(\mu+1) \rfloor$. Letting $\underline{x}$ denote $x \bmod (\mu+1)$, we can now rewrite Loop 11 as follows.

Loop 12:

```
μ = ⌊(M+N-2)/γ⌋
UU(0, *, *) = U(*, *)
DO 11 I = 1, μ
UU(I, 0, *) = U(0, *)
                ⋮
11 CONTINUE
    DO 88 I = 1, ∞
    DO  8 SIM FOR ALL (J̄', K̄) ε { (j', k) :
        0 ≤ j' ≤ μ, 1 ≤ k ≤ N }
 8  J̄(J̄', K̄) = J̄' + (μ + 1) * ⌊I/(μ + 1)⌋
    DO 77 Ī = γ*I + 2, γ*I + γ + 1
    S'_I = { (j', k) : 0 ≤ j' ≤ μ, 1 ≤ J̄(j', k),
        1 ≤ k ≤ N, 1 ≤ Ī - γ*J̄(j', k) ≤ M }
    DO 77 SIM FOR ALL (J̄', K̄) ε S'_I
    TT(J̄', Ī - γ*J̄(J̄', K̄) - K̄, K̄) = ...
    UU(J̄', Ī - γ*J̄(J̄', K̄) - K̄, K̄) = ...
77 CONTINUE
    I_c = I - μ
    IF (I_c < 1) GOTO 88
80 E = MAXIMUM { | TT(I_c, j, k) | : ... }
81 IF (E ≤ MAXERR) GOTO 99
88 CONTINUE
99 U(*, *) = UU(I_c, *, *)
```

The arrays UU and TT have dimensions $(\mu + 1) \times (M+2) \times (N+2)$ and $(\mu + 1) \times M \times N$, respectively. $\bar{J}$ is of dimension $(\mu + 1) \times N$.

Let us now compare Loop 12 with the rewriting obtained by applying the simple hyperplane method to the DO J/DO K loop of Loop 10. Just counting sequential iterations of the inner loop body, Loop 12 is faster by a factor of $(M+N-2)/\gamma \approx \mu$, assuming that the number of iterations of the outer loop is large compared to μ. However, Loop 12 requires $\mu + 1$ times as much storage. The choice of γ therefore provides a simple space-time tradeoff.

For Loop 12 to be the better choice, we must have enough memory space, and enough processors for exploiting the resulting parallelism, so that we can choose $\mu \gg 1$. Moreover, the number of iterations of the outer loop must be large enough to make up for the overhead of initializing the array UU and executing statement 99.

Non-Deterministic Loops

Let us now compare Loop 12 with the rewriting we would have obtained had we been able simply to use the pipelined hyperplane method on the innermost DO I/ DO J/DO K loop of Loop 10. Loop 12 is similar to a pipelined hyperplane rewriting, except that it uses the three-dimensional array UU instead of the original array U. Introducing UU adds significantly to the overhead of the rewritten loop.

We had to use UU for the following reason. Suppose the convergence condition $E \leq MAXERR$ is met on the iteration of the I loop for $I = I_c$. Then execution of the inner loop body would already have begun for $I = I_c + 1$, $I = I_c + 2, \ldots$, and $I = I_c + \mu$. The subarray $UU(I_c, *, *)$ still contains the value of U computed for $I = I_c$, which is the value $\underline{U}$ must have upon exit from the loop. Had we not used UU to save $\mu+1$ consecutive versions of U, then the values of some of these elements would have been destroyed before we knew that they were the final values. (This problem did not arise in Loop 7 because we knew in advance the final value of I.)

However, it actually would not matter if some of these values of U were replaced by the values computed for $I > I_c$, since the computation is convergent. The "incorrect" values would be even better approximations to the true values then the "correct" ones. All the overhead caused by introducing the array UU is unnecessary! The compiler is forced to use UU because the programmer specified that the computation must stop immediately after the first iteration in which the convergence criterion is met. The programmer was forced by the programming language to specify his program this way.

For most convergent iterative computations, it does not matter if some extra calculations are performed after the convergence criterion is met. However, present programming languages require that the iterations stop at a precisely specified point. I will therefore introduce a new indeterminate looping construction of the following form:

```
     REPEAT α UNTIL AFTER (exp)
          loop body
α  CONTINUE
```

where exp is a boolean expression. It has the following interpretation

```
β  CONTINUE
          loop body
     IF (.NOT. exp) GOTO β
          partially execute one or more further iterations of the loop body
α  CONTINUE
```

Partial execution of an iteration involves executing one or more of its assignment statements.

The REPEAT UNTIL AFTER loop allows the compiler considerable freedom in its execution. In particular, superfluous operations may be performed. This can be useful for any kind of parallel computer, not just for an array computer. Pipe-lining successive iterations of a loop is a technique commonly used on many parallel computers -- for example, on the CDC 7600. The REPEAT UNTIL AFTER loop permits it to be done more efficiently because new values can be generated without waiting for the outcome of a convergence test.

Now suppose that Loop 9 had been written with a REPEAT UNTIL AFTER statement as follows.

```
     REPEAT 88 UNTIL AFTER (E ≤ MAXERR)
  1  E = 0
     DO 88 J = 1, M
        ⋮
88   CONTINUE
```

This loop could again be rewritten as Loop 10, except that the loop exit in statement 81 is now a non-deterministic one: after the IF condition is found to be true, the inner DO J/DO K loop body may be executed for further values of I, J, and K before the GOTO 99 is executed.

We next add the I coordinate to TT, as we did in Loop 11, but we leave U alone. We then proceed as above, except applying the pipelined rather than the simple hyper-plane method to the inner DO I/DO J/DO K loop. This yields the following rewriting (taking $\Upsilon = M$).

Loop 13:

$\mu = \lfloor (M+N-2)/M \rfloor$

DO 88 I = 1, ∞

DO 77 $\overline{I}$ = M*I + 2, M*I + M + 1

DO 9 SIM FOR ALL $\overline{K} \, \varepsilon \, \{1,...,N\}$

9 $\overline{J}(\overline{K}) = \lfloor (I - 1 - \overline{K})/M \rfloor$

$\mathcal{J}_{\overline{I}} = \{ k : 1 \leq k \leq N, 1 \leq \overline{J}(\overline{K}), \text{ and } \overline{I} - M \leq M*\overline{J}(k) + k\}$

DO 77 SIM FOR ALL $\overline{K} \, \varepsilon \, \mathcal{J}_{\overline{I}}$

$TT(\overline{J(\overline{K})}, \overline{I} - M*\overline{J}(\overline{K}) - \overline{K}, \overline{K}) = ...$

$U(\overline{I} - M*\overline{J}(\overline{K}) - \overline{K}, \overline{K}) = ...$

77 CONTINUE

$I_c = I - \mu$

IF (I_c < 1) GOTO 88

88 E = MAXIMUM { $|TT(I_c, j, k)|$: ... }

81 IF (E ≤ MAXERR) GOTO 99

88 CONTINUE

99 CONTINUE

The DO SIM loops satisfy SR. We can store the array U as before, and store the array TT so that TT(i, j, k) is in memory module k mod P (allocation [#(1, 2), (3)]).

Let us compare Loop 13 with the rewriting we would obtain by applying the simple hyperplane method to the inner DO J/DO K loop. Loop 13 has only $M/(M+N-2)$ times as many sequential iterations of the inner loop body (assuming that the number of iterations of the outer loop body is $>> (M+N-2)/M$). It requires $1 + \lfloor (M+N-2)/M \rfloor$ times as much space to store the array TT.

The General Case

I now consider the following generalization of Loop 10.

Loop 14:

DO β $I^1 = 1, \infty$

DO α $I^2 = \ell^2, u^2$

$\vdots$

DO α $I^n = \ell^n, u^n$

| inner loop body |

α CONTINUE

| exit test |

β CONTINUE

γ CONTINUE

I assume that the DO $I^2/\ldots/$DO I^n loop satisfies the hypotheses for applying the simple hyperplane method, so none of the variables $I^2,\ldots,I^n$ are missing from the inner loop body. I also assume that no variable generated in the exit test may occur in the inner loop body, and that there are no GOTOs out of the exit test except to β or γ. Otherwise, the exit test may consist of arbitrary code. If this is a non-deterministic loop (obtained from a REPEAT UNTIL AFTER loop), then extra iterations of the inner loop body are permitted.

The first step is to rewrite Loop 14 in the form of

Loop 15:

$$\mu = \lfloor \sum_{i=2}^{n} a_i * (u^i - \ell^i)/a_1 \rfloor$$

| prologue |

DO β $I^1 = 1, \infty$

DO α $I^2 = \ell^2, u^2$

$\vdots$

DO α $I^n = \ell^n, u^n$

| inner loop body |

α CONTINUE

$\quad I_c = I^1 - \mu$

$\quad$ IF $(I_c \leqslant 1)$ GOTO β

$\qquad \boxed{\text{exit test}}$

β CONTINUE

γ CONTINUE

$\qquad \boxed{\text{epilogue}}$

Using the procedure described below. (The a_i will be defined later.) For convenience, I assume that I^1 does not occur anywhere inside the DO I^1 loop in Loop 14. If
it does, some of the following operations can sometimes be eliminated.

Let $\mathcal{I}$ denote the index set [p. 85] of the DO $I^2/.../$DO I^n loop. (In the case
of arbitrary DO limits, we must also assume that $\mathcal{I}$ is a loop constant for DO I^1
loop.) For a deterministic loop, the following procedure is applied to all non-
scalar variables V occurring in the inner loop body. For a non-deterministic loop,
it is applied only to the variables V generated in the inner loop body and used in
the exit test.

Let $\mathcal{G}$ denote the set of all generations of V occurring in the inner loop body.
Let $< f, g >$ denote the sets computed for the DO $I^2/.../$DO I^n loop [p. 87]. Our
assumptions imply that each $< f, g >$ set consists of a single element. A use f of V
is called a <u>current</u> use if it appears in the exit test, or else it appears in the
inner loop body for some $g \in \mathcal{G}$ with $< g, f > = \{X\}$ either (i) $X > \vec{0}$ or (ii) $X = \vec{0}$
and $g \rightarrow f$ [p. 90]. Otherwise, f is called a <u>prior</u> use. A current use is one which
uses a value that was generated during the current iteration of the I^1 loop. In
Loop 10, the current uses of U are U(J-1, K) and U(J, K-1), and the rest are prior
uses. All uses of TT are current ones. Let $\mathcal{C}$ denote the set of current uses, $\mathcal{P}$
the set of prior uses, and $\mathcal{U}$ the set of all uses.

Loop 15 is obtained from Loop 14 by performing the following steps for each
such V.

1. Rewrite the inner loop body so that each $g \in \mathcal{G}$ is executed for all elements in $\mathcal{I}$. E.g., the statement

$\quad$ IF (exp) V(...) = ...

can be rewritten as

$\quad$ V(...) = IF (exp) THEN ...

$\qquad\qquad\qquad$ ELSE V(...).

2. If $\mathcal{P} \neq \emptyset$, then add the following to the prologue.

VV(0, *,...,*) = V(*,...,*).

3. Let $\mathcal{A}$ be any set containing [p. 86] $\bigcup_{f \in \mathcal{U}} T_f(\mathcal{I}_f) - \bigcup_{g \in \mathcal{G}} T_g(\mathcal{I})$, where $\mathcal{I}_f$ is the
appropriate index set for the use f. (If f appears in the inner loop body, then

$\mathcal{J}_f = \mathcal{J}$.) If $\mathcal{A} \neq \phi$, then add the following loop to the prologue.

    DO δ I = 0, μ

    DO δ SIM FOR ALL $(E^2, \ldots, E^n) \in \mathcal{A}$

δ VV(I, $E^2, \ldots, E^n$) = V($E^2, \ldots, E^n$)

(As in the DO 11 loop of Loop 12, this DO SIM may have to be rewritten as several separate DO SIMS in order to satisfy SR.)

    4. If $\mathcal{B} \neq \phi$ and V is used after exiting from the loop, then add the following to the epilogue.

    V(*,...,*) = $\dot{\text{VV}}$(I$_c$, *,...,*)

    5. For each occurrence f of V of the form V($e^2, \ldots, e^n$):

        (i) If $f \in \mathcal{C} \cup \mathcal{B}$ then replace f by the occurrence: (a) VV($I^1, e^2, \ldots, e^n$) if f is in the inner loop body, or (b) VV($I_c, e^2, \ldots, e^n$) if f is in the exit test.

        (ii) If $f \in \mathcal{P}$ then replace f by the occurrence VV($I^1-1, e^2, \ldots, e^n$).

    6. Define VV to be an array of dimensions $d^1 \times \ldots \times d^n$, where $d^1 \geq \mu+1$ and $d^2 \times \ldots \times d^n$ are the dimensions of V.

Having constructed Loop 15, we obtain the a_i by applying (i) the simple hyperplane method if the loop is deterministic, or (ii) the pipelined hyperplane method if the loop is non-deterministic, to the DO $I^1/\ldots/$DO I^n inner loop. The new index variables J^i are then defined by (1), and the DO $I^2/\ldots/$DO I^n loop of Loop 15 is rewritten as follows.

<u>Deterministic Inner Loop.</u> Case 1: $j \neq 1$, so $I^1 = J^2$.

$$R_{I^1} = \{(jj, j^3, \ldots, j^n) : 0 \leq jj \leq \mu,$$
$$\ell^{(i)} \leq j^i \leq u^{(i)}\}$$

DO δ SIM FOR ALL $(JJ, J^3, \ldots, J^n) \in R_{I^1}$

δ J^2(JJ, $J^3, \ldots, J^n$) = JJ + $(\mu+1) * \lfloor I^1/(\mu+1) \rfloor$

DO α $J^1 = \sum_{i=1}^{n} a_i \ell^i, \sum_{i=1}^{n} a_i u^i$

$$\mathcal{S}_{J^1} = \{(jj, j^3, \ldots, j^n) \in R_{I^1} : \ell^j \leq$$
$$J^1 - a_1 J^2(jj, j^3, \ldots, j^n) - \sum_{i=3}^{n} a_i J^i \leq u^j\}$$

DO α SIM FOR ALL $(JJ, J^3, \ldots, J^n) \in \mathcal{S}_{J^1}$

    | inner loop body |

α CONTINUE

The inner loop body is obtained from that of Loop 15 by first replacing I^1 by JJ, then using (1') to substitute for the other I^i, then replacing J^2 by J^2(JJ, $J^3, \ldots, J^n$). Storage allocation is the same as for Loop 4.

Case 2: $j = 1$, so $I^i = J^i$ for $i \geq 2$. The DO α loop is rewritten just as in Loop 4, except that for any occurrence in the inner loop body of a variable VV introduced by the above procedure, the first subscript is evaluated <u>mod</u> $\mu+1$.

<u>Non-Deterministic Loop</u>. Case 1: $j \neq 1$. The DO α loop is rewritten just as in Loop 8, except that the first subscript of any occurrence of an introduced variable VV is evaluated <u>mod</u> $\mu+1$.

Case 2. $j = 1$. This is handled the same way as for a deterministic loop.

CONCLUSION

The techniques described above can be used to implement the hyperplane method in a compiler for an array computer. The simple hyperplane method is currently being implemented in the FORTRAN compiler for the Illiax IV. The pipelined hyperplane method will probably be of little value to a compiler for any current programming language. However, future languages should allow non-deterministic loops exits, and should encourage their use for convergent iterative computations. The pipelined hyperplane method will be a useful technique for compiling such a language for an array computer.

REFERENCES

[1] L. Lamport, "The Parallel Execution of DO Loops," <u>Comm. ACM</u> <u>17</u>, 2 (Feb., 1974), pp. 83-93.

[2] D.E. McIntyre, "An Introduction to the Illiac IV Computer," <u>Datamation</u>, <u>16</u>, 4 (April, 1970), pp. 60-67.

[3] R.E. Millstein, "Control Structures in Illiac IV Fortran," <u>Comm. ACM</u> <u>16</u>, 10 (October, 1973), pp. 621-627.

SYNTACTIC RECOGNITION OF PARALLEL PROCESSES IN FORMALLY DEFINED COMPLEXES OF INTERACTING DIGITAL SYSTEMS

PAMELA Z. SMITH and D.R. FITZWATER
Computer Sciences Department
University of Wisconsin
Madison, Wisconsin 53706

SUMMARY

A formal universe has been developed in which representations of asynchronously interacting digital systems are interpreted by a deterministic automaton. It is presented in [1] and extended to include observers in [2]. It is intended to provide a machine-independent notation in which design problems -- and the tools to solve them-- can be formulated and communicated, as well as making it possible to study the properties of a design before commitment to the details of a particular implementation. The description language is based on Post production systems, with two unusual features: a mechanism for inter-system communication, and a vehicle for representing abstraction.

Some interesting assertions can already be proven about complexes of formally defined systems [3]. The state of a system is represented by a set of strings called process states. Johnson's work shows that, as a property of the way operators are applied to process states, regular languages are excellent characterizations of state structures. By applying the operators of a system to selected regular languages, he arrives at a finite description of all the computations, finite or infinite, that can ever be generated by the system. Based on these results we define a finite graph model of a system complex. This graph, called a finite process structure (fps), can be derived algorithmically from the representation of the system complex -- it requires neither simulation nor human interpretation. Each node in an fps belongs to one system of the complex, and is a disjoint regular language to which process states of that system may belong. The nodes are connected by directed arcs (some have multiple components because of interactions between states) describing the effects of operators in generating a process state set from its predecessor. A complete explanation of fps's is given in [4].

We use an fps to identify processes by syntax alone, making possible the automatic analysis of large-scale designs. Given a system complex and an fps describing it, a process is defined as a set of regular languages, one for each system in the complex, such that (1) the regular language for a system is a union of nodes in the fps for that system, (2) process states in a system belong to the process if and only if they belong to the regular language corresponding to that system, and (3) no arcs cross the process boundary except interactions (multiple-component arcs with at least one origin node on either side of the process boundary) [4]. This definition is actually very close to the well known one in [5], differing from it mainly because we have the use of multiple -- and more flexible -- state spaces (each system has its own), and because our processes can communicate. Formalized communication is valuable because it enables us to study interactions between computationally manageable units rather than having to define a larger process containing the interacting ones.

Analysis of a system complex may begin with its basic process structure, which is a unique partition of its states into the smallest parallel processes whose properties allow them to be analyzed separately from their environments. These properties, syntactically recognizable from the fps, are that all the states of the process exist in the same system, and that side effects from other processes cannot occur. The successive states of a basic process can be modeled by a finite state machine.

Process structure as defined depends on the choice of fps nodes. An infinite number of fps's describe a system, ranging from those with low resolution (few nodes, each representing a large language) to those of high resolution (many small nodes), and forming a lattice in which there exists an fps describing any part of the system in any level of detail. We use these facts to discover the basic process structure of the system flexibly and efficiently, by starting with a low-resolution fps and selectively raising its resolution. It is shown in [6] that, because of the invariancies of basic process structure along a unidirectional path through a lattice, only the structure of the basic process in which resolution is raised (by splitting a node into smaller ones) can change. Thus each successive node split entails an increment of knowledge about the basic process structure of the system, but the search can be directed where the designer most requires detail, and can be cut off whenever the value of additional detail does not justify the cost of obtaining it.

REFERENCES

[1] D.R. Fitzwater, and P.Z. Smith, A Formal Definition Universe for Complexes of Interacting Digital Systems, Comp. Sci. Dept., University of Wisconsin, #184, (June, 1973), 47 pp.

[2] P.Z. Smith, and D.R. Fitzwater, A Concept of Equivalence Between Formally Defined Complexes of Interacting Digital Systems, Comp. Sci. Dept., University of Wisconsin, #213, (April, 1974), 30 pp.

[3] R.T. Johnson, Proving Assertions about the State Structure of Formally-Defined, Interacting Digital Systems, University of Wisconsin (1973), 160 pp., partially available in Comp. Sci. Dept. Tech. Report #193.

[4] P.Z. Smith, and D.R. Fitzwater, Finite Process Structures, Comp. Sci. Dept., University of Wisconsin, #213, (June, 1974), 78 pp.

[5] J.J. Horning, and B. Randell, "Process Structuring", Comp. Surveys , (March, 1973), pp. 5-30.

[6] P.Z. Smith, and D.R. Fitzwater, Efficient Analysis of the Process Structures of Formally Defined Complexes of Interacting Digital Systems, Comp. Sci. Dept., University of Wisconsin, #219, (August, 1974), 67 pp.

A CONTROL STRUCTURE FOR PARALLEL PROCESSING

SUBRAMANYA K. SHASTRY
Moore School of Electrical Engineering
University of Pennsylvania
Philadelphia Pa. 19104

Abstract -- This paper describes a control structure for the control of parallel processors such that (1) at most one of the processors is engaged in its 'critical section' at any instant and (2) if a processor wants to enter a critical section it is eventually allowed to do so. The solution is described using APL programs and flowcharts. It does not assume the existence of 'indivisible' operations like 'TS' instruction of SYSTEM/360. It is observed that to control 'N' processors the number 'M' of 'N-WAY' switches required is given by:

$$M \geq 2 + \frac{\text{Ln } (n - 1)}{\text{Ln } 2}$$

INTRODUCTION

The motivation of this paper is the desire to solve some problems in the control of parallel processors. The 'mutual exclusion' or 'interlock' problem in the control of parallel processors has been studied by Dijkstra and many others [1] - [6]. Most of the solutions for this purpose assume the existence of 'indivisible' operations[a] like 'P-operation' and 'V-operation' on some common variables (or 'semaphores' as used by Dijkstra).

However, in some cases, it may not be possible to implement such indivisible operations truthfully. For example, in some computers (like, RCA SPECTRA 70/46), the communication between two programs can be achieved only through a common data area and only by the two operations 'read' and 'write'. In this case, the effect of P and V operations cannot be obtained easily.

This paper describes a control structure for the control of parallel processors such that (1) at most one of the processors is engaged in its 'critical section' at any instant and (2) if a processor wants to enter a critical section it is eventually allowed to do so.

Section (2) describes the problem in more detail and describes (using APL programs) a control structure for parallel processors using an indivisible instruction.

In section (3) a constructive solution for the control of parallel processors is obtained without the assumption of the existence of the indivisible operations

---

[a] An operation is called 'indivisible' if when two (or more) processors perform the operation 'simultaneously', the operation as a whole is to be regarded as done one after the other at least with respect to the changes in the environment caused by the operation.

described in section (2) . The solution is described using APL programs and flow-charts. Some familiarity with APL is assumed. If the reader is not familiar with APL, he is advised to refer to [7]. The '±' operator used in this paper is described in [8].

A CONTROL STRUCTURE USING AN INDIVISIBLE INSTRUCTION

As an example, assume that a variable 'TOTAL' specifies the number of active processors connected to a system at any instant. Now, consider the operation of incrementing the variable TOTAL when two processors 'A' and 'B' are connected simultaneously. The operation can be described by:

TOTAL ← TOTAL + 1

The processor 'A' performs the operation 'TOTAL + 1' and before assigning the result to TOTAL, the processor 'B' also may perform the same operation and then both of them assign the result to TOTAL. Because of this simultaneous action, one of the desired incrementation is lost.

Dijkstra assumes the existence of P and V operations on some common variables called 'semaphores'. These operations are defined by [3]:

"The V operation is an operation with one argument, which must be the identification of a semaphore. Its function is to increase the value of its argument semaphore by 1; this increase is to be regarded as an indivisible operation.

The P operation is an operation with one argument, which must be the identification of a semaphore. Its function is to decrease the value of its argument semaphore by 1 as soon as the resulting value would be non-negative. The completion of the P operation, i.e., the decision that this is the appropriate moment to effectuate the decrease and the subsequent decrease itself - is to be regarded as an indivisible operation."

If a P operation always follows a V operation then the semaphore value will never be negative and this assumption simplifies the definition of P operation to:

"The P operation is an operation with one argument, which must be the identification of a semaphore. Its function is to decrease the value of its argument semaphore by 1; this decrease is to be regarded as an indivisible operation."

This definition for P operation will be used in the description that follows.

The functions 'P1' and 'V1' in Fig. (1) describe the above P and V operations using an indivisible instruction described by the function 'TS' in Fig. (1). It is assumed that the two assignments on lines [1] and [2] of the function TS take place simultaneously. With this assumption, the explicit result of executing the function TS is the same as the value of the argument, and the resulting value of the argument is always 1. Note that the function TS uses the name of the variable, and not its value as the argument. That is why the assignment in the second line of the function TS has some meaning. The operator '±' used in the program takes as its argument a character vector and evaluates (or executes) the APL statement it (the argument) represents. For example, $'A \leftarrow 9'$ performs the operation: $A \leftarrow 9$. The function 'TS1' given in Fig. (2) is not functionally equivalent to the function TS of Fig. (1). In the function TS1, the value of the argument is changed locally since it is regarded as a local variable.

```
        ∇ Z←TS L
[1]        Z←⍑L
[2]        ⍑L,'←1'
        ∇


        ∇ L P1 X
[1]    ONE:→(1=TS L)/ONE
[2]        ⍑X,'←',X,'-1'
[3]        ⍑L,'←0'
        ∇


        ∇ L V1 X
[1]    ONE:→(1=TS L)/ONE
[2]        ⍑X,'←', X,'+1'
[3]        ⍑L,'←0'
        ∇
```

Fig. (1). An Indivisible Instruction and P and V Functions.

```
        ∇ Z←TS1 L
[1]        Z←L
[2]        L←0
        ∇
```

Fig. (2). This function is functionally not equivalent to the function TS
          of Fig. (1).'

The two functions P1 and V1 of Fig. (1) are similar except for line [2]. In one case, the value of the semaphore is decremented and in the other case, it is incremented.

When executing the function P1, for example, the processor (that has invoked it) dwells on line [1] of the function till it finds the switch in the reset condition. Since the result of executing the function TS always sets the switch and since the execution of that function is assumed to be indivisible, no two processors can execute line [2] of the function P1. After decrementing the semaphore, the switch is reset by the instruction on line [3]. If the reader is familiar with the Assembly

Language instructions of SYSTEM/360, then he can recognize that the function TS of Fig. (1) performs the same operation as the 'TS' instruction in SYSTEM/360. For example, the V operation described in Fig. (1) can be described by the assembly language routine given in Fig. (3).

```
ONE    TS   L              TEST AND SET
       BO   ONE            DWELL IF ALREADY SET
       AP   NAME,=p'1'     INCREMENT THE SEMAPHORE
       MVI  L,X'00'        RESET THE SWITCH
       BR   7              RETURN
NAME   DC   2P'0'          conatins the SEMAPHORE
L      DC   X'00'          SWITCH
```

Fig. (3). An Assembly Language Routine For the V operation described in Fig. (1).

A QUEUE of all processors contending for a critical section can be maintained and this is described by the functions 'P2' and 'V2' of Fig. (4). The function 'CS2' of Fig. (4) describes a control structure that controls the execution of the Critical Section. It is assumed that each processor has a unique identification specified by 'TSN' and only that processor at the top of the QUEUE (1 ↑ QUEUE) can enter the critical section.

A GENERAL CONTROL STRUCTURE

In this section a constructive solution for the control of parallel processors is obtained without the assumption of the existence of an indivisible operation like the function TS described in section (2). The solution consists of a program that replaces the function of the function TS of Fig. (1).

The assumptions made in the solution are:

1. There exists a data area which is common to all processors (called 'common data area' here onwards).

2. Initially all the locations in the common data area contain zeros.

3. A processor is identified in the common data area by a unique identification (TSN).

4. Any processor can store data into the common data area.

5. Any processor can load data from the common data area.

6. There is no way of communicating between any two processors except through the common data area and only by the operations (4) and (5).

7. The operation of writing data into the common data area is regarded as indivisible, i.e., when two (or more) processors simultaneously assign a new value

to the same common variable in the common data area, the assignments are to be regarded as done one after the other, the final value of the variable will be one of
the two values assigned, but never a mixture of the two.

```
      ∇ L P2 X
[1]   ONE:→(1=TS L)/ONE
[2]    ⍕X,'←',X,'-1'
[3]   QUEF←1↓QUEUE
[4]    ⍕L, '←0'
       ∇


      ∇ L V2 X
[1]   ONE:→(1=TS L)/ONE
[2]    ⍕X,'←', X,'+1'
[3]   QUEUE←QUEUE, TSN
[4]    ⍕L, '←0'
       ∇


      ∇ CS2
[1]    'L' V2 'NAME'
[2]   DWELL:→(TSN≠1↑QUEUE)/DWELL
[3]    ⍝ *** CRITICAL SECTION ***
[4]    'L' P2 'NAME'
       ∇
```

Fig. (4) P and V operations and the Control Structure using QUEUE.

8. Stopping of any processor is not allowed, either in the critical section or
during the 'initialization' process.

9. The speeds of the processors and the times for signals to propagate are
finite, but unbounded.

10. There is no master clock for synchronizing the operation of the system.

11. An upper limit for the number of processors to be controlled is known.

The initialization process mentioned in the assumption (8) corresponds to the
P and V operations described in section (2). For example, a processor should not
stop while executing the line [2] of the function P2 in Fig. (4).

Figure (5) gives a simple solution for the control of 'N' processors. In this
solution no two processors can enter the critical section simultaneously. To prove
this, notice that the set of processors that have found 'S2=0' (in the operation (3))

are the only ones that can enter the critical section, and the setting of the switch S1 can correspond to at most one of the processors in this set (because of the assumption (3)). Subsequently, at most one of the processors can succeed in the test by the operation (5).

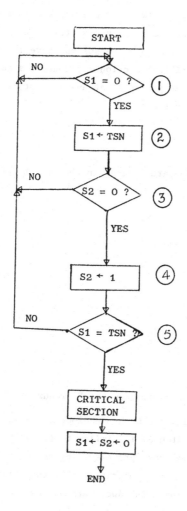

Fig. (5).

However, deadlock can occur. For example, if two processors 'A' and 'B' find 'S1 = 0' in the operation (1), thereafter, the processor 'A' was quick enough to complete the operations (2), (3) and (4) (while the processor 'B' completed the operation (2)), then the processor 'A' cannot enter the critical section because 'S1 = TSN' is false, and the processor 'B' cannot enter because S2 is already set (by the processor 'A' in the operation (4)). Deadlock.

The switches S1 and S2 used in the Fig. (5) are located in the common data area, and the program CS1 given in Fig. (6) (which corresponds to the flowchart of Fig. (5)) can be invoked by any processor at any instant of time. The program itself may be resident in the common data area or each processor may have its own copy of the program in its working area. The critical section may contain a set of instructions which can be invoked by at most one processor at any instant of time. For example, this may contain the set of instructions:

NAME ← NAME + 1

QUEUE ← QUEUE, TSN

where the variables NAME and QUEUE are located in the common data area (see also the function P2 in Fig. (4)).

$$\triangledown\ CS1$$

[1] $ONE: \rightarrow (S1 \neq 0)/ONE$

[2] $S1 \leftarrow TSN$

[3] $\rightarrow (S2 \neq 0)/ONE$

[4] $S2 \leftarrow 1$

[5] $\rightarrow (S1 \neq TSN)/ONE$

[6]   ♀ *** CRITICAL SECTION ***

[7] $S1 \leftarrow S2 \leftarrow 0$

$$\triangledown$$

Fig. (6). The program corresponding to the Flowchart of Fig. (5).

The solution of Fig. (7) eliminates the deadlock of the solution in Fig. (5). In this solution, the 'N-WAY' switch S2 is similar to the switch S1, but is set only if it was not already set by some other processor (by the operation (4)). If the switch S1 is changed before the test in operation (5), the original value is bound to be restored by the operation (8). The dwell around the operations (5) and (6) lasts till one of the processors resets the switch S1.

Deadlock is completely avoided in this solution. To prove this, notice that S1 can be changed only by the operations (2) and (8). If the switch S1 does not correspond to any one of the processors that have found 'S2 = 0' (in operation (3)), it must have been changed by one of the processors that eventually perform the operations (7) and (8). The switch S1 can be changed (by the operation (8)) only by that processor which has the same identification (TSN) as the current setting of S1. The operation (8) thus ensures that the last processor that has set or changed the switch S2 in performing the operation (4)) will enter the critical section.

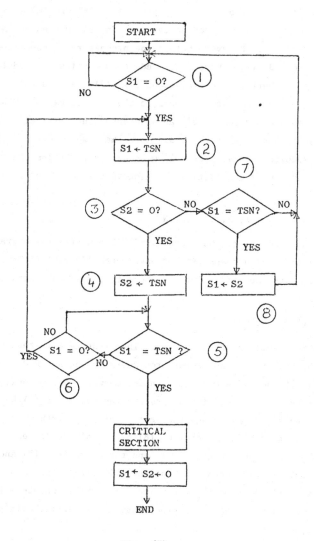

Fig. (7).

However, the mutual exclusion is not guaranteed in the solution of Fig. (7), i.e., two or more processors can enter the critical section at any instant[b]. For

---

[b] Note, however, that if there are only two processors contending for the critical section, then the mutual exclusion is guaranteed in the solution of Fig. (7). This solution can then be regarded as functionally equivalent to the solution of Dekker for two processes [3].

example, consider the case when three processors 'A', 'B' and 'C' completed the operation (1) simultaneously. Thereafter, the processors 'A' and 'B' completed the operations (2) and (3) simultaneously, and then the processor 'A' was quick enough to complete the operations (4) and (5) (the processors 'B' and 'C' still have not started the operations (4) and (2) respectively). Now the processor 'A' can safely enter the critical section. However, before the processor 'A' completes the critical section, the processor 'B' might have completed the operation (4) and the processor 'C' was quick enough to perform the operations (2), (3), (7) and (8). At this moment, the setting of switch S1 corresponds to the identification (TSN) of the processor 'B', and so the processor 'B' can also enter the critical section. Therefore, this solution is not safe if there are more than two processors that perform the operation (1) simultaneously. The following analysis obtains the maximum number of processors that may enter the critical section in the solution of Fig. (7).

Let

$$P = \{p_i\} \qquad i = 1, 2, \ldots, N$$

denote the set of all processors that have found 'S1 = 0' (in the operation (1)), and $Q \subset P$ be the set of all processors that have found 'S2 $\neq$ 0' (in the operation (3)). If $|S|$ represents the cardinality of the set S, then in general, at most 'K' processors given by:

$$K = \text{Min } (1 + |Q|, |P| - |Q|) \tag{1}$$

can enter the critical section at any moment. The first term in the above expression is derived from the fact that none of the processors in the set P-Q (i.e., the set of processors that have found 'S2 = 0') can change the switch S1 and only one of the processors in this set can succeed in the test by the operation (5) before any of the processors in the set Q can change the setting of the switch S1 by the operation (8). Subsequent execution of the operation (8) by one of the processors in the set Q can allow a processor $X \subset P-Q$ (that dwell around the operations (5) and (6)) to enter the critical section. This process can continue till all the processors in the set Q have completed the execution of the operation (8). The second term in the above expression is because at most $|P| - |Q|$ processors can enter the critical section even though $1 + |Q| > |P| - |Q|$.

The equation (1) can be rewritten as an inequality:

$$1 \leq K \leq \frac{|P| + 1}{2} \tag{2}$$

If the upper limit on the number of processors is known, then the structure of Fig. (7) can be expanded till 'K = 1'. Thus, using two switches, a maximum of two processors can be controlled; using three switches, a maximum of three processors can be controlled and so on. In general, 'M' switches (where M > 1) can control

$$2^{M-2} + 1$$

processors (with 'K = 1', i.e., one and only one processor is allowed to enter the critical section at any moment). In other words, to control 'N' processors, the number 'M' of 'N-WAY' switches required is given by:

$$M \geq 2 + \frac{Ln\ (n - 1)}{Ln\ 2} \tag{3}$$

The general structure of the control mechanism for the control of 'N' processors using 'M' switches is given in Fig. (8).

The two functions 'P3' and 'V3' given in Fig. (9) perform the same function as the corresponding functions P2 and V2 in Fig. (4). However, instead of using the function TS, the functions P3 and V3 use the function 'INITIALIZE' given in Fig. (10) which corresponds to the flowchart of Fig. (8). The control structure represented by the functions CS3 in Fig. (11) can be used for the control of parallel processors without the assumption of the existence of an indivisible operation.

CONCLUSIONS

The control structure given in section (3) is much more expensive than the one given in section (2). It is definitely advantageous to have built-in indivisible operations like TS instruction of SYSTEM/360 on some of the variables in a common data area. It can also be seen from the programs of Fig. (4) that if the time required for a P or a V operation is more than the time required for the execution of the critical section, then it is possible that the faster processors can take absolute control over the critical section. For example, if the speed ratio between two sets of processors is 10:1, then even though the slow processors contend to enter the critical section with the fast processors at the same time, they may spend more time in dwelling around the first two instructions of the program in Fig. (3) and the probability that one of them may enter the critical section is given by:

$$\frac{1}{P + Q \times 10}$$

where 'P' is the number of slow processors and 'Q' is the number of fast processors that contend for the critical section at any instant. The above probability is even less in the solution of Fig. (11) because each processor has to execute many more instructions than that in the solution of Fig. (4). Therefore, the solution developed in section (3) can be useful only if the invokation of the critical section is less frequent. This solution is used in the initial version of APL 70/46 (implemented for RCA SPECTRA 70/46) for the communication between APL programs (for example, in the implementation of the APL commands:)PORT,)MSG and)MSGN).

In comparing the solution given in section (3) with that of Dijkstra [1], the following points can be noted:

144

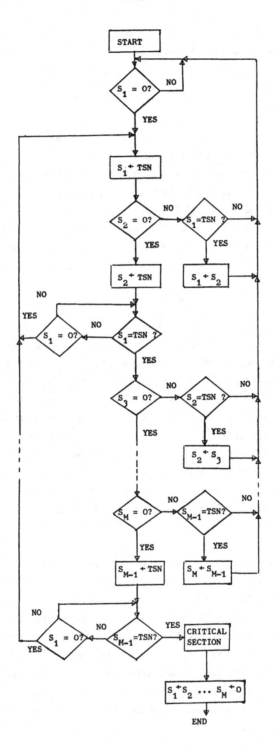

Fig. (8).

```
    ∇ S P3 X;M;TSN
[1]   ⍝GET THE IDENTIFICATION.
[2]    TSN←I29
[3]   ⍝MAXIMUM NUMBER OF SWITCHES.
[4]    M←⌈2+(●N-1)÷●2
[5]    INITIALIZE
[6]    ⍎X,'←',X,'-1'
[7]   ⍝REMOVE THE ENTRY FROM QUEUE.
[8]    QUEUE←1↓QUEUE
[9]    ⍎S,'←Mρ0'
    ∇

    ∇ S V3 X;M;TSN
[1]   ⍝GET THE IDENTIFICATION
[2]    TSN←I29
[3]   ⍝MAXIMUM NUMBER OF SWITCHES.
[4]    M←⌈2+(●N-1)÷●2
[5]    INITIALIZE
[6]    ⍎X,'←',X,'+1'
[7]   ⍝ADD THE PROCESSOR TO QUEUE.
[8]    QUEUE←QUEUE, TSN
[9]    ⍎S,'←Mρ0'
    ∇
```

Fig. (9). P and V operations without the use of Indivisible Instructions.

```
      ∇  INITIALIZE
[1]      ⍝ DWELL IF THE SWITCH IS ALREADY SET.
[2]      ONE:→([1]≠0)/ONE
[3]      ⍝  INITIALIZE.
[4]      TWO:I←1
[5]       S[I]←TSN
[6]      ⍝  IF THE SWITCH IS SET GOTO RESET S[I].
[7]      BEGIN:→(S[I+1]≠0)RESET
[8]      ⍝ SET THE SWITCH.
[9]       S[I+1]←TSN
[10]     ⍝ IF THE SWITCH IS SAME AS THE IDENTIFICATION,
[11]     ⍝ GOTO SET THE NEXT SWITCH
[12]     TEST:→(S[I]=TSN)/GOOD
[13]     ⍝ OTHERWISE, DWELL TILL THE SWITCH S[I] IS CHANGED
[14]     ⍝ OR TILL THE SWITCH S[1] IS RESET.
[15]      →(S[1]≠0)/TEST
[16]      →TWO
[17]     ⍝ CHANGE ONLY IF S[I] = TSN.
[18]     RESET:→(S[I]≠TSN)/ONE
[19]      S[I]←S[I+1]
[20]      →ONE
[21]     ⍝ REPEAT.
[22]     GOOD:→((I←I+1)<M)/BEGIN
[23]     ⍝  ** ENTER THE CRITICAL SECTION **.
      ∇
```

Fig. (10). The program that corresponds to the flowchart of Fig. (8).


```
      ∇ CS3
[1]      'L' V3 'NAME'
[2]      DWELL:→(TSN≠1↑QUEUE)/DWELL
[3]      ⍝ *** CRITICAL SECTION ***
[4]      'L' P3 'NAME'
      ∇
```

Fig. (11). The control structure using the P and V operations of Fig. (9).

1. The solution of Fig. (8) is much simpler than the solution of Dijkstra because of fewer switches.

2. In Dijkstra's solution, it is necessary to assign a number 'I' to a processor so that the corresponding switches 'B[I]' or 'A[I]' in the common data area can be recognized by any of the processors. This is usually not difficult, but was

impossible in SPECTRA 70/46, without going into the level of system design. Of course, the switch TSN is a form of identification, but if this switch has to be used in the solution of Dijkstra, the whole common data area will be filled with the switches 'B' and 'C' because TSN can take as many as 10000 different (or more) values. Therefore, Dijkstra's solution could not be used for the communication of APL programs in APL 70/46, without going into the system level of design.

ACKNOWLEDGEMENTS

The author would like to thank his colleagues, members of the CIS staff of Moore School, and Dr. Ghandour for their helpful suggestions.

REFERENCES

[1] E.W. Dijkstra, "Solution of a problem in concurrent programming control," Communications of ACM, Vol. 8, (September 1965), pp. 569.

[2] E.W. Dijkstra, "The Structure of 'THE' Multiprogramming System," Communications of ACM, Vol. 11, (May 1968), pp. 341-346.

[3] E.W. Dijkstra, "Cooperating Sequential Processes" in Programming Languages, F. Genuys, (Ed.), Academic Press (1968).

[4] D.E. Knuth, "Additional Comments on a Problem in Concurrent Programming Control," Communications of ACM, Vol. 9, (May 1966), pp. 321-322.

[5] T.E. Bredt, "Analysis and Synthesis of Concurrent Sequential Programs," Technical Report #6, Stanford University, (May 1970).

[6] V.G. Cerf, "Multiporciessors, Semaphores, and a graph model of Computation," Ph.D.Thesis, Computer Science Department, University of California, (April 1972).

[7] A.D. Falkoff, and K.E. Iverson, APL/360 Users Manual, IBM, (1968).

[8] A.D. Falkoff, and K.E. Iverson, APLSV User's Manual, IBM Philadelphia Scientific Center, (1973).

TOWARD THE DESIGN OF A NETWORK MANAGER
FOR A DISTRIBUTED COMPUTER NETWORK[a]

J. H. ROWAN, D. A. SMITH, AND M. D. SWENSEN
Ground Systems Group
Hughes Aircraft Company
Fullerton, California   92634

Abstract -- This paper describes a controlling entity called the Network
Manager which integrates and controls the activities of a network of distributed
processes. The processes may be realized by special-purpose hardware devices,
minicomputers, large-scale processing systems, or a combination of these. The Network Manager presents a well-defined hardware and software interface to the processes and provides control functions which are executive or operating system functions
found in traditional software systems. Where appropriate, these functions are
optimized by implementing them in hardware. The control functions are delineated
in detail in this paper along with the basic hardware configuration of the Network
Manager.

INTRODUCTION

Current military data systems are designed around a large central computer
which performs all or at least most of the data processing functions required by the
system. In order to offload the central processor and increase system performance,
some systems have incorporated "smart" sensors such as radar video processors. The
cost of the software invested in systems built around a large central computer has
reached such a level that it is almost cost prohibitive to replace the computer
with a more modern machine. Thus, this type of system is not capable of growing
both efficiently and cost effectively to meet the ever increasing demands of the
tactical environment.

The current trend in the architecture of military data systems is to distribute
the data processing functions among several processing components based on the natural partitioning of the data system functions (e.g., display, sonar, radar, communications, data base management, and weapon control functions). The resulting
configuration is a distributed computer network.

This paper specifies a controlling entity, called the Network Manager (NM),
which integrates and controls the activities of distributed processes. The processes
may be realized by special-purpose hardware devices, minicomputers, large-scale
processing systems, or a combination of these. The NM presents a well-defined hardware and software interface to the processes which it controls. This paper is based

(a) This research was supported by the Naval Electronics Laboratory Center,
San Diego, California, under Contract No. N00123-73-C-2130.

on a study, supported by the Naval Electronics Laboratory Center, that specified a controlling entity for a generalized distributed command and control system [1]. In general, the results are applicable to other types of military data systems as well as to commercial data processing systems.

The specific configuration considered is a centralized computer network in which the NM interfaces directly with a number of subordinate devices which are the controlled processes. A current research project is extending the NM's capabilities to allow it to be one of possibly several identical controlling entities in a distributed computer network.

FUNCTIONAL DESCRIPTION

Preliminary Remarks

The NM coordinates the operation of a number of functional nodes which comprise the system network. Each functional node is called a _process_. A process may be realized by a special-purpose hardware device or by a programmed device, as long as the interface requirements are met. Each process is physically connected to the NM at an interface called a _port_. The port provides a path for control information and data to and from the NM. Four things can take place "simultaneously" (i.e., interleaved in time) at the interface: input and output of control information to and from the NM, as well as input and output of a data block. The port interface is designed to be readily implemented with the standard Naval Tactical Data System interface.

The control information that passes between the NM and the processes is in the form of a _control statement_. The control statement consists of four words and may be transmitted as an entity or as a header for a data block to be routed from one process to another via a _data bus_. There are two classes of control statements. A _request_ (REQ) control statement is sent from a process to the NM, while an _interrupt_ (INT) control statement originates in the NM and is sent to a process.

In order to handle the control statements and route information between processes, the NM contains the following elements:

1. _Master program machine_ (MPM) -- The MPM is a microprogrammed device which ultimately responds to all requests. The microprogram which is executed by the MPM is called the _master program_.

2. _Local memory_ (LM) -- The state of the system is recorded in a set of data structures in the LM. The master program references these data structures and updates them in response to various events (e.g., requests and timer expirations) that occur.

3. _Process interface units_ (PIUs) -- A PIU provides the hardware interface between a process and the other elements in the NM.

4. _Data buses_ -- Control statements and data blocks are routed between the PIUs, the LM, and the MPM via a data bus.

5. Timers -- The message timer is used for scheduling messages to be sent at particular times. The task deadline timers (one per port) monitor the deadline of the highest priority task at each port; each timer signals a task deadline expired event if the highest priority task at that port exceeds its deadline time. (Deadline scheduling is discussed below.)

6. Resolution mechanism (RM) -- Competing requests from the processes and timers are temporarily held in the RM which decides what event the master program will recognize next.

Corresponding to each possible system event, there is a segment of micro-code in the master program, called an algorithm, which performs the necessary operations. The RM selects one event at a time which is completely processed by the corresponding master program algorithm before the next event is recognized. In order to minimize the Network Manager's response time, data block transfers from process to process are handled independently of the master program. The master program determines if a transfer can be accomplished, initiates the transfer, and then continues with its algorithm. The actual transfer is accomplished by mutual cooperation of the PIUs and a data bus. When the transfer is completed, a system event is generated which causes another algorithm to be executed. This algorithm completes the bookkeeping associated with the block transfer.

A message is the unit of communication among processes interconnected by the NM and represents an event in time with an associated variable quantity of data. Each message begins with a header which gives the NM all the information it needs to handle the message. Messages are routed from sender to receiver by using a destination code, which can be thought of as a "mailbox" code. The sender specifies the destination he wishes to send the message to; the receiver receives only a message addressed to the destination that the receiver specifies. In order to facilitate the transmission of small amounts of data or synchronization information, the NM distinguishes between short messages, which contain two words of data, and long messages. Since the receiver may not know what kind of message will be sent next, the same control statement is used to receive either kind of message. The sender, however, declares whether he is sending a long message or a short message. For a long message, the sender specifies the address and length of the message in his own memory; for a short message, the data (two words) is placed directly in the control statement. When both the sender and receiver are ready for transmitting a long message, a block transfer is started from the sending process to the receiving process via a data bus. Both the sender and receiver of a long message are delayed until the message transfer is completed. When a task sends a short message, however, the NM attempts to continue execution of the sender without delay. This is not done indefinitely because of the possibility of filling up the LM with short messages. A number is associated with each destination queue which bounds the number of short messages stored for which the sender is allowed to continue. When the number of such

short messages reaches the maximum, then senders of additional short messages are
delayed like senders of long messages.

Each process is assumed to be a multiprogrammed device with the individual
multiprogrammed activities being called tasks. The NM schedules the execution of the
tasks in each process based on the data structures maintained in the LM. A TASK
field is provided in most INT control statements. This field indicates the next
task which is to be executed in the receiving process. The scheduling algorithm
employed is deadline scheduling; each task has a deadline (which may be "infinite"),
and the ready task with the earliest deadline is the one which runs next. As mentioned previously, a task can become unready by waiting to receive a message, waiting to send a long message, or by sending a short message to a full destination
queue.

It a task is waiting for a message and its deadline expires, then the NM syn-
thesizes a short message which it flags appropriately and sends to the task. If the
task is running or waiting to send a message, then the NM assumes that the task will
eventually try to receive a message and flags the overrun in its local data structures. When the task next tries to receive a message, it receives an appropriately
flagged short message. Messages are also given deadlines, and the NM delivers
messages in the order of their deadlines. If the deadline of a message expires,
this is flagged and the receiver is notified when the message is delivered. The
receiver is also notified whether or not the sender was able to continue executing
immediately. If the sender was delayed, this can be construed to mean that the
receiver should in some way "hurry up" and process the messages faster.

The Standard Process

The standard process is the "virtual" device that is assumed to interface with
the NM at a port. By definition this device interacts with the NM in the most
efficient manner possible and utilizes NM services to the best possible advantage.
The formulation of the standard process was intentionally biased to anticipate implementation using a computer with the following properties: an independent input/
output channel, an uninterruptible supervisor state for the processor, and a processing load which is multiprogrammed. Naturally, simpler architectures can be con-
ceived which present the same interface to the NM, and which may or may not utilize
all of the available NM services.

The standard process itself has three states: running an application task,
running a local supervisor algorithm, or idling. In the first state, the process is
performing useful work and can be interrupted at any time by a NM INT control statement which places the process in the local supervisor state. The local supervisor
state is uninterruptible; in this state the process executes a finite algorithm
selected by the particular INT control statement. This state can also be entered
by request from an application task, for example, to generate a REQ control statement to the NM. (In some systems this may not be necessary for REQs, but it is

still necessary to have such a state so that incoming INT control statements do not overlay each other.) When the process sends a REQ to the NM, it is in general not discernible whether the requesting task will be delayed by the NM task scheduling capability or not. Therefore, the process leaves the local supervisor state and enters the idling state; in this state the process performs no useful work (or perhaps background work), but it is again interruptible by an INT from the NM.

NM Request Buffers and Control Statements

A request buffer is a structured data type which is used for a variety of purposes by the master program. Each REQ control statement submitted to the NM by a process is first placed in a request buffer, and each INT control statement issued to a process is first constructed in a request buffer and then output. In addition, when requests for NM action cannot be immediately satisfied, they are generally kept in the form of a REQ control statement in a request buffer.

A request buffer consists of a one-word link field, referred to as the NEXT field, followed by four words of data. Waiting requests are kept in ordered lists, or queues, where the ordering is dynamically accomplished using the NEXT field of the request buffers. Generally a known variable holds the address of the first buffer in the list, and the NEXT field of each buffer holds the address of the following buffer. The last buffer in the list has a special value, NIL, in the NEXT field; this value can be dynamically recognized since it does not represent a valid address.

The four data words of a request buffer hold a control statement which is broken down into fields. The identity and meaning of the fields depends on the particular control statement. The control statements and their fields are summarized in Table 1. When a REQ control statement is kept internally in a queue to represent an unfulfilled request, some of the fields are redefined. These variants are discussed in the subsection "NM Local Data Structures" in connection with the corresponding queues.

Control Statements

This subsection describes in detail the control statements that are used during general system operation. Control statements used for system initialization are described in reference [1]. Figures 1 and 2 illustrate the formats of the REQ and INT control statements. The OP field in each statement contains a code which represents the particular control statement and distinguishes the formats from each other.

The REQ-RECEIVE-MSG control statement indicates to the NM that the issuing task is ready for a message addressed to the specified destination queue. The TASK field indicates the requesting task. The DEST field indicates the desired destination queue. The ADDR and LTH fields describe the message buffer area in the process's memory; the message provided is guaranteed not to exceed the area length. The

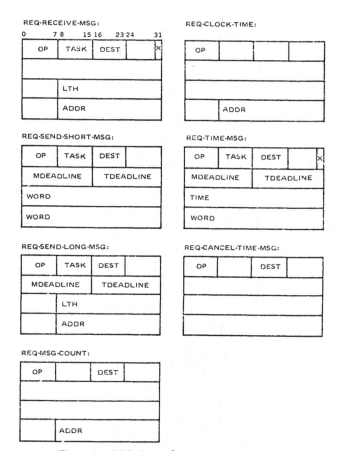

Figure 1. REQ Control Statement Formats

154

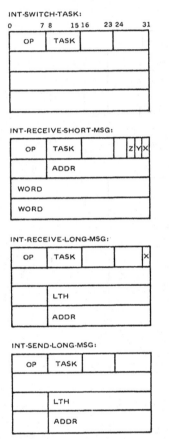

Figure 2. INT Control Statement Formats

address and length are used in subsequent INT control statements which deal with
this particular message transfer. The X bit has a special meaning. If it is set,
this means the task has met its previous deadline and the NM should therefore cancel
that deadline. When a message becomes available for the task, a new task deadline
should be computed and assigned to the task. If the X bit is not set, then the old
deadline remains in force even if the task must wait for a message.

The REQ-SEND-SHORT-MSG control statement indicates to the NM that the issuing
task has a message for the specified destination queue. The TASK field indicates
the requesting task. The DEST field indicates the desired destination queue. The
TDEADLINE field holds the task deadline to be imparted to the receiving task when
the message is transmitted, and is expressed as a time increment from when the message is transmitted. This deadline will not be imparted to the receiving task unless
the receiver exercises this option in the REQ-RECEIVE-MSG control statement. The
MDEADLINE field is used to express a deadline for the transmission of the message,
and is expressed as a time increment from when the send request is made. The remaining two words constitute the short message.

The REQ-SEND-LONG-MSG control statement is identical to the REQ-SEND-SHORT-MSG
control statement except that the two data words are replaced by the ADDR and LTH
fields which describe the message in the process's memory.

The REQ-MSG-COUNT control statement is used to interrogate the status of a
destination queue without delaying the task. The DEST field indicates the desired
destination queue. The ADDR field specifies a two-word area in the process's memory which is to receive the count of the number of messages in the queue and, if the
count is positive, the deadline of the next message. The information is returned in
an INT-RECEIVE-SHORT-MSG control statement.

The REQ-CLOCK-TIME control statement is a request to the NM to read the NM's
time-of-day clock. The ADDR field indicates where the time value is to be placed in
the process's memory. The master program reads the clock, formulates an INT-RECEIVE-
SHORT-MSG control statement containing the time value and specifying the address in
the process's memory, and sends this control statement to the requesting process.

The REQ-TIME-MSG control statement is a request for a message to be sent to the
specified destination queue after the delay of a specified time interval; the requesting task normally continues immediately, but it may then delay itself by requesting to receive this message. The TASK field indicates the requesting task, and
the DEST field specifies the desired destination queue. The X bit indicates the
meaning of the TIME field. If the bit is set, the TIME field represents a time interval measured from when this request is made. If the bit is not set, then the
TIME field represents an absolute time. The MDEADLINE and TDEADLINE fields have the
same meaning for the scheduled message as they do for a short message sent by a REQ-
SEND-SHORT-MSG control statement. The message actually sent consists of two words:
the time value for when the scheduled message entered the destination queue, and the

remaining data word from this control statement.

The REQ-CANCEL-TIME-MSG requests the NM to cancel a message scheduled by a REQ-TIME-MSG control statement, as described above. The DEST field specifies the destination queue. The precise function of this request is to delete the earliest scheduled time message addressed to the specified queue.

The INT-SWITCH-TASK control statement directs the process to switch to a specified application task, indicated by the TASK field. If this is the same task that was most recently running on the process, then this command is logically a No-Op, but it is left up to the process to optimize the task switch if this involves the swapping of task registers, etc. This control statement is also used by the NM as an "acknowledge" signal to release the process from the idling state and resume execution of the requesting task.

The INT-RECEIVE-SHORT-MSG control statement indicates that a requested message is available, and that it is a short message. This may immediately follow a REQ-RECEIVE-MSG, or it may be some time later when the message is sent. (Not every short message is generated by a REQ-SEND-SHORT-MSG; a short message also results from a task overflow, a REQ-MSG-COUNT, a REQ-CLOCK-TIME, or a REQ-TIME-MSG.) The ADDR field specifies the address in the process's memory where the message is to be placed. The remaining two words constitute the short message. The X bit is the "message overflow" bit; if it is set, this indicates that the message deadline specified by the sender of the message has expired. The Y bit is the "task overflow" bit; if it is set, this indicates that the receiving task has overrun its current task deadline. The Z bit is the "buffered" bit. If it is set, this indicates that the task which sent this message was able to continue immediately without waiting for the message to be received (i.e., the message was "buffered" within the NM). If this bit is not set, it indicates that this short message was sent by another task, but the maximum number of buffered short messages for this destination queue had been reached, so that the sending task had to be delayed. This may be construed to mean that the receiving task should "hurry up" by modifying its processing algorithm or perhaps by ignoring messages. Since the receiver may not be the highest priority task in the receiving process, the TASK field designates the next task to be executed.

The INT-RECEIVE-LONG-MSG control statement indicates that a requested message is available to be transmitted. This may immediately follow a REQ-RECEIVE-MSG, or it may be some time later when the message ie sent. The LTH and ADDR fields describe the area in the process's memory where the message is to be placed. The X bit is the "message overflow" bit. Since this control statement indicates that the message transmission can begin, the receiving task cannot yet continue. The TASK field designates the task that is to run while the transfer is taking place.

The INT-SEND-LONG-MSG control statement is used in response to the REQ-SEND-LONG-MSG control statement, either immediately or some time later when a receiver becomes ready. The ADDR and LTH fields describe the message in the process's memory. Since this control statement indicates that the message transmission can begin, the sending task cannot yet continue. The TASK field designates the task that is to run while the transfer is taking place.

NM Local Data Structure

For convenience of discussion the variables, arrays, and linked lists within the NM's local memory are grouped into "data structures". Each of these data structures corresponds conceptually with a functional capability of the NM or represents a collection of logically related information. They are shown graphically in Figure 3 and are described in the remainder of this subsection.

Free Buffer Pool. Initially the NM local memory is formatted into variables, arrays, and a pool of unused or "free" request buffers. These free buffers are linked in a single chain. The variable FREE always points to the first free buffer if there are any free buffers, otherwise it has the value NIL. The variable N-FREE always has a non-negative integer value which is equal to the number of request buffers in the free chain.

Task Information Table. Information describing each task in the system is kept in an array called the task information table (TINT). Each entry in the table consists of several variables or fields which describe the corresponding task. We will speak of these fields as arrays in their own right when it is convenient to do so.

The NEXT-TASK field holds a value which is either zero or the index of another task. This field is used to dynamically link together, in order of decreasing priority (increasing deadline), those tasks which run at the same port. The last task in this chain has a zero value in this field.

The WAITING-REQUEST field is used whenever the task is not ready to run. If the task is waiting, this field holds the address of the corresponding request buffer in the NM. If the task is ready to run, then this field has the value NIL. This field is therefore used to decide if the task is eligible for execution. This field is also used when the task's deadline expires. In this case, the master program can determine if the task is waiting to receive a message and, if so, formulate a short message which indicates the overrun condition.

The DEADLINE field holds the absolute time value of the task's current deadline. This field indicates an "infinite" deadline time if there is no current deadline.

The OVERFLOW field is used to indicate that the task has overrun its deadline, but has not yet been informed. When the task's deadline expires and the task is not currently waiting for a message, the next message the task receives will indicate the overrun.

Port Information Table. Information describing each NM port is kept in an array called the port information table (PIT). Each entry in the table consists of several variables or fields which describe the corresponding port. The SEND-TASK

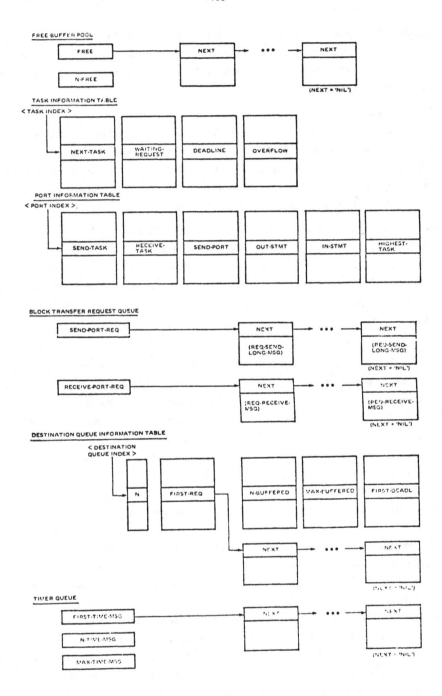

Figure 3. NM Data Structures

field for a port is zero if the input channel of that port is free. If the channel is busy with a block transfer or has been allocated to a particular block transfer, then this field holds the index of the sending task for the transfer. This task is in the process attached to this port, of course. (The "input channel" manages a block transfer out of the corresponding process into the NM.)

The RECEIVE-TASK field for a port is zero if the output channel of the port is free. If the channel is busy with a block transfer or has been allocated to a particular block transfer, then this field holds the index of the receiving task for the transfer. This task is in the process attached to this port. (The "output channel" manages a block transfer out of the NM into the corresponding process.)

The SEND-PORT field for a port is used when the corresponding process is receiving a block transfer. When the transfer terminates, an internal request is generated which informs the master program of the number of the port which received the block transfer. The master program uses this field to determine the sending port which participated in the transfer.

The OUT-STMT field for a port holds the address of the request buffer which holds the INT control statement currently being output at this port. If the NM has temporarily exceeded the rate at which the process can accept INTs, this buffer will be linked to a chain of all the INT control statements which the master program has prepared for this port.

The IN-STMT field for a port holds the address of the request buffer which has just been filled with an input control statement. This field is given a value by the PIU, since only the PIU knows which buffer it has been filling. The master program uses this field to locate the control statement.

The HIGHEST-TASK field for a port holds the task index of the task at that port with the highest priority (nearest deadline). The rest of the tasks at that port are chained from this task using the NEXT-TASK field (in the TINT). Recall that the ready tasks are distinguished by their WAITING-REQUEST field which has the value of NIL. The highest priority ready task in this chain is the one that is running.

Block Transfer Request Queue. The block transfer request queue is actually two parallel chains of request buffers. The variable SEND-PORT-REQ points to a chain ordered by message deadlines of REQ-SEND-LONG-MSG control statements. The variable RECEIVE-PORT-REQ points to a chain of REQ-RECEIVE-MSG control statements. Each of these requests is a "receive" which has been matched with a corresponding "send" and together they represent a request for an input channel, an output channel, and use of a data bus.

The fields of these enqueued control statements are slightly modified. The X bit in each receive request is now the message overflow bit. Each send and receive request has a bit, Y, which indicates that the corresponding port channel has been allocated to the transfer. When both of these bits are true, both ports have been allocated and the transfer can begin. Since the DEST field in each control statement is no longer needed, it is replaced with a PORT field which indicates the port being requested for the data transfer.

Destination Queue Information Table. Information describing each destination queue is kept in an array called the destination queue information table (DQIT). Each entry in the table consists of several variables or fields which describe the corresponding destination queue. The field N is used to denote the number of requests in the destination queue. For N equal to zero, there are no requests. If N is positive, then the FIRST-REQ field points to a chain of send requests, sorted in priority order (increasing message deadline). If N is negative, then the FIRST-REQ field points to a chain of receive requests, sorted in priority order (increasing task deadline of receiver tasks).

For positive N the MDEADLINE fields of the enqueued send requests are modified so that each represents a time increment from the deadline of the previous request. The absolute deadline time of the first message in the queue is held in the FIRST-DEADL field for the destination queue.

For a REQ-SEND-SHORT-MSG control statement enqueued in a destination queue, the NM employs two previously unused bits, Z and W, as logical flags. The Z bit indicates whether or not the short message is a buffered short message. The W bit indicates if the short message was generated by the NM as a time interval message.

The N-BUFFERED field indicates the number of REQ-SEND-SHORT-MSG control statements in the destination queue for which the sender was allowed to continue executing immediately. The field MAX-BUFFERED holds a value which N-BUFFERED is not permitted to exceed. If they are equal and another short message is sent, then the sender is delayed as is done when the message is a long message. The sender becomes ready again when the message is delivered to a receiver.

Timer Queue. The timer queue is used for scheduling messages requested by the REQ-TIME-MSG control statement. The variable FIRST-TIME-MSG points to a chain of request buffers. This chain consists of all the REQ-TIME-MSG control statements, sorted in order of increasing scheduling time (i.e., the time at which the corresponding message is to be sent). For requests which request a message after a time interval, the absolute time is computed when the request is processed and placed in the TIME field of the control statement. The message scheduling hardware timer is always set to cause an "interrupt" when it is time to send the first message in the timer queue.

The N-TIME-MSG variable indicates the number of REQ-TIME-MSG control statements in the timer queue for which the sender was allowed to continue executing immediately. The MAX-TIME-MSG variable holds a value which N-TIME-MSG is not permitted to exceed. If they are equal and another time message request is sent, then the sender is delayed. When the time message request leaves the timer queue and enters the appropriate destination queue, the sender becomes ready, providing the destination queue's

N-BUFFERED variable is less than its MAX-BUFFERED variable. The time message request enqueued in the time queue has a bit, Z, which indicates whether or not the request was buffered. The Z bit is also used to denote buffering when the time message is placed in the destination queue.

NM Master Program Algorithms

Four kinds of events cause execution of a master program algorithm. These are end of control statement output (END-CS-OUT), end of data block transfer (END-DB-OUT), end of a control statement input (END-CS-IN), and the end of a timer interval (TIMER-ELAPSED). The END-CS-OUT event invokes a single algorithm, as does the END-DB-OUT event. The END-CS-IN event invokes one of several algorithms, corresponding to the actual control statement. The TIMER-ELAPSED event invokes either the MSG-TIMER-ELAPSED algorithm or the TDEADLINE-ELAPSED algorithm, depending on whether the interrupting timer is the message timer or one of the task deadline timers, respectively.

The REQ-SEND-SHORT-MSG, REQ-SEND-LONG-MSG, and REQ-RECEIVE-MSG algorithms are described in Tables 2 through 4. The other master program algorithms are documented in reference [1]. These algorithms abbreviate a few frequent operations which are apparent from context. The words "enqueue" and dequeue" represent the common operations on a linked list, i.e., inserting and removing an element from the chain. The phrase "issue control statement" is a compound action: if the specified port is not outputting a control statement, the output is started on the specified control statement; if the specified port is busy with an output control statement, then the new control statement is chained to the current control statement (and any others that may be enqueued to the port). The END-CS-OUT event will later cause waiting control statements to be output in the order they were issued.

BASIC HARDWARE CONFIGURATION

The basic hardware configuration of the NM is presented in this section. The configuration presented is preliminary in nature and will be finalized after (1) additional capabilities have been considered for incorporation into the NM, and (2) a detailed performance analysis of the NM has been completed.

Block Diagram

The major components of the NM are shown in Figure 4. (For simplicity the timers and RM are not shown.) The NM contains one or more identical buses which route information among the PIUs, the MPM, and the LM. A bus interface unit (BIU) forms a logical connection between a PIU, the MPM, or the LM and a bus. The BIUs are identical, and additional buses can be added without affecting the design of the BIU.

A system clock is distributed to all components of the NM, thus eliminating many "hand shaking" operations which would otherwise occur during information

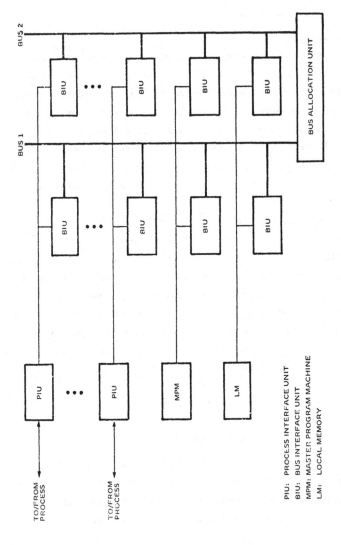

Figure 4. NM Block Diagram

PIU: PROCESS INTERFACE UNIT
BIU: BUS INTERFACE UNIT
MPM: MASTER PROGRAM MACHINE
LM: LOCAL MEMORY

transfers along a bus. All logic signals are derived from this common clock source. Each of the buses can be allocated to a requesting unit (PIU, MPM, or LM) during every clock period. The units generate bus request (BR) signals which are monitored by the bus allocation unit (BAU). The BAU assigns each bus to one of the requesting units.

Bus Allocation

The BAU receives the BR signals from each of the units on the bus and generates bus granted (BG) signals which are routed from the BAU to the BIUs. Whenever a unit wishes to gain access to a bus, it activates its BR line. The BAU monitors all of the BR lines and determines, based on an internal priority assignment, which unit will gain access to each bus. Once a unit gains access to a bus, it keeps the bus until the unit's BR signal becomes inactive. Requests for bus access during a particular clock period are made during the previous clock period. In this way, bus allocation is overlapped with information transfer along the bus.

The selection logic in the BAU is of two types; a round-robin selection for requests from the PIUs, and a fixed priority selection for requests from the MPM and the LM. Requests from the MPM and the LM take priority over requests from the PIUs, with the MPM having the highest priority. The BAU is capable of assigning all buses simultaneously.

Local Memory

The LM is a high speed random access memory which maintains the NM's local data structures. These data structures are accessed by the PIUs or by the MPM via a data bus. A preliminary estimate for the memory size is 8192 32-bit words. The cycle time of the memory must be one system clock period (approximately 200 nanoseconds).

Master Program Machine

The MPM is a microprogrammed processor which executes the algorithms of the master program. The MPM manipulates the data structures located in the LM. The MPM communicates with the PIUs and the LM via the data buses. It also interfaces with the RM and the timers.

SUMMARY

This paper describes in detail a controlling entity, called the Network Manager (NM) for a centralized computer network. The NM controls and coordinates the activities of the processes that interface with it. A process is realized by a hardware processing element such as a special or general-purpose computer. Control statements and data structures in the NM are presented in this paper which: (1) allow the NM to route information in the form of messages from one process to another, (2) enable the NM to schedule the execution of tasks in each process, and (3) allow the processes to synchronize their activities with respect to a real-time clock source. The basic hardware configuration of the NM is also presented, including a description of the bus structure which allows the various units in the NM to communicate with each other.

CURRENT RESEARCH

A current research and development project at Hughes Aircraft Company is extending the basic capabilities (message routing, task scheduling, and timing service) of the NM and incorporating additional capabilities into the design of the NM. The project objective is to develop a NM which can be one of possibly several identical controlling entities in a distributed computer network. The additional capacilities include: (1) an external interrupt handling capability which allows the NM to directly receive and dispatch various types of external interrupts, (2) a network monitoring capability which allows the performance of the system to be monitored, (3) a configuration/reconfiguration management capability which allows the NM to maintain the current configuration of the system and to reconfigure the system in the event of a failure, (4) a secure data capability which protects the data in the system against unauthorized disclosure, modification, restriction, or destruction, and (5) a system initialization capability which allows the processes and the data structures in the NM to be initialized.

REFERENCE

[1] J. R. Fogarty, J. H. Rowan, D. A. Smith, and M. D. Swensen, Hardware Command and Control System Study, Ground Systems Group, Hughes Aircraft Company, FR 74-11-02-A (February, 1974), 124 pp.

Table 1

Summary of Control Statements and Their Fields

REQ-RECEIVE-MSG (TASK, DEST, X, LTH, ADDR)
REQ-SEND-SHORT-MSG (TASK, DEST, MDEADLINE, TDEADLINE, word, word)
REQ-SEND-LONG-MSG (TASK, DEST, MDEADLINE, TDEADLINE, LTH, ADDR)
REQ-MSG-COUNT (DEST, ADDR)
REQ-CLOCK-TIME (ADDR)
REQ-TIME-MSG (TASK, DEST, X, MDEADLINE, TDEADLINE, TIME, word)
REQ-CANCEL-TIME-MSG (DEST)
INT-SWITCH-TASK (TASK)
INT-RECEIVE-SHORT-MSG (TASK, Z, Y, X, ADDR, word, word)
INT-RECEIVE-LONG-MSG (TASK, X, LTH, ADDR)
INT-SEND-LONG-MSG (TASK, LTH, ADDR)

Table 2

REQ-SEND-SHORT-MSG Algorithm

If N < 0, then:

- N ← N+1; dequeue receive; ready receiver task.
- If new deadline requested, then set deadline.
- Fix receive request (INT-RECEIVE-SHORT-MSG); copy message; issue control statement.
- Fix send request (INT-SWITCH-TASK); issue control statement.

Else:

- N ← N+1; enqueue request.
- If N-BUFFERED < MAX-BUFFERED, then increment N-BUFFERED by 1 and flag request as buffered, else unready task.
- Get buffer (INT-SWITCH-TASK); issue control statement.

Table 3

REQ-SEND-LONG-MSG Algorithm

If N ≥ 0, then:

- N ← N+1; enqueue request; unready sender.
- Get buffer (INT-SWITCH-TASK); issue control statement.

Else:

- N ← N+1; dequeue receive.
- If new deadline requested, then set deadline.
- If send port available, then mark SEND-TASK (of port) and set port assigned bit.
- If receive port available, then mark RECEIVE-TASK (of port) and set port assigned bit.
- If send and receive ports available, then:
    - Fix send request (INT-SEND-LONG); check length; issue control statement.
    - Fix receive request (INT-RECEIVE-LONG); check message deadline overflow; check length; issue control statement.

  Else:
    - Enqueue both; check message deadline overflow; unready task.
    - Get buffer (INT-SWITCH-TASK); issue control statement.

Table 4

REQ—RECEIVE—MSG Algorithm

If task deadline overflowed, then:

- Fix request (INT-RECEIVE-SHORT); set task overflow bit; issue control statement.
- Clear overflow.
- If new deadline requested, then clear deadline.

Else:

- If new deadline requested, then clear deadline.
- If N $\leq$ 0, then:
    - N $\leftarrow$ N-1; enqueue request; unready task.
    - Get buffer (INT-SWITCH-TASK); issue control statement.

  Else:

    - N $\leftarrow$ N-1; dequeue send request.
    - If new deadline requested, then set deadline.
    - If short message, then:
        - Fix request (INT-RECEIVE-SHORT); copy message; check message deadline overflow; check buffered bit; issue control statement.
        - If buffered, then:
            - Decrement N-BUFFERED by 1.
            - Free buffer.

          Else:

            - Ready sender.
            - If switch sender task, then:
                - Fix send request (INT-SWITCH-TASK); issue control statement.

              Else:

                - Free buffer.

      Else:

        - If send port available, then mark SEND-TASK (of port) and set port assigned bit.
        - If receive port available, then mark RECEIVE-TASK (of port) and set port assigned bit.
        - If send and receive ports available, then:
            - Fix send request (INT-SEND-LONG); check length; issue control statement.
            - Fix receive request (INT-RECEIVE-LONG); check message deadline overflow; check length; issue control statement.

          Else:

            - Enqueue both; check message deadline overflow; unready task.
            - Get buffer (INT-SWITCH-TASK); issue control statement.

THE TYPESET-10 MESSAGE EXCHANGE FACILITY
A CASE STUDY IN SYSTEMIC DESIGN

MICHAEL J. SPIER
Software Engineering Department
RICHARD L. HILL, TIMOTHY J. STEIN, DANIEL BRICKLIN
TYPESET-10 Development Group[a]
Digital Equipment Corporation
146 Main Street
Maynard, Massachusetts 01754

Abstract -- This paper describes the design considerations which led to the successful implementation of an interprocess communication mechanism, named the Message Exchange Facility (MX). The software implemented Message Exchange Facility provides services analogous to those of the hardware bus. It is the central link that binds a collection of synergistic asynchronous processes into a single systemic entity, the Digital Equipment Corporation's TYPESET-10 computerized newspaper production system. The peculiar functional constraints and requirements - dictated by TYPESET-10's specialized runtime environment - confronted us with a very difficult, and at the same time highly challenging, design problem. In this paper, the emphasis is placed on the decision making process leading from the statement of the problem to a specific technical solution.

PREAMBLE

TYPESET-10 is dedicated commercial text processing system, especially developed by Digital Equipment Corporation to automatically handle all phases of newspaper production (barring the actual printing, of course). Essentially, it has an input side in which raw text is entered in various convenient modes (interactive, batch, real time), and an output side from which emerges the composed text, ready for the printing press. This description is, of course, over simplified; depending on the specific installation, a typesetting machine may be directly connected to - and automatically driven by - TYPESET-10, or the connecting medium may consist of punched paper tape output which must manually be fed into the typesetting machine.

---

[a]This paper describes the research and design considerations which were applied to the development of an actual software product. The technical contents of this paper may not be construed to imply a product commitment by Digital Equipment Corporation, and is subject to change without notice. TYPESET-10 is a standard trademark of Digital Equipment Corporation.

Also, the composed text may or may not have to be manually paginated before it can actually be declared to be in press ready form.

TYPESET-10 is a multiple-user, parallel processing system. Its logical core consists of a 'text crunching' justification and hyphenation program which operates in sequential batch mode. In order to maintain an optimal flow of text throughput, both input and output sides each consist of one or more autonomous sequential processes which execute in asynchronous parallelism relative to one another. The distributed throughput capacity of all of these individual processes provides the total desired systemic throughput. We view the system as a single logical program, whose various dedicated modules operate in temporal concurrency. We developed an interprocess communication mechanism, TYPESET-10's Message Exchange Facility (known by the acronym MX), which is the central and vital link binding these various autonomous activities into a functional systemic entity.

The professional Literature abounds with descriptions of mechanisms for interprocess communication and/or synchronization. The bibliography furnished at the end of this paper testifies to the number of such publications. As argued by Spier[25], such mechanisms are custom tailored to their specific implementation environments as well as to their specific runtime requirements. The mechanism described in this paper is no exception to that rule; it was carefully designed to meet specific requirements pertaining to the usage to which it was to be put.

Given a pair of mutual exclusion process synchronization primitives such as Dijkstra's P and V[14], the mechanics of interprocess communication essentially resolve into a proper implementation of a buffered producer/consumer message exchange function, a subject which has been covered extensively in the Literature (e.g., Bernstein et al[2], Betourne et al [3], Brinch Hansen [4], Chambers [9], Courtois et al [11], Dijkstra [14,15], Gilbert and Chandler [16], Habermann [17], Horning and Randell [18], Lampson [20], Pouzin [21], Spier and Organick [22], Spier [23,24] Sorensen [28], and Wood [31]). To reiterate on these implementation details as ap - plied to yet another variety of interprocess communication mechanism would, in our opinion, be of very little interest to the reader.

On the other hand, in view of the fact that these mechanisms are typically one-of-a-kind constructs which are carefully tailored to meet some very specific functional requirements within the implementation context of some very specific runtime environment [25,27], we believe it to be of interest to describe the decision process which led to the functional definition of such a mechanism. This paper, then, elaborates on the design considerations which led to the definition and implementation of the TYPESET-10 Message Exchange Facility.

THE TYPESET-10 SYSTEM

TYPESET-10 is a dedicated, special purpose multiprogramming system for the computerized production of newspaper compositions. The system is effectively being used

by a number of our customers for the daily production of their newspaper. Implemented on the Digital Equipment Corporation's DECsystem-10 computer [13], the system
may be viewed as essentially consisting of three asynchronous components, as illustrated by Figure 1, being: (1) the input component, (2) the text processing component,
and (3) the output component.

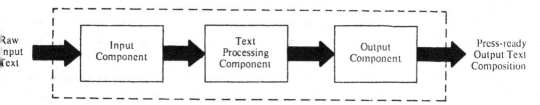

Figure 1. A global view of the TYPESET-10 system, consisting of three
asynchronous functional components. The encapsulating (broken-
line) rectangle represents the system as a text input-to-output
processing 'black box'.

As a matter of fact, each of these components may effectively consist of a number n of autonomous asynchronous sequential processes (where n is equal to, or greater than one, but may well be - at least temporarily - equal to zero). Each process
performs some dedicated operation. On the input side of the system, we may have any
one or more of the following dedicated processes:

- CLASAD the iterative Classified Advertising program, through which classified
  ads are received over the telephone by a human operator and are immediately
  keyed into the system. Several CLASAD processes may concurrently be active.
- COPYED the interactive Copy Editor program, through which news stories are keyed
  into the system, and/or edited, by human operators. Several COPYED processes
  may concurrently be active.
- PRUFED the interactive Proof Editor program, where newspaper editors may inspect and edit an already existing text. Several PRUFED processes may concurrently be active.
- WIPTIN the Wire and Paper Tape Input program provides batch-mode input of
  punched paper tape texts. These texts are either manually punched by keyboard
  operators, or automatically punched by wire service equipment. Several tape
  input processes may concurrently be active. The live wire service information
  may optionally be fed directly into the computer system via WIPTIN.

The text processing component of TYPESET-10 is a program named JUSTIF which
operates in batch mode, being a sequential high-speed 'text-cruncher' that transforms the raw input texts into hyphenated and justified compositions which may then
be input directly into actual text typesetting machines. These typesetting machines
are typically of two varieties: (1) hot metal machines (i.e., linotypes), and (2)

photocomposition machines. Several JUSTIF processes may concurrently be active.

The output component consists of as many autonomous asynchronous processes as there are typesetting machines, each process driving a single typesetting machine either directly (i.e., typesetting machine is actually wired into the computer system) or indirectly (i.e., the process punches out a paper tape which is then manually fed into the typesetting machine).

The simplistic illustration shown in Figure 1 merely represents the conceptual text flow through a 'black box' system (represented by the encapsulating broken-line rectangle). The exact functional structure internal to the 'black box' is a priori indeterminate, depending on the specific requirements of the individual customer installation, and possibly varying from hour to hour within each customer installation.

Not shown in Figure 1 are various other asynchronous processes which may be activated at various times depending on specific needs. The Reports and Manifests process compiles reports about the daily activities. The Auto-Delete process is periodically activated to delete old texts which are no longer needed. The Classified Ad Pagination process is activated to assemble all of the classified advertisements - which were entered into the system via CLASAD - into a sorted multiple-column press composition. And a special supervisory process allows the composition room supervisor to manually interact with the system, in order to observe and control the internal data flow.

Each TYPESET-10 system is custom tailored to the specific installation in which it is to run. This is primarily dictated by the installation's output equipment (e.g., whether the installation has hot-metal or photo-composition typesetting machines and whether the machines are directly wired into the computer or indirectly driven through the intermediary of punched paper tape, etc.), as well as by its text input equipment (e.g., are texts entered interactively via COPYED, or in batch-mode via WIPTIN, etc.).

THE COMPOSING ROOM

The newspaper's composing room is literally the kind of 'boiler room' environment as depicted by the popular literature and the movies. A place of hectic and seemingly chaotic activity, it operates virtually around the clock. Yet this apparent chaos has a method to it; at some point in time, it resolves into a state of completion where the next edition is in press-ready form, whereupon the presses start to roll and the finished newspapers are bundled up, ready for delivery.

One absolute rule prevails:

THE PAPER WILL BE PRODUCED!

It is absolutely inconceivable that the paper might not get produced at all! No excuse on earth would possibly justify such an eventuality. Given that the paper's production is contingent upon the proper functioning of the computer system, each TYPESET-10 computer installation is equipped with sufficiently redundant hardware (i.e., dual processor machine, several memory banks, multiple dismountable disk units, etc.) to allow the computer system to survive any single hardware component malfunction.

Another inflexible rule is:

THE PRESSES START ROLLING

AT A PREDETERMINED ABSOLUTE TIME!

The newspaper delivery system is an elaborately scheduled affair, and the trucks back into the loading ramps at precisely predetermined hours to pick up their loads of newspapers. A ten minute delay in starting the printing presses is a catastrophe for which someone will be held accountable; and again, no excuse could possibly justify such a breach of schedule.

Figure 2 illustrates the TYPESET-10 system as seen from the composing room employee's point of view. Being ignorant of the computer and its internal 'magic', the composing room employee is aware of two mechanisms only, being: (1) the text input device, e.g., an interactive terminal, or a paper tape reader, and (2) the text output device, e.g., an actual typesetting machine, or a papertape punch.

In the employee's mind, a certain text is either physically resident in the input device or else it is physically resident in the output device. For example, suppose that a keyboard operator enters a news story via the interactive COPYED program. So long as the story is being entered and/or edited, it seemingly resides within the input terminal, literally. When the story seems satisfactory and ready for print, the operator issues a typesetting command which sends the story to be hyphenated, justified and typeset. Once the command is issued, then to all intents and purposes – insofar as the keyboard operator is concerned – the story has physically removed itself from the input terminal, and is now physically resident within the typesetting machine. The keyboard operator dismisses that story from his (her) mind, and concentrates on entering the next news story.

Figure 2. TYPESET-10 as seen by the composing room employee.

In reality, the command which sends the story on its way to the typesetting machine translates, internally, to an interprocess signal indicating to JUSTIF that the story should be hyphenated and justified. The JUSTIF process is an autonomous sequential batch activity which hyphenates and justifies a single story at a time. When the keyboard operator issues the typesetting command, that command appends a new request to JUSTIF's input queue of texts which are to be processed. Following justification, JUSTIF issues an interprocess signal to some output process driving a

typesetting machine, causing the respective text to be queued up for actual typesetting.

LOSS OF SIGNAL

Given that data flow within TYPESET-10 is governed by the Message Exchange
Facility which links the various internal asynchronous activities, it is evident that
the Message Exchange must have inherent properties of determinism and reliability to
exclude any possibility of failure, be it hardware or software originated.

Let us investigate the effects of loss of signal. Suppose that the system
crashes sometime after the keyboard operator issued the typesetting command, and before that specific story has actually been output by the typesetting machine. If
such a crash could cause loss of signal, rupturing the causal chain of asynchronous
process activations, then the story will forever have been lost within the computer
system's limbo.

Given the reality of the newspaper's composing room, there is no practical way
in which such loss of signal might be detected through human means. Consider the
following:

- PRODUCTION MODE: The system is processing thousands of individual texts each
  day, and the emphasis is on attaining a maximal textflow throughput per time
  unit. Texts (such as news stories, classified advertisements, stockmarket
  quotations, editorials, syndicated columns etc.) are asynchronously handled by
  operators whose full time activity consists of processing as much text as possible.

  On the input side, a keyboard operator may be entering a story text at a
  rate of some 120 words per minute. When the text has satisfactorily been entered, the operator issues a typesetting command for that story, and immediately
  proceeds to enter the following text. A paper tape reader operator feeds
  punched paper tapes into a reader; upon detection of an end-of-tape condition an
  automatic typesetting command is issued, and the operator proceeds to enter the
  following paper tape. Texts may even enter the system without any human intervention whatsoever, through a directly connected live news service wire; upon an
  end-of-text condition, an automatic typesetting command is issued.

  On the output side there may typically be typesetting machine operators
  whose sole activity consists of removing finished compositions from the typesetting machine. Given the asynchronous nature of our system, there is no
  direct correlation between the sequence of entering texts and the sequence of
  output compositions. There is no way by which an input operator (if any) may
  predict when a given text will effectively be output, nor on what specific output device.

- SIGNAL QUEUEING: As interprocess signals pertaining to a single text are

propagated throughout the system, from one asynchronous process to another, the
signals may be queued up pending recognition by the respective receiving process.
Because of specific runtime conditions, temporary queues may build up causing
bottleneck effects which may delay the processing of certain texts. The fact
that a given text has not been finally output within a certain period of time
is no indication that it will not eventually emerge from some typesetting machine. In other words, while it is possible to ascertain that a given text did
successfully complete its journey through the system, it is a priori impossible
to ascertain that some other text has effectively been lost somewhere along the
way.

• TEXT NAMING CONVENTION: In view of the immense volume of transitory text which
is daily being processed by the computer system, there is no practical way in
which to assign meaningful file system names to texts. By necessity, each text
is given a unique symbolic file system name which is automatically and arbitra-
ily generated by the system. The only reason for having such names is to allow
for file retrieval by the various programs which have to access the text.

The Message Exchange Facility's primary function is to channel these unique
symbolic names from one asynchronous activity to another; we may think of such a file
system name as being a token, and of the interprocess signal as being the vehicle
which moves the token from one autonomous process to another. Loss of signal could
be viewed as the loss of a token; loss of a token effectively implies the loss of the
text which the token represents.

Now suppose that a loss of signal occurred, and that a certain story will therefore never be output on the typesetting machine. This will be detected - in the last
minute prior to press time - in the form of a conspicuously blank space, with no corresponding story to fill that gap. Admittedly, that story could be typeset in a matter of minutes, provided that we knew its file system name, which typically we do not
know because that name is a unique concoction generated by the system, for the system's internal purposes. And lest we be accused at this point of having misdesigned
TYPESET-10, let us point out that there exist various procedures by which such a lost
story can be retrieved. Nonetheless, such retrieval could take time, be it only ten
minutes, and this delay could be sufficient to jeopardize the timely starting of the
presses!

The inevitable conclusion is that the Message Exchange Facility must be 100%
fault tolerant insofar as runtime conditions are concerned. If the system crashes,
for whatever reason, no loss of signal must occur. When the system is started,
signal propagation must continue as if the crash had never occurred. Moreover, this
principle must apply not only to a total system crash, but also to a partial one.
Suppose that a new and (allegedly) improved version of some specific program (say
JUSTIF) were installed. Further suppose that despite the most meticulous pre-release
testing and validation procedures, this new JUSTIF contains an undetected bug which -

not surprisingly - chooses to manifest itself in the middle of an actual customer
production session. The JUSTIF process dies, however the remainder of the system
continues with its operation. It should now be possible to start running the previous version of JUSTIF - which is known to be reliable - without risking any loss
of signal.

The possibility of such a partial system crash precludes the notion of a system
restart, given that all other ongoing activities were unimpaired and should not be
perturbed. Thus, the Message Exchange signalling mechanism must allow for the arbitrary killing and start-up of any asynchronous process in the system, while guaran-
teeing against loss of signal due to interference with the activities of any such
process.

INTERPROCESS LINKAGE

Certain interprocess communication mechanisms are cognizant of the concepts
'process' and 'process_identity' where signalling is accomplished through some function of the form:

$$SIGNAL \text{(process\_identity,message)};$$

We had to reject this kind of interface, because - as explained in the previous section - we had to anticipate the arbitrary termination of some process and the re-
sumption of the terminated process' activity by a newly created process. Also, we
could not restrict the number of discrete processes engaged in some specific activity.
Suppose that TYPESET-10 normally runs a single JUSTIF process which handles the
justification and hyphenation of queued-up texts, one story at a time. Further suppose that this queue builds up to a point where the single JUSTIF process is no
longer capable of catching up with it. The composing room supervisor should have the
ability to start up a second (or, for that matter, a third or fourth) JUSTIF process
so as to increase the amount of CPU resource dedicated to text hyphenation and justification.[a] Were our interprocess signaling mechanism to address itself to some
specific process' identity, the ability to start a second JUSTIF process would no
longer be easily implementable (if at all).

We have therefore chosen to base our mechanism on the 'mail-box' concept, as
proposed by Spier[22,23], where a mailbox is a sharable repository of interprocess
messages, dedicated to some specific function. The mailbox named 'justif' contains
all the interprocess messages concerning texts which have to be justified. The mailbox named 'delete' contains messages concerning texts which should be deleted at
some predetermined future point in time. The mailbox named 'typeset' contains mes-

---

[a]Given that it is a file-to-file processor, JUSTIF must by necessity spend a certain amount of time in I/O wait state. The amount of time required for text justification is consequently bound by the amount of time necessary to perform the appropriate I/O operations. The activation of an additional JUSTIF process will effectively augment the system's hyphenation and justification throughput capacity.

sages concerning texts which have to be output on a typesetting machine, etc. Each mailbox has a sufficiently large queueing capacity so as to reconcile the speed discrepancies among the asynchronous communicating processes.

A potential loss of signal may be caused by simple programming bugs, where a message is addressed to a non-existent mailbox, and hence possibly dissipates into the blue. To guard ourselves against this eventuality, we designed our Message Exchange Facility to be completely addressable by association. One addresses the 'justif' mailbox by literally specifying a call parameter which is the character string 'justif'. The Message Exchange Facility contains a table of symbolic mailbox names, one of which must match the specified character string parameter. The same principle applies to all other control items. The functional interfaces of the Message Exchange Facility are all logical rather than literal, and the actual mechanics of the facility are unknown to its caller. If the facility is called with an improper symbolic parameter which does not match the symbolic names known to the facility, the offending process is immediately stopped and put into a debugging-mode halt state. Given that a new system is exhaustively tested prior to its release, the assumption is that all such interprocess mis-linkage bugs will be intercepted and corrected during the testing phase.

Assuming, even, that such a bug is not intercepted prior to delivery, but manifests itself at the customer's installation during an active production session, then we still guarantee against loss of signal, given that the signal was not issued at all and that this condition was promptly intercepted and reported. The prevailing authority (composing room supervisor, chief operator, chief programmer) may then remove the offending program from the system, re-install its proven predecessor, and re-issue the interprocess signal. In other words, we do not claim to produce impeccably correct software, although we do try very hard to do so; we do, however, guarantee that occasional software errors will not cause an undetected loss of signal. Thus, while the Message Exchange Facility is designed to be fault tolerant insofar as runtime conditions are concerned, it is designed to be fault intolerant insofar as coding errors are concerned.

The coding error fault intolerance applies to loss of signal only! We have no way of checking that a program which should address itself to mailbox 'a' does not address itself to mailbox 'b' instead, so long as 'b' is a valid mailbox name. On the other hand, we were not overly concerned about this type of coding error, given that the TYPESET-10 software is produced by a dedicated team of conscientious programmers which would not intentionally miscode such a reference; rather, we were concerned about some innocent typographical error which could conceivably lead to an elusive and hard to find loss-of-signal bug.

Note that this reference-by-association is simply the runtime application of long established assembly/compilation techniques, where the assembler/compiler complains about references to undeclared symbolic names.

MESSAGE SCHEDULING

The interprocess communication mechanisms that we may find described in the Literature typically provide for a First In, First Out message queueing service. In our specific case, such simple queueing could not be adopted; rather, we needed an interprocess communication mechanism where messages could be received in an order dictated by their specific scheduling parameters, as distinct from the order in which they were sent. Consider the following cases;

- JUSTIF Normally, JUSTIF will process queued texts in the order in which they were sent. The interactive CLASAD program, however, needs immediate justification services from JUSTIF. Namely, the CLASAD operator typically receives classified advertisement placements over the telephone, and is supposed to be able to quote to the customer - who is on the other end of the telephone line - the price of the ad. That price can only be derived from the number of lines actually occupied by the finally printed ad. The operator has to type the text of the ad into the system, issue a justification command, and wait for the ad to be processed by JUSTIF, following which the system will display the accurate price. It must therefore be possible for JUSTIF to identify any pending requests for the processing of classified advertisements, and service those requests promptly, in order that CLASAD's response wait time be kept as short as possible.

- TYPESET A typesetting machine is normally equipped with a limited number of typeface setups. These setups may be changed, manually, as the need arises. A text which is queued up for actual typesetting may require a typeface setup which is not currently available on any of the machines, thus the text cannot be output, for obvious reasons. The process which drives a particular type-setting machine can therefore only accept texts requiring typeface setups which are currently available on the machine. The process must be able to ignore temporarily all texts requiring typeface setups which are currently unavailable on the machine. When the typeface setup of some machine has been manually changed, all pending requests corresponding to the new setups must automatically be recognized and serviced.

- RESCHEDULING We had also to take into account the possibility that some eleventh-hour change in scheduling may take place. For example, a last minute news story may have to replace some previously scheduled less important story. In such a case, the preempted story may well be in some intermediate processing stage within the system; the composing room supervisor must have the ability to intercept and kill the preempted story in order to relieve the system of this unnecessary computational burden. For another example, it should be possible for the composing room supervisor to issue a rescheduling command which would give the highest service priority to a certain class of texts (e.g., to all stockmarket quotation texts) because of reasons having to do with the actual newspaper production.

To achieve these goals, each interprocess signal contains a special scheduling parameter, whose value is set by the signalling process. What this value is, and how it is to be interpreted depends on the specific mailbox used. Given that each mailbox is associated with a specific function, it has a distinct set of scheduling parameters which are appropriate for that function, and which are known by convention to both the signalling and the receiving process (see 'IPC-Setup' in Spier and Organick [22] and in Spier [23]). The receiving process may inspect the entire collection of scheduling parameters pertaining to all of the queued up messages, and select for reception that message which has the highest scheduling priority. The selection algorithm itself, which is local to the receiving process, may be modified dynamically at runtime, to provide the rescheduling capability mentioned earlier.

IMPLEMENTATION CONSIDERATIONS

The most important implementation consideration had to do with the guarantee against loss of signal. We have therefore decided to keep the mailboxes as disk resident files, so as to guarantee their continued existence across potential system crashes (be they total or partial). Experience had shown that the incidence of a physical disk-head crash - resulting in physical damage to stored information - is at most once every two years, and may in all probability be totally avoided through conscientious and meticulous equipment maintenance procedures. Moreover, the consequences of even this slight chance of mishap may be greatly reduced by the periodic saving of mailboxes which are copied onto another independent backup disk unit.

Having dismissed this consideration from our minds, we had to consider the issue of mailbox integrity. Assuming that the sending of a message entailed the disjoint writing of two individual disk records, the possibility existed that a system crash would occur after the first record was written, yet prior to the writing of the second record, resulting in a meaningless and inconsistent state of the mailbox, hence in loss of signal. We had to guarantee that the writing of the mailbox file be done as a single, indivisible action (see Dijkstra [14] and Spier [23]). This implied that we had to be cognizant of the 'disk record' concept, and - in turn - led to the design decision to delimit any amount of information within the mailbox to the actual size of a TYPESET-10 disk record, which is currently set at 128_{10} words (each word being a 36-bit quantity).

Each mailbox consists of two major items, being: (1) the mailbox directory, and (2) the mailbox information. The state of the mailbox is determined from its directory, exclusively. The directory, which occupies exactly one disk record, contains three threaded lists, as follows:

- EMPTY LIST The list of empty message slots which can be used for message
  signalling.
- ACTIVE MESSAGE LIST List of messages which have been signalled but not yet
  received.
- INACTIVE MESSAGE LIST List of messages which have been received but not yet
  deleted. As will be described in the following, message reception does not
  cause the automatic deletion of that message from the mailbox, but only its removal from the list of active messages to the list of inactive ones.

The directory has a fixed capacity a maximum of 500_{10} queued-up messages, this
capacity having been dictated by the physical size limitation inherent to a single
disk record. When a message is signalled, the following actions take place:

step-1:   Open the specified mailbox file under mutual exclusion conditions. The
          operating system monitor provides mutual exclusion services whereby only
          a single process at a time may gain access to a file [13].

step-2:   Read in the mailbox's directory record.

step-3:   Locate an available message slot in the Empty List.

step-4:   Determine the physical file record corresponding to the available message
          slot, and read in that record. The operating system has provisions allow-
          ing for the random accessing of individual file records [13].

step-5:   Write the message into that block and output the block back onto disk.

step-6:   Update the mailbox's directory, appending the new message to the Active
          Message List.

step-7:   Write the directory record back onto disk, and release the mailbox file
          from its mutual exclusion state.

Message reception follows an essentially identical ritual, where in step-3 one
locates a message in the Active Message List, and where in step-6 the received - but
not yet deleted - message is removed from the Active Message List to the Inactive
Message List. As can be clearly seen, the state of the mailbox is determined by its
directory only. Suppose that message signalling is attempted, and that the system
crashes somewhere between step-1 and step-7. With the exclusion of a disk-crash - a
low probability eventuality which we find tolerable - the entire directory record
either has or has not been written back onto the disk. If it has, then the message
was successfully signalled; if it has not, then the mailbox's directory is in its
former consistent state and the signalling simply did not take place.

Given that we consider the writing of the directory record to be an indivisible
operation, the mailbox may be either in the pre-step-7 state or in the post-step-7
state, but never in an inconsistent inbetween state. If signalling has succeeded,
then an appropriate completion code is returned to the signalling process. Failure
to receive such a successful completion code constitutes prima facie evidence that
the signalling did not take place, and results in the alerting of the operator and/or

composing room supervisor.

Thus, the Message Exchange Facility's guarantee against loss of signal is predicated on the following three conditions: (1) the message must have been signalled successfully, in the sense that step-7 must have been carried to successful completion, (2) the possibility of a physical disk-head crash does not arise, and (3) the Message Exchange Facility program is properly coded and free of bugs. Concerning this last point, it is clearly evident that the Message Exchange's desired properties of determinism and reliability are inextricably related to the correctness of its actual implementation; to this end, we have coded MX using our especially developed structured programming and program validation techniques (see Spier [26,27]), paying the most meticulous attention to the program's implementation and to the validation of its correct behavior.

THE MESSAGE EXCHANGE FUNCTIONS

In describing the various Message Exchange Facility functions, we make use of the syntactic notation proposed by Spier [27]:

$$cp := FUNC([I_1, I_2, \ldots, I_m], [O_1, O_2, \ldots, O_n]);$$

where:

- cp is a completion predicate variable whose value is set by the invoked function. By convention, condition cp=0 is interpreted as a successful completion code. If the value of cp is non-zero, that non-zero value is interpreted as a diagnostic code indicating: (1) that the function activation failed, and (2) what the specific reason for failure was.

- $FUNC$ is the name of the invoked function.

- $[I_1, I_2, \ldots, I_m]$ is the (possibly null) list of input arguments.

- $[O_1, O_2, \ldots, O_n]$ is the (possibly null) list of output arguments.

The following symbolic names are used in order to refer to specific call arguments. They represent the corresponding data structures:

- mailbox is a symbolic mailbox name in character string form (e.g., 'justif', 'typeset' etc.).
- schedule is an array of symbolic scheduling parameters, in character string form. Their exact value is determined by the specific nature of each individual mailbox. The array may be of zero-length, implying that no explicit scheduling is specified, in which case default parameters are provided.
- message is an array of words constituting the bulk information which is to be signalled. The Message Exchange Facility simply treats this item as a single block of bulk data, without inspecting or interpreting its value.

- msg_name   is a guaranteed unique message name which is generated by the Message Exchange Facility. The value of this name is structured in such a manner as to provide a direct access pointer to the message itself, within the mailbox.
- mbx_state   is an array of pairs {s,n} where s is a schedule item (i.e., an array of symbolic scheduling parameters) and n is an msg_name item (i.e., a unique message name). The mbx_state array may be of zero-length, indicating that there are no active messages in the mailbox.
- msg_origin   is an array of system-generated control information specifying the origin of a message (e.g., name of sending program (such as PRUFED), name of sending process, name of sending operator (if any), time at which message was sent, etc.).

The main Message Exchange functions are listed below. Note that a function name is prefixed with the corresponding facility's acronym (in this case 'MX') in accordance with our structured programming conventions [26]:

cp:=*MX_SIGNAL*([mailbox, schedule, message],[msg_name]);

cp:=*MX_STATE*([mailbox],[mbx_state]);

cp:=*MX_RECEIVE*([mailbox,msg_name],[msg_origin, message]);

cp:=*MX_DELETE*([mailbox,msg_name],[ ]);

cp:=*MX_RESTORE*([mailbox],[ ]);

Note that all control-item input parameters are symbolic names, recognized (within MX) by association. Any failure to identify such a control item (with the exception of an msg_name input argument) is interpreted as a runtime mis-linkage bug, causing an immediate abort of the offending process.

The signalling of a message is straightforward and self-evident from the functional specification of *MX_SIGNAL*. Note that *MX* returns the unique msg_name to the signaller. As can be seen from the remaining functions, this unique message name is the only means of retrieving a message from a mailbox; by returning this unique name value to the signaller, we allow the signalling process to retrieve its own message at a later point in time (e.g., for the purpose of ascertaining whether or not the message has actually been received within a finite period of time).

A receiving process is typically of a cyclic nature. Figure 3 is a stylized representation of the logic of a typical receiving process, expressed in a free-form programming 'language' notation. For reasons of convenience, we have dispensed with explicit variable declarations in order to enhance the algorithm's lucidity. The while statement refers to an unspecified completion code value returned in cp. The *SLEEP* function implies process deactivation pending message reception in the specified mailbox.

```
receiver:begin
     cp:=MX_RESTORE([mailbox],[ ]);
loop: while (mailbox contains active messages)
          begin
               cp:=MX_STATE([mailbox],[mbx_state]);
               {apply selection algorithm to scheduling parameters and select
                highest priority message by choosing an appropriate msg_name}
               cp:=MX_RECEIVE([mailbox,msg_name ,[msg_origin,message]);
               {do the appropriate processing of the message}
               cp:=MX_DELETE([mailbox,msg_name], [ ]);
          end;
          cp:=SLEEP([mailbox],[ ]);
          goto loop;
end;
```

Figure 3: Formalized representation of the logic of a receiving process.
         Note the start-up of a receiving process always implies an
         initial call to *MX_RESTORE*, which has the effect of restoring
         all messages which were received - but not yet deleted - to
         the Active Message List, to insure against loss of signal due
         to the interruption of message processing.

As mentioned, message reception does not imply the immediate removal of the
message from the mailbox, but rather its removal from the Active Message List and its
addition to the Inactive Message List. The *MX_STATE* function returns information
pertaining only to active messages, ignoring the messages belonging to the Inactive
Message List. The *MX_DELETE* function removes the specified message from the Inactive Message List, effectively deleting that message from the mailbox. Thus, if
the system (or merely that specific receiving process) crashes between the reception
of a message and its deletion, the message itself is guaranteed to be still in the
mailbox, albeit in an 'invisible' state. Note that a receiving process always
starts its activity by issuing an *MX_RESTORE* directive, whose purpose it is to append
the entire Inactive Message List to the mailbox's Active Message List , and to reset
the Inactive Message List to null. Thus, the casual starting of the system, or the
starting of a specific process that had crashed, will effect the reactivation of any
message whose processing was not successfully completed. At worst, we may have
processed a certain message twice, which will be easily detectable by the composing
room employees (in the form of redundant text composition). We will, however, never
lose a message signal due to such a crash!

THE TECHNICAL REALITIES

Our purpose in making this presentation was to describe a real-life case study, showing how given product requirements and design considerations have led us to a specific technical solution. We therefore presented the functional interface of the Message Exchange Facility in an idealized fashion, which we felt to be most meaningful to the reader.

In reality, once these functional specifications were arrived at, we applied further ingenuity to the actual implementation in order to make the mechanism as runtime efficient as possible. Even though we did not elaborate on these additional technicalities - which would only detract from the paper's readability - we decided to present the following technical details, in order to give the reader an idea of the kind of refinements which were further incorporated into this mechanism.

By virtue of the cyclic nature of the receiving process, it is evident that each call to *MX_DELETE* is followed by a call to *MX_RECEIVE*. Because of the inevitable input/output operations required by each mailbox access (dictated by the fact that the mailboxes are disk resident), such a mailbox access entails a non-trivial expenditure in time. We therefore expanded the *MX_RECEIVE* function to have an additional input argument named old_message which is the unique name of the previous message (i.e., the message which was successfully processed during the previous iteration through the receiving process' cycle). Thus the *MX_RECEIVE* function provides the dual services of deleting the previous message from the Inactive Message List, while at the same time returning the newly selected message in the normal manner. This allowed us to dispense with the explicit call to *MX_DELETE* (although that function, itself, has of course been retained in its described form). Also, the mailbox structure is by far more elaborate than suggested earlier. For example, all of the *MX_STATE* information is concentrated in a single physical locality (within the mailbox) to provide for the highspeed extraction of that information.

Thus, the actual implementation of the mechanism is satisfactorily efficient; each mailbox access takes on the average 4-5 physical disk accesses (including the implicit disk accesses performed by the operating system monitor for the purpose of retrieving the mailbox file), and needs an average of 30ms worth of *CPU* time. Compared to the actual system resource requirements for the text processing activities, the overhead incurred by this specific implementation of the Message Exchange Facility is effectively insignificant.

As mentioned, an interprocess signal usually transmits to the receiving process the file system name of a text. As it turns out, a non-trivial portion of the texts handled in the newspaper business is of very limited size (e.g., a classified advertisement, a single headline, a short news bulletin). We therefore provided for the transmission of bulk data as part of the *MX* message (the amount being limited by the physical size of a single disk record, for reasons given earlier), and all texts which fit into a single message capacity are automatically transmitted as part of the message. Thus, all short texts need not be stored away in individual files, providing significant savings in runtime overhead.

We have additional *MX* functions such as *MX_PURGE* which resets an entire mailbox to its empty state, and *MX_LIST* which provides a very detailed and verbose listing of the contents of a mailbox, for inspection purposes. Also, we have a special supervisory process which accepts interactive commands from the composition room supervisor's console, enabling the supervisor to manually intervene in the inter-process message traffic as necessity arises.

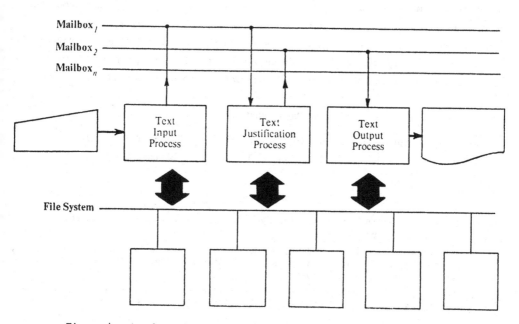

Figure 4: A schematic representation of the TYPESET-10 system as a software analogy to a hardware architecture.

As shown by Figure 4, the effect of our implementation is to provide the software analogy of a classical hardware architecture, where the various mailboxes may be thought of as being signal buses and where the file system may be thought of as being the data bus; we may think of the various autonomous processes as being 'black box' plug-in modules, each of which may arbitrarily be plugged in and out of the system without affecting the autonomous behavior of all other active modules.

In the description of the receiving process' logic (i.e., Figure 3), all function activation were of the

    cp:=*FUNC*([input arguments],[output arguments]);

form, even though no testing of the cp completion predicate values was demonstrated (as mentioned, we refrained from incorporating into that model program any technicalities which would have detracted from its lucidity). Concerning this completion predicate value, a case of interest is that where following an invocation of *MX_STATE* a suitable message name is selected, to be used as the input argument for the *MX_RECEIVE* function that follows. A possible failure code from *MX_RECEIVE* would indicate that the specified message could not be located on the Active Message List. This case is typical of the situation where we have several processes engaged in the same concurrent activity (for example, the two JUSTIF processes mentioned earlier), and where - because of some race condition - two or more processes selected the very same message for reception, whereupon one of them managed to attain the mailbox first and receive that message. In that case, all other processes - which attempted to get that very same message - are cognizant of that race condition, and select some other message for processing. We mention this fact in order to emphasize the synergistic[a] nature of our processes; these processes may simply be activated (i.e., 'plugged in') in the most arbitrary manner, whereupon they automatically engage in an interference-free cooperative effort to throughput as much data as possible across the system. □

ACKNOWLEDGEMENT

We wish to express our thanks to the members of the TYPESET-10 development group, who have contributed to the successful completion of this project.

REFERENCES

[1] R. M. Balzer, Ports - A Method for Dynamic Interprogram and Job Control, in Proc. 1971 SJCC, pp. 485-490.

[2] A. J. Bernstein, G. D. Detlefsen, R. H. Kerr, Process Control and Communication, in Proc. 2nd ACM Symposium on Operating Systems Principles, Princeton University, October 1969, pp. 60-66.

[3] C. Betourne, et al, Process Management and Resource Sharing in the Multiaccess System ESOPE, in Comm. of the ACM, 13 12(1970), pp. 727-733.

[4] P. Brinch Hansen, The Nucleus of a Multiprogramming System, in Comm. of the ACM, 13 4(1970), pp. 238-242.

[5] P. Brinch Hansen, Structured Multiporgramming, in Comm. of the ACM, 15 7(1972), pp. 574-578.

[6] P. Brinch Hansen, A Comparison of Two Synchronizing Concepts, in Acta Informatica, 1 3(1972), pp. 190-199.

[7] P. Brinch Hansen, A Reply to Comments on 'A Comparison of Two Synchronizing Concepts', in Acta Informatica, 2 2(1973), pp. 189-190.

[8] R. H. Campbell, The Specification of Process Synchronization by Path Expressions, in Proc. Symposium on the Theoretical and Practical Aspects of Operating Systems, IRIA, Rocquencourt (France), April 1974, pp. 93-106.

---

[a] From Webster's New Collegiate Dictionary:
synergism n, Cooperative action of discrete agencies such that the total effect is greater than the sum of the effects taken separately.

synergistic adj, having the capacity to act in synergism.

[9] J. M. Chambers, A User Controlled Synchronization Method, in Operating Systems Review, ACM SIGOPS 7 2(1973), pp. 16-25.

[10] C. Carr, S. Crocker, V. Cerf, Host/Host Communication Protocol in the ARPA Network, in Proc. 1970 SJCC, pp. 589-597.

[11] P. J. Courtois, F. Heymans, D. L. Parnas, Concurrent Control with 'Readers' and 'writers', in Comm. of the ACM, 14 10(1971), pp. 667-668.

[12] P. J. Courtois, F. Heymans, D. L. Parnas, Comments on 'A Comparison of Two Synchronizing Concepts', in Acta Informatica, 1 4(1972), pp. 375-376.

[13] Digital Equipment Corporation, The PDP10 Assembly Language Handbook, Maynard, Massachusetts, (1974).

[14] E. W. Dijkstra, Cooperating Sequential Processes, in Programming Languages, F. Genuys (ed.), Academic Press (1968), pp. 43-112.

[15] E. W. Dijkstra, Information Streams Sharing a Finite Buffer, in Information Processing Letters, 1 (1972), pp. 179-180.

[16] P. Gilbert, J. W. Chandler, Interference Between Communicating Parallel Processes, in Comm. of the ACM, 15 6(1972), pp. 427-437.

[17] A. N. Habermann, Synchronization of Communicating Processes, in Comm of the ACM, 15 3(1972), pp. 171-176.

[18] J. J. Horning, B. Randell, Process Structuring, in ACM Computing Surveys, 5 1 (1973), pp. 5-30.

[19] J. B. Johnston, The Structure of Multiple Activity Algorithms, in Proc. 2nd ACM Symposium on Operating Systems Principles, Princeton University, October, 1969, pp. 80-82.

[20] B. W. Lampson, A Scheduling Philosophy for Multiprocessing Systems, in Comm. of the ACM, 11 5(1968), pp. 347-360.

[21] L. Pouzin, Network Protocols, in Proc. NATO Advanced Study Institute, University of Sussex, Brighton, England, September 1973.

[22] M. J. Spier, E. I. Organick, The Multics Interprocess Communication Facility, in Proc. 2nd ACM Symposium on Operating Systems Principles, Princeton University, October 1969, pp. 83-91.

[23] M. J. Spier, Process Communication Prerequisites, or the IPC-Setup Revisited, in Proc. 1973 Sagamore Conference on Parallel Processing, Syracuse University, pp. 79-88.

[24] M. J. Spier, The Experimental Implementation of a Comprehensive Intermodule Communication Mechanism, in Proc. 1973 Sagamore Conference on Parallel Processing, Syracuse University, pp. 89.

[25] M. J. Spier, A Critical Look at the State of our Science, in Operating Systems Review, ACM SIGOPS 8 2(1974), pp. 9-15.

[26] M. J. Spier, The TYPESET-10 Codex Programmaticus, internal publication, Digital Equipment Corporation (1974).

[27] M. J. Spier, Etude Systemologique de la Maitrise de Complexite, Appliquee a la Synthese des Systemes Informatiques, in preparation (1974).

[28] P. G. Sorensen, Interprocess Communication in Real-Time Systems, in Proc.
      4th ACM Symposium on Operating Systems Principles, T. J. Watson Research
      Institute, October 1973, pp. 1-7.

[29] H. Vantilborgh, A. Van Lamsweerde, On an Extension of Dijkstra's Semaphore
      Primitives, in Structure et Programmation des Calculateurs, Seminairs, IRIA,
      Rocquencourt (France),(1973), pp. 31-40.

[30] N. Wirth, On Multiprogramming, Machine Coding and Computer Organization, in
      Comm. of the ACM, 12 9(1969), pp. 489-498.

[31] C. M. Wood, An Example in Synchronization of Cooperative Processes: Theory
      and Practice, in Operating Systems Review, ACM SIGOPS 7 3(1973), pp. 10-18.

OPTIMAL RESOURCE ALLOCATION AND SCHEDULING AMONG PARALLEL PROCESSES[a]

ART LEW
Department of Information
and Computer Sciences
University of Hawaii
Honolulu, Hawaii 96822

Abstract -- The problem of optimally allocating limited resources among competing processes may be formulated as a problem in finding the shortest path in a
directed graph, provided a quantitative measure of the performance of each process
as a function of its resource allocation can be suitably defined. If this measure
is also a function of time, scheduling problems arise so that optimal allocations
become time-varying and may depend upon various precedence relations or constraints
among the processes. Dynamic programming approaches to such allocation and scheduling problems are presented in the context of parallel processing.

INTRODUCTION

In this paper we discuss some optimization problems that arise in the study of
parallel processing systems. (For an overview, see [1,2].) Informally, a process
is an entity ("task" [3]) that requires resources from a supervisory operating system in order to execute. These resources include, at the least, processing time and
memory locations. Once allocated requested resources (possibly in part only), execution of a process may be initiated. Execution may then terminate autonomously, or
else by force in the case of preemptibility, upon which held resources are returned
to the system. A process is <u>active</u> during the intervals of time between initiations
and terminations. Its resource requirements, and its allocation, may vary while active. When a process has no further resource requirements, we say it is completed;
a process once activated is incomplete until then. A parallel processing system is
one where incomplete processes may coexist (be concurrent). If active processes may
coexist, we say the system is multiprocessing; otherwise, we say multiprogramming.

The general problem with which we are concerned is that of <u>optimally</u> allocating
resources among competing parallel processes. By "optimal" we mean with respect to
formal quantitative criteria, usually chosen subjectively. This subjectivity arises
because our models must compromise between the detailed complexities demanded by re-
alism and the simplifying assumptions necessitated by practicality. Furthermore,
numerous figures of merit have been suggested -- e.g. throughput, turnaround time,
processor utilization, memory fragmentation -- which may be incommensurable and even
conflicting. The difficulties present such a major obstacle that most parallel

---

[a]Supported by the U.S. Army Research Office.

processing operating systems do not seek optimality, but rather are heuristically "tuned" (perhaps by simulation) for good or efficient performance. It is uncertain how "tuned" allocations would compare with theoretically "optimal" ones, as the problem of determining the latter has gone largely unresolved. We address it herein.

Our underlying assumption regarding the nature of resources is that a limited quantity exists for allocation at any time, so that not all processes can be granted their resource requirements simultaneously. We also assume that resource units are indistinguishable, so that the main problem is deciding upon the sizes of allocations. If a process must be granted its full requirement in order to execute, we say it is "peremptory". Allocations among peremptory processes may be made generally on the basis of common scheduling considerations. A nonperemptory process can execute given only a part of its resource requirements, at a cost relative to its performance given a full allocation. This (partial) allocation cost provides the basis for allocation decisions among nonperemptory (and peremptory) processes.

In Section 2, we discuss the basic (static) allocation problem, where allocation costs are (for each process) given functions of the sizes of the allocations. This problem can be formulated as that of finding the shortest path in a directed graph, and solved, for example, by dynamic programming. In Section 3, we consider the more realistic time-varying problem, where allocation costs are functions of time as therefore optimal allocations are also. Reallocation costs must then be introduced. Scheduling problems also arise since processes can be delayed (inactive) if resources are withheld. In Section 4, we investigate "control" aspects of scheduling in the resource allocation context. In particular, we describe methods for treating precedence constraints, redundancies, and deadlocks. We conclude with a discussion of the applicability and limitations of the formulations presented herein.

The basic objectives of this paper are theoretical and pedagogic rather than practical. We wish to establish here how formal mathematical oprimization techniques can be applied in principle to a variety of important parallel processing allocation problems. A consideration of pragmatic aspects, which must be related to a specific application (i.e. a specific type of resource and environment), is deferred. We remark that the application which motivated this study is memory allocation in paging systems [4]. A survey of numerous other application areas is also presented: these include storage partitioning or overlaying, page allotment and replacement, dynamic table allocation, buffer allocation, CPU and file scheduling, and decision table conversion.

2. THE STATIC ALLOCATION PROBLEM

We formulate here the basic problem of allocating a finite set of resources among independent parallel processes in an "optimal" manner. Optimality must, of course, be relative to a specified (generally subjectively chosen) quantitative criterion. Let $c_k(q_k)$ denote a nonnegative real measure of the expected performance of process P_k given an allocation of integral size q_k. We assume that the "allocation cost" $c_k(q_k)$ for each process P_k is independent of $c_j(q_j)$ for any other process P_j; this is a "separability" assumption. Suppose there are N processes $\{P_i\}$ and M total units of a single resource type, (Vector equations can be written for multiple resource types; however, optimal algorithms then generally become impractical for dimensionality reasons.) Then the optimal (minimal-cost) <u>static</u> resource allocation problem may be formally stated as

$$\min_{\{q_k\}} \sum_{k=1}^{N} c_k(q_k), \quad \text{subject to} \quad \sum_{k=1}^{N} q_k \le M,$$

where we require $0 \le q_k \le M$ for each k. We remark that the separability assumption permits us to allocate resources to processes sequentially in any arbitrary order.

For convenience, we introduce a dummy process P_0 representing unused resources, so that the inequality constraint above may be replaced by an equality $\sum_{k=0}^{N} q_k = M$; $c_0(q_0)$ is thus a measure of inefficient utilization of resources. If for any reason all resources must be allocated, we may let $c_0(q_0) = \infty$ for $q_0 > 0$, $c_0(0) = 0$. We may of course let $c_0(q_0) = 0$ for all q_0 if nothing else. The introduction of P_0 permits withholding of resources as may be necessary to avoid deadlocks or other scheduling problems.

In order to solve the discrete optimization problem we have posed, we first reformulate it abstractly as one of finding the shortest path in a graph. A dynamic programming solution to this routing problem is then given.

2.1. <u>Routing Problem Formulation</u>

Let $P = \{P_0, P_1, \ldots, P_N\}$ be an augmented (as described above) set of competing processes, and M be the number of units of available resources. Let $c_k(q)$ be given, $q = 0, 1, \ldots, M$, for each $k = 0, 1, \ldots, N$.

<u>Definition</u>. An <u>allocation graph</u> $G = (V,E,C,\ell)$ is a labelled directed graph [5,6], where V is a set of vertices, E is a set of arcs, C is a set of arc labels, and ℓ is a labelling function, defined as follows:

(a) $V = \{[k,i] \mid k \in \{0, 1, \ldots, N+1\}, i \in \{0, 1, \ldots, M\}\}$;

(b) $E = \{(a,b) \mid a = [k_a, i_a] \in V, b = [k_b, i_b] \in V, k_b = k_a + 1, i_b \le i_a\}$;

(c) C = set of nonnegative real numbers (arc lengths);

(d) $\ell: E \to C$ such that $\ell(a,b) = c_{k_a}(i_a - i_b)$.

Each vertex $[k,i]$ is associated with the <u>state</u> of having i units of available resources, some portion of which is to be allocated to process k, where allocations are made sequentially in order of the indices (justified by the separability assumption). An arc $([k,i],[k+1,i-q])$ represents the state transition resulting from allocating q units of resources to process k, at a cost $c_k(q)$ given by the arc label. A path is a sequence of arcs (or allocations) whose length (cost) is the sum of the individual arc labels.

Proposition 1. The optimal static allocation problem is equivalent to the problem of finding the shortest path in the allocation graph from vertex [0,M] to vertex [N+1,0].

The allocation graph has $(N+2)(M+1)$ vertices and $(N+1)(M+1)(M+2)/2$ arcs; of these, 2 M vertices and $M(M+1)$ arcs cannot lie on the shortest path. It may also be characterized as irreflexive, asymmetric, and transitive.

Example 1 (Storage Partitioning). Let us suppose that the resource to be allocated is main memory space. Our underlying assumption here is that each process (program) can execute in a range of partition sizes, where the cost (efficiency) of its execution is a function of the partition size -- as is the case in an overlaying environment. Let $c_k(q_k)$ be defined as the expected number of overlay calls made by program P_k (proportionate to its expected execution time) given an allocation of size q_k. This function can be determined from a knowledge of the frequency of jumps (calls) in the program [7] and its overlay structure [8]. (A discussion of how the overlay structure for a particular program might be determined, a special kind of "packing" problem, is given in [9].)

2.2 Dynamic Programming Solution

An allocation graph is an acyclic directed graph with nonnegative labels, so numerous methods are available for determining its shortest path [10]. We adopt here the method of dynamic programming [5,11,12], which is relatively inefficient but is readily generalizable (as we shall see).

For G as defined above, let $f(v)$ be the length of the shortest path from any vertex v to vertex [N+1,0]; let $f(v) = \infty$ if no such path exists.

Lemma. $f(a) = \min_{b \in E_a} \{\ell(a,b) + f(b)\}$, where $E_a = \{b \,|\, (a,b) \in E\}$.

This recursive functional equation follows directly from Bellman's Principle of Optimality [11]. By definition of f, we also have the terminal condition $f([N+1,0]) = 0$. The solution to the routing problem can then be found in the process of determining $f([0,M])$. The functional equation is to be first solved "backwards" starting from the terminal condition, followed by a "reconstruction" process to identify the arcs in the shortest path.

The algorithm, applied canonically, requires on the order of 2NM memory locations for the function f, and on the order of $NM^2/2$ addition and comparison operations; subscripting operations are neglected. (Recall that the number of vertices is of order NM). The complexity of the problem is less than that associated with finding shortest paths in arbitrary graphs since the allocation graph is transitive.

3. TIME-VARYING ALLOCATIONS

In general, $c_k(q_k)$ is a time-varying function, $c_k(q_k,t)$, in which case reallocations should be made "every so often", at a set of discrete reallocation times
$\{t_1, t_2, t_3, \ldots\}$. In discretizing time, we assume that the functions $c_k(q_k,t_i)$ accurately represent the allocation costs during the entire time interval (t_i,t_{i+1}).
One approach to making time-varying allocations is to resolve the basic routing problem at each time t_i. That is, we may let $c_k(q_k) = c_k(q_k,t_i)$, obtaining the optimal
allocation $q_k^*(t_i)$ for process P_k in the interval (t_i,t_{i+1}). The time-varying allocation problem can thereby be reduced to a sequence of (time-independent) static allocation problems. We call this the _sequential_ allocation procedure.

Example 2 (Page Allotment). Let us suppose that the resource to be allocated
is page frames in a paging system. The policy of granting each program its "working
set size" [13] is inadequate for several reasons, one of which is that of determining
this size in the first place. Of more significance is the fact that the policy is
not optimal, being designed primarily to prevent "thrashing" [14], not necessarily
to obtain best performance. The fact that time-varying allotments are generally
better than fixed allotments is established in [15] under Gaussian working set assumptions. Let $c_k(q_k,t)$ be defined as the expected page-fault cost of program P_k
given a page frame allotment of size q_k at time t. This function may be determined
using the cost evaluation method of [16, Example 3b] or [17] for any given (realiz-
able) replacement algorithm assuming a Markov program model. Methods for estimating
the function based upon structural rather than probabilistic information are discussed in [4].

3.1. Reallocation Times

The times at which resources should be reallocated depends upon many factors.
In nonpreemptive systems, reallocations would only take place when a process runs to
completion. In preemptive systems, however, reallocation times would be determined
by scheduling considerations, depending upon, for example, such factors as time-
slices, process blockings, or performance measurements. We assume herein a given
scheduling environment where reallocation times are not controllable variables (with
respect to the optimal resource allocation problem). This does not imply that reallocation times are fixed; they may happen to be so in time-slicing systems, but
they may arise nondeterministically otherwise.

Reallocation times need not be known _a priori_ if instead the allocation cost
functions $c_k(q,t_i)$ can be determined at each time t_i. The sequential allocation procedure may be used in this event. Furthermore, the costs may depend not on t_i but on
i, in which case the times need not be known at all. If a priori knowledge of the
set of reallocation times $\{t_i\}$ is given, and if $\{c_k(q,t_i)\}$ are pre-calculable functions, then the optimal allocations $\{q_k^*(t_i)\}$ can be precomputed (prior to t_1). We
show in the next section that q_k^* can be determined as a function not just of t_i but

also of the allocations at time t_{i-1}, so that reallocations can be made adaptively.

An "optimal" set of reallocation times, in the sense of minimizing unnecessary or unprofitable reallocations, can be found in principle as follows. We first assume that time is a discrete variable equal to integral multiples of a basic time unit (e.g., the computer instruction cycle time or some larger quantum), and that the allocation cost functions can be determined for each instant of time. The allocation problem can then be solved, yielding a sequence of allocations $q_k^*(t_i)$. An "optimal" set of reallocation times would then be given by the set $\{t_i \mid \exists k \ni q_k^*(t_i) \neq q_k^*(t_{i-1})\}$. Alternatively, we may consider the set $\{t_i \mid \exists k \ni c_k(q_k(t_{i-1}), t_i) - c_k(q_k^*(t_i), t_i) > V_o\}$. A priori calculation of these sets is considered impractical, but heuristic approximations may prove feasible. On the other hand, we may monitor the performance of the system and make reallocations only when the performance drops below some prespecified level (a system parameter, cf. [18]). A more formal approach is described below.

3.2 Reallocatión Costs

In the above, we have neglected the fact that each reallocation of resources can only be done at a price -- in part because of the overhead required to change the amount of resources allocated to any process, and in part because of the calculations required to re-solve the routing problem. The latter, which we term the "re-evaluation" cost, is assumed herein to be a constant V_1 (which can be approximated by "analysis of algorithms" techniques [6]); this cost appears best minimized by performance monitoring, as mentioned above. The cost of "transferring" resources is a constant V_2 plus a function of the amount of change and/or the magnitude of the new (or old) allocation. Let $h_k(q, \delta q, t_i)$ be the total reallocation cost (including constants V_1 and V_2) incurred in changing the allocation of process P_k from $q_k(t_{i-1}) = q - \delta q$ to $q_k(t_i) = q$ at time t_i. We assume here a priori knowledge of the functions h_k and c_k. We note that if h_k is a monotonic function of δq, unprofitable reallocations would tend to be minimized.

Suppose reallocation decisions are made at the finite set of times $\{t_1, t_2, \ldots, t_L\}$. Let $Q_i = (q_0(t_i), \ldots, q_N(t_i))$ be the <u>allocation state</u> of the system at time t_i, $C(Q_i, t_i) = \sum_{k=0}^{N} c_k(q_k(t_i), t_i)$ be its associated cost, and $H(Q_i, \delta Q_i, t_i) = \sum_{k=0}^{N} h_k(q_k(t_i), \delta q_k(t_i), t_i)$, where $\delta Q_i = (\delta q_0(t_i), \ldots, \delta q_N(t_i))$. The cost of an initial allocation state Q_1 followed by a single transition (reallocation) to state Q_2 is given by

$$H(Q_1, Q_1 - Q_0, t_1) + C(Q_1, t_1) + H(Q_2, Q_2 - Q_1, t_2) + C(Q_2, t_2).$$

We write $\delta Q_\ell = Q_\ell - Q_{\ell-1}$, and define $Q_0 = 0$. The cost of L transitions is then

$$\sum_{\ell=1}^{L} [H(Q_\ell, \delta Q_\ell, t_\ell) + C(Q_\ell, t_\ell)],$$

which is to be minimized over the set $\{\delta Q_1, \ldots, \delta Q_L\}$. This new L-stage allocation problem can also be solved by means of dynamic programming.

Let $F(Q,\ell)$ be the minimum achievable allocation cost of $L+1-\ell$ transitions for an original allocation Q; i.e.

$$F(Q,\ell) = \min_{\{\delta Q_i\}} \{ \sum_{i=\ell}^{L} [H(Q_i,\delta Q_i,t_i) + C(Q_i,t_i)] \}$$

for $1 \leq \ell \leq L$, where $Q_{\ell-1} = Q$ and $F(Q,L+1) = 0$ for all Q.

<u>Proposition 2.</u> The optimal solution can be found by solving the dynamic programming functional equation

$$F(Q,\ell) = \min_{\delta Q} \{ [H(Q+\delta Q,\delta Q,t_\ell) + C(Q+\delta Q,t_\ell)] + F(Q+\delta Q,\ell+1) \},$$

with terminal condition $F(Q,L+1) = 0$, for the value $F(0,1)$. Let $\delta Q*(Q,\ell)$ yield the minimum value $F(Q,\ell)$; $\delta Q*(0,1)$ is the optimal initial allocation, and subsequent re-allocations can be determined adaptively by the usual "reconstruction" process.

This algorithm increases the computational burden by a multiplicative factor of LN (not just L). Practicality of the dynamic programming procedure thus is quite dubious, so that suboptimal heuristic programming algorithms become attractive. Such alternatives will not be discussed here.

If H and C are independent of t and $H(Q,0,t) = 0$, then the minimizing values δQ_ℓ are all zero, and the problem reduces to the simple static case, as expected. If $H \equiv 0$, then the L-stage allocation problem may be replaced by a sequence of static (single-stage) allocation problems, the sequential procedure discussed previously.

<u>Example 3</u> (Dynamic Table Allocation). Let us suppose again that main memory space is the resource to be allocated, and also that sequential (as opposed to linked) memory locations are required by each process for, for example, dynamic tables. In addition to allocation cost c_k as in Example 1, proportional now to a probability of overflow, we associate a cost h_k for relocating blocks of memory. This latter cost can be determined by "analysis of algorithm" techniques. A heuristic procedure for adjusting allocations and repacking memory is given in [6, Section 2.2.2]. Repacking costs can be reduced by computing new allocations differently so as to minimize the amount of shifting ("transplantation" [19]) required. Relative to this, the dynamic programming procedure assumes the worst case where every table must be shifted.

<u>Example 4</u> (Buffer Allocation). Let us suppose that memory is the resource to be allocated, but now in buffer units. We assume that the buffers are partitioned into disjoint buffer pools, each of which may be used by a process-set (of producers and consumers [20]). The performance of each process-set is a function of the size of its pool, proportionate to the amount of idle time associated with waiting processes when the buffer pool is filled. This can be calculated by statistical methods as in [21]. The cost of transferring buffer units from one pool to another depends in general upon the number of units, and may be measured in terms of the time required for this overhead. When buffer pools are circularly linked [6, Section 1.4.4], this overhead time is primarily that of pointer changing.

3.3 Cost of Inactivity

A process P_k is considered "inactive" at the times when $q_k(t) = 0$, at a cost $c_k(0,t)$. We say also that execution of the process P_k is "delayed" until at least time t_{i+1} if $q_k(t_i) = 0$. This may not, of course, be tolerable for certain processes. If any or all processes are required to be active in the time interval (t_i, t_{i+1}), $c_k(0,t_i)$ may be set arbitrarily high. Where there are insufficient resources, then a cost of inactivity may be defined based upon scheduling criteria. Priorities may be assigned a priori, or be functions of common parameters such as arrival times, deadline times, processing times (completed or remaining), storage demands, and so forth [22]. We remark that this formulation requires that the costs of inactivity $c_k(0,t_i)$ be made commensurable with nonvacuous allocation costs $c_k(q,t_i)$, $q > 0$.

Example 5 (CPU Scheduling). Our discussion of resource allocation problems has mostly been general, without specification of the resource. CPU processing time is, of course, one very important type of resource, which formally can be allocated among N independent processes. If processors cannot be shared, nor allocated to more than one process at a time, then we may let $c_k(0,t_i)$ be the cost of inactivity for process k for the interval (t_i, t_{i+1}), and $c_k(1,t_i) = 0$. The costs $c_k(0,t_i)$ can be defined according to common scheduling parameters, so that the minimum (or maximum) one will always be scheduled next whenever a processor is available. It should be emphasized that this approach minimizes the criterion $\sum_i \sum_k c_k(q_k, t_i)$ (for separable costs), as opposed to the more common criteria of minimal schedule length and mean time or number in system [23].

In the absence of other criteria, we may let $c_k(0,t_i) = c_k(1,t_i)$. Since $c_k(q,t_i)$ is generally a monotonically decreasing function of q, processes would thereby be prevented from having an allocation of only one. Higher "activation thresholds", $\tilde{q}_k$, lower bounds on allocations necessary for activation of P_k, may be set by letting $c_k(0,t_i) = c_k(\tilde{q}_k, t_i)$. These thresholds may be based upon a prespecified level of performance-cost, C* (a system parameter), which should not be exceeded. If $c_k(1,t_i) \leq C*$ for each k and i, no thresholds need be set since each process can be allocated only one unit of resource (not necessarily concurrently), while still achieving the given performance level. If $c_k(1,t_i) > C*$ for some k and i, then let $\tilde{q}_k$ equal the largest integer q for which $c_k(q,t_i) > C*$. (This always exists for decreasing cost functions which equal zero at some point -- say, when q = M, the total amount of resources in the system.)

We remark in conclusion that by allowing $q_k(t)$ to be zero, our formulation automatically yields the optimal "degree of multiprogramming" (number of active processes). After solving for the optimal set of allocations, $\{q_k*(t_i) | 1 \leq k \leq N\}$, the optimal degree of multiprogramming for the interval (t_i, t_{i+1}) is simply the number of nonzero $q_k*(t_i)$.

3.4 Stochastic Costs

In our foregoing development, we have assumed that $\{c_k(q,t_i)\}$ are precalculable deterministic independent functions. This may not be realistic for several reasons. First, $c_k(q,t_i)$ may not accurately "predict" $c_k(q,t)$ over the entire interval (t_i,t_{i+1}), especially since it must be calculated at time t_i or earlier. Second, the cost may depend upon nondeterministic factors -- e.g., data dependencies or new process arrivals. Third, among others, the costs may be correlated in time, so that $c_k(q,t)$ and $c_k(q,t')$ are dependent for $t \neq t'$. While an exact formulation of allocation costs may be infeasible, a stochastic model offers an expedient alternative.

Let $C(Q_i,\delta Q_i,R_i)$ denote the cost of changing the allocation state to Q_i at time t_i, given that the previous allocation state was $Q_i - \delta Q_i$, where R_i is a random variable introduced to reflect uncertainties. Formally, we wish to minimize $\exp_{\{R_i\}}[\sum_i C(Q_i,\delta Q_i,R_i)]$ over all δQ_i. Then, generalizing Proposition 2, we have

$$F(Q,\ell) = \min_{\delta Q} \{\exp_{R_\ell}[C(Q+\delta Q,\delta Q,R_\ell) + F(Q+\delta Q,\ell+1)]\},$$

as expected. Here we have assumed that allocation state transitions are not subject to random influences.

Suppose now that the allocation state can change during the interval (t_i,t_{i+1}). This reflects the situation where processes can terminate and return their allocated resources to the system (process P_0) for possible reallocation to other processes prior to time t_{i+1}. (The latter processes may be selected from inactive ones if allocations to active processes cannot be forcibly changed until t_{i+1}.) We assume then that there is a given probability $\Pi_{Q_i Q_i'}(t_i)$ and cost $H_{Q_i Q_i'}(t_i)$ that the system changes from state Q_i to Q_i' in the interval (t_i,t_{i+1}). At time t_{i+1}, reallocation costs will depend upon Q_i' rather than $Q_i = (q_0(t_i), \ldots, q_N(t_i))$. This is an example of a Markovian decision process (of "D.H." type [5]).

Proposition 3. The optimal expected allocation cost can be found by solving

$$F(Q,\ell) = \min_{\delta Q} \{\exp_{R_\ell} [C(Q+\delta Q,\delta Q,R_\ell)] + \sum_{Q'} \Pi_{Q+\delta Q,Q'}(\ell) [H_{Q+\delta Q,Q'}(\ell) + F(Q',\ell+1)]\},$$

with terminal condition $F(Q,L+1) = 0$, for the value $F(0,1)$.

Example 6 (Page Allotment). Continuing Example 2, paging costs are measured in terms of page faults. We assume that the I/O required by a single page fault dominates the bookkeeping overhead for a reallotment. We now also assume that each program P_k has a given probability of terminating (blocking) during each interval (t_i, t_{i+1}), denoted $p_k(t_i)$. For the Markov program model of [16,17], this would be the probability of absorption. Suppose $c_k(q_k,t_i)$ is the page-fault cost given that process P_k executes during the entire interval (t_i,t_{i+1}) with a page frame allotment $q_k(t_i)$. The expected time of termination may be given by $t_{i+1} - p_k(t_i)*(t_{i+1} - t_i)$, thereby reducing the page-fault cost by the same factor $p_k(t_i)$; so we let $h_k(t_i) = -p_k(t_i)*c_k(q_k,t_i)$. Then $\Pi_{Q_k Q_k'}(t_i) = p_k(t_i)$ and $H_{Q_k Q_k'}(t_i) = h_k(t_i)$, where $Q_k = (q_0(t_i), \ldots, q_k(t_i), \ldots)$ and $Q_k' = (q_0(t_i) + q_k(t_i), \ldots, 0, \ldots)$.

As anticipated, the complexity of the allocation problem increases greatly as more realistic factors are considered. In practice, simplifying assumptions will become necessary for computationally feasible algorithms to be applicable. In the above for example, if stationarity of Π and time-independence of the costs are assumed (perhaps by using time averages), then Howard's iterative procedure [24] is especially attractive.

Example 7 (Page Replacement). We remark that the page replacement problem [25] may also be formulated as a Markovian decision process, and solved by Howard's method. (See [16,26].)

4. SCHEDULING AND CONTROL

We have already observed that scheduling problems arise naturally when allocations of resources (other than CPUs) may vary with time. If resources are withheld from a process, for example, forced inactivity or delays result in favor of other processes. Allocation and scheduling decisions are thus clearly interrelated; an optimal "schedule" must minimize the sum of allocation costs over time, subject now to constraints of various types. In the following sections, we discuss how certain "control" aspects of scheduling may be treated in the context of non-CPU resource allocation. (For a discussion of CPU scheduling, unrelated to other resources, see [2,23].) The problems we consider no longer assume independent processes.

4.1 Process Coordination

When parallel processes are not independent, so that they interfere if executed concurrently [27], allocation decisions should take into account the dependencies. For example, if processes are partially ordered according to a temporal precedence relation, for (say) determinacy reasons, then resources should be allocated at any point in time only to "eligible" processes whose predecessors have all been completed. If (cyclic) processes must satisfy synchronization or exclusion constraints, again only certain processes are "eligible" for resources. Formally, we may set the allocation costs for ineligible processes arbitrarily high, and use the foregoing procedures to distribute resources among the eligible processes. Allocation costs may be functions of time (or time indices), or else functions of the "state" of the system (e.g. values of semaphores or event-variables), or both. For example, the costs may be made functions of how "critical" processes are: a critical process is one on the longest path of a scheduling (PERT [5]) network. (Longest paths can, of course, be found by adapting shortest path algorithms.)

When allocation of resources is constrained by "soft" precedence relations among processes, where there may be preferred rather than absolute precedences (superseding other measures of allocation cost), a problem of a different nature arises. We may in this case associate a higher cost with one ordering of two processes than another, where we assume these costs are independent of the sizes of the allocations. Let

$\{P_1, \ldots, P_N\}$ denote the set of processes. Given $\{C_{ij}\}$, the cost of P_i having precedence over P_j, the optimal ordering of the processes can be found by solving a "traveling-salesperson" routing problem -- e.g. by dynamic programming. Let $f_k(A,P_i)$ be the minimum cost of finally executing process P_k, preceded by all processes in the subset A, starting with the execution of process P_i in A. Initial and terminal conditions can be added by letting a_i and b_i be the costs of starting and ending, respectively, with process P_i; these would be zero if there are no constraints or preferences.

Proposition 4. The optimal ordering of processes can be found by solving

$$f_k(\{P_{s_1}, \ldots, P_{s_\ell}\}, P_i) = \min_j \{C_{ij} + f_k(\{P_{s_1}, \ldots, P_{s_\ell}\} - \{P_i\}, P_j)\},$$

for $f_k(\{P_1, \ldots, P_N\}, P_k)$ given that $f_k(\{P_i\}, P_i) = b_i$. The $j \in \{s_1, \ldots, s_\ell\}$ which yields the minimum in the above designates the process to be executed immediately following P_i. The initial process is given by $\min_k [a_k + f_k(\{P_1, \ldots, P_N\}, P_k)]$, with succeeding processes determined by reconstruction.

Example 8 (File Scheduling). Given a queue of processes wishing to access a file, the dominant cost factor is usually device-dependent [28]. In any event, the optimal ordering of processes can be determined as above, where $\{C_{ij}\}$ are the access times associated with servicing P_j immediately after P_i, a_i is the cost of servicing P_i initially (based on the initial state of the device), and $b_i \equiv 0$. We note that if all C_{ij} are taken to be zero, the first process to be serviced would be that having the shortest access time (cf. [29]); a statistical analysis of various file scheduling policies appears in [30].

Suppose that $P_{i_1}, P_{i_2}, \ldots, P_{i_N}$ is an optimally ordered sequence of processes. Then resources should be allocated to processes in that order. If the processes may be concurrent, resources may be allocated in toto first to P_{i_1}, then to P_{i_2}, and so forth, until the supply is exhausted; the latter processes then generally are delayed. Alternatively, or if they must be concurrent, allocation costs may prescribe the apportionment as before. If two processes may not be concurrent, then the lower priority one is ineligible until the higher priority process completes.

4.2 Redundant Processes

The situation may arise in parallel processing applications where a set of processes has "redundancies". A process, for example, may no longer be necessary depending upon the outcomes of certain other processes, so that it would be wasteful to execute the former process first. If decisions as to whether or not to execute processes depend upon others, we have a new scheduling problem, which may be formalized as follows.

Given a set of processes $\{P_1, \ldots, P_N\}$, let $V_i = \{v_{i1}, \ldots, v_{ir_i}\}$ be a set of "outcomes" associated with P_i. Execution of P_i selects one element of V_i as its outcome, say v_{ij}; we denote this by writing $e(P_i) = v_{ij}$. Let $C(P_i|R)$ be the cost of executing P_i given that the predicate R is true. Define $f_k(\{P_{s_1}, P_{s_2}, \ldots, P_{s_k}\} | R_k)$ as the minimum achievable cost of execution having the k remaining processes $\{P_{s_1}, \ldots, P_{s_k}\}$ given that R_k is true.

<u>Proposition 5.</u> The optimal ordering of processes can be found by solving

$$f_k(\{P_{s_1}, \ldots, P_{s_k}\} | R_k) = \min_i \{C(P_i | R_k) + \sum_{j=1}^{r_i} f_{k-1}(\{P_{s_1}, \ldots, P_{s_k}\} - \{P_i\} | R_k \wedge e(P_i) = v_{ij})\}$$

for $f_N(\{P_1, \ldots, P_N\} | .\text{TRUE.})$ given that $f_1(\{P_i\} | R_1) = C(P_i | R_1)$. The $i \in \{s_1, \ldots, s_k\}$ which yields the minimum in the above designates the process to be executed next (at stage k; k = N, ..., 1) given that R_k is true.

We observe that R_k is the intersection of predicates of the form $e(P_i) = v_{ij}$ for P_i not in the set $\{P_{s_1}, \ldots, P_{s_k}\}$ of processes executed at the earlier stages, k+1, ..., N. If $\{P_{s_1}, \ldots, P_{s_k}\}$ consists only of redundant processes given the outcome R_k, then $C(P_i | R_k^1) = 0$ for each such process. Otherwise, we may let $C(P_i | R_k) = c_i * \Pi(R_k)$, where c_i is the execution cost (resource requirement) of process P_i, and $\Pi(R_k)$ is the probability that R_k occurs. (The latter depends upon likelihoods of various outcomes; equi-likelihood may be assumed if probabilistic information is not available.)

With the above definition our dynamic programming procedure yields the hierarchical order of process executions which minimizes the expected total cost associated with a set of redundant processes. It should be emphasized that the ordering is not linear, but is of tree form. We remark, in conclusion, that sequencing constraints (for precedence reasons, as in the prior section) can be incorporated in this new algorithm by restricting the minimum in the functional equation to be taken only over those P_i in $\{P_{s_1}, \ldots, P_{s_k}\}$ which can be executed prior to each of the remaining processes.

<u>Example 9</u> (Decision Tables). The algorithm presented above may be used to convert extended-entry decision tables to optimal computer programs (cf. [31]). To minimize time, let c_i be the time required to evaluate "condition" P_i and $\Pi(R_k)$ be the probability that the specified combination of condition values R_k obtains. $C(P_i | R_k) = 0$ if the "subtable" associated with R_k has a common action set. To minimize space, let c_i be the space required to evaluate P_i, and $\Pi(R_k) = 1$ if the probability of R_k is nonzero, else $\Pi(R_k) = 0$. (The latter formulation also applies to the problem of minimizing the weighted number of internal nodes in a tree (cf. [6, Section 2.3.4.5]); an extension to the problem discussed therein of minimizing weighted path lengths is possible.)

4.3 <u>Deadlock Avoidance</u>

If we assume nonpreemptible resources, or more weakly that there is a nonzero lower bound on the amount of resources a process can be allocated once activated (possibly a time-varying bound), then requests for additional resources by processes cannot be granted on demand without risk of a "deadlock" [32,33]. A deadlock avoidance criterion may rule out the shortest path in the allocation graph as an acceptable solution to the optimal resource allocation problem. In this event, a "safety" constraint may be formally added to the optimization problem. For example, suppose we require knowledge of the maximum resource requirement, M_k, of each process P_k.

<u>Proposition 6</u>. The set of allocations $\{q_k(t_i)\}$ is safe if

$$(\forall j) \; M_j - q_j(t_i) \leq q_0(t_i) + \sum_{k \in K_i} q_k(t_i);$$

$$K_i = \{k \,|\, q_k(t_i) = M_k\}.$$

We therefore should minimize $\sum_k c_k(q_k, t_i)$ subject both to $\sum_k q_k = M$ and the above. We remark that this new constraint is quite conservative; the universal quantifier can be replaced by a sequence of existential ones if the inequality is evaluated recursively with $q_0(t_i)$ increased by $q_j(t_i)$ each time the inequality holds (cf. [20]). We remark, in addition, that while some overhead is required to evaluate constraint relations, the computational requirements of dynamic programming algorithms are generally reduced significantly by their addition.

An alternative approach to the above is the direct utilization of dynamic programming to determine the k-th shortest path, for k = 1, 2, ... [34]. The smallest k for which the k-th shortest path does not violate the safety criterion then yields the desired solution. We note that if no such path exists, the system is initially deadlocked. In this event, one or more of the deadlocked processes must be "aborted" to effect a recovery, at a cost which should be minimized (cf. [32]).

One method of preventing deadlocks where there are different types of resources is to require that processes use the resources in a fixed order. Given this ordering of resources, the problem of optimally ordering processes is a "flow-shop" problem [23]; a dynamic programming solution of this problem for two resource types appears in [12].

5. CONCLUSION

In this paper, we have investigated the general problem of <u>optimally</u> allocating resources among parallel processes. Our objective has not been the derivation of new mathematical results, but rather the application of old ones to new problem areas. Specifically, we have applied the method of dynamic programming [11] to various aspects of the resource allocation problem, taking into account the special nature of computer "parallel processing" systems (as opposed to typical "operations research" contexts [35]). Sections 2 and 3 were devoted to the determination of optimal allocations relative to quantitative measures of the performance-cost of executing independent processes as functions of the sizes of their respective allocations.

We have also observed that "scheduling" problems arise when non-CPU resources are to be allocated. Processing time is, of course, also a resource which must be allocated, so an optimal policy should, in principle, consider processor utilization criteria in addition to the non-CPU resource allocation costs. One approach to "balancing" the two criteria is to attempt to keep the system operating at a pre-specified constant level of performance [13]; it has been noted that efficient utilization may lead to poor response [13,36] and also be "unfair" [36]. Another approach is to minimize some scalar function of multiple criteria as in [37], which forces us to make commensurability assumptions (e.g. time and space, as measured in terms of $). The "Procrustean" nature of such assumptions has led to alternatives (e.g. [38]) which we are presently exploring.

In the meantime, we have considered the situation where "scheduling" decisions are to be made solely on the basis of (non-CPU) resource allocation costs rather than processor utilization. Most scheduling literature assume the opposite. When there are "control" constraints (e.g., precedences, redundancies, and deadlocks) among dependent processes, considerations of allocation costs are commonly neglected. Section 4, however, discusses optimal resource allocation in this new context.

We have surveyed numerous examples of applications in this paper. A detailed study of one (paging) is in progress. Establishment of the practical value of the formal models presented herein awaits further developments. While our formulations have been in terms of conventional dynamic programming, more efficient algorithms may be necessary and are available. In addition, heuristics [39] and approximations [40] may be adopted for practicality reasons, leading, of course, to suboptimal solutions. However, we expect such solutions to be generally superior to informally obtained ones.

In summary, we have suggested a number of new analytical approaches to important resource allocation problems. The main limitations of such formal quantitative approaches are realistic formulations or identifications of costs, states, other parameters, and their functional dependence (a problem shared by informal approaches, although to a lesser extent), and computational complexity. The main advantage is the potential attainment of optimal or near-optimal performance (possible otherwise only by chance, without knowledge thereof). At the least, knowledge of theoretical bounds ("benchmarks") provides a means for evaluating other allocation procedures.

REFERENCES

[1] H. Lorin, Parallelism in Hardware and Software: Real and Apparent Concurrency, Prentice-Hall, (1972).

[2] E.G. Coffman, Jr., and P.J. Denning, Operating Systems Theory, Prentice-Hall, (1973).

[3] IBM, "IBM System/360 Operating System Concepts and Facilities," Form. No. GC28-6535.

[4] A. Lew, "Memory Allocation in Paging Systems," Proc. ACM Annual Conf., (1973), pp. 232-235.

[5] A. Kaufmann, Graphs, Dynamic Programming, and Finite Games, Academic Press, (1967).

[6] D.E. Knuth, <u>Fundamental Algorithms</u>, Addison-Wesley, (1968).

[7] J. Kral, "One Way of Estimating Frequencies of Jumps in a Program," <u>Comm. ACM</u>, (1968) pp. 475-480.

[8] IBM, "IBM System/360 Operating System Linkage Editor and Loader," Form No. C28-6538.

[9] D.P. Bovet, and G. Estrin, "On Static Memory Allocation in Computer Systems," <u>IEEE Trans. Comp.</u>, (1970), pp. 492-503.

[10] S.E. Dreyfus, "An Appraisal of Some Shortest-path Algorithms," <u>ORSA</u>, (1969), pp. 395-412.

[11] R.E. Bellman, and S.E. Dreyfus, <u>Applied Dynamic Programming</u>, Princeton U. Press, (1962).

[12] M. Held and R.M. Karp, "The Construction of Discrete Dynamic Programming Algorithms," <u>IBM Syst. J.</u>, (1965), pp. 136-147.

[13] P.J. Denning, "The Working Set Model for Program Behavior", <u>Comm. ACM</u>, (1968), pp. 323-333.

[14] P.J. Denning, "Thrashing: Its Causes and Prevention," Proc. AFIPS FJCC, (1968), pp. 915-922.

[15] E.G. Coffman, Jr., and T.A. Ryan, Jr., "A Study of Storage Partitioning Using a Mathematical Model of Locality," <u>Comm. ACM</u>, (1972), pp. 185-190.

[16] G. Ingargiola and J.F. Korsh, "Finding Optimal Demand Paging Algorithms," <u>J. ACM</u>, (1974), pp. 40-53.

[17] M.A. Franklin, and R.K. Gupta, "Computation of Page Fault Probability from Program Transition Diagram," <u>Comm. ACM</u>, (1974), pp. 186-191.

[18] W.W. Chu, and H. Opderbeck, "The Page Fault Frequency Replacement Algorithm", Proc. AFIPS FJCC, (1972), pp. 597-609.

[19] S. Even, A. Pnueli, and A. Lempel, "Permutation Graphs and Transitive Graphs," <u>J. ACM</u>, (1972), pp. 400-410.

[20] E.W. Dijkstra, "Co-operating Sequential Processes," in <u>Programming Languages</u> (Ed. Genuys), Academic Press, (1968), pp. 43-112.

[21] D.P. Gaver, Jr., and P.A.W. Lewis, "Probability Models for Buffer Storage Allocation Problems," <u>J. ACM</u>, (1971), pp. 186-198.

[22] H. Hellerman, "Time-sharing Scheduler Strategies," <u>IBM Syst. J.</u>, (1969), pp. 94-117.

[23] R.W. Conway, W.L. Maxwell, and L.W. Miller, <u>Theory of Scheduling</u>, Addison-Wesley, (1967).

[24] R.A. Howard, <u>Dynamic Programming and Markov Processes</u>, MIT Press, (1960).

[25] R.L. Mattson, J. Gecsei, D.R. Slutz, and I.L. Traiger, "Evaluation Techniques for Storage Hierarchies," <u>IBM Syst. J.</u>, (1970), pp. 78-117.

[26] A. Lew, "Comments on 'Finding Optimal Demand Paging Algorithms'," Dept. of Info. and Comp. Sci., Univ. of Hawaii, TR No. ARO-19, (1974).

[27] J.L. Baer, "A Survey of Some Theoretical Aspects of Multiprocessing," <u>ACM Comp. Surv.</u>, (1973), pp. 31-80.

[28] IBM, "Direct Access Storage Devices and Organization Methods," Form No. C20-1649.

[29] P.J. Denning, "Effects of Scheduling on File Memory Operations," Proc. AFIPS SJCC (1967), pp. 9-21.

[30] T.J. Teorey, and T.B. Pinkerton, "A Comparative Analysis of Disk Scheduling Policies," <u>Comm. ACM</u>, (1972), pp. 177-184.

[31] L.T. Reinwald, and R.M. Soland, "Conversion of Limited-Entry Decision Tables to Optimal Computer Programs I: Minimum Average Processing Time," J. ACM, (1966), pp. 339-358.

[32] E.G. Coffman, Jr., M.J. Elphick, and A. Shoshani, "System Deadlocks," ACM Comp. Surv., (1971), pp. 67-78.

[33] R.C. Holt, "Some Deadlock Properties of Computer Systems," ACM Comp. Surv. (1972), pp. 179-196.

[34] R. Bellman, and R. Kalaba, "On kth Best Policies," J. SIAM, (1960), pp. 582-588.

[35] F.S. Hillier, and G.J. Lieberman, Introduction to Operations Research, Holden-Day, (1967).

[36] R.G. Hamlet, "Efficient Multiprogramming Resource Allocation and Accounting," Comm. ACM, (1973), pp. 337-343.

[37] A. Thesen, "Scheduling of Computer Programs for Optimal Machine Utilization," BIT, (1973), pp. 206-216.

[38] R.M. Beeson, and W.S. Meisel, "Optimization of Complex Systems with Respect to Multiple Criteria," Proc. IEEE-SMC Symp., (1971), pp. 144-149.

[39] D. Michie, J.G. Fleming, and J.V. Oldfield, "A Comparison of Heuristic, Interactive, and Unaided Methods of Solving a Shortest-route Problem," in Machine Intelligence 3 (Ed. Michie), American Elsevier, (1968), pp. 245-255.

[40] A. Lew, "Successive Approximations and Dynamic Programming," Proc. 5th Asilomar Conf. on Circuits and Systems, (1971), pp. 79-82.

A RECOGNIZER AND POST-RECOGNIZER FOR OPTIMIZING EXECUTION TIMES OF PROGRAMS

P.F. REYNOLDS and K.M. CHANDY
Department of Computer Sciences
The University of Texas at Austin
Austin, Texas 78712

SUMMARY

Ramamoorthy and Gonzales [4] have shown that a parallelism-induced reduction in the real time required to execute a program is offset by task activation overhead if task durations are too small. In the case of parallelism recognizers this means that run time scheduling costs may be greatly increased if a recognizer partitions a program too finely. One method of resolving this tradeoff between task size and scheduling overhead is to implement a post-recognizer that arranges tasks for optimum scheduling. We shall discuss a static recognizer post-recognizer system that has as a design goal the detection and optimal prescheduling of dependent tasks.

The recognizer and post-recognizer are necessarily interdependent, but each has specific duties. The recognizer attempts to detect the maximum amount of parallelism in a given program in order to produce a task graph for the post-recognizer; it is not concerned with scheduling. The post-recognizer attempts to arrange tasks for optimal scheduling in order to yield a graph most suitable for scheduling; it does not detect parallelism. Together they produce a graph of optimally sized tasks so a simple scheduler, often a list scheduler [2], may be used.

Major characteristics of our recognizer are derived from the recognizers of Ramamoorthy and Gonzalez [3] and Tjaden and Flynn [5]. Recognition is performed at the instruction level in FORTRAN programs using the criteria established by Bernstein [1]. Output of the recognizer is a successors list for each instruction and lists of conditional and unconditional branches. Successors are determined for each instruction for all possible logical paths except those paths deemed redundant or too short. Unresolvable data dependencies, procedural dependencies [5] and subroutine calls are the major source of wait-for conditions.

Since logical paths frequently lead to loops, methods for terminating the recognition process had to be developed. Treating all branching conditionals as binary conditionals (three-branch conditionals can be expanded to two binary conditionals) most FORTRAN-like algorithmic languages can be graphically represented with the following node and arc definitions: 1) Conditional nodes -- one node for each conditional -- each having two outpointing arcs and one inpointing arc, 2) Transfer nodes -- nodes representing labelled statements -- each having one outpointing node and any number greater than zero of inpointing arcs, 3) Labelled arcs -- one arc for each segment of code logically between the above node types. Labelled conditionals can be represented as a transfer node and conditional node with a null arc between them. Proofs have been developed by the authors to demonstrate that a third recursive visit to either of the above node types is sufficient for establishing all possible data dependencies back to the last conditional node visited.

Various methods for maximizing inter-instruction independence are employed in the recognizer. Data dependencies are established through unconditional and conditional branches; essentially unconditional branches are ignored. Algorithms have been developed for determining if array references either inside or outside of DO loops conflict with other references. Since a static recognizer usually cannot determine the possible values of variables, the array reference checking algorithms depend primarily on array references differing by a constant and their not having statements which change subscript variable values lying between them.

The post-recognizer groups tasks together attempting to reduce the number of additional constraints created by the coalescing process. For instance, supposing there were six independent tasks all of which required one unit of processing time, and two identical processors. Then the minimum total execution time is three units. Suppose the six tasks were coalesced to form three independent larger tasks, each of which required two time units. Now the minimum execution time (if preemption is not allowed) is four time units. Thus the process of coalescing delays total execution time by one unit of time if there is no overhead involved. In the paper we describe two distinct types of constraints called extrinsic and intrinsic constraints and suggest methods for coalescing tasks so as to minimize the increase in execution time.

Acknowledgement: This work was supported by NSF Grant No. GJ-35109. The authors would like to thank Dr. Mario Gonzalez for his help.

REFERENCES

[1] A.J. Bernstein, "Analysis of Programs for Parallel Processing", IEEE Trans. on EC (October, 1966), pp. 12-34.

[2] E.F. Coffman, and P.J. Denning, Operating Systems Theory, Prentice-Hall, (1973)

[3] C.V. Ramamoorthy, and M.J. Gonzalez, "A Survey of Techniques for Recognizing Parallel Processable Streams in Computer Programs," Proc. AFIPS Fall Joint Computer Conf. (1969), pp. 1-15.

[4] C.V. Ramamoorthy, and M.J. Gonzalez, "Parallel Task Execution in a Decentralized System," IEEE Trans. on Computers, (December, 1972), pp. 1310-1322.

[5] G.S. Tjaden, and M.J. Flynn, "Representation of Concurrency with Ordering Matrices", IEEE Trans. on Computers, (August, 1973), pp. 752-761.

ANALYTIC AND IMPLEMENTATION CONSIDERATIONS OF TWO-FACILITY SEQUENCING IN COMPUTER SYSTEMS[a]

S.S. REDDI
Laboratory for Computer Science and Engineering
Department of Electrical Engineering
Rice University
Houston, Texas 77001

SUMMARY

There has been extensive investigation in the field of sequencing algorithms which achieve overlap processing but up to date simulation is the only tool that has been used to answer questions regarding the effectiveness of such algorithms when implemented in computer systems. In implementation of sequencing algorithms one encounters questions regarding overhead times due to the algorithms, improvements in program execution times because of the algorithms, situations where the algorithms degrade the performance of the computer system because of their excessive overheads, etc. Also one has to consider the effects of overlapping overhead times with execution times of the jobs (programs) on the performance of the system. In the following we consider an optimal sequencing algorithm of Ref. [1] and show how some of these questions can be answered analytically when this algorithm is implemented in a computer system. Though it is not claimed that the presented approach can be applied to any other sequencing algorithm easily, it is hoped that our efforts increase the understanding of the aspects of implementation of sequencing algorithms and hence lead to better simulation methods in the future.

The sequencing problem considered is the following. There are n independent jobs 1,2,3, ..., n and two facilities F_1 and F_2. Each job goes through F_1 and F_2 and in that order. Job i requires a_i and b_i units of processing time on F_1 and F_2 respectively. (Note in a computer system F_1 and F_2 may correspond to a processor and an I/O unit respectively. Then we are overlapping process and I/O times.) A schedule $(i_1, i_2, ..., i_n)$ represents the situation where the processing sequence of jobs is $i_1, i_2, ..., i_n$ on both facilities. Then LEMMA 1 (Johnson): A schedule $(i_1, i_2, ..., i_n)$ minimizes the completion time of all jobs if $\text{Min}(a_{i_p}, b_{i_q}) \leq \text{Min}(a_{i_q}, b_{i_p})$ for $p < q$. Further $(i_n, i_{n-1}, ..., i_2, i_1)$ maximizes the completion time of the jobs.

Assume the jobs are numbered so that $Smn = (1,2, ..., n)$ minimizes the completion time. $Smx = (n, n-1, ..., 2, 1)$ maximizes the completion time. $C(S)$ is the time to complete any schedule S. Let $Tmx = C(Smx)$, $Tmn = C(Smn)$ and $T = Tmx - Tmn$.

THEOREM 1: Let $a_{i_1} \geq a_{i_2} \geq \cdots \geq a_{i_n}$, $\quad i_p \neq i_q$ for $p \neq q$

and

$\qquad\qquad b_{j_1} \geq b_{j_2} \geq \cdots \geq b_{j_n}$, $\quad j_p \neq j_q$ for $p \neq q$.

---

[a]This research was supported by the National Science Foundation under Grant GJ-36471.

Define $m = \lceil n - 2/2 \rceil$

$\qquad$ Amx $= a_{i_1} + a_{i_2} + \ldots + a_{i_m} \quad$ for $n > 2$

$\qquad$ Amn $= a_{i_{m+2}} + a_{i_{m+3}} + \ldots + a_{i_n} \qquad$ for odd n,

$\qquad\qquad = a_{i_{m+3}} + a_{i_{m+4}} + \ldots + a_{i_n} \qquad$ for even $n > 2$

$\qquad$ Amx $=$ Amn $= 0 \quad$ for $n = 2$.

Similarly define Bmx and Bmn by replacing A, a and i by B, b and j respectively. Define $\Delta =$ Amx $-$ Amn $+$ Bmx $-$ Bmn for odd n

$\qquad = $ Amx $-$ Amn $+$ Bmx $-$ Bmn $+$ Max$(a_{i_{m+1}} - a_{i_{m+2}}, b_{i_{m+1}} - b_{i_{m+2}})$ for even n.

Then $\Delta \geq T$. Also the upper bound is tight since there exists a job set for which $\Delta = T$.

$\qquad$ Note $E = \lfloor n/2 \rfloor (a^* + b^*) \geq \Delta$ where $a^* = $ Max$(a_i) - $ Min(a_i) and $b^* = $ Max$(b_i) - $ Min(b_i). E can be computed with $7n/2$ operations [2]. Hence by virtue of Theorem 1, it is preferable not to compute an optimal schedule when $OV(n) > E$ where $OV(n)$ is the overhead to compute an optimal schedule for n jobs.

$\qquad$ Now we consider the following implementation procedure which attempts to overlap overhead and execution times. Initially $k \leq n$ jobs are considered and an optimal processing sequence for these k jobs is calculated. During execution of any single job, it is possible to consider w more jobs and decide an optimal execution sequence for these jobs. Then we combine the existing processing sequence with the newly computed optimal sequence to obtain a composite optimal sequence. As an example, consider 5 jobs 1,2,3,4,5 (the optimal sequence is (1,2,3,4,5) and assume they are stored in the sequence (4,5,2,1,3). Let $k = 2$ and $w = 2$. We consider the first two jobs 4 and 5 and decide the optimal processing sequence (by Johnson's algorithm) to be (4,5). When job 4 is in execution, jobs 2 and 1 are considered and the optimal sequence is determined to be (1,2). Then (1,2) is combined with the existing optimal sequence of unprocessed jobs, which is (5) in this case, to obtain (1,2,5). Thus we see for this example the processing sequence becomes (4,1,2,3,5). We say the stored sequence (4,5,2,1,3) is transformed to (4,1,2,3,5) for $k = 2$, $w = 2$.

$\qquad$ Calculation of t, the number of stored sequences that are transformed into optimal sequence (1,2, ..., n) is equivalent to enumeration of permutation with restricted positions [3]. Define $\eta = t/n!$. Then it is preferable to consider implementation procedure with parameter k over direct calculation of optimal schedules when $OV(n) - OV(k) > \Delta_k$ where Δ_k is Δ for jobs 1,2,...,n-k+1. Also $OV(k) + Tmn + (1-\eta) \cdot \Delta_k \geq EC$ where EC is the expected completion time under the implementation procedure.

REFERENCES

[1] S.M. Johnson, "Optimal Two- and Three-Stage Production Schedules with Set-Up Times Included," N.R.L.Q., (March,1954), pp. 61-68.

[2] D. Knuth, The Art of Comp. Proq., Vol. 3, 1972.

[3] J. Riordan, An Introduction to Combinatorial Analysis, Wiley, (1958), 244 pp.

COMPUTER MODELS WITH CONSTRAINED PARALLEL PROCESSORS

T.W. KELLER and K.M. CHANDY
Department of Computer Sciences
University of Texas at Austin
Austin, Texas 78712

SUMMARY

This paper presents the development of approximate, rather than exact, solutions to queueing network models of parallel processors in computer systems incorporating passive resource behavior which are easily (hence economically) obtained.

Models are characterized by the active processors, CPU's and I/O's, and the passive processors, PP's and channels. The CPU's and I/O's are characterized by job processing rates. In contrast to the active processors, PP's and channels are not characterized by rates but by the way they are allocated by the operating system in order to insure the proper functioning of the CPU and I/O devices. For a complete description of a PP see Thornton [3].

A central server model is frequently used to model a multiprogrammed computer system. In this model, jobs queue up for the CPU, receive a CPU burst of mean duration $1/\mu$ and then queue up (with probability P_i) for an I/O processor i to receive a mean processing burst of $1/\lambda_i$. The service time distributions for all processors are assumed exponential. Unfortunately, this simple-minded model ignores the degradation to system performance due to contention between jobs for PP's and channels to effect I/O processing upon the I/O devices. We describe how one of these features, PP contention, is incorporated into a more general model, and its impact upon modeling parallel processors.

Upon completing a CPU burst, a job must queue up for a PP, as a PP is required for I/O processing. Upon receiving a PP it then waits for a channel to the desired I/O device, is assigned a channel, and then holds the channel until the I/O processing is completed. Upon completion the channel and PP are released and made available to other jobs. Channel behavior is not presented here for the sake of brevity. For our purposes, I/O processing for a job will consist of the assignment of a PP, and the entering of an I/O queue i whose server processes jobs with a mean (exponential) service rate of λ_i, the inverse of the average channel i holding time. Consider such a model (which we will call the extended central server model) with degree of multiprogramming M with N PP's. In the model, PP's can be thought of as tokens, with a job being refused admittance to a channel queue without a token. Tokens are dispensed (when available) to a job awaiting I/O. Tokens are not released by jobs until they exit the channel queue upon completion of service, at which point the tokens are returned to the pool of N tokens. If $N \geq M$, no contention for PP's exists and the model reduces to the central server model. For the frequently realistic case of N < M, contention exists and is modeled by the following technique.

The complexity of the extended central server model is reduced by approximating it by a two queue model in which the I/O queue is equivalent, in terms of job throughput, to the many channel queues. This I/O queue will be termed the "composite" queue, with service rates parameterized by the following technique. The composite queue's service rate is taken to be a function of the number of jobs in the queue. This functional rate $\lambda(n)$, where n is the number of jobs in the queue, is obtained numerically for each n by eliminating the CPU queue in the central server model and evaluating the resulting model's throughput as the degree of multiprogramming n is varied from 1 to N. This throughput is $\lambda(n)$. This process may be conceptualized as finding out the overall I/O throughput in the original model for n jobs, where n is the total number of jobs in the I/O queues.

The "composite" model is analyzed using Markov (local balance [1]) analysis and is determined numerically via a queueing network analysis program ASQ [2] implemented at the University of Texas at Austin. The details of the analysis are not included in this summary. Experiments indicate that the solutions for CPU throughput and utilization in the composite (approximate) model are within a few percent of the exact solutions.

This technique has greater application than merely that of modeling passive resource contention in computer systems models. Most generally, this technique is applicable to any queueing network model with the constraints inherent in the discussion in which the total number of customers active in any subsystem of parallel processors is limited.

Systems with different kinds of functional processors are becoming common. Queueing models of computer systems must include models of multiple and parallel processors. This work is a step in that direction.

Acknowledgement: This work was supported by NSF Grants GJ-1084 and GJ-35109. The authors would like to thank Dr. Mario Gonzalez for his help.

REFERENCES

[1] K.M. Chandy, "The Analysis and Solutions for General Queueing Networks," Proc. 6th Annual Princeton Conf. on Information Sc. and Sys., Princeton University, N.J. (March 1972), pp. 224-228.

[2] T.W. Keller, ASQ Manual - User's Guide to a Program for the Automatic Analysis of Queueing Network Models, Comp. Sc., University of Texas TR-27, 1973.

[3] Thornton, J.F., Design of a Computer -- the Control Data 6600, Scott, Foreman & Co. (1970).

IMPLEMENTATION OF DATA MANIPULATING FUNCTIONS
ON THE STARAN ASSOCIATIVE PROCESSOR

LYAL H. BAUER
Rome Air Development Center
Griffiss AFB, N.Y. 13441

Abstract -- Parallel processing data manipulating functions have been widely discussed in the literature. These functions are used to move data from one processing element to another in a parallel manner. A large subset of these functions (shift, flip, shuffle, spread, replicate, close-up) have been implemented as macros on the STARAN S-1000 Associative Processor. An end off shift was found to require 3W to 8W instruction cycles (W is the field width in bits). Other functions have been implemented requiring $\log_2 N$ (N = string length) end off shift operations. Execution times are minimum when string lengths are a power of two. Data manipulation execution times are typically greater than the time required for an array add instruction but much less than required for an array multiply. Aspects of the STARAN architecture as related to the data manipulating functions are discussed.

1. INTRODUCTION

This paper describes the implementation of data manipulation functions on RADCAP the RADC STARAN Associative Processor (AP). Timing results, a sample problem, and suggestions for improvements are also given.

Data Manipulating (DM) functions are defined as those functions required for preparing operands so that a high degree of parallel processing can be maintained [1]. These functions are usually used to transmit data from one processing element to another. (A processing element (PE) is one memory and arithmetic unit.) Data manipulation functions are vital in such areas as matrix operations, FFT and a wide variety of application programs [2,3].

2. SYSTEM DESCRIPTION AND IMPLEMENTATIONS OF DM FUNCTIONS

If the processing elements are envisioned as being stacked one on top of another then they can be numbered 0 to N-1 and we can talk about the effect of certain data manipulating functions by noting that a certain operand went from PE[I] to PE[J]. Figure 1 shows the RADC associative processor in this context. There are four arrays at RADC (up to 32 arrays can be utilized by STARAN) each consisting of 256 PE's by 256 bits. Associated with each array is a flip network that allows data to be read or stored in the bit slice mode (a bit i of each PE) or the word mode (all bits of a PE). There is also a mixed mode of accessing that will be discussed later [4]. M is the mask register that enables subsets of PE's to participate in instructions,

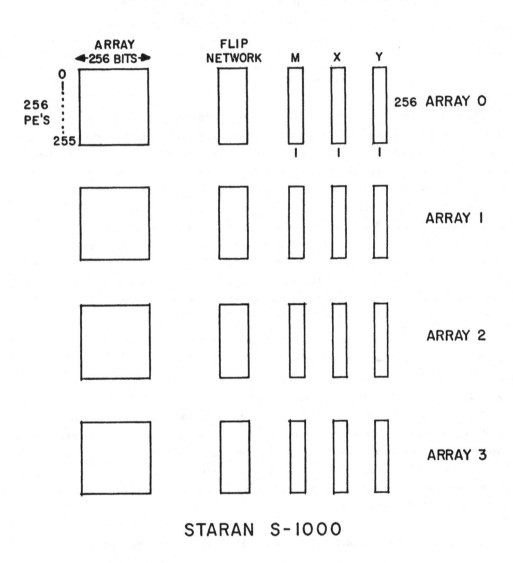

Figure 1. RADC Associative Processor Arrays

while X and Y are response store registers used for holding the responders of a
search and for temporary results.

As an example, assume a shift down of 1 modulo 256 is desired. The results of
this DM function is to transmit an operand from PE[I] to PE[I+1] with PE[255] transmitting an operand to PE[0]. Since STARAN is bit oriented, this generally means
transferring one bit slice at a time until the entire field width of the operand is
covered. The formal macro definitions of many DM functions were presented at the
1972 Sagamore Computer Conference and will not be repeated here [5]. However, the
definitions should be clear from the following examples of DM functions as implemented on STARAN.

At this point, a word about the flip network is in order. As mentioned before,
the flip network allows multi-dimensional access of the STARAN arrays (Figure 2).
It also can perform thousands of different permutations on a 256 bit string of bits.
Although its primary purpose is to provide multi-dimensional accessibility, many of
the permutations are useful as DM functions. Some of these permutations are described
below:

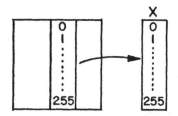

**BIT SLICE TRANSFER
INTO X RESPONSE STORE-
ONLY ONE ARRAY SHOWN**

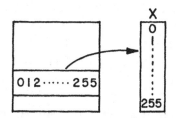

**WORD MODE TRANSFER
INTO X RESPONSE STORE-
ONLY ONE ARRAY SHOWN**

**NOTE: ALL ARRAYS CAN
PERFORM THIS OPERATION
IN PARALLEL**

Figure 2. Accessing the Staran Array

Definition: A subset (substring) flip of M is defined as dividing a string of P bits into N equal substrings and flipping (mirroring or turning end end) each subset of length P/N (see Figure 3). Some permutations have the same logical effect as

ORIGINAL STRING	FINAL STRING	ORIGINAL STRING	FINAL STRING
0	3	0	3
1	2	1	2
2	1	2	1
3	0	3	0
4	7	4	7
5	6	5	6
6	5	6	5
7	4	7	4
		8	11
		9	10
		10	9
		11	8

SUBSTRING FLIP OF 4-STRING OF 8 BITS, 2 SUBSETS

SUBSTRING FLIP OF 4-STRING OF 12 BITS, 3 SUBSETS

Figure 3. Substring Flips

if a series of subset flips were performed on the string. For example:

Permutation Number	Succession of Subset Flips
1	NONE
2	2 flip of 2
3	4, 2 flip of 4 followed by flip of 2
4	4
5	8,4
6	8,4,2
7	8,2
8	8
:	
22	32,16,8,4,2
:	
256	256,128,64,32,16,8,4,2

Another set of permutations are similar to the ones just mentioned but the word flip is replaced by shift end around m modulo n (subset size of n). For example, one permutation is a shift end around of 8 on every 16 PE's followed by a shift end a-round of 2 on every 4 PE's. Although these permutations appear as many permutations performed in "stages", they actually are performed by one STARAN machine instruction.

There are 8 instruction bits for a "flip" constant, another 8 bits (in a regis-ter) for a "shift" constant and one bit for mirroring (optionally allowing a 256 bit flip as another permutation). All of these bits can be specified independently but some of the permutations are not unique and the author does not have a closed form solution for all possible permutations. This area requires more investigation.

Each array also has the ability to load a response store register from array memory, from another response store register, or from itself with the contents shifted down by a power of two. Shifts up of a power of two require two instructions since a shift up is obtained by mirroring, shifting down a power of two (one instruction) and finally mirroring again. All shifts up require at least two mirrors but the last mirror can sometimes be performed along with another shift instruction. The first mirror is always performed during a shift instruction. Since STARAN can shift both up and down, non-power of two shifts can be performed efficiently. For example, a shift of 127 is made up of a shift down of 128 and a shift up of 1 (both powers of two). Logical operations can also be specified (AND, OR, and many others) between an input source (array, X or Y) and a response store register (X or Y).

These flip permutations, mirroring, shifting and logic can all be performed in succession by one machine instruction in as little as 150 nS (per bit slice).

Examples of specific implementations of DM functions should give the reader a feel for the power of these machine instructions. For illustration, string lengths of less than 256 will be used. PT will stand for power of two.

Regular Functions

Shift - End off shifts, total or substring, are all performed in the same way, only the mask changes for the various options. A bit slice is accessed from memory while being shifted a PT and stored in X. If the shift amount is a PT, X is then stored masked into the array. Since the shifting is done while accessing the bit slice, this function time is determined only by the basic access and masked store times of the array. If the shift amount is not a power of two, X is shifted the re-maining amount and then stored (masked) into the array (see Figure 4). This opera-tion is iterated in a hardware loop over all bit slices constituting the operand.

End around shifts are similar to end off shifts. For subsets that are a PT in length, STARAN can perform end around shifts of a PT as it reads from the array if aligned on the correct boundary (see Figure 5). The STARAN hardware performs subset flips or shifts on PT subsets starting at PE[0]. This defines the hardware bounda-ries. If the user specifies a string that is not on a hardware boundary, an initial

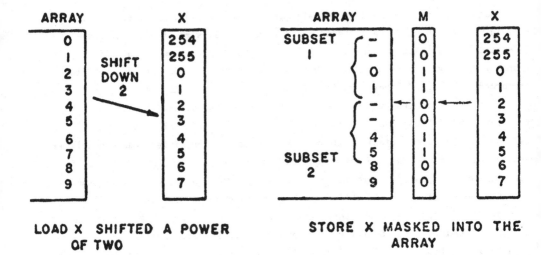

LOAD X SHIFTED A POWER OF TWO

STORE X MASKED INTO THE ARRAY

Figure 4.   Substring End Off Shift of 2
with Substring Size of 4

alignment (shift) is required. Non-PT shifts on PT substrings are handled just as
end off shifts were. End around shifts on non-PT substrings are obtained by performing two end-off shifts - one down and one up. Since end off shifts are fast, they
are used as building blocks for other DM functions.

Flip - Flipping PT substrings is also fast because the flip can perform this
permutation directly. All that is needed is to assure that the substrings are a-
ligned on the correct boundary (same as substring end around shifts). If the substrings are not on the correct boundaries, a simple end around shift (subset 256) is
performed.

Spread - Spread is made up of successive end off shifts, the number being $\log_2$
(# substrings). See Figure 6. The method shown is general, but when the spacing is
a PT, execution time is less. Certain spreads can be obtained in exactly the same
way a shuffle is implemented. These spreads are even faster (see shuffle).

Close - Close is also made up of end off shifts and is exactly the reverse of
spread.

Replicate - Replicate is used in many associative algorithms and fortunately is
quite efficient on STARAN. Contiguous replicate is obtained by doing a spread and
then a spaced replicate. Spaced and total replicate are performed in the same manner,
only the mask is different. Total replicate will be used as an example.

Consider a total string length that is a PT (Figure 7). A bit slice is selected
from the array, logically ANDed with the mask in the Y response store and ORed with
X (X was previously cleared), all by one machine instruction (Step 1, Figure 7). X
is then shifted a PT (the string length) and logically ORed with itself (Step 2, Figure 7). X is shifted by ever increasing powers of two and ORed with itself until the

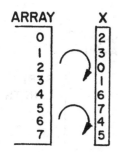

END AROUND SHIFT
ON POWER OF TWO
SUBSTRINGS SHIFTED
A POWER OF TWO-
INITIAL STRING ON
CORRECT BOUNDARY

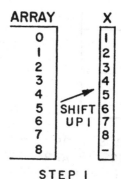

STEP I
END AROUND SHIFT ON
PT SUBSTRINGS – INITIAL
STRING NOT ON CORRECT
HARDWARE BOUNDARY

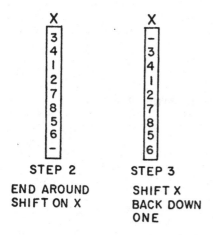

STEP 2
END AROUND
SHIFT ON X

STEP 3
SHIFT X
BACK DOWN
ONE

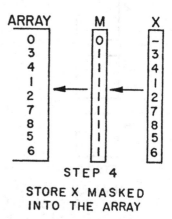

STEP 4
STORE X MASKED
INTO THE ARRAY

Figure 5. End Around Shifts Illustrating
Boundary Alignment Requirements

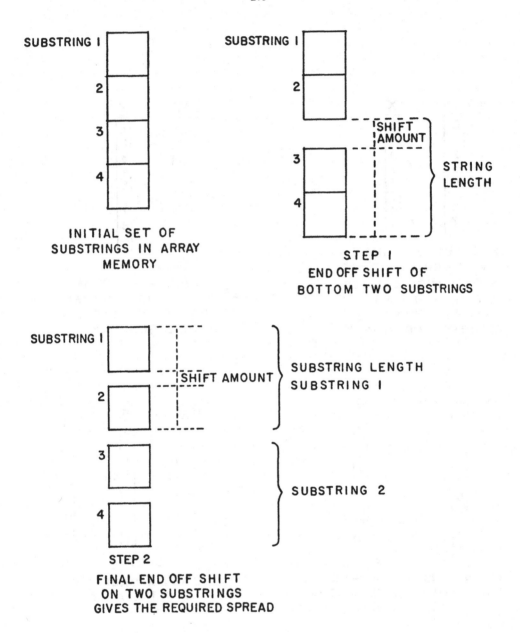

Figure 6. Performing a Spread on Four Substrings

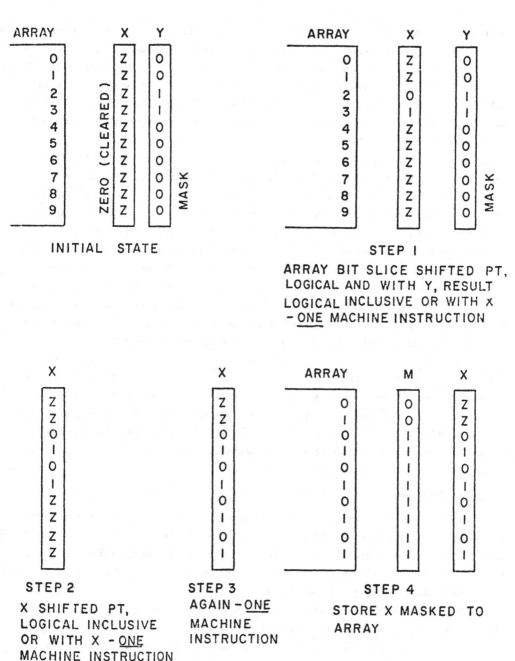

Figure 7. Replicating a String of Two Bits Starting at PE [0].
Replication Factor is 5.

desired replication factor is obtained. X is then stored masked into the array.

For non-PT string lengths, the procedure is nearly the same. X is loaded as in Step 1 of Figure 7, Y is then loaded with X shifted a PT. Y is then shifted if need be. X is ORed with Y shifted a final PT. This sequence repeats until the non-PT total string length is replicated the correct number of times. Each new bit slice that is accessed must be preceded by a clear X (done concurrently with another set up instruction) and a restore Y (the mask).

Shuffle - a shuffle can be visualized as a series of end around shifts (Figure 8) This method can be used to produce non-PT shuffles but STARAN's flip network offers a faster method for PT shuffles. The required PT end around shifts are slowed down because the substrings are not on the correct boundaries, thus requiring an initial shift for alignment and a final shift to restore the correct order. This problem can be eliminated by using one of the many flip permutations that produces an end around shift of selected substrings not on the correct boundary (Figure 9). With proper masking, the desired end around shift is efficiently obtained as follows: Y is loaded with a mask corresponding to the present "stage" or number of substrings to be shifted. X is double flipped (see Figure 9) and stored masked back into X all in one machine instruction. Finally, the shuffled X is stored back into the arrays.

Move - Move transfers a "block" or a set of contiguous locations to another location. By using the multi-dimension access memory, all the bits of a field in a PE are loaded into X (word mode). A destination PE is addressed and all the bits of the source field are placed into the destination field. This macro operates sequentially on PE's but parallel on the field width (all bits of a field are transferred at once). Since the move only consists of loads and masked stores, its time is also determined by the basic input-output time of the array.

Irregular Functions

Compress - Compress is similar to move except that the Y response store contains a dynamic run time mask that indicates which PE's are to be considered as sources for the "irregular close" (Figure 10). It is sequential on PE's but parallel on field width. An associative "step instruction" is used to step to each Y bit in turn. This "step instruction" requires 150 nS to execute.

Expand - Expand is the counterpart of compress and is implemented in a like manner. Expand and compress can be done only in one array at a time. (All other functions can be executed on all arrays at once.) Later we will see how global (on all arrays) DM functions can be used to advantage.

3. TIMING RESULTS

Timing results are given in Table 1. As a reference, an add of two 32 bit integers requires 30 microseconds while a multiply of two 32 bit integers requires 960 microseconds. Listed beside some of the timings are execution times of the same

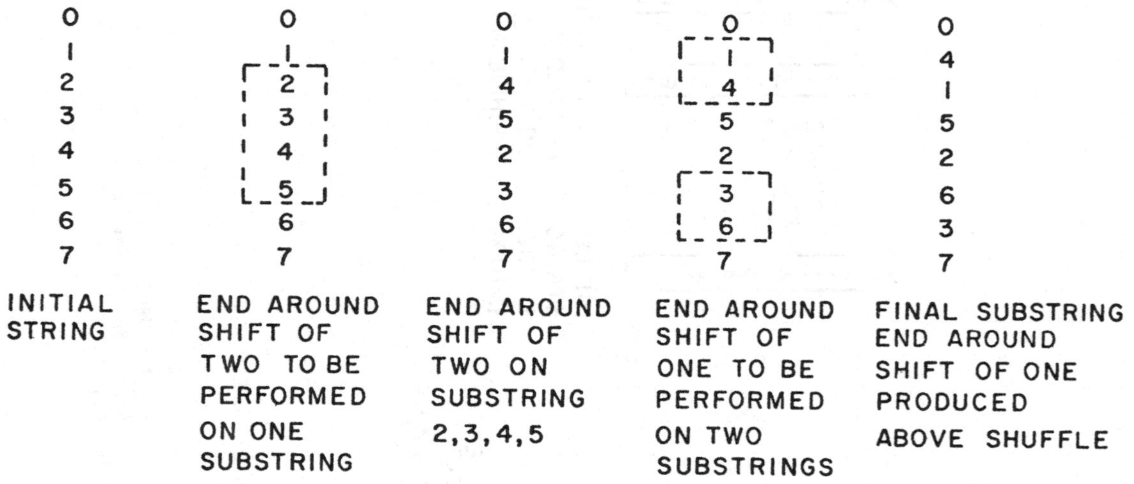

INITIAL STRING	END AROUND SHIFT OF TWO TO BE PERFORMED ON ONE SUBSTRING	END AROUND SHIFT OF TWO ON SUBSTRING 2,3,4,5	END AROUND SHIFT OF ONE TO BE PERFORMED ON TWO SUBSTRINGS	FINAL SUBSTRING END AROUND SHIFT OF ONE PRODUCED ABOVE SHUFFLE
0	0	0	0	0
1	1	1	4	4
2	2	4	5	1
3	3	5	2	5
4	4	2	3	2
5	5	3	6	6
6	6	6	7	3
7	7	7		7

Figure 8.   Shuffle by Way of End Around Shift

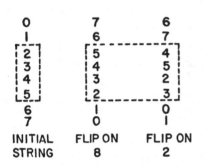

INITIAL STRING   FLIP ON 8   FLIP ON 2

FLIP ON SUBSTRINGS OF 8
FOLLOWED BY A FLIP ON
SUBSTRINGS OF TWO – <u>ONE</u>
MACHINE INSTRUCTION GIVES
END AROUND SHIFT OF 2,3 & 4,5 –
SEE UPPER RIGHT

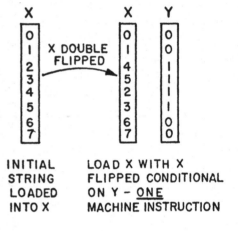

INITIAL STRING LOADED INTO X   LOAD X WITH X FLIPPED CONDITIONAL ON Y – <u>ONE</u> MACHINE INSTRUCTION

Figure 9.   Double Flip Used to Produce
End Around Shifts for Use in
Shuffle

TABLE 1. TIMINGS OF SOME DM FUNCTIONS ON STARAN

	Power of Two Functions (uS)	Same* Function Via Move	Non-Power of Two Functions (uS)	Same* Function Via Move	Comments
COMPRESS 32 Responders			39.5		No mask needed
FLIP					
256 Bit SL	15.8				No boundary alignment
128 Bit SL, 64 SS, Origin 0	20.6				Boundary Alignment
40 Bit SL, 10 SS, Origin 11	39.9	28.2		28.2	Move is faster
50 Bit SL, 10 SS, Origin 11			271.3		
100 Bit SL, 10 SS, Origin 0			262.1	61.5	
REPLICATE TOTAL					
8 Bit SL, Replicate 32	36.1				Fills entire array
7 Bit SL, Replicate 7			62.6	25.2	42 PE's moved via Move Macro
8 Bit SL, Replicate 7	28.5	21.8			
SHUFFLE					
256 Bit SL, Shuffle factor = 1	73.6				Worst case for PT SL and PT shuffle factor
256 Bit SL, Shuffle factor = 4	57.4				
MOVE					
5 PE's	3.8				
32 PE's	16.8				For 32 PE's takes same time as load and store in bit slice mode
SPREAD					
16 Bit SL, 8 SS, Spacing = 5	50.9	13.1	62.1	13.1	
16 Bit SL, 8 SS, Spacing = 2			41.5	10.1	
21 Bit SL, 3 SS, Spacing = 9					

*Timings of the same function implemented via a modified move macro sequential on PE's - Parallel on field width.

TABLE 1. TIMINGS OF SOME DM FUNCTIONS ON STARAN (Cont'd)

	Power of Two Functions (uS)	Same * Function Via Move	Non-Power of Two Functions (uS)	Same * Function Via Move	Comments
SHIFT END AROUND					
90 Bits, 30 SS, Shift 2, Origin 11	20.9				Non-PT shift with PT SL needs alignment
40 Bits, 10 SS, Shift 3, Origin 0	32.2				
40 Bits, 10 SS, Shift 3, Origin 2			42.8		
SHIFT END OFF					
Any Shift Down	17.0				About 32 times faster than end off shift
Any Shift Up	20.0				
MIXED MODE					
1 Out of 32 Shift of "1"	0.55				

SS = # Substrings
SL = String Length
All functions timed with 32 bit fields

*Timings of the same function implemented via a modified move macro - sequential on PE's - parallel on field width.

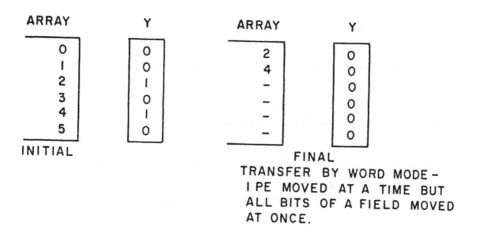

Figure 10. "Irregular Close" or Compress

function implemented by way of the move macro (sequential on PE's but parallel on fields). With a 32 bit field width, it is usually faster to move PE's word sequentially rather than one bit slice at a time. Most of the algorithms described so far have an execution time proportional to the product of the $\log_2$ of some parameter (e.g., string length) and the field width. Consideration of this product and the number of PE's to be moved enables a macro time decision to be made as to which algorithm is faster. Move is really beneficial in some non-PT areas such as flipping non-PT substrings.

Shift

Shift down of a PT down is one of the fastest functions (17 microseconds) because the data manipulation is done as each bit slice is read from array memory (17 microseconds for 32 bits gives 0.53 microseconds/bit slice). A 15% improvement in speed was attained by carefully arranging the sequence of instructions within the hardware loop iterating over each bit slice in the field. (When two array operations — load or store — were separated by a non-array instruction the improvement was realized.)

The 17 micorseconds is comprised roughly of a 150 nS read plus a set up mask and store masked instruction (total about 400 nS) for each of the 32 bit slices in the field width. Non-PT shifts require more instructions in the loop with an attendant longer execution time. The exact number of instructions in the loop for an end off shift is a function of the shift amount, the average being 4-5 for non-PT shifts.

Execution times for end around shifts vary depending on the shift amount as well as on the possibility of a shift for alignment on PT boundaries. Shifts on the total array (all 256 bits) are faster since a mask is not required.

Flip

Flips on PT substrings are very fast because the flip network performs this permutation naturally. Non-PT flips are performed by flipping all 256 bits and storing each substring individually - not particularly fast. Here the move is really helpful — sequential on PE's but parallel on field width.

Spread and Close

Most spreads and closes are made up of end off shifts. (See shifts for timing.) Some spreads can be performed by way of the shuffle since shuffle divides a string length in two and "spreads" the top half down and the bottom half up.

Replicate

For total (spaced) replications whose string length (substring length) is a PT, the execution time is minimal.

Shuffle

Shuffle has been implemented only for those cases with substring lengths and shuffle factors equal to a PT. Non-PT shuffles can be done by performing appropriate end around shifts. $\log_2$ (string lengths) - $\log_2$ (shuffle factor) - 1 operations are required for a shuffle. An operation is load Y with a mask, permute X, and store masked into X - just two instructions.

Move

Move is sequential on PE's and parallel on field width. Move could also have been implemented in a bit slice manner exactly as an end off total shift. Move sequential on PE's is faster if the number of PE's to be moved is less than the number of bits in the field width (for moves of a PT). The execution time of a move is linearly related to the number of PE's to be moved and is independent of the move distance and the field width.

Compress

The irregular functions are basically a move with the address of the source PE found associatively (one machine instruction).

Mixed Mode

An end around shift was performed in mixed mode. Mixed mode allows one to access N bits from every Nth PE so long as the total number of bits equals 256 and N is a PT. For example, suppose a problem allows one to subset the PE's so that every 32nd PE is active (8 PE's per array). A field of 32 bits from each of the 8 PE's can be accessed to form a 256 bit string (see Figure 11). Thus only 1/32 PE's are utilized but 32 times as many bits are manipulated in parallel in each active PE. So a shift end around of "1" on the 8 PE's really amounts to a shift of 32 with respect to the total array. This shift of "1" (32) can be performed as the data is read from memory (in mixed mode). Only two instructions are required - one mixed mode read with

A R R A Y

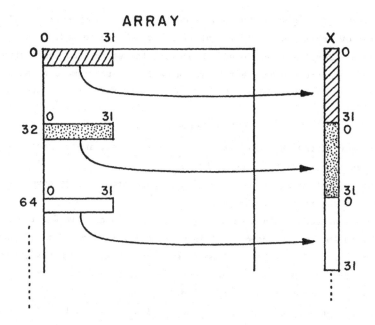

Figure 11. Mixed Mode Access

a PT shift and a mixed mode store giving a total execution time of 0.55 microseconds. (This is about 32 times faster than the 17 microseconds required to treat all 32 bit slices individually.) See [2] for more details on mixed modes.

4. AN EXAMPLE

An example of how the data manipulation functions can be globally used on all arrays will now be presented.

Consider a matrix multiplication, where matrix A is to multiply matrix B. Let A have dimensions I x K and B have dimensions K x J. With only one array, the flow chart for the associative solution [2] requires K iterations. An iteration is composed of two replicate functions, a parallel add and a parallel multiply. By using N STARAN arrays, the number of iterations can be reduced to $\lceil (K/N) \rceil$. Not only are the arithmetics reduced by adding more PE's (arrays) but also the required number of DM replicate functions are also reduced by the same factor. Since each STARAN array has the same DM capacity, these "global" DM functions can be used to advantage.

Other options are possible with the DM functions described. For example, using the word mode allows DM functions to be performed horizontally. To visualize the word mode turn each array 90 degrees and perform the DM functions as illustrated before. Upon completion, restore the array orientation.

DM functions with logic can also be performed with little or no additional execution time. For example, a "shuffle negative field" will perform a shuffle and complement each bit in the same amount of time as a shuffle. Likewise, a "replicate absolute field" or "shift two's complement field" can be performed. Mixed Mode DM functions have already been mentioned. Presently the source and destination fields for all DM functions are the same but they can easily be programmed to be different with no increase in execution time.

5. IMPROVEMENTS

Although many of the DM functions are relatively fast, improvements can be made. Software improvements consist of the following:

1. A thorough study should be made of the flip network to discover other useful permutations that it might perform.
2. The DM functions could have been written equally as well for the PIO (parallel input-output processor). This would allow the use of a PIO port register as a scratch bit slice to hold temporary results or a mask, reducing the execution time of many functions. It would also allow DM functions to be performed as background processing.
3. If a problem can be organized so that at least some DM functions operate on all 256 bits, time can be saved since a masked store to the array is not required.

Hardware modifications beneficial to DM functions are as follows:

1. For non-PT DM functions an arbitrary shift amount in one machine instruction would greatly help. The non-PT DM function execution time would generally approach the PT DM function execution time for many functions.
2. Extra response stores would be well appreciated. Log_2 (# PE's in one array) response stores would be ideal but this is probably too much to ask. One or two may be practical. Even a few bits of scratch memory (150 nS read/write) would help.

6. CONCLUSION

Implementation of the DM functions on STARAN were discussed and timings were presented. Data manipulation can be performed by manipulating each bit slice (parallel on PE's) or by moving one PE at a time but all bits of a field in parallel. Most DM functions execute between one half and two times the array add execution time. An illustration of how the DM functions can be globally executed was given. Suggestions for improvements are: 1. A detailed study of the flip network to uncover more permutations that may be useful to DM functions. 2. Implementing the DM functions in the PIO. 3. Adding more response store registers, and 4. Performing an arbitrary shift in one machine instruction.

REFERENCES

[1] T. Feng, "Data Manipulating Functions in Parallel Processors and Their Implementations", IEEE Trans. on Computers, (March 1974), pp. 309-318.

[2] W.T. Cheng, and T. Feng, "Solving Some Mathematical Problems by Associative Processing", Proceedings of the 1972 Sagamore Computer Conference on RADCAP and Its Applications, (August 1972), pp. 169-206.

[3] H.S. Stone, "Parallel Processing with the Perfect Shuffle", IEEE Trans. on Computers, (February 1971), pp. 153-161.

[4] E.P. Stabler, "Mixed Mode Arithmetic for STARAN", Proceedings of the 1974 Sagamore Computer Conference on Parallel Processing (August 1974).

[5] C.D. DeFiore, A.A. Vito, and L.H. Bauer, "Toward the Development of a Higher Order Language for RADCAP", Proceedings of 1972 Sagamore Computer Conference on RADCAP and Its Applications (August 1972), pp. 11-112.

MIXED MODE ARITHMETIC FOR STARAN [a]

E. P. STABLER
Department of Electrical and Computer Engineering
Syracuse University
Syracuse, N. Y.

SUMMARY

The array memory of STARAN can provide data to the arithmetic processing equipment in bit serial mode, word mode or mixed mode. In the mixed mode system analyzed here the memory provides 32 words of 32 bits for parallel processing. It is different from the normal bit mode operation for STARAN in which the system processes a single bit of each of the 1024 data words at a given moment.

The STARAN system analyzed here has an array memory size of 1024 x 1024 bits, which is segmented into 4 subarrays of 256 x 1024. In bit mode arithmetic, a single bit of each of 1024 words is processed simultaneously. For the mixed mode we assume a data word length of 32 bits so that up to 32 data words, each of 32 bits can processed simultaneously. Word lengths of 16, 24 or any other length may be processed similarly. It is intuitively clear that the bit mode of operation will have a good level of utilization of the equipment when the number of data words approaches 1024. In application problems which do not present so many data words for parallel processing, it is desirable to process simultaneously all the bits of a smaller number of data streams. Fortunately the array memory is designed to support either alternative. However, the processing logic available was designed principally to support bit mode arithmetic. Even so, the analysis of mixed mode arithmetic given here shows that large increases in speed and efficiency of utilization can be obtained using mixed mode arithmetic. In many application areas efficient processing of 32 element vectors will yield better overall results than the method which yields efficient processing of 1024 element vectors.

One method of speeding up the add process on an average basis is to use the process known as Mercer's adder. A carry vector and a partial sum vector are repeatedly combined until the carry vector becomes zero and the addition is complete. On an average basis the longest bit propagation path while adding two 32 bit numbers is about 5 bits. In the case that there are 32 such additions in parallel the longest average carry propagation length is increased to 11. The add time for mixed mode is proportional to the carry propagation length rather than the word length. The add time for bit serial add of 32 bit numbers is 32 μsec. The mixed mode add time is 15 μs average. The results for subtraction are similar.

[a] The work reported here was performed at Syracuse University and was supported by the Air Force Rome Air Development Center under Contract F30602-72-C-0281.

The high speed array logic multiply algorithms achieve multiply times which are proportional to the number of bits in the multiplier (n). If these algorithms can be implemented in some manner on the STARAN array we would expect multiply times proportional to n instead of n^2, as is the case for bit mode arithmetic.

The major idea behind many of the high speed multiply algorithms is the postponement of the completion of the add operations to the very end. Hence many add operations are in various states of progress. In the STARAN case the partial sum is stored as two n bit numbers whose sum is the true partial sum. The true sum is formed only when all the addends have been entered. Multiplication of pairs of 32 bit words to form 64 bit products takes 953 μsecs. in bit serial mode. The same calculation takes 240 μsec. in mixed mode.

Unfortunately the division process cannot be speeded up in the same manner as the multiply because in division algorithms the next step depends on the outcome of the previous one. A non-restoring division algorithm using the add-subtract process described earlier was implemented. Some speed improvement was obtained because the addition/subtraction is faster than the bit serial version. The divide time for bit serial mode is 1285 μsec. The mixed mode divide time is 830 μsec.

The STARAN memory control accepts 8 bit addresses so there are 256 distinct addresses available independent of the mode. In bit serial mode the 256 addresses are addresses of individual bits in the data words. Hence the hardware allows reference to any bit in any one of 8 32 bit words. The limitation to 8 words as a severe constraint in many applications. It can be overcome by masking and data movement with some loss in time. In the mixed mode case the 256 distinct addresses refer to 256 distinct 32 bit words which will be adequate in most cases. However, in mixed mode if bits must be selected from the data words masking is required.

The arithmetic processing speed of STARAN can be increased using mixed mode arithmetic. In this case the natural parallelism of the system is 32 rather than 1024 as in the conventional bit serial mode. Modification of the processing hardware to support mixed mode arithmetic, as well as bit serial would yield further increases in speed.

AAPL: AN ARRAY PROCESSING LANGUAGE[a]

JOHN G. MARZOLF
Department of Electrical and Computer Engineering
Syracuse University
Syracuse, New York 13210

Abstract -- AAPL is a dialect of APL designed to be more amenable to compilation than the standard version of APL. The principal differences include the use of name prefixes, the ability to accept a limited character set for denoting the primitive functions, some variations and restrictions on the use of the program-branching primitive, and some additional I/O primitives. The reasons for each of these modifications are discussed in detail, as well as the implications for transportability between the two dialects. An implementation of AAPL has been undertaken for the STARAN Associative Processor. An outline of this implementation and a progress report on the work is presented.

INTRODUCTION

APL as currently defined by the APL/360 implementation (see [1] and [2]) seems to be a natural candidate for a high-level language for SIMD-type parallel processors [3]-[5]. For a number of reasons, however, it does not appear that it can be conveniently compiled. For instance, the context-sensitive nature of a number of primitive symbols leaves their semantics ambiguous until execution time. Specifically, there are a group of primitive symbols which are used to denote two completely different functions depending on the number of arguments supplied with the symbol.

An example would be the cross (ordinary multiplication sign), which can be used monadically (i.e., with only a right argument) to represent the signum function, or it can be used dyadically (i.e., with both a left and right argument) to denote the multiplication function. In any given context the precise function intended can be determined by examining the source code to the left of the symbol. If there is some primitive scalar function on the left, then the cross has no left argument and hence is the signum function. If there is a right parenthesis or a number to the left of the cross, then it is known to be dyadic and thus is the multiplication function. For these cases the meaning is uniquely determined when the source code is entered. Such an arrangement allows compilation, provided one omits consideration of the memory management required for storage of the result.

The complication sets in when a name or identifier appears to the left of the

---
[a]This work was supported in part by Rome Air Development Center under Contract No. F30602-72-C-0281.

cross. There is no way of knowing, prior to the actual execution of the statement, whether this name will represent (at execution time) a variable value or a monadic defined function call - and that makes all the difference. Another difficulty in compiling APL stems from the absence of declaration statements in the language. This makes memory management a very complicated process.

One obvious response to these difficulties is to run APL interpretatively. Not only does this solve the problems mentioned, but it also buys a whole host of little extras that are very convenient for interactive programming. On the other hand, it entails a certain loss of execution efficiency. This is counter-productive to the increased computational throughput expected from parallel processing.

The solution that is proposed here is to introduce a dialect of APL (to be called AAPL, for 'An Array Processing Language') which can be more readily compiled, yet will remain as close as possible to the basic structure of standard APL. This permits parallel processing programs to be interactively written, tested and debugged on existing APL systems, and then transferred to the parallel processing systems for production use. It also provides the parallel processing programmers with a tested set of array oriented algorithms that have been developed by the APL programmers.

THE DESIGN OF AAPL

There appear to be two solutions to the problem of using the same symbol to represent two different functions, namely (1) change one of the symbols, or (2) provide naming conventions which explicitly identify the class of a name used on the left of the ambiguous symbol. The first solution is the obvious one, but it adds the additional burden of having to provide more primitive symbols - perhaps to the extent of creating a symbol set that will become unwieldy. This objection could be removed by a variation employing reserved words for certain of the primitive functions. In this case there is the more serious objection that it would be difficult to transport programs between the two dialects of APL. For this reason the second of the proposed solutions was chosen for AAPL. This also solves the related problem of detecting the syntax error in an attempted assignment of a value to a niladic function name or a label.

All names in AAPL are given alphabetic prefixes which specify the name-class of the object identified. There are five name-classes, and each is distinguished by a two letter prefix as shown in Table I. This means that all AAPL names are a minimum of three characters long. The first two must be a proper prefix and the remaining characters should be chosen according to the ordinary naming rules of APL. Such a procedure causes AAPL names to form a subset of APL names. Provided the names used in standard APL programs are chosen from that subset, all programs can be interchanged without alteration between the two dialects.

The selection of a two letter prefix scheme (rather than a one letter arrangement) was related to the desire of freeing AAPL from the I/O device restrictions imposed by the ordinary APL symbol set. In discussing this problem it should be noted that AAPL is intended to be a dialect of APL, and hence should differ from it as little as possible. On these grounds it was decided that the AAPL symbol graphics would be those of standard APL. However, the AAPL compiler would be designed to accept mnemonics as well as the standard symbols, since this would broaden the base of I/O devices that could be used with the system.

There have already been a number of proposals for such a set of mnemonics [6]-[8], but they generally employ a preceding escape character to differentiate the mnemonics from a similarly constructed APL name. In addition, the escape sequence is designed to be processed by the system input routine. This means that the conversion from the supplied mnemonic to the proper internal representation is made wherever the escape convention is encountered. In other words, if the escape sequence were used within a character literal, it would be converted by the system to the appropriate internal representation of the graphic for which it was the mnemonic. This is a suitable arrangement provided one is willing to allow the internal character count of some arrays to be different from that of their graphic representations. This is an anomaly which is avoided in AAPL.

There are no mnemonic escape characters used in AAPL. If the input is coming from a device capable of generating only a subset of the APL symbols, then those are the only symbols the device can enter into the system. What AAPL does permit, and which is not permitted in standard APL, is an alternate way of indicating to the compiler what precise computation is intended by the programmer.

The AAPL programmer may replace many of the standard APL graphics with a two letter mnemonic, which, because of the prefixing scheme chosen, cannot be confused with a name. When these mnemonics are entered from any device (including a device capable of entering the full APL symbol set) they are entered into the system precisely as the symbols for which they are the graphics (not as the symbols for which they are the mnemonics). The difference comes when the AAPL compiler encounters them. At this point they are translated into the proper execution code according to their mnemonic meaning.

For this reason not every APL graphic has a mnemonic representation, but only those that denote an executable operation, or are used as compiler directives, such as the lamp to indicate a remark. The mnemonics recognized by the AAPL compiler are shown in Table II. They are all two letter mnemonics, except for the letter N which is used to denote the hi-minus. This is treated as an exception since it is used as part of a numeric representation to denote a negative value, and is analogous to the use of the letter E in exponential format. In addition, the ASCII circumflex and the PL/1 logical NOT (hooked-minus) are considered as stylized versions of the hi-minus.

In cases where two mnemonics are shown for a given primitive, they are so provided to improve the readability of the mnemonic source code, but they may be used interchangeably. The intended meaning is determined by the compiler following the same procedures it would use if the primitive graphic had been employed.

Using this set of mnemonics, the only symbols required to write any AAPL function would be the letters, digits, parentheses, period, quote, and space. This permits AAPL programs to be entered from virtually any I/O device. The only features not provided by the mnemonics are the first-axis functions (for rotate, compress, expand, reduction, and scan), and the trace and stop control vectors. The omission of the first axis functions is not serious since they may be obtained from the indexed versions of these functions. The trace and stop control facilities are debugging aids, and it was not considered necessary to include them in a production oriented system.

Three new primitive functions have been added to allow the full use of all available I/O devices. These primitives are not assigned graphics from the standard APL symbol set so as not to conflict with any future assignments. They are available only as mnemonics. There is one input function (IN) which is monadic and takes a two component vector for its right argument. This argument specifies a file number and a component number which is the logical identifier of a physical device and a specific record. The assignment of a logical identifier to a given physical file is made by one of the I-beam functions. This also opens the file. The result generated by the input function is the value of the data object identified by its right argument.

There are two functions provided for generalized output; OU is the mnemonic for bare output and OT denotes terminated output. These functions are identical except for a final new-line character (carriage return plus line feed) that is supplied by the system at the end of each OT output request. Both functions are dyadic. The left argument specifies a logical file and component (similar to the file/component specification of the input function) and the right argument provides the data object to be output. Like other APL primitives, the output functions generate a result, which in this case is the value of the right argument. In other words, ignoring the physical output produced, these functions act as if they were the identity function. An alternate way of viewing these two functions is as a specialized case of the assignment function where the left argument is the logical name of a shared variable [9].

The problem of memory management in the absence of dimension declarations is solved by subterfuge. Although subsequent versions of AAPL may wish to attack this problem directly, the present version solves it by a get-space routine that does the job at execution time. This means that there is not a unique correspondence between the variable names and their physical memory addresses. Data values are located through a data descriptor table. Once some experience is gained with this implementation it will be possible to determine if a better solution to the problem is demanded.

There has been an improvement in the efficiency of the branching mechanism supplied with standard APL. Since the whole question of a proper set of control structures for APL is under investigation (see, for example, [10] and [11]) the arrangement described here should be seen as only an interim solution. Although the GOTO is not eliminated (indeed, it remains the kernel of the whole control system) it is made subject to a number of restrictions designed to provide more efficient execution. As a by-product these restrictions significantly improve one's ability to trace the flow of control through a program.

There are only three types of syntax allowed when using the branch arrow. It may be used

(1) with a single label or the number 0,

(2) with an indexed label list, or

(3) with a single label or the number 0, followed by the mnemonic IF, followed by any AAPL expression that evaluates to a 1 or 0.

This means that the target(s) of any branch is (are) always visible at the source level. Although this is more restrictive than the ordinary APL usage, it avoids the possibility of a variable name or function name completely obscuring the destination of the branch.

The indexed label list mentioned in the second type of branch is constructed by simply juxtaposing a number of labels (or the number 0) as if they were the elements of a numeric vector, and then indexing this string. This is the format required by the AAPL compiler, but it is not permitted in APL. Nonetheless, its semantic equivalent may be easily obtained in APL by catenating the labels, enclosing them in parentheses and indexing the resulting expression. This multiple branch provides the "case selection" capability used by structured programming languages to execute one of a number of alternate program blocks.

The third type of branch uses a new primitive (IF) which is nothing more than the compression function with its arguments reversed, together with the restriction that its left argument must be a single label or the number 0. Although this function is not available in standard APL as a primitive, it is easily introduced as a user defined function. Indeed, there are no real transportability problems between the two dialects because of these branching restrictions. All that is required is that these restdictions also be followed in the standard APL programs.

THE IMPLEMENTATION OF AAPL

An implementation of AAPL is in progress for the STARAN Associative Processor at Rome Air Development Center. The AAPL compiler is itself written in AAPL. It

235

communicates with the I/O devices through a supervisor module written in MACRO-11
assembly code. This module runs on a PDP-11 which acts as the sequential control
unit for STARAN. The supervisor module uses the basic I/O facilities of the DOS-11
batch operating system, and presents the AAPL compiler with a source program in a
form called PCODE. This is a print-code, and is merely an extension of ASCII to
allow for the APL graphics, including the overstrikes.

The AAPL compiler translates the PCODE source program into an object module in
a form called QCODE. If the source program is a function definition, then the object module is merely stored in the control memory. Otherwise the compiler acts as
a load-and-go system, deleting the object module when execution is complete.

QCODE is the AAPL execution code, and is basically a form of threaded code
[12]. The QCODE machine is a stack oriented virtual machine composed of two main
modules, one running on the sequential processor (SP) and the other on the associative processor (AP). There is also an interface module to manage the inter-
processor communications via the interrupt system and shared memory (which is actually AP control memory that is accessible to SP).

The system attempts to overlap as much as possible of the SP and AP execution.
The SP module fetches the object code, decodes it, performs the necessary housekeeping, and makes a call to AP for an array operation. While AP is satisfying this
request, SP proceeds to the next object code.

The SP module consists of about 100 routines, of which about 70 have been
written and tested. These routines have all been written in MACRO-11. The AP module is written in APPLE, which is the assembly language for the STARAN associative
processor. Only a few of these routines have been completed.

The initial tests on the system have used a sequential simulation in place of
the AP module. While it is not possible at this time to provide detailed performance statistics, preliminary tests using a stand-alone PDP-11/45 are extremely en-
couraging. For instance, the AAPL branch outperforms the APL branch (running on an
IBM 370/155) by better than 4-1. This is an actual elapsed time measurement without
an adjustment for the different intrinsic speeds of the two machines.

TABLE I. NAME PREFIXES

Prefix	Name Class
VA	Variable
LA	Label
NF	Niladic function
MF	Monadic function
DF	Dyadic function

TABLE II. AAPL MNEMONICS

Graphic	Name	Mnemonic	Graphic	Name	Mnemonic
+	Plus	PL	↑	Take	TA
−	Minus	MI	↓	Drop	DR
×	Times (Signum)	TI,SG	⍋	Grade Up	GU
÷	Divide	DV	⍒	Grade Down	GD
*	Exponentiate	XP	/	Compression (Reduction)	CM,RD
⌈	Maximum (Ceiling)	MX,CE	\	Expansion (Scan)	XN,SC
⌊	Minimum (Floor)	MN,FL	⊥	Base Value	BV
|	Residue (Absolute Value)	RS,AB	⊤	Representation	RP
⊛	Logarithm	LG	⍎	Execute/Evaluate	EX
!	Factorial(Binomial Coef)	FA,BC	⍕	Format	FM
○	Circular Fns (Pi Times)	CI,PI	⌹	Matrix Divide	MD
<	Less than	LT	←	Assign/Is	IS
≤	Less than or Equal	LE	[	Left Bracket	LB
=	Equal	EQ	]	Right Bracket	RB
≥	Greater than or Equal	GE	;	Semicolon	SM
>	Greater than	GT	I	I-Beam	IB
≠	Not Equal	NE	▯	Quad	QD
∧	And	AN	▯	Quote-Quad	QQ
∨	Or	OR		Input	IN
⍲	Nand	NA		Output-Bare	OU
⍱	Nor	NR		Output-Terminated	OT
~	Logical Not	NT	∘	Null/Outer Product	OP
?	Question Mark	QU	∇	Del	DL
,	Catenate (Ravel)	CA,RA	⍱	Locked Del	LD
ρ	Rho	RH	→	Go To	GO
ι	Iota	IO		IF	IF
ε	Epsilon	EP	:	Colon	CL
⍉	Transpose	TR	⍝	Lamp/Remark	RM
φ	Rotate	RT	‾	Hi-minus	N

REFERENCES

[1]   APL/360-OS and APL/360-DOS User's Manual, IBM Publication GH20-0906 (1970).

[2]   Sandra Pakin, APL-360 Reference Manual, Science Research Associates, Inc.,
      (1972), 192 pp.

[3]   Kenneth J. Thurber and John W. Myrna, "System Design of a Cellular APL
      Computer", IEEE Transactions on Computers (April, 1970), vol. C-19, No. 4,
      pp. 199-212.

[4]   A. Hassitt, J. W. Lageschulte, and L. E. Lyon, "Implementation of a High Level
      Language Machine," Communications of the ACM (April, 1973), vol. 16, No. 4,
      pp. 291-303.

[5]   A. D. Falkoff and K. E. Iverson, "The Design of APL", IBM J. Res. Develop.
      (July, 1973), vol. 17, pp. 324-334.

[6]   Tom McMurchie, "A Limited Character APL Symbolism", APL Quote-Quad
      (November, 1970), vol. 2, No. 4, pp. 3-4.

[7]   P. E. Hagerty, "An APL Symbol Set for Model 35 Teletypes", APL Quote-Quad
      (September, 1970), vol. 2, No. 3, pp. 6-8.

[8]   Glen Seeds, "APL Character Mnemonics", APL Quote-Quad (Fall, 1974), vol. 5,
      No. 2, pp. 3-9.

[9]   A. D. Falkoff and K. E. Iverson, APLSV User's Manual, IBM Publication SH20-
      1460 (1973).

[10] R. A. Kelley, "APLGOL, an Experimental Structured Programming Language",
      IBM J. Res. Develop. (January, 1973), vol. 17, pp. 69-73.

[11] M. A. Jenkins, A Control Structure Extension to APL, Department of Computing
      and Information Science, Queen's University, Kingston, Ontario, Technical
      Report No. 21, (September, 1973), 13 pp.

[12] James R. Bell, "Threaded Code", Communications of the ACM (June, 1973),
      vol. 16, No. 6, pp. 370-372.

THE EVOLUTION OF A PARALLEL
ACTIVE TRACKING PROGRAM

MICHAEL W. SUMMERS and DAVID F. TRAD
Rome Air Development Center (ISCA)
Griffiss AFB, N.Y. 13441

Abstract — Processing active radar data is a real time function with potentially high data rates. As the data rate increases, iterative sequential tracking routines become critically time consuming. These properties and the inherent parallelism of the tracking algorithms make active tracking an ideal application for parallel processing.

This paper documents the parallel implementation of an active tracking computer program. Program design considerations are discussed, with particular regard to their impact on accuracy, speed of execution, and memory utilization. This study is part of a larger effort currently underway at Rome Air Development Center (RADC), to evaluate the capabilities offered by parallel computer architectures.

1. INTRODUCTION

The underlying objective of the Rome Air Development Center Associative Processor (RADCAP) Project is to investigate solutions to data processing problems which strain conventional approaches due to high data rates and heavy processing requirements. The approach being taken consists of a detailed analysis and assessment of a specific application which is representative of a class of real-world problems which have current and near future relevance to the USAF data processing requirements. It was considered desirable to select an application which provided a suitable evaluation medium for the comparisons of performance between an associative processor and a conventional sequential processor architecture. The data processing functions inherent in the USAF Airborne Warning and Control System (AWACS) Project provide an excellent application area for RADCAP test bed investigations. This paper describes a parallel implementation of an active tracking function which resembles active tracking as performed in AWACS.

This study will use the RADCAP test bed facility, which consists of a STARAN associative array processor (AP) coupled to a Honeywell Information System (HIS) 645. The hardware and software comprising this test bed facility are described in references [1] and [2].

2. TEST PROBLEM SELECTION

Initial considerations in the selection of a meaningful application to be analyzed as part of the RADCAP program were based on several criteria. Such an application should span a wide range of data processing functions including real-time data processing with its attendant concurrency of processing and input/output, command/control functions, display processing facilities and algorithms amenable to parallel/associative processing. AWACS was a natural choice and provided the additional advantage of data availability for both input and result validation. However, the intent was not to implement the entire set of AWACS data processing functions, since this was considered too ambitious an initial undertaking. Hence, a representative subset of AWACS was regarded as a suitable alternative. The plan then was to select a simple function, perform the required analysis and comparisons, and follow these by more complex functions. Active tracking was the initial function selected.

Active tracking, as an AWACS data processing function, was implemented by two different computer programs at the time the test problem selection was made.

The first alternative considered was the Ground Tracking Computer Program (GTCP). GTCP is a completely operational surveillance system, which in addition to active tracking, includes coordinate conversion, passive tracking and display functions. The input data, collected in a real-world environment, is classified. Similarly, many of the algorithms implemented by the GTCP are classified. The bulk of the system was coded using FORTRAN, while assembly language was used to code portions of the system for speed of execution.

The second alternative considered was the Integrated Tracking and Surveillance (ITAS) program. The implementation of ITAS includes only the active tracking function and while the algorithms resemble those used in the GTCP, they are unclassified. The input data, also unclassified, is generated within ITAS. The entire system is coded using FORTRAN.

Both the GTCP and ITAS execute in a sequential processor environment.

The selection of ITAS resolved several potential problems. First, it was felt that the active tracking function of the GTCP could not be handled within the time frame allotted for this phase of the RADCAP program. The subsystem interface within the GTCP would be more difficult, hence more time consuming. Secondly, the RADCAP testbed facility does not operate in a classified environment. Thirdly, the collection of real-world data for input to GTCP could prove to be difficult and time consuming.

A careful look at ITAS showed that it would be relatively easy to isolate the data generation portion from the actual active tracking portions. This was desirable since only the active tracking routines would be monitored. Additionally, greater flexibility would be provided in the generation of input data allowing any number of targets to traverse any desired paths, thus providing greater control over the experiment and facilitating program checkout and extension to handle more tracks.

3. ITAS

The active tracking function to be implemented on RADCAP can be divided into two main areas: association/correlation, to select the most appropriate radar return for each track, and the actual smoothing of the track by a Kalman filter [3].

Association/correlation consists of a sequence of several steps which are performed on each radar return to select that report which is "closest" to the predicted track. Association is performed as the first step in the selection process by forming some range and azimuth boundaries (or windows) within which a report must fall in order to be considered further. One of four windows is selected, depending on the correlation history of the preceding scans. Range rate is also checked to see if it falls in an acceptable window. A return falling within the selected windows is further tested to see if it falls too far in front of the predicted point; if it does, it is rejected. Next comes a test to see if the observed change in range rate and range both have the same sign.

The detailed correlation process then begins with the formation of more refined non-maneuver windows in range and azimuth, using measurement error and expected track error from filter covariances. Reports falling inside these windows are labelled as non-maneuvering and the one closest to the predicted track is selected for smoothing. Closeness is judged by normalizing the measured error to the expected error and summing azimuth, range and range rate components.

If no return appears in the non-maneuver window, associated returns are tested to see if they could have come from a maneuvering target. Maneuvering windows are formed by allowing the target to accelerate, decelerate, and turn parallel and perpendicular to the range vector. Reports passing this test are labeled maneuvering and tested for closeness. The closest correlated return is then passed to the filter.

A track is initiated from two data points. Subsequent reports which correlate with the track are then used to smooth it. Two 2 x 2 Kalman filters are used to smooth the X and Y components of target position. A disturbance or filter "drive" is computed on the basis of correlation data. This drive is used to prevent filter divergence and to help follow maneuvers. Then the covariance matrix is updated; smoothing coefficients are computed, and the track and covariance matrix are updated. If range rate measurements are available, the range rate and the smoothed speed are used to determine the new heading of the target.

4. TEST PLAN

The previous section has defined the model of the AWACS active tracking functions to be used in the comparison of parallel and sequential processing. The test plan which is described in the following paragraphs defines the input scenario to be used and specifies what parameters are to be measured in these initial comparison tests.

The performance measurements of both association/correlation and smoothing/prediction will be based on the following parameters:

1. Number of tracks processed per scan

2. Number of false reports per scan

3. Ratio of the number of returns to the expected number of returns for all
   tracks (blip to scan ratio)

4. Target maneuvers

Performance measurements will be made for the test cases identified in Tables 1
and 2. All cases will be measured for fifty tracks over sixty radar scans. Cases 1
through 9 will be measured for non-maneuvering targets and cases 10 through 12 will
be measured with each target making a 90 degree turn after twelve radar scans. Case
13 will be measured for non-maneuvering targets of ten groups with five targets in
each group. Each group of targets has different initial conditions. Case 14 is similar to case 13, but will be measured for maneuvering targets. Each group target will
make a 90 degree turn. The turn direction and acceleration and time of turn will be
different for each group. Average times to process a single track will be computed
for each case. These average times will be used to estimate the time required to
process 10, 100, 200, 500 and 1,000 tracks for each case.

5. ITAS - PARALLEL IMPLEMENTATION

Efficient rewriting of an application program for another computer requires an
understanding of the application as well as the target machine. This is particularly
true when both the language of the new program and the architecture in which it will
execute are new and different.

In ITAS, much of the exploitable parallelism is inherent and obvious. Still a
great deal is to be gained by thorough investigation of the serial algorithms. The
more apparent parallelism is provided by FORTRAN "do loops" on tracks and on radar
reports. More subtle, second order parallelism exists by virtue of the x-y component
calculations of the Kalman filter. However, in order to fairly demonstrate the capability of an Associative Processor to perform the tracking function, the parallel implementation must be more than a straightforward translation of serially structured
algorithms. The serial approach to the problem must be analyzed and, wherever pro-
fitable, restructured to fully exploit the parallel architecture.

Basic changes to the structure of ITAS were somewhat limited by the desire to
perform essentially the same functions and the need to clearly validate results.

As outlined in Section III, the active tracking function performed by ITAS can
be divided into two distinct areas, association/correlation, and smoothing and prediction.

In the serial implementation the sequence of association tests are performed by
passing each report's data sequentially over each established track to match each
track with at most a small group of contending reports. Thus, if there are N tracks
and M reports, N x M iterations are required. In the parallel case, two modes of
operation are apparent, parallel on tracks (parallelism N) or parallel on reports
(parallelism M). On a given radar scan, the percentage of the established tracks

TABLE 1 DESCRIPTION OF ITAS TEST CASES

Case No.	False Reports per Scan	Blip to Scan Ratio	Initial Conditions of AWACS Aircraft			
			X – Pos. (N. Miles)	Y – Pos (N. Miles)	Speed (Knots)	Heading* (Deg.)
1	10	.32	0.0	0.0	360.0	0.0
2	10	.60				
3	10	.90				
4	50	.32				
5	50	.60				
6	50	.90				
7	150	.32				
8	150	.60				
9	150	.90				
10	50	.32				
11	50	.90				
12	150	.90				
13	50	.60				
14	50	.90				

*Heading angle measured from Positive X-axis or the true east in counterclockwise direction.

TABLE 2 TARGET INITIAL CONDITIONS OF ITAS TEST CASES

Case No.	Target No.	X - Pos (N. Miles)	Y - Pos.* (N. Miles)	Speed (Knots)	Heading (Deg.)	Turn Begin Time (Hrs.)	Turn Angle (Deb.)	Turn Dir. (L or R)	Accel. thru Turn (G)
1,2, 3,4, 5,6, 7,8 9	1	177.0	177.0	500.0	180.0	--	--	--	--
	2		175.0						
	3		173.0						
	.	.	.						
	.	.	.						
	50		79.0	500.0	180.0	--	--	--	--
10,11, 12	1	177.0	177.0	500.0		0.03	90.0	RH	3.0
	2		175.0						
	3		173.0						
	.	.	.						
	.	.	.						
	50		79.0	500.0	180.0	0.03	90.0	RH	3.0
13	1-5	177.0	177.0 - 171.0	500.0	180.0	--	--	--	--
	6-10	-177.0	177.0 - 171.0	500.0	90.0				
	11-15	-100.0	100.0 - 92.0	500.0	90.0				
	16-20	100.0	100.0 - 92.0	1200.0	180.0				
	21-25	0.0	50.0 - 42.0	500.0	180.0				
	26-30	-50.0	50.0 - 42.0	500.0	135.0				
	31-35	170.0	0.0 - -8.0	500.0	270.0				
	36-40	-170.0	0.0 - -8.0	500.0	90.0				
	41-45	50.0	-50.0 - -58.0	1000.0	315.0				
	45-50	0.0	-100.0- -108.0	700.0	0.0				

*The initial Y-position of each target is separated by 2 miles.

TABLE 2 TARGET INITIAL CONDITIONS OF ITAS TEST CASES (Cont'd)

Initial Conditions of Targets

Case No.	Target No.	X - Pos (N. Miles)	Y - Pos.* (N. Miles)	Speed (Knots)	Heading (Deg.)	Turn Begin Time (Hrs.)	Turn Angle (Deg.)	Turn Dir. (L or R)	Accel. thru Turn (G)
14	1-5	177.0	177.0 - 171.0	500.0	180.0	0.03	90.0	RH	3.0
	6-10	-177.0	177.0 - 171.0	500.0	90.0	0.06		RH	3.0
	11-15	-100.0	100.0 - 92.0	500.0	90.0	0.12		LH	2.0
	16-20	100.0	100.0 - 92.0	1200.0	180.0	0.09		RH	3.0
	21-25	0.0	50.0 - 42.0	500.0	180.0	0.11		LH	2.0
	26-30	-50.0	50.0 - 42.0	500.0	135.0	0.05		LH	2.0
	31-35	177.0	0.0 - -8.0	500.0	270.0	0.08		RH	2.0
	36-40	-177.0	0.0 - -8.0	1000.0	90.0	0.04		LH	2.0
	41-45	50.0	-50.0 - -58.0	500.0	315.0	0.07		RH	2.0
	46-50	0.0	-100.0 - -108.0	700.0	0.0	0.10		LH	3.0

*The initial Y-position of each target is separated by 2 miles.

which will typically be detected is determined by the "blip to scan" ratio of the radar. In addition to these "real" reports, a variable number of "false" reports determined by the "false alarm" rate, will inevitably be detected. Since the total number of reports, both real and false, is likely to be greater than the number of established tracks, we can typically expect M to be greater than N. This would indicate that performing the association tests parallel on reports would be the best choice yielding N iterations, parallelism M. That is in fact the case initially, but as successive association tests screen out false reports, the number of surviving reports, and hence the degree of parallelism M, for any given track decreases rapidly. For our test cases the maximum number of reports surviving the first two association tests, range and azimuth, was as low as two percent of the original M reports.

To solve this problem the parallel version of ITAS performs the first two association tests parallel on reports and the remaining tests parallel on tracks. The tests which are done parallel on tracks must be repeated for each report which survived the previous test. Therefore the number of repetitions of each track-parallel test is dependent upon the maximum number (for our test cases this maximum number was three after the first two association tests) of reports surviving the previous test.

The next step is correlation which applies more refined, dynamic windows to further screen reports prior to the closeness determination. The serial version of ITAS must calculate the non-maneuver correlation windows individually for each track. This task is performed only once in the parallel version eliminating the repetitive nature of the serial code. Following the application of these non-maneuver windows, maneuver correlation must be performed in some instances as described in Section 3.

The calculation of the sophisticated maneuver correlation windows and their application occurs only for those tracks with one or more reports which survived association, but failed non-maneuver correlation. Typically, this represents only a small subset of the established tracks, and therefore most of the track parallelism is lost during maneuver correlation. Since maneuver correlation represents a significant amount of time consuming code, alternatives have been investigated. If a radar report, which failed non-maneuver correlation, were simply assumed to have passed maneuver correlation, two results are possible. First, if the report would indeed have passed maneuver correlation, then the assumption was correct, and no problems arise. On the other hand, if the report would have been eliminated by maneuver correlation, then this report could incorrectly be passed to the Kalman filter by virtue of being the only surviving report or in a rare situation by being "closer" than a remaining non-maneuver report. This would lead to different predictions for speed and position for the affected track than would have arisen had the report been eliminated.

A scheme for handling this situation and thereby eliminating maneuver correlation involves maintaining two copies of each track history. One copy chooses its closest report only from among the reports which passed non-maneuver correlation, assuming any other reports failed maneuver correlation. The second copy chooses from all reports which passed association assuming that those which failed non-maneuver correlation would have passed maneuver correlation. The copy of the track based only on non-maneuver correlated returns is assumed to be correct until the question is resolved on a subsequent scan.

This scheme is currently being implemented and its performance as a substitute for maneuver correlation will be closely evaluated. Since this method requires more array-memory for the dual track history variables, it must yield a considerable saving in execution time to warrant its inclusion in the program.

In both the serial and the parallel versions of ITAS, the final step in association/correlation is the "closeness" determination described in Section 3. This best fit test serves to reduce the number of contending reports to at most one. Smoothing and prediction now begins and the remainder of the scan processing can be done in parallel on those tracks with surviving reports. Smoothing and prediction is accomplished via a Kalman filtering process briefly described in Section 3. In this portion of the algorithm the planar radar data has been converted from its original polar coordinates to Cartesian coordinates. The vast majority of variables, both intermediate and history, which appear in this algorithm are calculated and used in similar ways for both the x and y components. Therefore a great deal of what can be termed second order parallelism can be exploited with two processing elements active for each track. The x and y components of a particular variable can be derived in parallel for all tracks. This yields an order of parallelism twice the number of active tracks for most of the smoothing and prediction process.

6. PROGRAMMING CONSIDERATIONS

Two related programming considerations which arose early in the effort were the acquisition of data and the allocation of the various types of available memory.

The data representing the test cases described in Tables 1 and 2 was recorded on magnetic tape as part of the serial execution of ITAS. Using the testbed facilities, the tape was converted from ASCII to fixed point binary and put in a form suitable for use as input to the active tracking program executing on STARAN. This data is then transferred, as needed, from the HIS-645 to the PDP-11 disk storage subsystem, a peripheral accessible to STARAN. At execution time this data is read into a buffer in STARAN bulk core memory, one scan at a time. Parallel Input/Output (PIO) control [1] is activated to perform the core to array (3) transfer concurrent with processing in array (0) under AP control. The scan's worth of data is then transferred in parallel from array (3) to array (0).

The four arrays are functionally organized with all computation occurring in array (0). Arrays (1), (2), and (3) are used to simulate a parallel mass memory backup store with array (3) doubling as an input data buffer.

The layout of the processing array (0) changes dynamically, but the following basic layout is used in each processing element of array (0).

0		255
Variable sized argument fields	Buffer area	Masks

The layout is fixed for array (1) which contains the history variables for the Kalman filter. Only the values of the variables change from scan to scan, the positions and sizes of the fields are unaltered. Array (2) is used primarily to hold intermediate variables which must be saved temporarily in the course of both association/correlation and the Kalman filter.

Array (3) serves two different purposes. First, it serves as an I/O buffer for incoming radar reports. This data is transferred from bulk core memory to array (3) by the PIO while Kalman filter calculations are underway in array (0). Then as the first step in the next scan the data is transferred in parallel to array (0), and Association begins the cycle again. The second use of array (3) is as back up memory during association/correlation. It should be pointed out that all STARAN arrays possess identical capability and the functional organization described above was derived to meet the particular objectives of this evaluation.

The high speed semiconductor memory in STARAN is used to hold frequently called system and user subroutines and to store program constants for rapid access.

Resident in bulk core memory is the executing program itself and the radar data input buffer mentioned previously. Memory allocation decisions are not frozen at this time, but the above description represents the structure of what will be the first operating model of the parallel version of ITAS.

Another of the more important programming decisions involved the choice between fixed point and floating point arithmetics. The fixed point arithmetic subroutines execute considerably faster than the software floating point available on the RADCAP STARAN. Also, floating point requires a fixed field size of 32 bits whereas fixed point allows the size of the array fields to adjust to the particular accuracy requirements and dynamic range of each variable. Inherent in this flexibility of fixed point variable fields is the requirement for detailed knowledge of the characteristics of each variable. The anticipated gain in the execution time of fixed point was considered worth the additional coding time required and fixed point arithmetics using variable sized fields with varying binary point position was selected.

The extensive macro capability of the MACRO APPLE [2] assembler greatly aided the coding effort by allowing the programmer to essentially add new user defined mnemonics to the assembly language. Many macros are used in the parallel version of ITAS to perform commonly repeated tasks in the areas of input and output, data manipulation, debugging, and the set up and call of user subroutines. Some of these ITAS macros meet a particular requirement of the application at hand and have remained resident in the ITAS user's macro library. Many macros developed for ITAS are of general interest and have been added to the system macro library, essentially providing an extension to the assembly language for all RADCAP users. Most of the macros added to the system macro library are used to establish the calling sequence and format the arguments for a related subroutine. For example, macros were developed to set up and call the trigonometric SINE, COSINE, and ARCTANGENT subroutines also developed for ITAS. These macros and the associated subroutines represent significant additions to the AP programming language as a byproduct of the active tracking application effort.

7. CONCLUSIONS

The primary requirement of the parallel version of ITAS is that it must perform accurately in comparison with the serial validation data. Preliminary results from the debugging of track initialization and association/correlation indicate that the fixed point fields thus far defined are providing adequate accuracy. The effect of rounding errors on subsequent scans has yet to be fully analyzed, but the accuracy of track history variables has been defined as critical to this process.

No timing results are obtainable at this time since the smoothing and prediction function is incomplete and association/correlation is not yet thoroughly debugged. All support software has been debugged and is currently operational. Upon completion, the parallel version of ITAS will undergo performance evaluation.

This evaluation will be based on the following monitor data for each test case in both the serial and parallel version.

      a.   Wall clock start to end time

      b.   Total CPU time

      c.   Association/correlation CPU time

      d.   Smoothing and prediction CPU time

CPU times for association/correlation and smoothing and prediction will be plotted against the blip to scan ratio and the false alarm rate for all test cases. Suitable extrapolations will be made for both the serial and parallel implementation.

8. SUMMARY

This paper has traced the evolution of a parallel active tracking program from problem definition through coding. The active tracking function has been briefly described and the case for a parallel approach has been outlined. The concentration has been on the mapping of a representative sequential tracking program into a more efficient parallel version to execute on the STARAN Associative Processor at RADC.

A FORTRAN program called ITAS (Integrated Tracking and Surveillance) was selected as a representative sequential implementation of the tracking algorithms. The major elements of ITAS are association/correlation and smoothing and prediction (Kalman filter).

Association consists of gross comparisons in an attempt to pair one report with each track. Correlation then employs more refined tests to determine if the radar report does in fact correlate with the associated track. The sequential implementation and the parallel version developed have been presented.

The smoothing and prediction routine employs Kalman filtering to update each track and based on the smoothed position and velocity, to predict the next-scan target position. The sequential version of ITAS must perform smoothing and prediction once for each track with a correlated return for the scan. The parallel version described performs this task only once per scan and in addition exploits the second order parallelism inherent in the Kalman filter algorithms.

The STARAN arrays have been apportioned to fully exploit the parallelism of the tracking function while attempting to simulate parallel mass memory I/O operation.

The last major section of the paper documents the important programming decisions and the rationale behind them. Included in this section is a discussion of the choice of fixed point vs. floating point arithmetics and the flexibility and complexity of writing a parallel program with array fields of varying length and different binary point positions.

The paper concludes with the status of the effort and a discussion of some preliminary results.

REFERENCES

[1] K.E. Batcher, "STARAN/RADCAP Hardware Architecture", Proceedings of the 1973 Sagamore Conference on Parallel Processing, (August, 1973) pp. 147-152.

[2] E.W. Davis, "STARAN/RADCAP System Software", Proceedings of the 1973 Sagamore Conference on Parallel Processing, (August 1973), pp. 153-159.

[3] J.J. Burke, "Understanding Kalman Filtering and Its Application in Real Time Tracking Systems," ESD-TR-72-312, (July, 1974).

IMPLEMENTATION OF THE AWACS PASSIVE TRACKING
ALGORITHMS ON A GOODYEAR STARAN

BRIAN W. PRENTICE
Boeing Computer Services
Space & Military Applications Division
Seattle, Washington 98124

Abstract -- The AWACS Passive Tracking algorithms are being implemented on the
Goodyear STARAN computer installation at RADC. Difficulties encountered during the
implementation due to the limitations of the hardware architecture and system software are identified. The design concepts which were used to minimize these difficulties are discussed. Possible improvements to the hardware and software which may
be of benefit to futute applications programmers are recommended.

INTRODUCTION

Research into parallel processing is currently being conducted at Rome Air Development Center. The objective of this research is to determine the extent to which
associative processors can be used to solve some military applications, with high
data rate requirements, which are beyond the scope of conventional serial processors.
A Goodyear STARAN 1000 associative processor is being used for this research study.
As a part of this study, suitable programs from the Advanced Warning and Control System (AWACS) software have been selected. Performance comparisons of these selected
programs coded for both the STARAN and an IBM 360/65 will be conducted. One of the
selected programs performs the AWACS passive tracking function.

A program which implements the AWACS passive tracking algorithms on the RADC
STARAN computer system is described in this paper. The passive tracking process
which forms the basis for the program's requirements is briefly described. The design objectives of the program and the design concepts which were used to achieve
these objectives are presented. Possible improvements to the RADC computer system's
hardware and software which may be of benefit to future applications of this type
are recommended.

PASSIVE TRACKING APPLICATION BACKGROUND

One of the primary functions of the AWACS surveillance system is to provide
tracking data on airborne targets. Tracking can be divided into two categories.
These are active tracking and passive tracking. Active tracking is accomplished by
using radar sensors which measure the range, range rate and azimuth of targets. Passive tracking is accomplished by using target azimuth information only. The target
locations are determined from passive data by using triangulation. Two methods of
passive tracking are employed. The first method, known as self-passive tracking,

requires the AWACS to fly in a closed loop. When a second AWACS is available, its radar measurements can be combined with those of the primary AWACS. This method is known as cooperative passive tracking.

Passive tracking is primarily used to locate and track jamming targets from measurements of the azimuth of the radiation source. The radar returns which are referred to as strobes provide azimuth and strobe width data. A target normally operates its jamming equipment intermittently. When the jammer is off, active radar reports from the target may be obtained. The passive tracking algorithms take advantage of this additional information.

A block diagram of the passive tracking process is shown in Figure 1. The passive tracking algorithms describe four major functions. Each of these functions is performed for each radar scan. After the radar data has been read for a particular scan, the position and speed of each tracked target is predicted for the current scan using past scan histories. Each observed strobe is then associated with a particular track by selecting the closest predicted track azimuth to each observed strobe azimuth. Observed strobes are then correlated to tracks using a computed correlation window. Smoothing of azimuth or azimuth and range is then performed on each track and the smoothing filter updated. If cooperative passive tracking is employed, additional association, correlation and smoothing is performed on the secondary AWACS data. Ghosts produced by multiple intersections of radar strobes are also identified in this case.

Inputs to the program consist of the coordinate positions of each AWACS obtained from the aircraft's navigation and guidance equipmant and the azimuth and strobe width data for each observed target obtained from the aircraft's radar. The program's output consists of the position and speed of each tracked target. The inputs are received and the output computed for each radar scan.

The prediction of the position and speed of each target is described by the following matrix computation:

$$\hat{X}_{i+1} = \Phi\hat{X}_i$$

where

X_i is the true state vector for a given target at time t

$\hat{X}_{i+1}$ is the estimated state vector χ at time t + Δt

and

Φ is the state transition matrix for one time interval Δt.

The covariance matrix P is computed by the following equation:

$$P_{i+1} = \Phi P_i \Phi^T + \Gamma Q \Gamma^T$$

where

Q   is the covariance of disturbance

and

Γ is the transition matrix for the effect of disturbance over Δt.

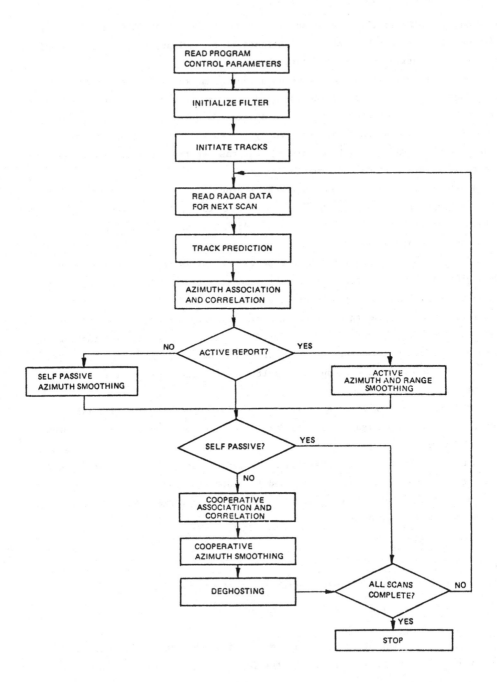

Figure 1. Passive Tracking Block Diagram

Association of the observed target returns with target tracks is performed by finding the best fit between observed and predicted strobes. The correlation window around the predicted strobes is computed from the AWACS position, predicted target position and the estimated measurement variances. An observed strobe is considered to correlate to a particular track if it falls wholly or partially within the computed correlation window for that track. After correlation, each observed strobe is smoothed by a Kalman filter and the filter and covariance matrices are updated. The following equations describe these operations.

$$\chi = \chi + \kappa(\alpha - \hat{\alpha}) \qquad \text{(state vector)}$$

$$\kappa = \frac{PH^T}{HPH^T + R} \qquad \text{(Kalman filter)}$$

$$P = P - CKHP \qquad \text{(Covariance)}$$

where

K   is the Kalman gain matrix

α is the observed strobe azimuth or range

$\hat{\alpha}$ is the predicted strobe azimuth or range

H   is the Jacobian matrix

R   is the covariance of measurement errors

and

C   is a scalar correction factor.

H and K are computed from the position coordinates of the AWACS, the predicted position coordinates of the target and estimates of measurement error. Different equations describe the computation of H and K for self, cooperative and active smoothing. When n targets are tracked cooperatively, n^2 strobe intersections are possible. Only n of these intersections represent true targets. By comparing range, velocity, and acceleration of targets against given reference values, a quality index can be generated. This index is used to identify and reject ghosts.

DESIGN OBJECTIVES

The purpose of the parallel implementation of the AWACS passive tracking algorithms is to provide a means by which performance measurements could be made on the STARAN. The performance of the STARAN program is to be compared with the performance of a conventional serial program written for an IBM 360/65. The serial version of the program is written in FORTRAN and uses floating point arithmetic. In order to obtain meaningful performance comparisons, it was decided that the parallel program should also use floating point arithmetic.

The implementation of the STARAN program also provides a means by which general parallel programming techniques could be explored. In addition, any problems with the current STARAN system software and hardware architecture which limited the program design could be identified.

The main objective of the program design is to exploit three types of parallelism, namely, 1st order parallelism, 2nd order parallelism and the simultaneous operation of the three main STARAN processors.

In general, the operations required to associate, correlate and smooth any particular observed target strobe are the same as those required for any other observed target strobe. Thus they deserve to be performed simultaneously. This is the first order parallelism inherent in the problem. One objective of the passive tracking design is to perform the operations on all radar returns received in a particular scan in parallel.

The equations describing the passive tracking algorithms also contain a considerable amount of second order parallelism. Thus portions of sequential operations may be performed simultaneously. Equations (1) and (2) below are used in the calculation of the correlation window.

$$D = (B - Y)^2 \cdot C_1 - 2(B - Y)(A - X) \cdot C_2 + (A - X)^2 \cdot C_3 \tag{1}$$

$$E = (B - Y)^2 + (A - X)^2 \tag{2}$$

C_1, C_2, C_3, D, E, X and Y are vectors with elements corresponding to the radar returns. It can be seen that by replicating the A and B values and by appropriate alignment of the vectors, the calculations of $A - X$ and $B - Y$, $(A - X)^2$ and $(B - Y)^2$ and $(A - X)^2 \cdot C_3$ and $(B - Y)^2 \cdot C_1$ can be performed in parallel. Since movements of consecutive blocks of data within the STARAN arrays is fast in comparison to perfroming floating point arithmetic operations, the exploitation of 2nd order parallelism is also a design objective.

A block diagram of the RADC computer system is shown in Figure 2. The system contains four independent processors (Associative, Parallel I/O, Paging and Sequential). At the heart of the system are four 256 x 256 bit associative arrays. These arrays are controlled by the associative array processor. This processor has 16,384 words of bulk core memory, three 512 word high speed page memories and a 512 word high speed data buffer. The page memories usually contain the main control program and the high speed data buffer is used for rapid access of data. The parallel I/O (PIO) processor with 512 words of memory is used for array to array data transfers and data transfers between the arrays and bulk core or the high speed data buffer. The paging processor is used to load the high speed page memories. Finally, the sequential processor with 8192 words of core is used to drive the peripherals (disk, card reader, line printer, paper tape I/O and typewriter) and to generate and debug programs for all other processors. The processors can be synchronized through external function logic using interlocks. A Honeywell 645 is also interfaced to the system.

The third objective of the passive tracking design is to operate the STARAN processors simultaneously in order that data transfers could be overlapped with array arithmetic. During each radar scan, the program is required to read radar

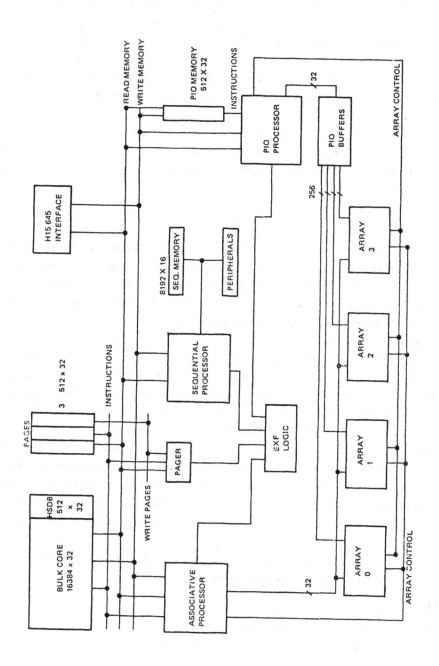

Figure 2. RADC STARAN Block Diagram

data and write target descriptions. Since the total input and output is too large to be held in the STARAN memory, input and output records for each radar scan must be held on the disk. To effect overlapping the radar data input for scan I + 1 is transferred from the disk to bulk core and the track description output for scan I - 1 is transferred from bulk core to the disk, using the sequential processor, while the associative and PIO processors perform the calculations for scan I. Data alignment transfers are also performed by the PIO processor to exploit the 2nd order parallelism in the problem, while the associative processor performs arithmetic on previously aligned data.

As a consequence, storage allocations dictated holding all array arithmetic and function routines required by the problem in page memory, all array transfer routines in PIO memory and the main control program in bulk core. The intent of all of these design objectives is to maximize the program's performance.

DESIGN CONCEPTS

The STARAN passive tracking program was designed to handle a maximum of 64 radar strobe returns for each radar scan. The processing of these inputs requires a set of routines to transfer 64 element vectors between the STARAN memories, associative arrays and disk and another set of routines to perform arithmetic and trigonometric computations on these vectors or groups of vectors in parallel within the associative arrays.

For each radar scan, radar inputs are transferred from the disk to a buffer in AP memory via sequential memory. Data transfers from this buffer to the associative arrays are then performed and calculation within the arrays is initiated. The array calculations consist of vector alignment within the arrays, to exploit 2nd order parallelism, and arithmetic and trigonometric calculations to be performed on the previously aligned vectors. In addition, transfers of temporary vectors generated by these computations are performed between the arrays and temporary storage areas in bulk core or the high speed data buffer (HSDB). When the processing of the radar scan is complete, the vectors containing the target track descriptions are transferred from the arrays to a buffer in AP memory and then from this buffer to the disk via sequential memory.

The data transfer and vector computation tasks required by the passive tracking program are assigned to the STARAN processors as follows:

Sequential Processor

Transfer of input records from disk to AP memory.
Transfer of output records from AP memory to disk.

PIO Processor

Data transfers from memory to the associative arrays.
Data transfers from the associative arrays to memory.

Vector alignment between the arrays.

Associative Processor

Arithmetic and trigonometric calculations are vectors.

Vector alignment within specified arrays.

The synchronization of the three processors during the passive tracking process is accomplished with the STARAN external function logic by setting, resetting, and testing interlock flip flops from each of the processors. Data transfers from the disk to the associative arrays pass through an input buffer. This buffer is loaded by the sequential processor and emptied by the PIO processor. The use of this buffer is synchronized by interlock 0. Interlock 1 is used to synchronize the output buffer in a similar manner during data transfers from the arrays to the disk. Figure 3 shows the sequential processor flow.

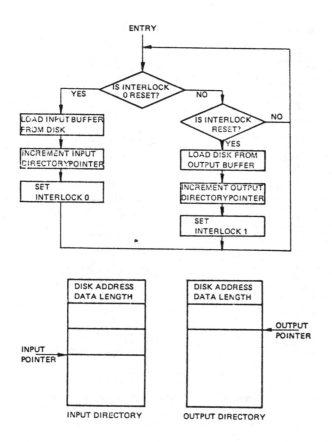

Figure 3. Sequential Processor Flow

During the passive tracking process, each array is assigned to either the associative processor or the PIO processor. The associative processor performs calculations on vectors of data while the PIO processor arranges data vectors on which future calculations will be performed. The array assignments between the associative and PIO processors are synchronized by interlocks 2, 3, 4 and 5. The associative processor program is arranged in logical blocks of code. Each of these blocks is terminated with a call to a PIO synchronization routine. The PIO processor program is also arranged in logical blocks of code and each of these blocks is terminated with a call to an AP synchronization routine. The corresponding blocks of code for the associative and PIO processors are executed simultaneously. The first processor to complete its block waits for the other before new array assignments are made and the next pair of code blocks are executed. Figure 4 shows PIO and AP synchronization flows.

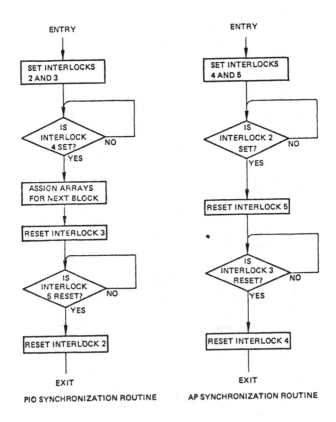

Figure 4. PIO and AP Synchronization Flows

The control program for the associative processor resides in bulk core and consists basically of calls to array arithmetic, trigonometric and comparison routines. These array computation routines are held in the high speed page memories. The control program for the PIO processor also resides in bulk core. This control program consists of interpretive code which controls the array data transfers. An interpreter which resides in PIO memory interprets this control program. The interpreter loads the PIO registers with parameters which specify the data transfer operation to be performed and then selects one of three general array transfer routines by loading the PIO program counter register. These array transfer routines also reside in the PIO memory. The sequential processor control program resides in sequential memory. I/O buffers are provided in sequential memory, bulk core and the high speed data buffer. These I/O buffers are used by routines which load the associative arrays with radar input from the disk and store track description output to the disk. The allocation of the passive tracking control programs is shown in Figure 5. This diagram also shows the control and synchronization of these programs.

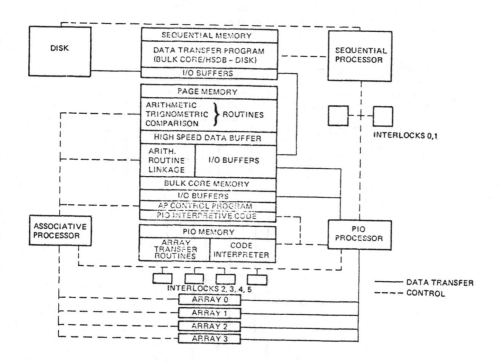

Figure 5. Program Allocation and Control

Array floating point arithmetic routines were written specifically for the passive tracking program. These routines perform addition, subtraction, multiplication, division and square root operations on any of eight fixed array fields. A floating point format was chosen to allow the use of the fast fixed point comparison routines to perform floating point comparisons. Ones complement arithmetic was also selected. The arithmetic routines have a two word calling sequence consisting of a branch and link to the routine followed by pointers to a fixed 8 word block in the high speed data buffer. The pointers define the two argument fields, the result field and a scratch field. The 8 words in the high speed data buffer block correspond to the eight 32 bit fixed array fields. Each word contains the column numbers of the most significant bit, the least significant bit and the most significant bit of the mantissa for its corresponding field. The floating point format and arithmetic routine linkage is shown in Figure 6.

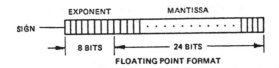

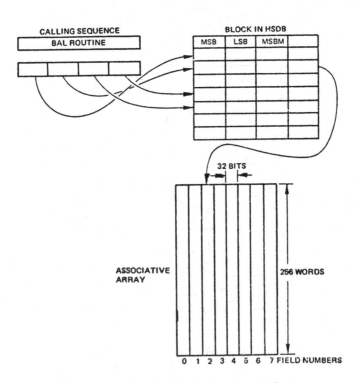

Figure 6. Floating Point Routine Linkage

Sine, Cosine and Arctangent routines were also written for the passive tracking program. These trigonometric routines use the floating point arithmetic routines and have similar calling sequences.

Three data transfer routines were required by the passive tracking program. These routines were coded for the PIO processor and perform array to array transfers, array to memory transfers and memory to array transfers. The associative arrays were divided into eight fields and each field was divided into four blocks. The blocks contain 64 32 bit words. The array to array transfer routine is used to transfer any block or group of blocks within a field of one array to any block or group of blocks within a field of any other array. The array to memory routine is used to transfer array data blocks to output buffers in either bulk core or the high speed data buffer. Array data block loading from input buffers in these memories is performed by the memory to array transfer routine. These routines are synchronized with their respective sequential processor disk routines. The ability to replicate a data value in an array block was also provided by the memory to array transfer routine.

Figure 7 shows how these data transfer routines are initiated by PIO interpretive code in bulk core. The interpretive code consists of consecutive three word blocks. Each of these blocks initiates a data transfer routine and supplies controlling parameters to the routine.

An example of how the associative and PIO processors jointly perform the passive tracking calculations within the associative arrays is presented in Figure 8. A section of FORTRAN code describing part of the active smoothing algorithm is given. This is followed by descriptions of the functions required by both the associative and PIO processors to implement this algorithm. The two processors are synchronized at the end of each section of code. The arrays are divided into 64 blocks and these blocks are numbered in row major order. The block numbers on which the operations are performed are enclosed in parenthesis and the subscripts denote selected arrays.

CONCLUSIONS AND RECOMMENDATIONS

During the design of the passive tracking program, the RADC STARAN computer systems hardware architecture and system software were examined for possible future improvements. Certain additions and modifications to the existing system were identified. These changes would have helped to achieve the program's design objectives, would have improved the program's performance and would have simplified the implementation of the design. The identified additions and modifications to the RADC STARAN system are summarized as:

o Improve the floating point package.

o Add hardware features to improve the performance of associative array transfers.

o Provide software routines which combine array arithmetic with array transfers.

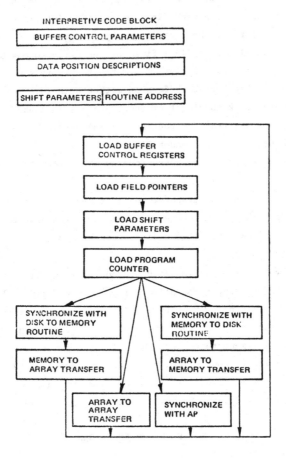

Figure 7. PIO Flow

263

DO 10I = 1, 64
RX(I) = X(I) - AWX
RY(I) = Y(I) - AWY
RSQ(I) = RX(I) * RX(I) + RY(I) * RY(I)

H(1,I) = RY(I)/RSQ(I)
H(2,I) = RX(I)/RSQ(I)
PHT(1,I) = P(1,1,I) * H(1,I) + P(1,2,I) * H(2,I)
PHT(2,I) = P(2,1,I) * H(1,I) + P(2,2,I) * H(2,I)
PHT(3,I) = P(3,1,I) * H(1,I) + P(3,2,I) * H(2,I)
10   PHT(4,I) = P(4,1,I) * H(1,I) + P(4,2,I) * H(2,I)

ASSOCIATIVE PROCESSOR   PIO PROCESSOR

SECTION 1

LOAD X, Y INTO $\begin{bmatrix} 1 \\ 9 \end{bmatrix}_1$

REPLICATE AWX, AWY IN $\begin{bmatrix} 2 \\ 10 \end{bmatrix}_1$

$\begin{bmatrix} 1 \\ 9 \end{bmatrix}_1 - \begin{bmatrix} 2 \\ 10 \end{bmatrix}_1 \rightarrow \begin{bmatrix} 3 \\ 11 \end{bmatrix}_1$

$\begin{bmatrix} 3 \\ 11 \end{bmatrix}_1 \times \begin{bmatrix} 3 \\ 11 \end{bmatrix}_1 \rightarrow \begin{bmatrix} 4 \\ 12 \end{bmatrix}_1$

$P(\cdot,1,\cdot) \rightarrow \begin{bmatrix} 1 \\ 9 \\ 17 \\ 25 \end{bmatrix}_2$

$P(\cdot,2,\cdot) \rightarrow \begin{bmatrix} 1 \\ 9 \\ 17 \\ 25 \end{bmatrix}_3$

SECTION 2

$\begin{bmatrix} 12 \end{bmatrix}_1 \rightarrow \begin{bmatrix} 5 \end{bmatrix}_1$

$\begin{bmatrix} 4 \end{bmatrix}_1 + \begin{bmatrix} 5 \end{bmatrix}_1 \rightarrow \begin{bmatrix} 6 \end{bmatrix}_1$

$\begin{bmatrix} 6 \end{bmatrix}_1 \rightarrow \begin{bmatrix} 14 \end{bmatrix}_1$

$\begin{bmatrix} 3 \\ 11 \end{bmatrix}_1 + \begin{bmatrix} 6 \\ 14 \end{bmatrix}_1 \rightarrow \begin{bmatrix} 7 \\ 15 \end{bmatrix}_1$

ASSOCIATIVE PROCESSOR   PIO PROCESSOR

SECTION 3

$\begin{bmatrix} 7 \end{bmatrix}_1 \rightarrow \begin{bmatrix} 2 \\ 10 \\ 18 \\ 26 \end{bmatrix}_2$

$\begin{bmatrix} 15 \end{bmatrix}_1 \rightarrow \begin{bmatrix} 2 \\ 10 \\ 18 \\ 26 \end{bmatrix}_3$

SECTION 4

$\begin{bmatrix} 1 \\ 9 \\ 17 \\ 25 \end{bmatrix}_{2,3} \times \begin{bmatrix} 2 \\ 10 \\ 18 \\ 26 \end{bmatrix}_{2,3} \rightarrow \begin{bmatrix} 3 \\ 11 \\ 19 \\ 27 \end{bmatrix}_{2,3}$

SECTION 5

$\begin{bmatrix} 3 \\ 11 \\ 19 \\ 27 \end{bmatrix}_2 + \begin{bmatrix} 4 \\ 12 \\ 20 \\ 28 \end{bmatrix}_2 \rightarrow \begin{bmatrix} 4 \\ 12 \\ 20 \\ 28 \end{bmatrix}_2$

SECTION 6

$\begin{bmatrix} 3 \\ 11 \\ 19 \\ 27 \end{bmatrix}_2 + \begin{bmatrix} 4 \\ 12 \\ 20 \\ 23 \end{bmatrix}_2 \rightarrow \begin{bmatrix} 5 \\ 13 \\ 21 \\ 29 \end{bmatrix}_2$

Figure 8. Example of Passive Tracking Code

o Provide a disk linked to the array buffers.

o Add hardware features to improve the performance of array to core transfers.

o Eliminate the PIO processor by combining its capability with that of the associative processor.

The current floating point package uses a floating point format which is compatible with the HIS 645 computer interfaced to the system. This format does not allow the use of the fast fixed point comparison routines to perform floating point comparisons. If the floating point format were changed to allow the use of the fixed point comparison routines, conversion routines for floating point transfers between the STARAN and the HIS 645 would be required, but an overall improvement in the performance of programs using floating point arithmetic would be achieved. The current floating point package is designed to reside in page memory and operates on variable array fields. The calling sequences generate long preambles, however. The floating point add and subtract routines generate 70 word preambles and the multiply and divide routines generate 20 word preambles. These long preambles severely restrict the size of a program which can be executed without core overlays. Floating point routines designed specifically for the passive tracking program which allow the use of the fixed point comparison routines, have 2 word calling sequences but operate on fixed array fields are described above.

In order to exploit 2nd order parallelism in the passive tracking program, alignment of blocks of consecutive 32 bit words within and between arrays was required. These block transfers of data between the associative arrays could be handled more efficiently if the ability to generate masks and the ability to perform general response store shifts were provided. Figure 9 shows how a general block transfer might be coded if these additional features were provided. The ability to shift a response store instruction according to the contents of a 10 bit shift register which is activated by a bit in either the load or store response store instructions is assumed. This shift register could share the data bus with the FPE and FL2 registers. The ability to generate a mask starting at a bit position held in a field pointer with a length contained in a field length counter is also assumed.

Array field arithmetic and comparison routines consist basically of loading array words or columns into response stores, performing logic within the response stores and then storing the resulting contents of the response stores into array words or columns. If these array computation routines were written to use general buffer transfer and shift operations, the data transfer routines described above could be incorporated into these computation routines. This would then allow a block of data in one array to be added to a block of data in a second array and the result stored in a third array. No restriction would be placed on the positions of these data blocks within their respective arrays. This concept would produce a powerful set of system routines which would be excellent for exploiting 2nd order parallelism within problems. In addition the requirement for a separate PIO processor would be

265

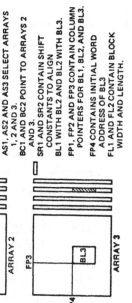

BL1 + BL2 → BL3

LOAD ARRAY SELECT REGISTERS (AS1, AS2, AS3)
LOAD BUFFER CONTROL REGISTERS (BC1, BC2)
LOAD SHIFT REGISTERS (SR1, SR2)
LOAD FIELD POINTERS (FP1, FP2, FP3, FP4)
LOAD LENGTH COUNTERS (FL1, FL2)
GENERATE MASK, USE AS3, FP4, FL2
0 → X   USE AS2
LOOP FL1 TIMES

X → Y   USE AS2
A → B   USE AS1, SR1, FP1
B → B   USE AS1, BC1
X ⊕ YB→X, Y ⊕ 3→Y   USE AS2
X ⊕ YA→X, Y ⊕ A→Y   USE AS2, FP2
Y → B   USE AS2, SR2
B → B   USE AS2, BC2
B → A   USE AS3, FP3

AS1, AS2 AND AS3 SELECT ARRAYS 1, 2 AND 3.
BC1 AND BC2 POINT TO ARRAYS 2 AND 3.
SR1 AND SR2 CONTAIN SHIFT CONSTANTS TO ALIGN BL1 WITH BL2 AND BL2 WITH BL3.
FP1, FP2 AND FP3 CONTAIN COLUMN POINTERS FOR BL1, BL2, AND BL3.
FP4 CONTAINS INITIAL WORD ADDRESS OF BL3
FL1 AND FL2 CONTAIN BLOCK WIDTH AND LENGTH.

Figure 10.   Field Arithmetic Combined with Array Transfer

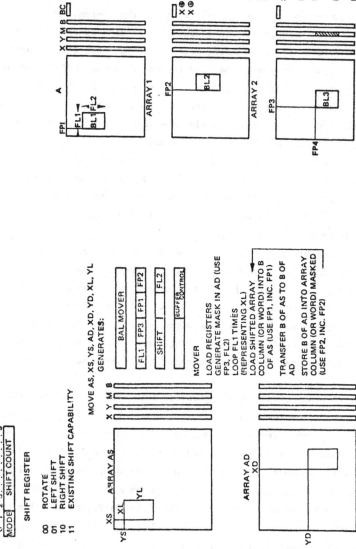

0 1 2 3 9
MODE | SHIFT COUNT

SHIFT REGISTER

00   ROTATE
01   LEFT SHIFT
10   RIGHT SHIFT
11   EXISTING SHIFT CAPABILITY

MOVE AS, XS, YS, AD, XD, YD, XL, YL
GENERATES:

BAL MOVER

FL1 | FP3 | FP1 | FP2
SHIFT | | FL2
BUFFER CONTROL

MOVER

LOAD REGISTERS
GENERATE MASK IN AD (USE FP3, FL2)
LOOP FL1 TIMES
    LOAD SHIFTED ARRAY COLUMN (OR WORD) INTO B OF AS (USE FP1, INC. FP1)
    TRANSFER B OF AS TO B OF AD
    STORE B OF AD INTO ARRAY COLUMN (OR WORD) MASKED (USE FP2, INC. FP2)

Figure 9.   Array to Array Transfers

eliminated.

The arrays on which the associative processor operates are selected by a 32 bit array select register. Three 16 bit registers are used to select arrays and control buffer transfers in the PIO processor. If the capability of the PIO processor is added to that of associative processor, the abiltty to control buffer transfers must be provided. One method of implementing this for a 16 array system would be to control the array selection with three 16 bit array select registers and to add a 4 bit buffer control register to each array in the system. Each associative array instruction would reference a particular array select register. Each bit of the array select register would correspond to a particular array in the system. The arrays on which associative array instructions operate would be selected by setting the appropriate bits in their referenced array select register. The 4 bit buffer control registers associated with each array would be used to connect array buffers and would hold the destination array number for buffer to buffer transfers. Figure 10 shows how these features might be used to code a fixed point add routine. Combining arithmetic with array transfers in this manner would save valuable array storage and would reduce the size and complexity of the control program.

The STARAN currently requires each masked store instruction to be preceded by a set up mask operation. This operation is required by the hardware but should not be the concern of the programmer. If the set up mask operation were activated by the hardware before performing each masked store instruction, the size of the basic system software programs could be reduced.

The passive tracking program uses the sequential processor and the PIO processor to transfer input from the disk to the arrays and to transfer output from the arrays to the disk. The technique used to perform these transfers was an attempt to simulate a disk linked directly to the array buffers. If a 256 parallel head disk had been included in the system and linked to the array buffers, the design of the passive tracking program would have been simpler, the time required to implement the program would have been reduced and the performance of the program would have been increased.

The STARAN has no means of performing parallel data transfers between the associative arrays and conventional memory. Currently all such transfers must pass through either a 32 bit common register or a 32 bit data part. One possible method of providing such parallel data transfers would be to include a 256x32 bit array in the system. This array should be capable of being accessed by the associative array instructions, by the AP memory instructions or by the sequential processor. The four accessing modes of this proposed transfer array are shown in Figure 11. The transfer array can be considered as either 32 columns or 32 eight word blocks for transfers to or from selected array response store registers. The transfer array would also be allocated a block of 256 memory addresses for transfers to or from AP control register groups or transfers to or from sequential memory or sequential processor registers. A transfer array with these capabilities would provide a versatile and fast

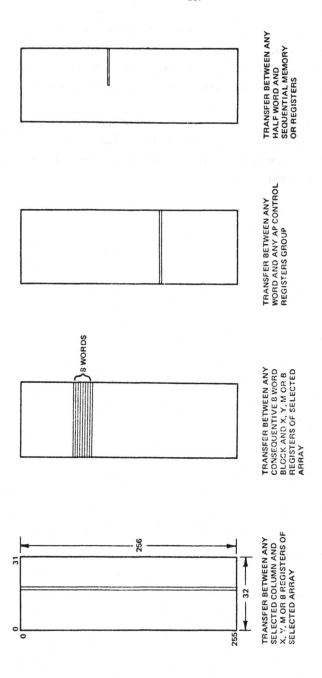

Figure 11. Access Modes of Transfer Array

means of performing data transfers between the associative arrays and the conventional memory modules in the system.

A block diagram of a parallel computing system which contains two control processors and which incorporates the additional features described above is shown in
Figure 12.

When addressing requirements for improved associative processors, it is suggested that consideration be given to the modifications identified above. It is felt
that these modifications would result in applications programmers being able to
achieve more efficient execution of their programs with less complex code.

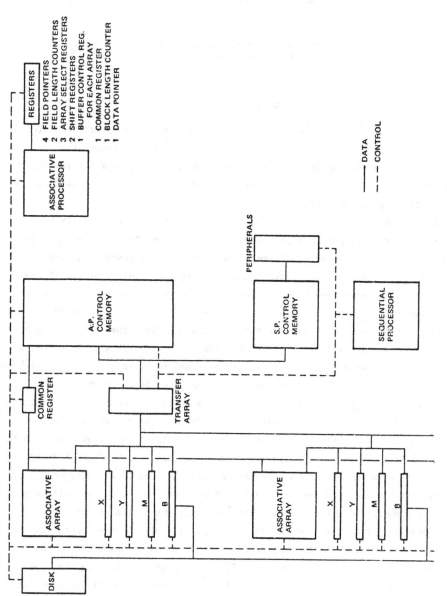

Figure 12. A Parallel Computing System Block Diagram

EXPERIENCES WITH AN OPERATIONAL ASSOCIATIVE PROCESSOR[a]

DAVID L. BALDAUF
Computer Network Systems
The MITRE Corporation
Bedford, Massachusetts 01730

SUMMARY

The MITRE Corporation has implemented a set of space object position prediction equations on the Goodyear Aerospace Corporation STARAN[b] S-1000 associative processor. This paper outlines the experience gained from this task. For information on STARAN hardware and software, the reader is directed to Goodyear Aerospace Corporation, STARAN Development Division.

The SGP4 (Simplified General Perturbation #4) system consists of forty-four equations with fourteen inputs and sixteen outputs. Computation is done in a sequential manner with no branches or conditional computations. No possible sources of parallelism exist within the equations. To utilize the parallelism of the STARAN, many sets of data are processed simultaneously. These equations are typical of a class of scientific computations involving non-iterative arithmetic operations.

Several approaches were examined for the implementation. The first approach was to process 1024 objects in parallel (256 words/array x 4 arrays). This idea was discarded because all of control memory would be needed to store the output variables. The second approach was to process 512 objects in parallel by dedicating two contiguous associative memory words to each object. This design needed a large amount of time to do input/output. The third design takes advantage of the ability to overlap I/O in PIO control with computation in AP control. The first two arrays are used for computation while the other two arrays are used as buffers. Each of the 512 objects still has two array words, one in a computation array and one in a buffer array. In this configuration, input and output is being done in the buffer arrays while computation is going on in the other arrays. This approach was chosen as the best.

The investigation of the best design took approximately 180 man-hours. The data area mapping was next done. This phase lasted about 150 man-hours. Coding was straightforward and took 60 man-hours. The 60 hours spent on debugging consisted mainly of the time required to debug the specially developed parallel input/output routines.

During the implementation effort some general impressions of the RADC system were obtained. The configuration seemed easy to work with, but the software produced

---

[a] The work described was sponsored by AF Systems Command/Electronic Systems Division / Information Systems Technology Application Office under Contract F19628-73-C-0001.

[b] TM, Goodyear Aerospace Corporation, Akron, Ohio.

was very inflexible to changes. The debugging facilities provided are a helpful aid
to the programmer. Some changes and additions would be useful, however. The addition of more breakpoints and the ability to set breakpoints in PIO control would be
useful. Another shortcoming is that there are no in-line debugging aids. In-line
traces and dumps could reduce on-line debugging time. The most important recommen-
dation for a hardware modification to the STARAN system is an increase in associative array word size. The addition of more storage per array word would eliminate
entirely the need to use control memory for temporary storage. In those applications
that use floating point arithmetic, floating point hardware would be very beneficial.
The addition of more control memory could make similar programs easier to implement.
In the present program the code and data could not fit into control memory and overlays were needed.

Most of the above recommendations are mainly based on the experience gained in
the experimental implementation of SGP4. The changes suggested below would benefit
any user of the RADC system. An improved paging system that takes control of the
pager out of the hands of the programmer would be very useful. A faster transfer
rate of data between control memory and array memory could greatly reduce the execution time of any program. The STARAN-Multics interface has several areas that could
be improved. There is very little immediate feedback obtained when using the STARAN
remotely. This deficiency is especially noticeable when a long procedure such as an
assembly is being executed. An interactive debugging session is virtually impossible.
On occasional system crashes no notice is given to the user. Also, no procedure
exists for loading the STARAN system through Multics. The ability to issue commands
to Multics while attached to STARAN would also be useful.

The experimental implementation of SGP4 on the RADC STARAN system has produced
many interesting and useful results. It is hoped that the information gathered can
be useful to system designers looking for an improved AP and to present and prospec-
tive RADC STARAN users.

MATRIX COMPUTATIONS ON AN ASSOCIATIVE PROCESSOR [a]

P.A. GILMORE
Goodyear Aerospace Corporation
Akron, Ohio

Abstract -- Stationary iterative techniques for solving systems of linear equations are reviewed, and an accelerated form of the Point-Jacobi method (referred to as parallel relaxation) is developed. Associative processors are introduced, and operational characteristics are described. The parallel relaxation method is structured for parallel execution on an associative processor, and parallel and sequential computational requirements are compared. The comparison shows a potential advantage for parallel execution which increases with the size of the system of equations. The results are extended to arbitrary stationary iterative techniques, and a practical parallel approach to SOR suggested.

Key Words and Phrases: Parallel processors, associative processors, parallel execution, linear equations, stationary iteration, iterative techniques.

1. INTRODUCTION

In a number of recent articles, the subject of parallel execution of matrix-oriented computations has been considered. We shall consider a particular type of matrix computation, the numerical solution of systems of linear equations by stationary iteration, and a particular type of parallel processor, the associative processor (AP). We shall show that the parallel arithmetic capability of an AP offers a computational advantage over conventional sequential processing for matrix computations. In the process we show also that certain matrix computations which are apparently sequential in nature can in fact be readily executed in parallel, a potential which has been seen to obtain for other types of computations [10].

We shall denote a system of linear equations in matrix form by $AX = B$, where $A = (a_{ij})$ is an $n \times n$ matrix of coefficients; $X = (x_1, x_2, \ldots, x_n)^T$ is an $n \times 1$ vector of unknowns; and $B = (b_1, b_2, \ldots, b_n)^T$ is an $n \times 1$ vector of real constants. Unless otherwise stated, we shall assume that A is nonsingular, real and symmetric with positive diagonal elements. The stationary iterative techniques with which we are concerned are the Point-Jacobi (PJ) and Gauss-Seidel (GS) methods; the accelerated successive overrelaxation (SOR) form of GS; and an accelerated form of PJ that we shall call parallel relaxation (PR).

---

[a] The work reported in this paper was supported in part by the Air Force Office of Scientific Research under Contract F44620-70-C-0100.

2. BACKGROUND

Systems of linear equations often derive from discrete approximations to partial differential equations. Iterative solution of such a linear system effects a cyclic sweep over the mesh points of the grid employed during which point-wise approximations to the solution of the differential equation are refined. For a wide class of problems, a successive displacement refinement procedure (Gauss-Seidel) is to be preferred over a simultaneous displacement procedure (Point-Jacobi) due to considerations of convergence rate and suitability of implementation on conventional, sequential, digital computers.

The advent of parallel processors on the digital computer scene suggests a review of the rationale by which computational techniques are selected. For suppose a parallel processor is available and a processing unit can be assigned to each point of a mesh (equivalently, to each variable of the corresponding system of equations) so that updating of mesh points (variables) can be carried on in parallel. Does the obvious potential for parallel execution inherent in the simultaneous displacement procedure make it the logical choice for parallel processing? And does the apparently sequential character of the successive displacement procedure render it unattractive for parallel execution? A reasonable answer to these and related questions requires additional analysis as we shall see.

3. STATIONARY ITERATIVE TECHNIQUES AND PARALLEL PROCESSING

In this section we shall briefly examine systems

$$AX = B \tag{1}$$

for exhibiting their iterative solution via parallel processing. Our assumptions regarding the n x n coefficient matrix A remain those of Section 1; namely, that A is nonsingular, real, and symmetric with positive diagonal elements. If we write Equation 1 in the equivalent form

$$X = MX + G, \tag{2}$$

we may specify iterative solutions to Equation 1 by selecting $X^{(0)}$, an initial approximation to X, and by iterating

$$X^{(k+1)} = MX^{(k)} + G. \tag{3}$$

The sequence $X^{(0)}$, $X^{(1)}$, $X^{(2)}$, ... generated by the iteration will, for suitable conditions, converge to a solution of Equation 1. A wealth of literature exists regarding necessary and sufficient conditions for the convergence of Equation 3 [1, 2,3]. The matrix M is called the iteration matrix. If it does not vary from iteration to iteration, the iteration is said to be stationary. If we split the coefficient matrix A as

$$A = D - E - F, \tag{4}$$

where D is a diagonal matrix and E(F) is lower (upper) triangular, then two equivalent forms of Equation 1 are given by

$$X = D^{-1}(E + F)X + D^{-1}B, \tag{5}$$

and

$$X = (D - E)^{-1}FX + (D - E)^{-1}B , \tag{6}$$

From the first form, we obtain the simultaneous displacement PJ iteration

$$X^{(k+1)} = D^{-1}(E + F)X^{(k)} + D^{-1}B ; \tag{7}$$

from the second form, we obtain the successive displacement GS iteration

$$X^{(k+1)} = (D - E)^{-1}FX^{(k)} + (D - E)^{-1}B . \tag{8}$$

A variety of authors have achieved rather striking success in developing an accelerated version of Gauss-Seidel, known as the successive overrelaxation (SOR) method and variations of it. We shall subsequently consider parallel execution of Gauss-Seidel and SOR.

Perhaps less well known is the theory associated with the acceleration of the Point-Jacobi iteration. This is due no doubt to the fact that for a wide class of applications problems the Gauss-Seidel or SOR approach is superior when implemented for sequential execution on conventional processors. The PJ iteration and accelerated versions of it are, however, computationally well suited to parallel processing and we shall examine such techniques in subsequent discussion.

A potentially accelerated form of the PJ iteration can be developed as follows. If we denote by $\tilde{X}^{(k+1)}$ the $(k + 1)$st estimate of the solution vector X given by PJ and then specify $X^{(k+1)}$ as a weighted average of $\tilde{X}^{(k+1)}$ and $X^{(k)}$, we have

$$X^{(k+1)} = \omega\tilde{X}^{(k+1)} + (1 - \omega)X^{(k)}. \tag{9}$$

In matrix form, this would be

$$X^{(k+1)} = \{(1 - \omega)I + \omega D^{-1}(E + F)\}X^{(k)} + \omega D^{-1}B. \tag{10}$$

We shall restrict $\omega > 0$ and refer to the iteration of Equation 10 as the parallel relaxation (PR) method. Evidently, if $\omega = 1$, PR reduces to PJ.

The question immediately arises as to what value of ω gives the maximum convergence rate and for what range of ω values is Equation 10 convergent. We defer discussion of these questions to Appendix A, which presents an easy derivation of the optimal ω are related discussions.

We note that the iteration matrix for Equation 10 retains a structural simplicity quite like that of the PJ iteration, and the PR iteration retains an evident amenability to parallel processing. In Section 4, we shall consider the implementation of PR on an associative processor and subsequently show that our results apply to the implementation of stationary iterations in general.

4. PARALLEL EXECUTION ON AN ASSOCIATIVE PROCESSOR

a. Introduction

The simultaneous displacement updating employed in the PR method is formally well suited to parallel processing. The practical question arises as to whether existing or near-term parallel processors are available for implementation of PR and, if so, what will be the parallel execution time and how does it compare with the execution time for sequential processing? Over the last several years, a number of parallel processor designs have been proposed [4-8]. Most of these designs are of theoretical interest only. At this writing only one - the STARAN[a] associative processor (AP) produced by Goodyear - is commercially available. The ILLIAC IV, which is currently under development by Burroughs Corporation and the University of Illinois, is now nearing completion. A number of other companies are working on parallel processors but dates for actual operation and commercial availability are uncertain.

The AP has been selected as the parallel processor on which to study the implementation of PR for parallel execution. Since its structure and operation are not widely known, Items b and c are devoted to a general description of the AP and its operation.

b. AP Structure

An associative processor (AP) is a stored program digital computing system capable of operating on many data items simultaneously. Both logical and arithmetic operations are available. The principal components of an AP system are typically as follows:

1. A set of associative memory arrays (AM) in which data are stored on which the AP operates. Typically, the arrays may each consist of 256 words, each with 256 bits, with read/write access in either the word or bit direction.

2. A response store configuration for each word of the AM, which provides arithmetic capability, read/write capability, and indication of logical operation results.

3. A data/instruction memory in which are stored the AP program (that is, the list of instructions executed by the AP) and data items required by (or generated by) the AP but not maintained in the AM.

4. A control unit that directs the AP to execute the instructions specified by the AP program; this control unit is similar to control units found in conventional computers. Communication channels are provided between the data/instruction memory and the sequential control unit and between both of these units and external devices.

A simplified representation of the AP is given in Figure 1.

c. AP Operations

We are principally concerned with the parallel execution of arithmetic operations in the AP and, to a lesser extent, with the transfer of data within the AP. An

[a] TM, Goodyear Aerospace Corporation, Akron, Ohio.

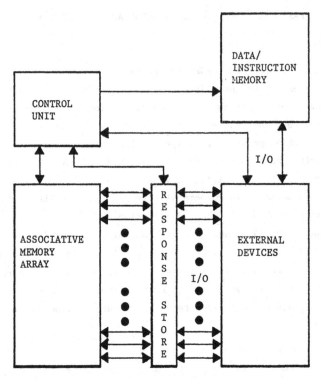

Figure 1. Simplified AP Structure

understanding of the AP's parallel arithmetic capability can be facilitated by considering Figure 2, which depicts the word/field structure of a hypothetical 10-word, 20-bit AM (refer to [9] for a full discussion of the AP's logical and arithmetic capability).

In Figure 2, each of the 20-bit words has been arbitrarily divided into two 5-bit fields and one 10-bit field. Other field assignments could have been made, and they need not be the same for all words. Field specifications are made by the programmer in accordance with computational and storage requirements at a given stage of the program; the specification is logical, not physical, and can be changed for any or all words at any point in the program by the programmer.

If, for $i = 1, 2, \ldots, 10$, we denote word i by w_i, the contents of Field 1 of w_i by $(F1_i)$, the contents of Field 2 by $(F2_i)$, and the contents of Field 3 by $(F3_i)$, then (at least) the following computations can be done in parallel (that is, simultaneously by word, sequential by bit). Such parallel computations are often called vector computations, since they involve like operations on corresponding elements of two vectors of operands:

$(F1_i) \oplus (F2_i)$

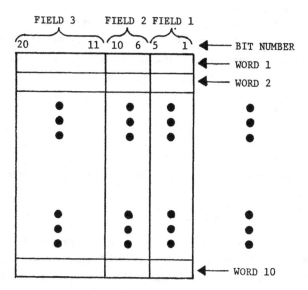

Figure 2. AM Structure

or

$$i = 1, 2, \ldots, 10 \quad \wedge \quad \oplus \quad \epsilon\{+, -, *, \div\}$$

$$(F2_i) \oplus (F1_i)$$

The field into which the results of the operations are stored is specified by the programmer. For example, the results of the $\pm$ operations could be stored in either Field 1, Field 2, or Field 3. We denote this, for example, by:

$$(F1_i) \pm (F2_i) \longrightarrow F1_i \qquad i = 1, 2, \ldots, 10,$$

or

$$(F1_i) \pm (F2_i) \longrightarrow F2_i \qquad i = 1, 2, \ldots, 10,$$

or

$$(F1_i) \pm (F2_i) \longrightarrow F3_i \qquad i = 1, 2, \ldots, 10.$$

In the first two specifications, the original values $(F1_i)$ or $(F2_i)$, respectively, would be destroyed; in the third specification, $(F1_i)$ and $(F2_i)$ would be unaltered.

In $*$ or $\div$ operations, a double-length product or quotient will be available. To save the double-length result, we would be restricted to placing the result in the double-length field, F3. For example,

$$(F1_i) * (F2_i) \longrightarrow F3_i \qquad i = 1, 2, \ldots, 10.$$

The original values $(F1_i)$, $(F2_i)$ would be unaltered. Operations such as those described above are referred to as within-word arithmetic operations. We also have available register-to-word operations and between-word operations.

In register-to-word operations, the contents of a specified field of a common register, denoted by CR, are used as an operand. A typical register-to-word operation would be:

$$(CR) * (F1_i) \longrightarrow F3_i \qquad i = 1, 2, \ldots, 10,$$

or

$$(CR) \pm (F1_i) \longrightarrow F2_i \qquad i = 1, 2, \ldots, 10 .$$

In between-word operations, the operand pairs derive from different words. For example, in the operation

$$(F1_i) * (F1_{i+2}) \longrightarrow F3_i \qquad i = 1, 2, \ldots, 8 ,$$

Field 1 of Word 1 is multiplied by Field 1 of Word 3, and the result is placed in Field 3 of Word 1; Field 1 of Word 2 is multiplied by Field 1 of Word 4, and the result is placed in Field 3 of Word 2 ..., Field 1 of Word 8 is multiplied by Field 1 of Word 10, and the result is placed in Field 3 of Word 8. Likewise, we could specify an operation such as

$$(F1_i) + (F2_{i+1}) \longrightarrow F1_i \qquad i = 1, 2, \ldots, 9 .$$

We note that, for between-word operations, the distance between words from which operand pairs are derived is constant; that is, with each Word i, we associate a Word $i \pm \Delta_.$.

Such between word operations are also executed in parallel. In many cases between-word operations are no more time consuming than within-word operations; in no case are they significantly more time consuming.

The bit-serial nature of AP operations results in long execution times if computation is considered on a per-word basis. The source of computational advantages for an AP lies in the AP's ability to do many, indeed thousands, of operations in a word-parallel fashion and thus give, for properly structured computations, effective per-word execution times that are very attractive. We might note that increased execution speeds are available via AP hardware options which include high-speed floating point hardware.

d. Parallel Relaxation Structure

For a linear system $AX = B$, the PR iteration is given by

$$X^{(k+1)} = \{(1 - \omega)I + \omega D^{-1}(E + F)\} X^{(k)} + \omega D^{-1} B . \tag{11}$$

We shall let the n x n PR iteration matrix be denoted by

$$P = (p_{ij}) = \{(1 - \omega)I + \omega D^{-1}(E + F)\} , \tag{12}$$

and we shall let the vector $\omega D^{-1} B$ be denoted by $G = (g_i)$. The elements of $P = (p_{ij})$ and $G = (g_i)$ do not change from iteration. The $k + 1$st estimates of x_i are computed as

$$x_i^{(k+1)} = \sum_{j=1}^{n} P_{ij} x_i^{(k)} + g_i, \qquad i = 1, 2, \ldots, n . \tag{13}$$

The structure of the computations in Equation 13 suggests storing data in an AP as shown in Figure 3, where we consider a 5 x 5 example.

		$x^{(k)}$	FIELDS		$x^{(k+1)}$		WORD
1	2	3	4	5	6	7	
g_1	P_{11}	x_1					1
	P_{12}	x_2					2
	P_{13}	x_3					3
	P_{14}	x_4					4
	P_{15}	x_5					5
g_2	P_{21}	x_1					6
	P_{22}	x_2					7
	P_{23}	x_3					8
	P_{24}	x_4					9
	P_{25}	x_5					10
g_3	P_{31}	x_1					11
	P_{32}	x_2					12
	P_{33}	x_3					13
	P_{34}	x_4					14
	P_{35}	x_5					15
g_4	P_{41}	x_1					16
	P_{42}	x_2					17
	P_{43}	x_3					18
	P_{44}	x_4					19
	P_{45}	x_5					20
g_5	P_{51}	x_1					21
	P_{52}	x_2					22
	P_{53}	x_3					23
	P_{54}	x_4					24
	P_{55}	x_5					25

Figure 3. AP Data Storage Scheme

The storage scheme employed involves redundant storage of current estimates of the variables x_1, x_2, $\ldots$, x_n. The redundancy is employed to gain computational speed; this will become clear in the following discussions.

We shall describe the operations required for one iteration in a step-by-step fashion with reference to corresponding figures depicting the contents of the AP memory.

For each word (1 through 25) in Step 1, we multiply the contents of Field 2 by the contents of Field 3 and store the product in Field 4. The resulting state of the AP memory is given in Figure 4.

Step 2 actually is a subroutine type of operation in which the sums $\sum P_{ij} x_j$ are formed in a treed operation that injects parallel computation into the basic summing process via parallel between-word addition. The summing subroutine is executed in parallel by the AP for each consecutive set of 5 (for the example, n in general)

1	2	3 $x^{(k)}$	4 FIELDS	5	6 $x^{(k+1)}$	7	WORD
g_1	p_{11}	x_1	$p_{11}x_1$				1
	p_{12}	x_2	$p_{12}x_2$				2
	p_{13}	x_3	$p_{13}x_3$				3
	p_{14}	x_4	$p_{14}x_4$				4
	p_{15}	x_5	$p_{15}x_5$				5
g_2	p_{21}	x_1	$p_{21}x_1$				6
	p_{22}	x_2	$p_{22}x_2$				7
	p_{23}	x_3	$p_{23}x_3$				8
	p_{24}	x_4	$p_{24}x_4$				9
	p_{25}	x_5	$p_{25}x_5$				10
g_3	p_{31}	x_1	$p_{31}x_1$				11
	p_{32}	x_2	$p_{32}x_2$				12
	p_{33}	x_3	$p_{33}x_3$				13
	p_{34}	x_4	$p_{34}x_4$				14
	p_{35}	x_5	$p_{35}x_5$				15
g_4	p_{41}	x_1	$p_{41}x_1$				16
	p_{42}	x_2	$p_{42}x_2$				17
	p_{43}	x_3	$p_{43}x_3$				18
	p_{44}	x_4	$p_{44}x_4$				19
	p_{45}	x_5	$p_{45}x_5$				20
g_5	p_{51}	x_1	$p_{51}x_1$				21
	p_{52}	x_2	$p_{52}x_2$				22
	p_{53}	x_3	$p_{53}x_3$				23
	p_{54}	x_4	$p_{54}x_4$				24
	p_{55}	x_5	$p_{55}x_5$				25

Figure 4. AP Storage Configuration after Step 1

words. The result of this summing operation is that in Field 4, Word 1 contains $\sum p_{1j}x_j$; Word 6 contains $\sum p_{2j}x_j$; ... , Word 21 contains $\sum p_{5j}x_j$. In general, for an n x n system, these sums would be accumulated in Field 4 of Words 1, n + 1, 2n + 1, ..., (n-1)n + 1. The resulting state of the AP memory is given in Figure 5.

For Words 1, 6, 11, 16, and 21 in Step 3, Field 1 is added to Field 5, and the sum is placed in Field 6; Field 6 of Words 1, 6, 11, 16, and 21, respectively, contains now the k +1st estimates of x_1, x_2, x_3, x_4, and x_5. The kth estimates are retained redundantly in Field 3. The resulting state of the AP memory is given in Figure 6.

In Step 4, we prepare for convergence testing. We first "line up" the kth and k + 1st values of the variables x_i. We do this by modifying the contents of Field 3; we read from Field 3 of Words 2, 3, 4, 5 the kth estimate of x_2, x_3, x_4, x_5 and write the values into Field 3 of Words 6, 11, 16, and 21. We are now ready to form the differences of the kth and k + 1st estimates. For Words 1, 6, 11, 16, and 21, Field 3 is subtracted from Field 6, and the difference is placed in Field 7. In Words 1, 6, 11, 16, and 21, respectively, Field 7 now contains the differences $x_1^{(k+1)} - x_1^{(k)}$, ..., $x_5^{(k+1)} - x_5^{(k)}$; we next execute Step 5, which forms absolute values.

		$x^{(k)}$		FIELDS		$x^{(k+1)}$		WORD
1	2	3	4	5	6	7		
g_1	p_{11}	x_1	$p_{11}x_1$	$\sum p_{1j}x_j$			1
	p_{12}	x_2	$p_{12}x_2$				2
	p_{13}	x_3	$p_{13}x_3$				3
	p_{14}	x_4	$p_{14}x_4$				4
	p_{15}	x_5	$p_{15}x_5$				5
g_2	p_{21}	x_1	$p_{21}x_1$	$\sum p_{2j}x_j$			6
	p_{22}	x_2	$p_{22}x_2$				7
	p_{23}	x_3	$p_{23}x_3$				8
	p_{24}	x_4	$p_{24}x_4$				9
	p_{25}	x_5	$p_{25}x_5$				10
g_3	p_{31}	x_1	$p_{31}x_1$	$\sum p_{3j}x_j$			11
	p_{32}	x_2	$p_{32}x_2$				12
	p_{33}	x_3	$p_{33}x_3$				13
	p_{34}	x_4	$p_{34}x_4$				14
	p_{35}	x_5	$p_{35}x_5$				15
g_4	p_{41}	x_1	$p_{41}x_1$	$\sum p_{4j}x_j$			16
	p_{42}	x_2	$p_{42}x_2$				17
	p_{43}	x_3	$p_{43}x_3$				18
	p_{44}	x_4	$p_{44}x_4$				19
	p_{45}	x_5	$p_{45}x_5$				20
g_5	p_{51}	x_1	$p_{51}x_1$	$\sum p_{5j}x_j$			21
	p_{52}	x_2	$p_{52}x_2$				22
	p_{53}	x_3	$p_{53}x_3$				23
	p_{54}	x_4	$p_{54}x_4$				24
	p_{55}	x_5	$p_{55}x_5$				25

Figure 5. AP Storage Configuration after Step 2

For Words 1, 6, 11, 16 and 21 in Step 5, we set Field 7 equal to the absolute value of the previous contents. The AP memory state resulting from Step 4 and 5 is given in Figure 7.

Step 6, like Step 2, actually is a subroutine type of operation. We actually do the convergence testing by doing a less-than comparand search in the AP. Effectively, we ask whether for all variables x_1, x_2, x_3, x_4, and x_5 the magnitude of the difference of the kth and k + 1st estimates is less than a specified tolerance. If so, we say convergence has been achieved, and the latest estimates would be printed out. If not, more iteration would be required, and we would pass to Step 7.

In Step 7, the new estimates for x_1, x_2, x_3, x_4, and x_5 are read out of Field 6 of Words 1, 6, 11, 16, and 21. Following each read, the x_i value is redundantly written into its proper position in Field 3.

In Step 8, iteration continues; we begin again at Step 1. More economical use of storage could be made in storing intermediate results. The storage scheme shown was selected for elucidation of AP operations, not optimal use of storage.

<u>e</u>. Computational Comparisons

The evident source of computational advantage for the AP lies in its parallel

1	2	3 $x^{(k)}$	4 FIELDS	5	6 $x^{(k+1)}$	7	WORD
g_1	p_{11}	x_1	$p_{11}x_1$	$\sum p_{1j}x_j$	$\sum + g_1$		1
	p_{12}	x_2	$p_{12}x_2$				2
	p_{13}	x_3	$p_{13}x_3$				3
	p_{14}	x_4	$p_{14}x_4$				4
	p_{15}	x_5	$p_{15}x_5$				5
g_2	p_{21}	x_1	$p_{21}x_1$	$\sum p_{2j}x_j$	$\sum + g_2$		6
	p_{22}	x_2	$p_{22}x_2$				7
	p_{23}	x_3	$p_{23}x_3$				8
	p_{24}	x_4	$p_{24}x_4$				9
	p_{25}	x_5	$p_{25}x_5$				10
g_3	p_{31}	x_1	$p_{31}x_1$	$\sum p_{3j}x_j$	$\sum + g_3$		11
	p_{32}	x_2	$p_{32}x_2$				12
	p_{33}	x_3	$p_{33}x_3$				13
	p_{34}	x_4	$p_{34}x_4$				14
	p_{35}	x_5	$p_{35}x_5$				15
g_4	p_{41}	x_1	$p_{41}x_1$	$\sum p_{4j}x_j$	$\sum + g_4$		16
	p_{42}	x_2	$p_{42}x_2$				17
	p_{43}	x_3	$p_{43}x_3$				18
	p_{44}	x_4	$p_{44}x_4$				19
	p_{45}	x_5	$p_{45}x_5$				20
g_5	p_{51}	x_1	$p_{51}x_1$	$\sum p_{5j}x_j$	$\sum + g_5$		21
	p_{52}	x_2	$p_{52}x_2$				22
	p_{53}	x_3	$p_{53}x_3$				23
	p_{54}	x_4	$p_{54}x_4$				24
	p_{55}	x_5	$p_{55}x_5$				25

Figure 6. AP Storage Configuration after Step 3

arithmetic capability. In a stationary iteration $X^{(k+1)} = MX^{(k)} + G$, not only can each element in the matrix product $MX^{(k)}$ be computed in parallel, but the scalar products required for each element can be computed in parallel and the subsequent summing process treed. Within AP capacity, only the treed summing process is explicitly dependent time-wise on n (the system size), and the requisite number of computational levels increases with $\ln_2(n)$. In contrast to this near-independence of n for parallel execution in an AP, sequential methods of execution will require an execution time varying with n^2 since each element of the product $MX^{(k)}$ will require up to n multiplies and there are n such elements. This basic advantage enjoyed by the AP evidently obtains for matrix multiplication in general where n^3 computational levels for sequential execution may be reduced to $\ln_2(n)$ for parallel execution. Any particular timing comparison between a sequential processor and an AP executing matrix operations will depend on the size of the matrices involved and basic speeds of the two processors.

Depending on the computer organization selected, the operations required in an iteration or sweep over the mesh will be executed either sequentially or in a parallel fashion. The number of iterations required for convergence is problem dependent. For the iteration described previously in Steps 1 through 8, the execution time for STARAN varies with the type of arithmetic employed and whether the standard STARAN or

1	2	3 $x^{(k)}$	4	5 FIELDS	6 $x^{(k+1)}$	7	WORD
g_1	p_{11}	x_1	$p_{11}x_1$	$\sum p_{1j}x_j$	$\sum^+ g_1$	$\left|x_1^{(k+1)} - x_1^{(k)}\right|$	1
	p_{12}	x_2	$p_{12}x_2$				2
	p_{13}	x_3	$p_{13}x_3$				3
	p_{14}	x_4	$p_{14}x_4$				4
	p_{15}	x_5	$p_{15}x_5$				5
g_2	p_{21}	x_1	$p_{21}x_1$	$\sum p_{2j}x_j$	$\sum^+ g_2$	$\left|x_2^{(k+1)} - x_2^{(k)}\right|$	6
	p_{22}	x_2	$p_{22}x_2$				7
	p_{23}	x_3	$p_{23}x_3$				8
	p_{24}	x_4	$p_{24}x_4$				9
	p_{25}	x_5	$p_{25}x_5$				10
g_3	p_{31}	x_1	$p_{31}x_1$	$\sum p_{3j}x_j$	$\sum^+ g_3$	$\left|x_3^{(k+1)} - x_3^{(k)}\right|$	11
	p_{32}	x_2	$p_{32}x_2$				12
	p_{33}	x_3	$p_{33}x_3$				13
	p_{34}	x_4	$p_{34}x_4$				14
	p_{35}	x_5	$p_{35}x_5$				15
g_4	p_{41}	x_1	$p_{41}x_1$	$\sum p_{4j}x_j$	$\sum^+ g_4$	$\left|x_4^{(k+1)} - x_4^{(k)}\right|$	16
	p_{42}	x_2	$p_{42}x_2$				17
	p_{43}	x_3	$p_{43}x_3$				18
	p_{44}	x_4	$p_{44}x_4$				19
	p_{45}	x_5	$p_{45}x_5$				20
g_5	p_{51}	x_1	$p_{51}x_1$	$\sum p_{5j}x_j$	$\sum^+ g_5$	$\left|x_5^{(k+1)} - x_5^{(k)}\right|$	21
	p_{52}	x_2	$p_{52}x_2$				22
	p_{53}	x_3	$p_{53}x_3$				23
	p_{54}	x_4	$p_{54}x_4$				24
	p_{55}	x_5	$p_{55}x_5$				25

Figure 7. AP Storage Configuration after Step 5

or a version with optional hardware is used. Options provide for hardware implementation of floating point (which is executed via a software package on the standard machine) and for faster fixed point operations.

In Table 1 we compare estimated execution times for STARAN with two sequential computers which we refer to as C1 and C2. The sequential computers are of modern design, of wide usage, and have floating point multiply times of 21.5 µsec and 4.5 µsec, respectively.

TABLE 1 - EXECUTION TIME IN MILLISECONDS FOR ONE ITERATION

Computer configuration	Time per iteration, msec System size		
	5 x 5	25 x 25	50 x 50
C1[*]	1.0	22.0	85.0
C2[+]	0.3	6.0	22.0
Standard AP 20 bit fixed point	0.6	1.1	1.6
Standard AP 32 bit floating point	3.0	4.3	5.2
Optional AP 32 bit floating point	0.4	0.9	1.4

[*]Computer 1 (C1): 21.5 µsec multiply.

[+]Computer 2 (C2): 4.5 µsec multiply.

Total problem execution time would increase with the number of iterations required and with system I/O and housekeeping operations. The times given are meant only as estimates for comparing parallel versus sequential execution and exhibiting the increasing advantage of parallel execution as system size increases.

f. General Stationary Iteration

In structuring the PR method for parallel execution on an AP, we have seen that associative processing exhibits a potential for computational advantage because of a reduction of n^2 computational levels to $\ln_2(n)$. One might object that such a comparison is misleading in that for sequential execution, GS and not PR usually would be chosen, and GS would probably give a better convergence rate with little penalty in terms of execution time per iteration. It also could be pointed out that GS can often be accelerated by employing SOR.

In answering such an objection, we might first observe that, in general, very little can be said about the relative convergence rates of PJ and GS. In fact, convergence of one method does not imply convergence of the other. We note further that the results of Appendix A allow the acceleration of PJ via PR in cases where theory for SOR has not yet been developed. But such answers do not get at the heart of the matter. The answer we must make is that the successive displacement GS or SOR methods can be executed in parallel.

The amenability of GS or SOR to parallel execution is, I believe, sometimes obscured by the widespread use of examples that introduce GS by exhibiting a numerical solution of, say, Laplace's equation over a rectangular grid. In such examples interior mesh points are cyclically updated using - for successive displacements - new pointwise estimates as they become available.

This sequential formulation of the computational procedure tends to convey the impression that new estimates must be computed sequentially if successive displacement updating is employed, the impression probably being strengthened by writing the updating equations in nonmatrix form. But although under sequential execution the computation of each new estimate in turn uses the most recently computed estimates, the chain of computations ultimately traces back to estimates available at the beginning of the sweep. The specification of this chain for each point or variable will allow the computations to proceed in parallel. In fact, we have already specified the chain of computations in the matrix formulation of GS, given by Equation 8; namely,

$$X^{(k+1)} = (D - E)^{-1} F X^{(k)} + (D - E)^{-1} B .$$

Evidently, GS can also be executed in parallel if we make the initial investment of computing $(D - E)^{-1} F$. In fact, any stationary iteration, SOR included, which we write as

$$X^{(k+1)} = M X^{(k)} + G$$

can be executed in parallel on an AP using the same computational procedure developed for PR. Parallel computation will require that the iteration matrix M be computed and stored in the AP, but once available, the AP execution time is independent of the analytical complexity of M. The question of how best to compute a particular M, either by parallel or sequential methods, is not considered here nor is the problem-dependent question of comparing total execution times for the several iterative methods considered. Our point is that apparently sequential techniques such as SOR can be executed in parallel.

But the potential for parallel execution does not imply practicality of execution, and the construction, storage and utilization of the iteration matrices required for GS or SOR would not seem in general to be practical. But this impracticality can be resolved in an approach which retains the theoretical attraction of GS or SOR and the computational advantage of parallel processing. The approach is based on a rather interesting property which obtains for a large class of coefficient matrices. We discuss this approach in greater detail in the following item.

g. Parallel Successive Displacement

Let us interpret the GS iteration in terms of the numerical solution of Laplace's equation for the unit square. We shall employ the familiar neighbor average approximation and a uniform mesh spacing of $h = 1/4$. We exhibit the mesh for the problem in Figure 8A with the interior mesh points indexed via a "typewriter" ordering.

For large meshes employing an ordering of this type, a typical interior point updated according to the GS convention would use, during a given sweep over the mesh, recently updated values for its north and west neighbors, but yet-to-be-updated values for its south and east neighbors. One can then view the iteration as using half-updated values all the time.

Now suppose we retain the same mesh, but order the interior points according to the "checkerboard" ordering of Figure 8b. Let us again employ the GS updating convention as we sweep over the mesh points. But we notice that on the first half of the sweep (Points 1 through 5 for the example mesh), although we want to use new estimates as they are generated, we are effectively thwarted by the fact that under the

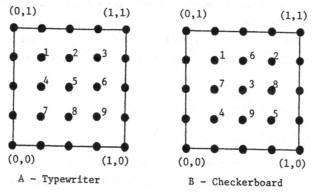

A - Typewriter   B - Checkerboard

Figure 8. Mesh Orderings for Unit Square

new ordering the updated points have not been neighbors. So we use no updated points half the time. By contrast, on the second half of the sweep (Points 6 through 9), we necessarily use nothing but new estimates in our updating procedure and we use all updated points half the time. This is because we were able to use a checkerboard ordering in which we effectively labeled points as red and black in such a fashion that (for the approximating stencil employed) red points had only black neighbors and conversely. This potential of the grid for a checkerboard ordering corresponds to Property (A) in the coefficient matrix of the related system of linear equations. The interesting thing for us here is that use of the typewriter and checkerboard orderings for GS (and SOR) give equivalent results in terms of convergence rate. In other words using half updated points all the time is equivalent to using all updated points half the time.

And we note that within each half of a GS sweep over a checkerboard-ordering grid, the arithmetic employed is effectively that of PJ and can easily be done in parallel. Hence back-to-back updatings of the first and last halves of the mesh points (variables) by simple parallel arithmetic is equivalent to a complicated sequential updating of all mesh points (whether actually done sequentially or by a parallel multiply of a precomputed iteration matrix). Now since for many of the large problems encountered in practice the number of mesh points (unknowns) greatly exceeds the number of processing units in any available parallel processor, nothing is to be lost by employment of the dual parallel updates of the checkerboard ordering scheme. The available processing units can be time shared by the red and black neighbors or subsets thereof. This approach allows full employment of available processors and simple, parallel PJ-type arithmetic in the execution of the apparently sequential GS or SOR methods. It is this approach which brings practical parallelism to the execution of the GS and SOR methods, by obviating the need to precompute an unwieldly iteration matrix.

Implementation of a red-black ordering scheme for parallel execution on an associative processor might be facilitated by employing an indexing scheme such as that given by the stencil of Figure 9, where a's indicate red points, b's indicate black points, and n is dependent on the number of mesh points in a row.

If we store current values for a_i and b_i in (say) Fields 1 and 2 of AP Word i, then parallel updating of a_i's followed by b_i's can be accomplished by the following data connections:

$$b_{i-1}, b_i, b_{i-n-1}, b_{i+n} \quad \text{---} \quad > \quad a_i$$

$$a_i, a_{i+1}, a_{i-n}, a_{i+n+1} \quad \text{---} \quad > \quad b_i$$

For practical problems, geometry and material dependent weighting constants for neighbor averaging at Point i can be stored in Word i. The between-words communication capability of the AP will allow the simultaneous data accesses necessary for parallel updating of mesh point values.

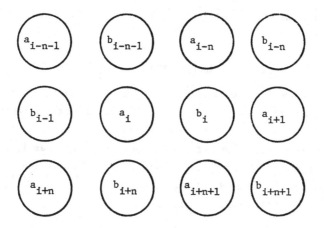

Figure 9. Red–Black Indexing Stencil

5. SUMMARY

We have considered the parallel implementation of stationary iterative techniques on an associative processor. Comparisons have been made between parallel and
sequential methods of execution and parallel methods were seen to offer a considerable reduction in requisite computational levels. It was observed that the parallel
processing capability of the AP is applicable not only to simultaneous displacement
techniques such as Point-Jacobi or parallel relaxation, but also to successive overrelaxation and, in fact, to stationary iteration in general.

6. REFERENCES

[1] R.S. Varga, "Matrix Iterative Analysis," Prentice-Hall, Inc., Englewood Cliffs,
N.J., (1962).

[2] E.L. Wachspress, "Iterative Solution of Elliptic Systems", Prentice-Hall Inc.
Englewood Cliffs, N.J. (1960).

[3] G. Forsyth, and W. Wasow, "Finite Difference Methods for Partial Differential
Equations," John Wiley and Sons, New York, N.Y., (1960).

[4] John Holland, "A Universal Computer Capable of Executing an Arbitrary Number of
Subprograms Simultaneously," Eastern Joint Computer Conference (1959).

[5] D.L. Slotnick, "The Fastest Computer," Scientific American, vol. 224, No. 2,
(February 1971).

[6] K.E. Batcher, "Sorting Networks and Their Application," Proceedings of the
Spring Joint Computer Conference, (1968).

[7] H.S. Stone, "Parallel Processing with the Perfect Shuffle," IEEE Trans. on
Computers, C-20, No. 2, (February 1971).

[8] J.A. Rudolph, "STARAN, A Production Implementation of an Associative Array
Processor," Proc. of the 1972 Fall Joint Computer Conference.

[9] GER-15636A, "STARAN Reference Manual," Goodyear Aerospace Corporation,
Akron, Ohio, (September 1973).

[10] P.A. Gilmore, "Structuring of Parallel Algorithms," J. of ACM, 15, No. 2
      (April 1968).

APPENDIX A – ACCELERATED POINT-JACOBI

In this appendix we further develop the notion of parallel relaxation introduced in Section 3. Our notation remains the same as do our assumptions regarding the coefficient Matrix A.

A potentially accelerated form of the PJ iteration can be easily developed as follows. If we denote $\tilde{X}^{(k+1)}$ the $(k + 1)$st estimate of the solution vector X given by PJ and then specify $X^{(k+1)}$ as a weighted average of $\tilde{X}^{(k+1)}$ and $X^{(k)}$, we have

$$X^{(k+1)} = \omega\tilde{X}^{(k+1)} + (1 - \omega)X^{(k)} . \tag{A-1}$$

In matrix form, this would be

$$X^{(k+1)} = \{(1 - \omega)I + \omega D^{-1}(E + F)\}X^{(k)} + \omega D^{-1}B . \tag{A-2}$$

We shall restrict $\omega > 0$ and refer to the iteration of Equation A-2 as the parallel relaxation (PR) method. Evidently, if $\omega = 1$, PR reduces to PJ.

The question immediately arises as to what value of ω gives the maximum convergence rate and for what range of ω values is Equation A-2 convergent. Let J denote the PJ iteration matrix:

$$J = D^{-1}(E + F) . \tag{A-3}$$

and let P denote the PR iteration matrix:

$$P = \{(1 - \omega)I + \omega J\}. \tag{A-4}$$

We denote the eigenvalues of J by S(J), read "the spectrum of J," and the eigenvalues of P by S(P). Our assumption that the coefficient Matrix A was real and symmetric implies that $S(A) \subset R$; that is, the eigenvalues of A are contained in R, the set of real numbers. The further assumption that A has positive diagonal elements implies that $S(J) \subset R$. We see this by noting that since the diagonal elements of A are positive, D^{-1} exists as do $D^{1/2}$ and $D^{-1/2}$, all being real. Now we may write $J = D^{-1}(E + F) = I - D^{-1}A$.

Since similarity transformations preserve eigenvalues, we have $S(D^{1/2}JD^{-1/2}) = S(J)$. But $\tilde{J} = D^{1/2}JD^{-1/2} = I - D^{-1/2}AD^{-1/2}$. Obviously, $\tilde{J}^T = \tilde{J}$; hence, $\tilde{J}$ is real and symmetric and $S(\tilde{J}) \subset R$. But $S(J) = S(\tilde{J})$; hence, $S(J) \subset R$. It follows from Equation A-2 that, if $\mu \varepsilon S(J)$ and $\lambda \varepsilon S(P)$ – that is, μ and λ are, respectively eigenvalues of J and P – we have the relation

$$\begin{aligned}\lambda &= \omega\mu + (1 - \omega) \\ &= 1 - \omega(1 - \mu) ,\end{aligned} \tag{A-5}$$

and since μ is real, so is λ. Since we are restricting $\omega > 0$, it is evident from Equation A-5 that, if the PR iteration is to converge, we must restrict $\mu \lessdot 1$. Within these restrictions, the optimum value of ω is that for which the spectral radius of P, denoted by $\rho(P)$, is minimized. Let us denote the ordered eigenvalues of J by $S(J) = \{\mu_1 \geq \mu_2 \geq \dots \geq \mu_n\}$ and denote the eigenvalues of P corresponding to μ_i by $\lambda(\omega, \mu_i) = 1 - \omega(1 - \mu_i)$. Then for $\omega = 0$, $\lambda(\omega, \mu_i) = 1$ for $i = 1, \dots, n$. For $\omega > 0$, $\mu_i < \mu_j > \lambda(\omega, \mu_i) < \lambda(\omega, \mu_j)$. Hence $\rho(P)$ is minimal for $\lambda(\omega, \mu_1) = -\lambda(\omega, \mu_n)$. We summarize these results in the following

Theorem

Let A be an n x n nonsingular matrix that is real and symmetric with positive diagonal entries and let the PJ iteration matrix for A have eigenvalues bounded from above by 1. Then, the optimum relaxation parameter for PR is given by:

$$\omega_{opt} = \frac{2}{2 - (\mu_1 + \mu_n)} . \tag{A-6}$$

An interesting feature of PR is that not only can it accelerate convergence of the PJ iteration, but it also can in some cases establish convergence. It is readily shown that, if the coefficient Matrix A is diagonally dominant, convergence of the PJ iteration is assured; diagonal dominance of A is, however, not a necessary condition. For convergence of PJ, a condition that is both necessary and sufficient is that the spectral radius of the iteration Matrix J be less than 1.0.

Let us consider a PJ iteration Matrix J with eigenvalues $S(J)$ bounded from above by 1.0. Now for any eigenvalue $\mu \epsilon S(J)$ the corresponding eigenvalue λ of the PR iteration matrix P is given by $\lambda(\omega, \mu) = 1 - \omega(1 - \mu)$. If we again denote the ordered spectrum of J by $S(J) = \{\mu_1 \geq \mu_2 \geq \dots \geq \mu_n\}$ where $\mu_1 < 1$, then for $\omega \epsilon (0, \infty)$ we have $\lambda(\omega, \mu_n) \leq \lambda(\omega, \mu_1) < 1$ always. To ensure $\lambda(\omega, \mu_n) > -1$, and hence convergence of the PR iteration, we need only restrict ω as follows:

$$0 < \omega < \frac{2}{1 - \mu_n} . \tag{A-7}$$

We see then that for linear systems for which the corresponding PJ Matrix J has eigenvalues bounded from above by 1.0, the convergence-destroying effects of negative eigenvalues whose magnitude exceeds 1.0 can be offset by proper selection of ω. As an example of the convergence-establishing properties of the PR iteration, consider the following matrix:

$$A = \begin{pmatrix} 6 & 1 & 2 & 1 & 3 \\ 1 & 5 & 4 & 0 & 1 \\ 2 & 4 & 8 & 1 & 2 \\ 1 & 0 & 1 & 4 & 3 \\ 3 & 1 & 2 & 3 & 8 \end{pmatrix}$$

The Matrix A is in no way diagonally dominant, and the eigenvalues of the associated PJ matrix are given by $S(J) = \{0.67596, 0.56931, 0.23783, -0.32066, -1.16243\}$. Evidently, the occurrence of the eigenvalue $\mu = -1.16243$ will cause divergence for the PJ iteration. However, the use of PR with ω in the range

$$0 < \omega < \frac{2}{1 + 1.16243} = 0.92488 \qquad \text{(A-8)}$$

will guarantee convergence. The optimal ω for this case is given by

$$\omega_{opt} = \frac{2}{2 - (0.67596 - 1.16243)} = 0.80435 \qquad \text{(A-9)}$$

These results are presented in Figure A-1. We note that in this case optimal convergence is achieved by underrelaxation.

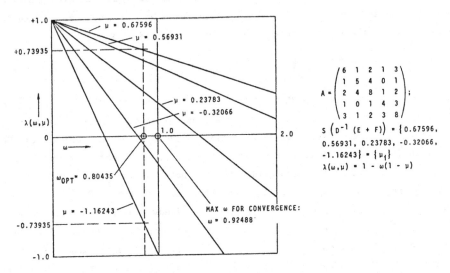

Figure A-1. ω-Dependent Eigenvalues for PR Iteration
Matrix $J = \{(1 - \omega) I + \omega D - 1 (E + F)\}$ for Given
Matrix A

The coefficient matrices with which we have dealt in the preceding discussion of the PR method have been assumed to be real and symmetric with positive diagonal elements. Very often, however, iterative solutions are sought for linear systems whose coefficient matrices possess Young's property (A). For such coefficient matrices, the eigenvalues of the corresponding PJ Matrix J occur either as zero or plus-minus pairs. In such cases, the maximum eigenvalue $\mu_1 \epsilon S(J)$, and the minimum eigenvalue $\mu_n \epsilon S(J)$ would be related as $\mu_1 = -\mu_n$, in which case the optimum ω for PR would given by

$$\omega_{opt} = \frac{2}{2 - (\mu_1 + \mu_n)} = 1 , \qquad \text{(A-10)}$$

and PR offers no advantage over PJ. In such cases, PJ still is attractive for implementation on parallel processors, and there exists the possibility for increasing the rate of convergence by utilizing semi-iterative techniques.

OPTIMAL SEARCHING ALGORITHMS FOR
PARALLEL-PIPELINED COMPUTERS[a]

DANIEL L. WELLER AND EDWARD S. DAVIDSON
Coordinated Science Laboratory
University of Illinois
Urbana, Illinois 61801

Abstract -- A new class of optimal search algorithms is presented for the classical problem of searching an ordered list. The appropriate algorithm is selected
as a function of the order,(s,p),of the target processor which may consist of p parallel processors each of which is an s level pipelined processor. The algorithms are
structured according to a new integer series, the W-series. The algorithms include
the binary search for processors of order $(1,1)$, the Fibonacci search for processors
of order $(2,1)$, and well-known parallel searches for processors of order $(1,p)$. Performance of the algorithms is evaluated. The algorithms are well-suited to computers
with interleaved or parallel memory banks.

1. INTRODUCTION

This paper is concerned with the classical problem of searching an ordered list
for a single desired item in the list. A class of optimal searching algorithms is
developed in which the specific algorithm to be used is a function of the architecture of the computer performing the search. These algorithms are analogous to the
binary search for a conventional sequential computer. Compact storage of the list
is assumed; i.e., no hash tables are used.

The fundamental step in searching is a <u>comparison</u> or memory <u>probe</u> which requires
one unit of time and compares the <u>key</u> or desired item with a particular item in the
list. The time for other operations associated with the search is considered to be
incorporated in the unit time for a comparison. Three-way comparisons are considered briefly at the end of Section II. Otherwise, only two-way comparisons are
considered. To be specific, the result of a comparison will be either that the key
is less than the list item (we say the comparison succeeds) or that the key is greater than or equal to the list item (we say the comparison fails).

Parallel-pipelined processors are becoming increasingly common, but their util-
ity has not been demonstrated for tasks which are normally highly sequential, such
as searching. In searching, the computational time for a comparison is almost negligible compared to the memory cycle time for retrieving a list item. The normal
solution to such problems in modern computers is to interleave the cycles of several

[a] This work was supported by the National Science Foundation under Grants GJ-35584X
and GJ-40584 and by the Joint Services Electronics Program under Contract DAAB-
07-72-C-0259.

banks of memory and/or to use a memory with a wide enough word to store several items in one memory word. In the former case, although the retrieval time remains constant, further items can be requested while the retrieval of a particular item is in process. In the latter case, several items can be retrieved simultaneously each cycle time. In the general case of an s-way interleaved p-wide memory, p items can be retrieved each 1/s of the cycle time. The comparison time, which is the interval from item request to completed retrieval, is constant and equal to the memory cycle time.

The development of new search algorithms which exploit the concurrency in present day computers is an important end in itself. In addition, it demonstrates the possibility of algorithm restructuring to introduce parallelism when presently known algorithms are highly sequential. The algorithms presented in this paper achieve maximum performance for searching on machines with parallel, interleaved memories. Furthermore, results indicate that a search which is cost-effective may require values of s and p greater than 1.

In our formal model, a parallel processor with p processors can initiate up to p comparisons at one time. A pipelined processor with s segments can initiate one comparison every 1/s units of time, thus allowing up to s comparisons to be in progress at one time. For full generality, a parallel-pipelined processor with p processors, each with s segments, is referred to as a parallel-pipelined processor of order (s,p). Such a processor can initiate p comparisons every 1/s units of time and may have up to p·s comparisons in progress at one time. Figure 1 shows a graphical view of this model for three processors. Each rectangle represents one comparison. For convenience we define a step of time to be 1/s units of time.

A search algorithm for a processor of a given order, chooses the time and placement of comparisons as a function only of the known outcomes of previously placed comparisons. A search algorithm is called optimal in the minimax sense if it minimizes, over all searching algorithms for a processor of a given order, the maximum time required to find any item in the list. A search algorithm is called optimal average if it minimizes, over all search algorithms for a processor of a given order, the average of the time required to find each item in the list. It is assumed here that the probability of searching for any item in a list of N items is a constant 1/N.

In the next section optimal search algorithms are presented for an arbitrary parallel-pipelined processor. In order to motivate that material we present here an intuitive derivation of an optimal search algorithm for a two segment pipelined processor. First let us consider the binary search which is known to be optimal on a conventional sequential computer. Suppose an ordered list is represented by a straight line of unit length and comparisons are represented by arrows. The outcome of a comparison is called successful if the key is to the left of the corresponding comparison (less than) and unsuccessful if it is to the right (greater than or equal). The first comparison is optimally placed at y, where y is as yet unknown. Figure 2

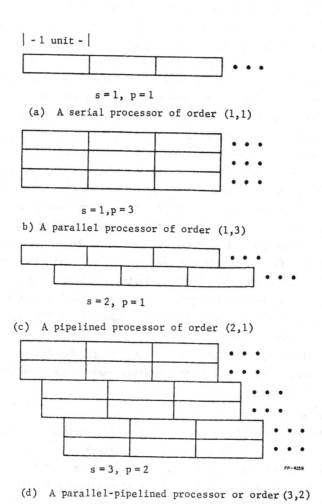

| - 1 unit - |

$s = 1, \ p = 1$

(a) A serial processor of order (1,1)

$s = 1, p = 3$

b) A parallel processor of order (1,3)

$s = 2, \ p = 1$

(c) A pipelined processor of order (2,1)

$s = 3, \ p = 2$

FP-4159

(d) A parallel-pipelined processor or order (3,2)

Figure 1. Model of Parallel-Pipelined Processors.

shows the divided list.

For the binary search with a serial processor we know the results of the first comparison when we make the second comparison. The second comparison is placed in either the y interval or in the 1-y interval, depending on the outcome of the first comparison. For a minimax optimal search we want a value of y that will minimize the maximum of y and 1-y. Obviously this occurs when $y = 1 - y$; i.e., $y = .5$. Thus the optimal serial search chooses the comparison in the middle of the remaining interval at each step; that is, the list is divided according to the binary series.

A similar argument can be presented for searching with a pipelined processor with two segments; i.e., a processor of order (2,1). The first comparison is optimally placed at y whose numerical value is as yet unknown. This comparison is shown in Figure 2. The second comparison must be placed before the outcome of the first comparison is known. Without loss of generality the second comparison is placed to the left of the first comparison. Placement of the second comparison is thus irrelevant if the first comparison is unsuccessful; i.e., if the desired item is in the 1-y interval. If the first comparison is successful, the desired item is in the y interval and the second comparison should be optimally placed at y^2, dividing the y interval into $y \cdot y$ and $y \cdot (1-y)$ subintervals. Figure 3 shows the list after the first two comparisons have been made. When the third comparison is placed, the outcome of only the first comparison is known. Thus, the third comparison is placed in the y^2 interval if the first comparison is successful and in the 1-y interval if the first comparison is unsuccessful. For a minimax optimal search we must minimize the maximum of y^2 and 1-y. This occurs at

$$y^2 = 1 - y,$$

which fixes y at $.618 \ldots = 1/\phi$, where ϕ is the golden ratio which generates the Fibonacci series (just as 2 generates the binary series).

The Fibonacci series, $F(1), F(2), \ldots,$ is defined to be $F(1) = F(2) = 1$ and $F(i) = F(i-1) + F(i-2)$, for $i > 2$. It is known that $y \cdot F(n) = F(n-1)$ to the nearest integer [4]. Thus a comparison at y cuts a list of $F(n)$ items into $F(n-1)$ items on the left and $F(n-2)$ items on the right. Therefore, the optimal search on a processor of order (2,1) is a Fibonacci search, which divides the list according to the Fibonacci numbers. Figure 4 graphically demonstrates this search algorithm.

This search algorithm is similar to the serial Fibonacci search described by Knuth [1] and the Fibonacci search procedure used to locate the maximum of a unimodal function using a serial processor [3], in that they all divide intervals according to the Fibonacci numbers. It is interesting to note that although the Fibonacci search is well-known, it was not previously known that it is optimal for a 2-segment pipelined processor.

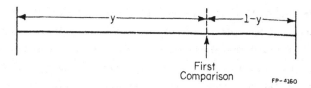

Figure 2. Placement of First Comparison.

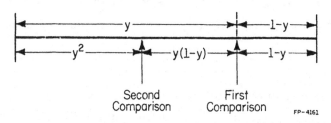

Figure 3. Placement of Second Comparison.

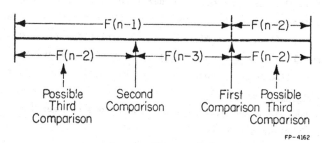

Figure 4. The Fibonacci Search.

II. MINIMAX OPTIMAL SEARCH ALGORITHMS

In this section optimal searching of an ordered list by a parallel-pipelined processor of order (s,p) is considered. The main result of this section is that the minimax optimal search is a W-search which divides a list according to the W-series (defined later) of the proper order.

A search algorithm shall be represented as a tree of possible comparisons. Leaf nodes shall be referred to as external or terminal nodes and are drawn as squares. Nonleaf nodes shall be referred to as internal nodes and are drawn as circles. A tree, representing a search algorithm for a list of N items, has N leaf nodes corresponding to the items in the list and consequently a root node labeled N. The ith leaf node from the left is labeled i and corresponds to the ith item in the list. Each internal node, labeled M, corresponds to a sublist of M items, namely the items associated with the M leaf nodes it generates. An internal node with k + 1 branches to offspring nodes is associated with k simultaneous comparisons ($k \leq p$). These k comparisons divide the sublist of M items into k + 1 sublists. Each offspring node of the internal node corresponds to one of these k + 1 sublists. The offspring nodes of an internal node specify the placement of the comparisons associated with that internal node. Each branch between two internal nodes is labeled with the number of steps of time between the comparisons associated with the two nodes. Each branch from an internal node to an external node is labeled s: the number of steps of time required to complete the comparisons associated with the internal node.

We now define an integer series which is central to optimal searching.

Definition 1: The W-series of order (s,p) is defined recursively as follows:

$$W(s,p,1) = W(s,p,2) = \ldots = W(s,p,s) = 1.$$

For n > s,

$$W(s,p,n) = W(s,p,n-1) + p \cdot W(s,p,n-s),$$

where s, p, and n are positive integers. For convenience $W(s,p,i)$ is defined to be zero for i < 1. □

If s and p are known from the context, we abbreviate $W(s,p,n)$ as simply $W(n)$. $W(s,p,n)$ is known as the nth W-number of order (s,p). It is interesting to note that the W-series of order (1,1) is the binary series, the W-series of order (2,1) is the Fibonacci series, and $W(1,p,n) = (p+1)^{n-1}$. The W-series describes optimal search algorithms in a natural way. A search algorithm of order (s,p) and size N defines a search for a list of size N on a processor of order (s,p) and can be represented by a search tree of order (s,p) and size N .

Consider now how big a decision tree of comparisons can get for a parallel-pipelined processor performing a search.

Theorem 1: No search tree can grow faster than the W-series from any node. □

This theorem is proved first by defining the level of a node as the sum of the branch lengths from the root node, plus the level of the root node, which is 1. Then it is proved that given any search tree of order (s,p) and some node in that tree at level L, that node generates $W(s,p,i)$ or fewer nodes at level L + i - 1. Each node represents the sublist of leaf nodes it generates. The level of a node minus one corresponds to steps of time. Therefore consider a sublist at some step of time t (with whose items no comparisons have been initiated) instead of its corresponding node at some level. Let $X(i)$ = the maximum number of distinct places a comparison could go at t + i - 1 (steps of time); i.e., one more than the maximum number of possible comparisons known at t + i - 1. If i = 1, ..., s then $X(i)$ = 1, but if i > s, then:

$$X(i) = 1 + \text{the maximum number of possible places that comparisons}$$
$$\text{could be placed from t to t + i - 1 - s.}$$

Then, since p comparisons can be made at once

$$X(i) = 1 + p \cdot \sum_{j=1}^{i-s} X(j).$$

Now consider $X(i) - X(i-1) = p \cdot X(i-s)$; that is, $X(i) = X(i-1) + p \cdot X(i-s)$. Thus the X(i) series is just the W-series. Therefore the maximum number of nodes at level $L + i - 1$ generated from a node at level L is W(i), and the theorem is proved.

The <u>height</u> of a search tree is the highest level of any node in the tree.

<u>Définition 2</u>: An optimal search tree of order (s,p) and size N is any search tree of order (s,p) and size N with the smallest height. []

Now using theorem 1, which tells us the maximum possible number of nodes at each level, and the easily proved fact that:

$$\sum_{i=1}^{n} W(s,p,i) = \frac{W(s,p,n+s) - 1}{p} ,$$

we can get the following result.

<u>Theorem 2</u>: An optimal search tree of order (s,p) and size N, where $W(s,p,n-1) < N \leq W(s,p,n)$, has a height $\geq n$. []

Theorem 2 says that any order (s,p) search of size N must have a worst case item that requires at least (n-1)/s units of time to find.

Now we define the W-tree and show that a W-tree of order (s,p) and size W(s,p,n) has height n and thus is optimal.

<u>Definition 3</u>: A W-tree of order (s,p) and size W(s,p,n) (referred to as a W-tree if the context is clear) is any tree that can be constructed by the following rules and only those trees.

1. Construct all nodes as circles.
2. Begin with a single node (the root node), labeled W(s,p,n). Let k = n.
3. Construct p + 1 offspring nodes with the leftmost branch to an offspring labeled 1 if W(s,p,k-1) > 1 else labeled s. The p rightmost branches to offspring nodes are each labeled s. Label the leftmost offspring node as W(s,p,k-1) and each of the p rightmost offspring nodes as W(s,p,k-s).
4. Do step 3 recursively for each node with label W(s,p,k) > 1.
5. Change all leaf nodes to squares and relabel them left to right in sequence with the positive integers. []

Figure 5 displays a W-tree of order (3,2) and size 13 and one of order (2,1) and size 8.

It is proved that all W-trees are search trees and that a W-tree of order (s,p) and size W(s,p,n) has a height n. Thus we have the theorem.

<u>Theorem 3</u>: All W-trees are optimal search trees. []

We define search trees to be <u>equivalent</u> if they are of the same order and size and they have the same number of internal and external nodes at each level, and we

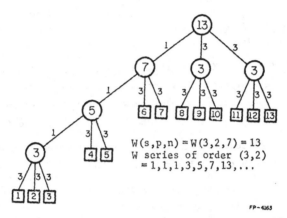

Figure 5a. A W-tree of Order (3,2) and size 13.

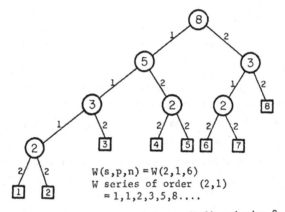

Figure 5b. A W-tree of Order (2,1) and size 8.

define search algorithms to be <u>equivalent</u> if the search trees representing the search algorithms are equivalent. We now define the W-search.

<u>Definition 4</u>: A W-search of order (s,p) and size W(s,p,n) is that search algorithm of order (s,p) and size W(s,p,n) that is represented by the W-tree of order (s,p) and size W(s,p,n). []

Then we immediately have the following theorem.

<u>Theorem 4</u>: A W-search of order (s,p) and size W(s,p,n) is the optimal search algorithm for a list of size W(s,p,n) on a processor of order (s,p). Furthermore no other nonequivalent search algorithm is optimal. []

We now generalize the W-search for lists of arbitrary size.

<u>Definition 5</u>: For every N there is an n such that W(s,p,n-1) < N ≤ W(s,p,n).

The W-search of order (s,p) and size N is the search algorithm of order (s,p) and size W(s,p,n) that is represented by the W-tree of order (s,p) and size W(s,p,n), with the following exception. Comparisons with items greater than the Nth item on the list are dummy comparisons that always indicate that the desired item is less than or equal to the list item. []

This definition means that we take the smallest W-tree of the proper order which has a size greater than or equal to N and remove all the leaves to the right labeled greater than N. By pruning the tree in a different way we could possibly get a better average search time, but any pruning will give the same worst case search time.

Theorem 5: Given a processor of order (s,p) and a list of size N, the W-search of order (s,p) and size N is an optimal search algorithm for that list on that processor. []

Figure 6 gives an example of a search tree representing a W-search for N not in the W-series.

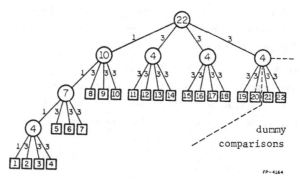

Figure 6. An Optimal Search Tree for a List of
Size 20 on a Processor of Order (3,3).

It is now possible to make a general statement about the search time for an optimal search.

Definition 6: wt(s,p,N) is the worst case search time (in units) for an optimal search of a list of N items on a processor of order (s,p). []

Theorem 6: Given a processor of order (s,p) and a list of size N, where W(s,p,n) < N ≤ W(s,p,n+1),

$$wt(s,p,N) = n/s. \quad []$$

Furthermore, the best case search time is very close to the worst case search time.

Theorem 7: In a W-search the time to find any item is within one unit (s steps) of the time to find any other item. []

Suppose now that we allow 3-way comparisons; that is, greater than-less than comparisons with a separate check for equality. The W'-series then describes mini-max optimal searching just as the W-series did for 2-way comparisons. <u>The W' series of order (s,p)</u> is defined as follows: $W'(s,p,1) = W'(s,p,2) =,...= W'(s,p,s) = 1$. For $n > s$, $W'(s,p,n) = W'(s,p,n-1) + p \cdot W'(s,p,n-s) + p$. It is easy to show that $W'(n) = 2 \cdot W(n) - 1$, for all s and p. Thus $W'(n) < 2 \cdot W(n)$. Since any processor can divide a list in half or better in one unit of time, the optimal worst case search time for a search with 3-way comparisons is at most one unit of time less than the optimal worst case search time for a search of the same list on a processor of the same order with 2-way comparisons.

A W-search of size $W(s,p,n)$ can be described as follows: the first p comparisons are placed to divide the list into a sublist of $W(s,p,n-1)$ items on the left and into p sublists of $W(s,p,n-s)$ items on the right. The next p comparisons subdivide the leftmost sublist similarly. This process continues until the item is located or the result of the mth set of p comparisons indicates that the desired item is not in the leftmost interval; i.e., the leftmost comparison among these p comparisons is unsuccessful. The search is then restarted beginning with the sublist of $W(s,p,n-(s+m-1))$ items which is known to contain the desired item.

The W-search of order (1,1) is the binary search. The W-search of order (1,p) is the well-known parallel search described by Karp and Miranker [2]. The W-search of order (2,1) is the Fibonacci search described in the first section. Other W-searches are new as is the proof of optimality for $s > 1$.

III. OPTIMAL AVERAGE SEARCHING

The main result of this section is that the average search time for the W-search is always within one unit of time of the average search time for an optimal average search.

The W-tree has the maximum number of internal nodes at each level and would be optimal in the average sense except that the branches to terminal nodes cause a slight increase in average search time. However, that end effect becomes a negligible part of the search time for large lists. Figure 7 shows an example of a W-search that is not optimal in the average sense.

For the following definitions and theorems we need the following symbols:

O.A.(N) - the average search time for an optimal average search of size N, and

W.A.(N) - the average search time for a W-search of size N.

<u>Definition 7</u>: An optimal average search algorithm of order (s,p) and size N is an average optimal search algorithm for a processor of order (s,p) and a list of size N. []

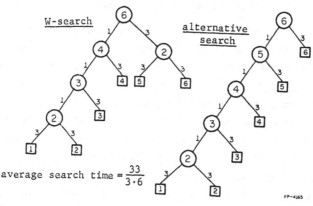

average search time $= \dfrac{33}{3 \cdot 6}$

average search time $= \dfrac{32}{3 \cdot 6}$

Figure 7. Searches of Order (3,1) and Size 6.

<u>Theorem 8</u>: The average search time for the W-search of order (s,p) and size N is within one unit of time of the average search time for an optimal search algorithm of order (s,p) and size N; that is,

W.A.(N) - O.A.(N) < 1 (units of time). []

To prove this we first define a T(n) tree (not a search tree). Suppose we have a W-tree of order (s,p) and size W(n). Such a W tree finds all the items between time (n-s)/s and time (n-1)/s. A <u>T(n) tree</u> is a W-tree of the proper order of size W(n) whose branch labels to leaf nodes have been decreased so that any item can be found at time (n-s)/s. Thus branch labels to leaf nodes are decreased by at most (s-1)/s units of time. If <u>T.A.(W(n))</u> is the average search time for a T(n) tree, then we have W.A.(W(n)) - T.A.(W(n)) $\leq$ (s-1)/s.

It can be shown that the T(n) tree has the maximum number of internal nodes at each level, and more leaf nodes at level n - s + 1 than allowable for a search tree. From this fact it can be proved that T.A.(W(n)) < O.A.(W(n)). Thus we have:

$$W.A.(W(n)) - O.A.(W(n)) < \frac{s-1}{s} \,.$$

Thus the theorem is proved for N = W(n).

Now suppose W(n) < N $\leq$ W(n+1). Now T.A.(W(n)) = (n-s)/s. Thus, (n-s)/s < O.A.(W(n)) $\leq$ O.A.(N). Also, W.A.(N) $\leq$ W.A.(W(n+1)) $\leq$ n/s, since the worst case search time for searching a W-tree of size W(n+1) is n/s. Putting these together we have (n-s)/s < O.A.(N) $\leq$ W.A.(N) $\leq$ n/s. Therefore:

W.A.(N) - O.A.(N) < 1

and the theorem is proved.

IV. ESTIMATING OPTIMAL SEARCH TIME

In this section methods for approximating the minimax optimal search time for an arbitrary processor will be presented. Also the speedup in search time relative to a binary search will be evaluated as a function of the order (s,p) of the processor doing the search. If we are searching a list of N items, a binary search takes $\lceil \log_2 N \rceil$ units of time. For a parallel computer of order (1,p), the optimal search algorithm divides the list into p + 1 equal length sublists at each unit of time. Since the length of the list is reduced by a factor of p + 1 at each time unit, any desired item can be located in $\lceil (\log_2 N)/(\log_2 (p+1)) \rceil$ units of time. The speedup thus approximates $\log_2 (p+1)$.

We know from Section II that if we are searching a list of size N, where $W(s,p,n) < N \le W(s,p,n+1)$, on a processor of order (s,p); then:

$$wt(s,p,N) = \frac{n}{s} \ .$$

The problem is that given N there is no known explicit formula for calculating n. Thus for a general solution we must approximate n. The most important result of this section is that the optimal worst case search time, relative to a binary search, for a processor of order (s,p) is:

$$s \cdot \log_2 \left(\frac{1}{y} \right) \ ,$$

where y is the real root of the equation $py^s + y - 1 = 0$.

Suppose G(y) is the generating function for the W-series. Then

$$G(y) = W(s,p,1) \cdot y + W(s,p,2) \cdot y^2 + W(s,p,3) \cdot y^3 + \ldots \ .$$

Then by methods similar to those used by Knuth [4] for the Fibonacci series we get:

$$G(y) = \frac{y}{1 - y - py^s} \ .$$

From this expression we can derive a formula for W(n) in terms of the roots of the equation $py^s + y - 1 = 0$.

<u>Theorem 9:</u> $W(s,p,n) = C_1 \left(\frac{1}{y_1} \right)^n + C_2 \left(\frac{1}{y_2} \right)^n + \ldots + C_s \left(\frac{1}{y_s} \right)^n$, where $C_1, \ldots, C_s$ are constants dependent on s and p; and $y_1, \ldots, y_s$ are the roots of the equation $py^s + y - 1 = 0$.[]

It is proved that the equation $py^s + y - 1 = 0$ has only one positive real root and that root is between 0 and 1. Suppose we call the positive real root y_1, then it can be shown that $y_1 < |y_i|$ where y_i is any other root. Using these facts along with the formula from Theorem 9 we can measure the growth rate of the W-series.

<u>Theorem 10:</u> $\lim\limits_{n \to \infty} \frac{W(s,p,n+1)}{W(s,p,n)} = \frac{1}{y_1}$, where y_1 is as stated above. []

In a similar fashion we can show that $\lim\limits_{n \to \infty} W(s,p,n) \cdot y_1^n = C_1$, where y_1 and C_1 are as stated above.

We now define performance improvement and show how it can be evaluated.

Definition 8: Performance improvement, I, for a processor of order (s,p) and a list of size N is defined as:

$$I(s,p,N) = \frac{wt(1,1,N)}{wt(s,p,N)} \cdot []$$

The performance improvement tells how many times faster a search can be done on a processor of order (s,p) than on a processor of order (1,1). Let $\underline{I(s,p)}$ = Lim I(s,p,N). Using previous results we get the following theorem.
N→∞

Theorem 11: $I(s,p) = s \cdot \log_2\left(\frac{1}{y_1}\right)$ where y_1 is the real positive root of the equation $py^s + y - 1 = 0$. []

Using this result we can approximate the optimal worst case search time as:

$$wt(s,p,N) \approx \frac{\log_2 N}{s \cdot \log_2\left(\frac{1}{y_1}\right)}, \quad \text{where } y_1 \text{ is as stated above.}$$

The question is how good is that estimate? The estimate is accurate in the limit as N → ∞. Furthermore, we believe that it is always within one unit of the actual search time, but no proof of this conjecture has been found.

A table showing I(s,p) for several values of s and p is shown below:

p\s	1	2	4	8	16	32
1	1	1.59	2.32	3.17	4.09	5.05
2	1.39	2	2.71	3.51	4.36	5.25
4	1.86	2.51	3.22	4	4.82	5.68
8	2.41	3.09	3.83	4.61	5.42	6.26
16	3.03	3.74	4.50	5.29	6.11	6.94
32	3.70	4.45	5.22	6.03	6.86	7.70

I(s,p)

These results are shown graphically in Figure 8. It is evident from the curves that any improvement ratio, I, can be attained through pipelining or parallelism or some mixture of the two. For example, an improvement of 3 or more can be obtained by processors of order (s,p) = (16,1), (8,2), (4,4), or (1,8) among others. An integer improvement of k can be obtained by $p = 2^k - 1$, s = 1. Improvement rises more steeply with increasing p than with increasing s.

To return to our original motivation of the problem as a memory utilization problem: what is the cost of s-way interleaving a memory? What is the cost of restructuring a memory to be p-wide (and possibly contain 1/p times the number of

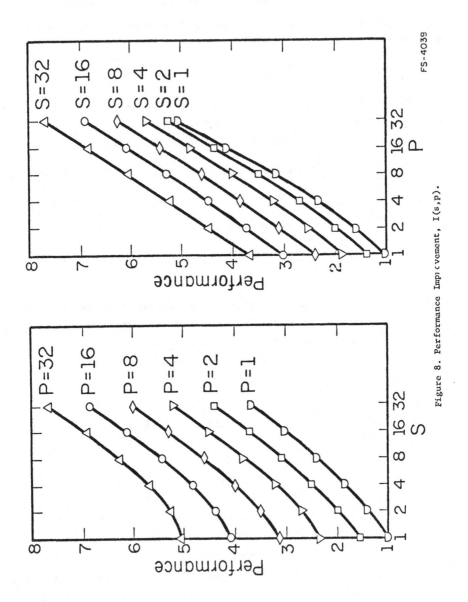

Figure 8. Performance Improvement, I(s,p).

FS-4039

words)? If an optimal search of the appropriate order is always used, the cost-effectiveness of searching on a parallel-pipelined processor of order (s,p) is $I(s,p)/C(s,p)$, where $C(s,p)$ is the cost of a restructured processor of order (s,p) relative to the original processor of order $(1,1)$ with the same memory cycle time. Values of s and p greater than 1 can well be cost-effective, even for searching. For example, it is unlikely that the percentage increase in system cost caused by two-way interleaving of a memory will exceed the 39% increase in performance. Similarly, the cost of providing a double-word memory is unlikely to exceed 59% of the original system cost.

It should be noted that any ordered list can be allocated to an s-way inter-leaved, p-wide memory for performing W-searches with no access conflicts. One advantage interleaving has over wide-word memories is the evenness of data flow and the preservation of the sequential nature of computation and decision making. This fact might lead one to conclude that generally increases in s are less costly than an equal increase in p. However, s must be increased more than p to achieve equal performance. These cost-performance tradeoffs are thus quite real and can only be evaluated with knowledge of current cost figures.

REFERENCES

[1] D.E. Knuth, <u>The Art of Computer Programming</u>, Vol. 3, Addison-Wesley, (1973), pp. 414-416.

[2] R.M. Karp and W.L. Miranker, "Parallel Minimax Search for a Maximum," <u>Journal of Combinatorial Theory</u>, Vol. 4, (1968), pp. 19-35.

[3] J. Kiefer, "Sequential Minimax Search for a Maximum," <u>Amer. Math. Soci. Proc.</u>, Vol. 4, (1953), pp. 502-505.

[4] D.E. Knuth, <u>The Art of Computer Programming,</u> Vol. 1, Addison-Wesley, (1969), pp. 81-82.

A NEW PARALLEL ALGORITHM FOR
NETWORK FLOW PROBLEMS

I-NGO CHEN
Department of Computing Science
University of Alberta
Edmonton, Alberta, Canada T6G 2E1

SUMMARY

Recently Chen and Feng [1] developed an algorithm for solving the maximum flow problem with an associative processor. The algorithm is based upon the matrix multiplication [3] which requires $0(n^3)$ computations sequentially and (n^2) computations with a parallel processor where n is the dimension of the matrix. In this paper, we present a new algorithm which requires about $0(n^2)$ computations sequentially, and $0(n)$ computations parallelly. This new algorithm is based on node-exclusion from a graph. Let N_1 be the source node and N_n be the sink node. A node N_k is <u>excluded</u> from a graph if (1) $C_{1k} = 0$, or (2) after the following operation:

$$\text{i.} \quad C'_{1j} \leftarrow \min. (C_{1k}, C_{kj}) \;\;.......\qquad (1)$$

$$\text{ii.} \quad C_{1j} \leftarrow C'_{1j}, \text{ if } C'_{1j} > C_{1j} \;\;....\qquad (1.2)$$

$$C_{1j} \text{ unchanged, otherwise } ...\qquad (1.3)$$

$$j = 2, 3, \ldots, n-1, \qquad j \neq k$$

where C_{ij} is an entry of the capacity matrix C. A node N_j is <u>returned</u> to a graph if it was excluded previously and then C_{1j} has been replaced due to the exclusion of any node as described in Eq. (1.2). A returned node can be excluded again. The procedure starts by first excluding N_1 and N_n and then excluding one by one the remaining n-2 nodes. Thus during the process, there are two classes of nodes, one contains those being excluded, and the other contains those waiting to be excluded. The process terminates when all nodes are excluded. The maximum flow is the final value of C_{1n}. To trace the path, we need a vector T initialized with 1. Every time the replacement of Eq. (1.2) takes place, $T(j) \leftarrow k$. The path can be easily traced back from $T(n) \rightarrow T(T(n)) \rightarrow \ldots$ until finally for some i, $T(i) = 1$. Since there is no negative capacity, there will be no negative cycles in the graph. Thus every time we run from N_2 to N_{n-1} the elements of the set of excluded nodes should be increased at least by one. With a parallel processor, the upper bound for our method is, therefore, (n-1)(n-2) comparisons plus another n comparisons for tracing the path. Compared to [1], our method does not require a matrix transpose operation in tracing the path. Moreover, although both methods have an upper bound of $0(n^2)$ in computing the maximum flow, in [1], the upper bound is also the lower bound, and in our case, the lower bound is 1, where N_1 and N_n are isolated from the rest. Computational experiments showed that for matrices varying from dense to 10% sparse, the average computations required for our method is about n. Our method differs to the Dijkstra's algorithm [2] in that we do not require finding the minimum out of n-1 elements which might be more time consuming with some parallel processors. The new algorithm can also be applied to solve for other problems of a flow network such as minimum cost, simple cycles, and negative cycles [4].

REFERENCES

[1] Y.K. Chen and Tse-Yun Feng, "A Parallel Algorithm for Maximum Flow Problem", Proceedings of the 1973 Sagamore Computer Conference.

[2] E.W. Dijkstra, "A Note on Two Problems in Connection with Graphs", Numerische Mathematik I (1959), pp. 269-271.

[3] M. Pollack, "The Maximum Capacity through a Network", OR 8(1960), pp. 733-736.

[4] I.N. Chen, "A Fast Method for Minimum Cost Flows", Tech. Rep. TR74-15, Dept. of Computing Science, University of Alberta,(August 1974).

PARALLEL PROCESSING BY VIRTUAL INSTRUCTION

CECIL KAPLINSKY
Computer Unit
Westfield College
(University of London)
London, NW3 7ST, England

Abstract -- An architecture involving at least one master CPU and many auxiliary processors is proposed to restore the balance between processor and store
systems in multi-programming systems.

The outline of the processor/store connections is given and the mode of operation is discussed. Parallelism is achieved by either parallel processing one task
or running many tasks in parallel.

It is shown that the system will run current high level programs making its own
decisions as to whether it is feasible to subtask a portion of the program. If any-
thing is subtasked it is treated as a virtual instruction to run on its own processor. This virtual instruction is mapped onto the auxiliary processors by an associative memory.

I INTRODUCTION

In this paper an architecture for a multi-processor multi-programmed computer
system is put forward. The proposed system will not only allow programs, which are
explicitly programmed to run on M processors, to take advantage of the multiple
physical processors but will also take advantage of any implied parallelism within
and between programs. This organization will then allow the explicitly parallel
programs to take full advantage of the many processors even if the number of available physical processors N is less than the number of parallel processors M, explicitly requested.

In Section II the justification for multi-processor systems is discussed while
the specific hardware proposal is outlined in Section III. Section IV discusses the
mode of operation of the system and the control systems necessary. A mechanism for
splitting programs written in a high level language into subtasks to take advantage
of the proposed system is put forward in Section V and a discussion of memory utilization in Section VI is followed by a concluding section.

II WHY MULTIPROCESSORS

The arguments for parallel processing and multi-computer systems have been put
forward many times, e.g. Ramamoorthy and Gonzalez [1] put forward five main advantages

1) Real time urgency.

2) Reduction of turnaround time of high priority jobs.

3) Reduction of memory and time requirements for housekeeping chores.

4) Increase in simultaneous service to many users.

5) Improved performance in a uni-processor multi-programmed environment i.e. overlapping of I/0 and processing.

However we would like to add a sixth argument; that of modularity. During the last few years integrated circuit packing densities have increased enormously which has resulted in the price of all electronic components falling sharply and this process can be expected to continue [2]. This decrease in price has not only affected the cost of the logical elements of computer systems e.g. processors and controllers but has also had an enormous impact on the cost of high speed random access memory (RAM). The drop in the price of RAM has not resulted in a lower system cost, rather more RAM is being put on each system. A similar trend is being seen in the cost of high speed backing store. Disk storage prices per bit, have fallen but systems now tend to have much more backing store than they used to have.

The net result of this process is that it is now technically and economically possible to add more storage, of all kinds, to a system when demand for computing rises if this is the bottleneck preventing an increase in throughput. However the problem of adding more processors, possibly the cheapest elements in the system, has not until now been solved due to the difficulties of organizing and controlling a multi-processor system. The system we propose would allow more processors to be added to increase the throughput of the system without needing any changes in the programs running on the system. In other words we propose a balanced system wherein the RAM capacity is balanced by the CPU demands upon it.

III THE PROPOSED HARDWARE SYSTEM

The architecture proposed is shown in Fig. 1.

The system consists of a large shared RAM, which is interleaved to achieve a high bandwidth and has at least two ports. Connected to this memory is a Main CPU (hereafter called the CPU) and a number of Auxiliary processors (AP's) each of which has its own private RAM. These private memories will be small compared to the main memory ($\sim$ 32K bytes). Most, if not all of the AP's will not differ, at least as virtual machines, from the CPU except in one respect. As the CPU will be required to switch between tasks relatively frequently it will have to be able to do this process efficiently. This implies that it will have a bank of local fast storage which it can use to store the status of each program[a] and change to another

---

[a] In order to increase the reliability of the system it should be possible for any of the AP's to access this information so that it could replace, albeit at a slower rate, the CPU when the latter was down.

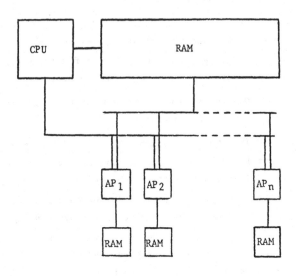

Fig. 1. The Proposed System.

program in a time comparable to its basic instruction time.

The bulk of the cost of this system, ignoring the peripherals, will still be largely dominated by the cost of the main bank of RAM. Ignoring the interconnection, packaging costs and using the prediction of Turn [2] as to future gate and memory bit prices we get the following figures for 1980.

For an 8 megabyte RAM	$200,000	
For an AP		
CPU ($\sim 10^5$ gates)	$500	
32K bytes RAM	$800	$1,300

These figures are not the costs of a system, rather the costs of packages to go on the system so they should be taken as relative, rather than absolute costs. Assuming 10 processors with interconnection and packaging costs 10 times that of the more regular store, the cost of the system is easily dominated by the Main RAM and it will pay us to add a processor and to idle it in order to maximize throughput rather than insist on maximum processor utliization.

This being the case some of the AP's may be specialized even if it means that they will idle for a high proportion of the time, but we shall examine this case later.

I/O arrangements have not been shown explicitly as it can be controlled in a number of ways - either by one or more of the AP's or the CPU in the conventional way or more probably by dedicating a specialized processor to the task [3].

IV MODE OF OPERATION OF THE SYSTEM

The easiest way to describe the way the system would operate is to draw a timing diagram (Fig. 2). In this diagram we plot the task each processor is actually running at any particular time. The letter above each line is the identifying letter of the particular task running on that processor.

If the tasks to be run by the CPU are numbered 0-M then a processor-time diagram would be as shown in Figure 2.

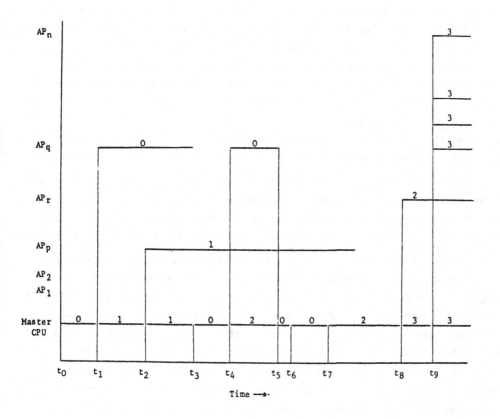

Fig. 2. Use of the System. The numbers above the horizontal lines represent process numbers.

Time Action

t_0 Task 0 enters the system and starts running on the CPU.

t_1 Task 0 requests that it be continued on one of its virtual processors. As the
mapping between virtual and real processor has not yet been established the
allocation procedure of the operating system is entered. (This mapping can be
done by an associative memory or by indirection.) The operating system will
then allocate a physical processor and set the link in the mapping mechanism.
The CPU then starts process 1.

t_2 Process 1 forks to a co-routine and runs on. (This co-routine could well be
an output routine.)

t_3 Process 0 has finished running on its AP and returns to the CPU. The work done
in the AP can then be regarded as a virtual instruction i.e. one instruction in
the main CPU instruction stream which is completed and then the main CPU re-
starts running the program.

t_4 Task 0 starts another virtual instruction and task 2 is started.

t_5 Task 0 returns to the CPU.

t_6 Task 0 starts another virtual instruction which has to be mapped onto the main
CPU, as it needs too much core to run on one of the AP's (of course the same
procedure could be used if there were no free AP's or if there were no AP's).
In the particular case of a set of parallel running co-routines the parallel
streams would be mapped onto a serial sequence of routines if there were no
AP's.

t_7 Task 2 is re-started.

t_8 A virtual instruction of task 2 is started and task 3 is started on CPU.

t_9 Task 3 splits into a series of co-routines one of which runs on the CPU.

This example illustrates the fact that the CPU will switch between tasks more
frequently than in a conventionally organized processor. As the system has a bank
of fast storage for this purpose, the actual switching between tasks should take
roughly the same time as any instruction once the identity of the next task is known.

One can make a choice between two strategies once an AP has finished a task,
either to ignore this knowledge until there is a natural break in the program running on the CPU or to switch the CPU back to the task it had started and which had
subsequently switched to an AP. We choose the latter strategy as we desire to clear
programs through the system as quickly as possible. Each AP communicates the fact
that it has finished its task to the CPU by interrupting it. If the scheduler is
running on the CPU then the next task can be activated by it. However in larger
systems it would be sensible to have the scheduler resident in an AP even if it were
idling for a large portion of the time. This need not necessarily be the case as a
scheduler can use a relatively large proportion of system time e.g. 7-1/2% on a
360/91 running large scientific jobs at a scientific laboratory [4]. The proposed

system will be swapping between tasks more often than in conventional systems not only because these tasks sub-divide more often but also because it is in effect scheduling more processors. It would not therefore be grossly underloading an AP if one were dedicated to scheduling in a multi-processor environment.

Although we do not primarily propose this system in order to minimise the time taken for a program to be run as do Gonzalez and Ramamoorthy [5], we can examine the possibility of using the system in this way. In their paper Gonzalez and Ramamoorthy show that the execution time of a program can be reduced by splitting it into a number of co-operating parallel sub-tasks if the time taken for scheduling the next task is less than 20% of the average sub-task time. If an AP were dedicated to scheduling then, effectively it could do part of the scheduling in parallel with the running task allowing very small sections of program to be run in parallel.

V SPLITTING A PROGRAM INTO A SUB-TASKS

Many people have discussed the problem of splitting a program into its sub-tasks [7]-[9], [1]. All of these papers essentially are looking for parallelism within a program, by considering it as a directed graph, without attempting to analyze the dynamics of the program. Indeed in many cases they explicitly state this as a deliberate part of the philosophy and "we have demanded that they treat the program as a set of strings without requiring or obtaining any information about what the program does". [6] This emphasis means that the program as a whole is treated for potential parallelism, a task that can be expensive in terms of time and memory required.

We start off by observing that programs spend a large proportion of their time within a loop or a set of nested loops. We justify this observation by

a) contending that if the program itself is not enormous and the program does not run for a trivially short time then it must repeat itself with a set of different or modified data.

b) Knuth [9] analyzed a set of 440 FORTRAN programs and found that typically, a program spent more than half of its running time in less than 4% of its program.

We propose that the computer should do an analysis of the flow of control of a program. First the program is divided into basic blocks, sequences of operations which are executed serially. Whenever control transfers into the basic block, all operations from the first to the last are executed in order [10]. A control flow graph is then constructed in which the nodes represent blocks and the edges represent control flow paths. Unlike other analyses of programs into graphs e.g. [1], [12] we weight these edges with a weighting proportional to the depth of loop from which the transition into the block was made. We are then primarily interested in the node, or set of nodes, which are the furthest weighted distance from any point. We state our hypothesis that it is indeed these sections of code in which the program will spend most of its time.

In order to test this hypothesis we have written a program to do a quick analysis of some FORTRAN programs which are in use at Westfield College. This program, which takes the simplistic view that the only basic blocks are SUBROUTINES or FUNCTIONS, produces the weighted connectivity matrix of the program to be analyzed.

The analysis shown (Fig. 3) is of a program which is a nonlinear minimization package written elsewhere and as expected the program would spend most of its time in FCN and the routines called from FCN. We have analyzed many programs and have drawn the following two conclusions: –

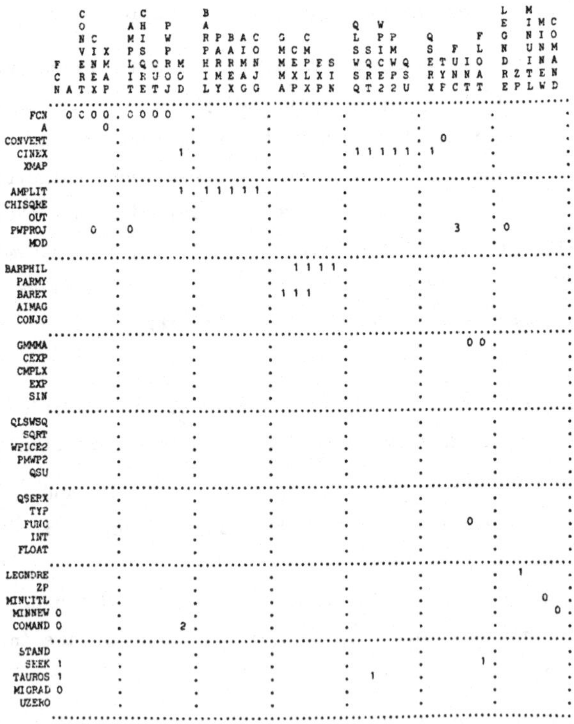

Fig. 3. An example of a weighted connectivity matrix. This is part of a sophisticated non-linear optimisation package.

a) either the nesting of the do-loops is well pronounced.

b) the nesting is not so pronounced but a few (5% – 10% of the total) small routines are called from many parts in the program.

Although this analysis could be produced by a separate analysis program all of the information is available to, or can easily be obtained by, the compiler. It would therefore be sensible for the compiler to produce, as part of its output from one of its early passes, a weighted connectivity matrix.

The compiler would then generate the virtual instructions mentioned above - i.e. regions of code which would fit into the private core of an AP. These areas would contain the code the furthest weighted distance from a calling point i.e. there would be a high probability that once this virtual instruction was entered, it would take an appreciable amount of time to traverse its loops. If it were desired to try and execute this program in parallel then it would be relatively straightforward using the techniques outlined by Allen [11] and the criteria of Bernstein [6] to split the program into parallel sub-tasks. The problem of analyzing these virtual instructions would be appreciably smaller than that of analyzing the whole program as we have effectively decomposed the program into smaller blocks within which we look for implied parallelism. We devote attention only to those portions of the program which will take an appreciable amount of time.

Aside from the above analysis for implicit virtual instructions and parallelism, it would be possible for the sophisticated programmer to explicitly use the parallelism of the system. It would then be straightforward to implement, on this system, the parallel compiler proposed by Conway in 1963 [12]. Conway in effect proposed a pipelined compiler where each stage in the pipeline is big e.g. lexical analysis, syntactic analysis, code generation. This organization would allow an enormous throughput of programs in the WATFOR type environment i.e. testing batches of programs where the compile time would be a significant portion of the total time taken by the program.

Another application may well be a set of runtime routines for an APL compiler. Many of these routines could be packed into the private RAM of an AP. The APL compiler would have them listed as a set of discrete virtual instructions which would gradually be loaded as they were used. Those routines which were not used need not be loaded.

In both the above cases, as in all cases where the programmer might explicitly use the parallelism, the programs produced could be run on single processor systems without any appreciable loss of efficiency.

VI MEMORY UTILIZATION OF THE SYSTEM

In the above discussion we have assumed that the system RAM can cope with the demands on it - a view that needs some justification. The normal effect of attaching many processors to a common bank of RAM is illustrated in Fig. 4, which is taken from [13].

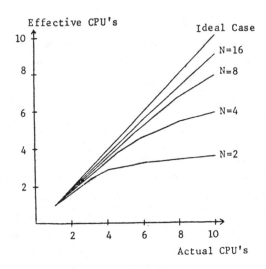

Fig. 4. Simulation results with shared main memory. The main memory is N-way interleaved.

In our system this problem is not so acute as the AP's fetch all their instructions, and most of their data from their private RAM's. We justify this statement by much the same argument as we used above in connection with the time spent in loops i.e.

a) either the program is performing a large number of operations on each datum or it will be I/0 bound getting the data into and out of the system e.g. Roberts & Wallace [14] reports that the lexical scanning of the FORTRAN compiler on the CDC 3200 makes 400 memory references, mainly program and local data for each symbol input, which may well be the only reference to the main RAM.

b) by examining the characteristics that have been measured for the working set size of a program. [15] - [16]. These studies show that for fairly large sections of programs, $\sim 10^5$ instructions, the working set can be restricted to about 20K bytes.

Should the system have so many AP's attached that either the main RAM or the highway be overloaded, we propose that the design allow for the insertion of cache memories between the AP's and the main RAM. This should reduce the number of actual references to main memory by an order of magnitude. The actual point at which this becomes necessary is difficult to predict as it depends on the ratio of processor to memory speeds as well as the proportion of memory references of the AP's to the main memory, but it should allow a large number of AP's to be attached before interference becomes a major factor. If we take Turn's [2] projection for 1980 again, we find that he is predicting that processor speeds and memory speeds will be roughly equal. A five way interleaved memory would then allow about 20-40 AP's to operate without much mutual interference if they kept their accesses to the public RAM to about 10% of all memory accesses (instruction plus data). If the memory were eight or sixteen way interleaved it would have ample capacity for the AP's plus an additional couple of master CPU's, if they were necessary, each running its own job stream, but using one common AP as the scheduler and allocator of physical processors.

CONCLUSION

We have proposed an extensible modular computer architecture to take advantage of the benefits that LSI technology will bring. Not only have we outlined a hardware system that could be expanded by at least 2 orders of magnitude but we have devised a software control system to meet these requirements. The software which controls the many processors may be summarized by the following:- having made an intelligent segmentation of the code, by using probable program localities, the system allocates a segment, which includes a processor, by dynamic remapping when the demand arises.

No account has been taken of the need for reliability or the potential for specialized processors in this paper but we shall return to these topics in future papers.

REFERENCES

[1] C. V. Ramamoorthy and M. J. Gonzalez, "A Survey of Techniques for Recognizing Parallel Processable Streams in Computer Programs," in 1969 Fall Joint Comput. Conf., AFIPS Conf. Proc., vol. 35, Montvale, N.J.: AFIPS Press 1969, pp. 1-7.

[2] R. Turn, "Computers in the 1980's - Trends in Hardware Technology," Information Processing 74, North Holland, Amsterdam, 1974, pp. 137-140.

[3] C. H. Kaplinsky, "The Universal Peripheral Controller - an intelligent buffered channel" Proceedings of the European Computing Conference, Online, 1974, pp. 659-670.

[4] W. Walkenshaw and A. J. Oxley (Ed), Computing and Automation Division Quarterly Report, 31 December 73 - 31 March 74, Computing and Automation Div., Rutherford Laboratory, RL-74-072 C78.

[5] M. J. Gonzalez and C. V. Ramamoorthy, "Parallel Task Execution in a Decentralized System," IEEE Trans. Comput. C.21, December 1972, pp. 1310-1322.

[6] A. J. Bernstein, "Analysis of Program for Parallel Processing," IEEE Trans. Electron. Comput. vol. EC-15, October 1966, pp. 757-763.

[7] W. H. Burkhart, "Automation of Program Speed-up on Parallel-Processor Computers," Computing 3, 1968, pp. 297-310.

[8] C. V. Ramamoorthy, J. H. Park and H. F. Li, "Compilation Techniques for Recognition of Parallel Processable Tasks in Arithmetic Expressions," _IEEE Trans. Comput._, C-22, November 1973, pp. 986-997.

[9] D. Knuth, "An Empirical Study of FORTRAN Programs," _Software - Practice and Experience_, vol. 1, 1971, pp. 105-133.

[10] K. Kennedy, "A Global Flow Analysis Algorithm," _International Journal of Computer Math._, vol. 3, December 1971, pp. 5-15.

[11] F. E. Allen, "Interprocedural Data Flow Analysis," _Information Processing 74_, vol. 2, North Holland 1974, pp. 398-402.

[12] M. E. Conway, "Design of a Seperable Transition-Diagram Compiler," _Com of ACM_, vol. 6, July 1963, pp. 396-408.

[13] J. E. Juliussen and F. J. Mowle, "Multiple Micro processors with Common Main and Control Memories," _IEEE Trans. Comput._, C-22, November 1973, pp. 999-1007.

[14] P. S. Roberts and C. S. Wallace, "A Micro programmed Lexical Processor," _Information Processing 71_, North Holland 1972, pp. 577-581.

[15] J. R. Spirn and P. J. Denning, "Experiments with Program Locality," _Proc. AFIPS Conf. Fall Joint Computer Conference_, 1972, pp. 611-621.

[16] I. Masuda, H. Shiota, K. Noguchi and T. Ohki, "Optimization of Program Organization by Cluster Analysis," _Information Process 74_, North Holland 1974, pp. 261-265.

AN APPROACH TO RESTRUCTURABLE COMPUTER SYSTEMS[a]

S. S. REDDI and E. A. FEUSTEL
Laboratory for Computer Science and Engineering
Department of Electrical Engineering
Rice University
Houston, Texas 77001

Abstract -- This paper develops the concept of resource structuring in an attempt to remove the structural rigidity present in a conventional computer system. It is claimed that the concept can lead to building better and more efficient computer systems. A language is developed to assist in resource structuring. The language can specify structures such as an arithmetic pipeline or an array configuration. It handles vector and matrix applications efficiently and can be used at the user as well as the system level. Resource structuring in a computer system has other advantages which include reduction of supervisory control on operand routing and transformation of the system to exhibit failsoft behavior. To implement structuring, tagged architecture is suggested and shown to be an eligible candidate.

INTRODUCTION

In this paper the concept of resource structuring is developed and claimed to be useful in improving the resource utilization and performance of the present day computer system. In order to facilitate implementation of the concept, a language is developed. The language is capable of specifying resource structures of interest such as an arithmetic pipeline of the TI ASC or an array structure of the ILLIAC IV [1,2]. The language is particularly well suited to vector and matrix applications (encountered in APL [3]) and can be used at the user as well as the system level. Introduction of the resource structure, together with the Iliffe concept of hardware recognition of information structure, may alleviate the existing information handling problems present in high performance computer systems like the ILLIAC IV, TI ASC, CDC STAR, etc., [4,5]. To implement resource structuring, tagged architecture is suggested since such an architecture has been acknowledged to be ideal for recognizing structural information [4,6].

RATIONALE FOR RESOURCE STRUCTURING

Recently some computer designers and architects speculated that the present day computer modeled after von Neumann's organization does not possess flexibility and cannot be adapted efficiently to the user's program structure. Iliffe suggested

---
[a] This research was supported by the National Science Foundation under Grant GJ-36471.

that the computer system, for any program, should store the data structure to reflect the information structure recognized by the system hardware [4]. It is claimed that such an approach increases the versatility of the present day computer. Wilner stated that in von Neumann-derived machines "memory cells and process registers are rigid containers which contort data and instructions into unnatural fields" and pointed out that the basic design objective behind Burroughs B1700 is to have 100 percent variability or the appearance of no inherent structure. Without inherent structure, he asserted, any definable language can be efficiently used for computing [7].

The structural rigidity experienced in any contemporary computer system can be directly attributed to the presence of the fixed control and communication links between the system resources. Since the user exerts no control over the structure of the system defined by the fixed links, he is faced with the problem of converting his program computation structure to suit the system structure. The conversion problem, at present, is not satisfactorily solved. Hence the conversion often leads to degraded system performance and poor resource utilization. If the user is provided with the capability of specifying and imposing the system structure he desires, his conversion problem will be relatively simplified. He will also be in a position to use the system resources efficiently. As an example consider a computer system whose resources are comparable, in terms of their computing power, to the processing elements of the ILLIAC IV. The array structure of the ILLIAC IV has been demonstrated to be useful in some matrix applications, but for some vector applications configuring the resources as a pipeline may ensure better resource utilization. The user, if provided with the capability of restructuring, can configure the resources as an array of a pipeline according to the problem on hand. This approach removes the structural rigidity present in the fixed array structure of the ILLIAC IV. Similarly, the hardware pipelines introduced in the TI ASC and CDC STAR computers can efficiently handle vector operations. However such pipelines do not perform well in implicit differencing schemes, Monte Carlo calculations or other "serial" situations. It would be preferable for the user to specify and create the pipelines and structures he needs.

In this paper it is suggested that the computer system be restructured to suit program requirements. The restructuring is done by establishing and/or deleting the control and communication links between the system resources. The term "Resource Structure" describes the system structure characterized by the existence or absence of the links between the resources. We claim that the ability on the part of the user to specify and impose his resource structure improves performance and resource utilization. The claim is partially supported by the existence of high performance computers with their specialized resource structures.

SPECIFICATION OF RESOURCE STRUCTURING

Specification of the resource structure is an important issue for our development. In the literature there have been attempts to specify resource structures, primarily by Bell and Newell [8]. They conceptualize resource structures by means of diagrams where links are represented by nodes labelled as Pc, Mp, K, etc. Their notation can represent most of the existing computers but becomes inadequate for complex systems (e.g., CDC STAR). In this paper the resource structure is specified by a language (introduced in Section 2). The primitives of the language can represent most of the resource structures of interest such as an arithmetic pipeline of the TI ASC or an array of the ILLIAC IV. The language enables the user to exercise control over the resource structure. The usefulness of the language lies in the fact that the user can experiment and develop efficient resource structures for his program. Furthermore he can gain invaluable information and insight by observing the interaction between the resource structure and the computation structure of his program. In the long run the language control over the resource structure can be replaced by hardware. Then the system will be capable of automatic restructuring.

ADVANTAGES OF RESOURCE STRUCTURING

Resource structuring has advantages other than improving system performance. It may prove to be a useful concept in organizing micro-processors and microcomputers [9]. Because of the rapid advances in the LSI technology, the availability of processors and computers on chips at low costs are or will be available. Resource structuring may be employed to assist the organization of the chips to solve a problem efficiently. In a similar context, it can also be used in minicomputer architecture. Sophisticated minicomputers like the SUE offer the user CPS's and memories as pluggable modules [10]. The communications between the modules are handled by a bus unit which is available as a printed circuit board. These advances dictate that the computer designer and the user should develop techniques for effectively utilizing the modularity of the computer resources. Resource structuring may prove to be helpful in developing the techniques.

Other advantages of resource structuring include the following:

. Resource structuring can save appreciable supervisory control on the part of the computer operating system. This can be illustrated by the following example. Suppose there are repetitive operations, like vector multiplications, to be performed. Before the operations are initiated, the structure of the resources is specified: for instance, let it be specified that the results of the functional unit F_1 should go to the functional unit F_2, etc. Since the resource structure will be kept the same throughout the operations, the operating system need not be concerned with the routing of the individual operations.

.   Since the resource structure reflects the program structure, the programmer controls or may determine the operations that the system components perform. This aspects helps in program debugging and machine fault location.

.   The resource structuring capability enables the computer system to exhibit graceful degradation in performance when any of the system components become inactive. The system's operation can be resumed after a restructuring in which the failed components are deleted and/or replaced.

It must be emphasized that restructuring cannot always improve system performance. Restructuring imposes overhead. Some of the overhead can be overcome by efficient scheduling and overlapping techniques. However, situations may still exist where the overhead cannot be completely overcome by the improvement in system performance. In these instances the computer system will deteriorate in performance. Only by means of analytic and simulation techniques, and future research, can we assess when resource structuring should be done.

LANGUAGE FOR RESOURCE STRUCTURING

The proposed language, Resource ALlocation and STructuring language (REALIST) handles resource structuring as well as allocation requirements. The resource allocation is included because it significantly affects the structuring. Once the resources are allocated to perform the tasks of a given program, the interdependence between the tasks dictates the resource structure. Some primitives of the language are shown in Table 1. The same table also shows the area of application for each primitive.

The types of the resources specified by the arguments of the primitives must correspond to the types of the physical resources present in the computer system. In this respect the language is similar to the job control language of an operating system [11]. The user can specify more resources than actually present for any type. In such situations the operating system has to supervise the sharing of the same resource by different operations. As an illustration, assume that the user specifies a pipeline consisting of an adder A1, followed by a multiplier M and then by an adder A2. If the computer system has only one adder A, it becomes necessary to supervise A. A has to handle the input and output streams for both A1 and A2. This approach, where the user can specify more resources than actually present, has the advantage that the user can be oblivious to the number of resources for any type. He does not have to modify his program to accommodate changes in the numbers. The approach also enables the system to become failsoft. On the other hand, excessive sharing of the same resource might lead to overloading of the operating system and degraded performance.

The resource structure specified by the privitives and the computation flow should be interlocked together to ensure correct and efficient execution of any program. The following subsections show how the interlock is effected. Note that the language only sets up resource structures. It is up to the operating system and the resources to enforce proper data alognment and communication.

VECTOR PROCESSING

APL provides features suitable for vector processing [3]. The primitive STREAM can handle the structuring requirements for many APL constructs.

Consider the simple vector operation $c \leftarrow a+b*d$, where a, b, c and d are vectors. The operation can be translated as:

$$A \leftarrow STREAM(\otimes, \uparrow_1 \uparrow_2; \oplus, \uparrow_3, \uparrow_1)$$

.
.

$$c \leftarrow A(b,d,a)$$

The statement $A \leftarrow STREAM(....)$ is declarative and not executable. When the statement $c \leftarrow A(....)$ is encountered (possibly by looking ahead), the system sets up a pipeline consisting of the functional units $\oplus$ (adder) and $\otimes$ (multiplier) as shown in Fig. 1. The input and output operand streams are identified by the upward and downward arrows respectively. The first two upward arrows correspond to b and d, the input streams to the multiplier. a and c, the input and output streams for the adder, are matched with the third upward and the downward arrows respectively. Note that the resources should be capable of interpreting and aligning the data streams. A method of establishing the links between the resources is considered in the section on implementation.

The arguments of STREAM can again be streams composed of functional units and data. They can also involve logical quantities.

$$A \leftarrow STREAM(X, \uparrow_1 \uparrow_2; Y, \uparrow_3 \downarrow_1)$$

$$Z \leftarrow IF \ L \ THEN \ Z1 \ ELSE \ Z2$$

$$B \leftarrow STREAM(A, \uparrow_1, \uparrow_2, \uparrow_3; Z, \uparrow_4, \downarrow_1)$$

.

$$a \leftarrow B(b,c,d,e)$$

X, Y, Z1 and Z2 are functional units. L is a logical quantity. $a, b, ..., e$ are vectors. The effect of executing the last statement is shown in Fig. 2.

Consider the APL statement $c \leftarrow +/(k*a)+b$ involving reduction and scalar dyadic operations. c and k are scalar variables. The statement can be decomposed as:

$$A \leftarrow STREAM(\otimes, \uparrow_1, \uparrow_2; \ominus, \uparrow_3; \oplus, \downarrow_1)$$

.

$$c \leftarrow A(k,a,b)$$

324

Some REALIST Primitives and Their Applications

Primitive	Application
STREAM PAR(.)STREAM	Vector Processing
ARRAY RING STRUC	Parallel and Overlap Processing
ENTITY	Definition of Resource Entities
ALLOC RELEASE ASSIGN	Allocation of Resources
LINK	Assignment of Bus Units
PRIORITY	Scheduling

TABLE 1

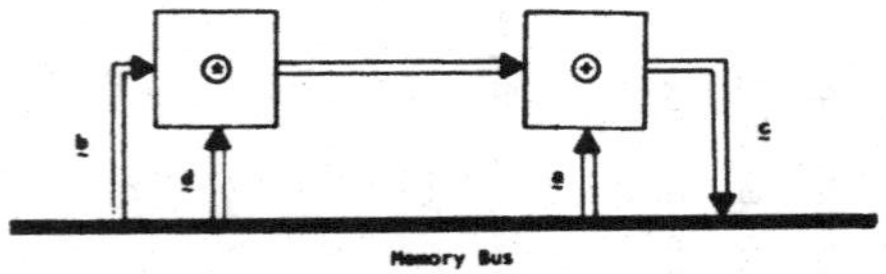

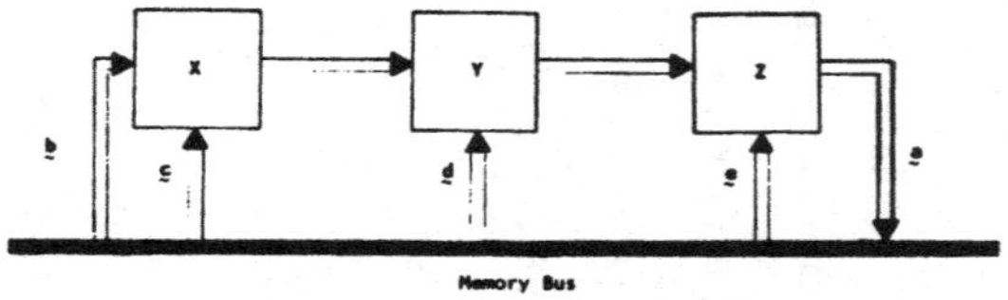

Fig. 2. An example of conditional arguments in STREAM.
Z is Z1 if L = 1. Otherwise Z is Z2.

Fig. 1. Pipeline structure set up for executing c=a*b*d.

It is assumed that the system has two adders $\oplus_1$ and $\oplus_2$. Fig. 3 shows the pipeline created for executing the final statement. Note that the system should be able to distinguish between scalar and vector operands for proper execution. (To make the data selfidentifying, tagged architecture can be used. A discussion on the suitability of this architecture in other aspects of restructuring is contained in another section.)

The last functional unit, $\oplus_2$, in the pipeline performs the APL's reduction operation. It has a vector input stream but a scalar output. When a functional unit is used to perform the reduction operation, it is said to operate in the "accumulator mode". Each resource must recognize whether or not it is operating in the accumulator mode. The system's ability to identify the types of data streams can be used in the recognition process.

It is often necessary to perform operations on specific vector components. The compression operator of APL is used for such purposes. Selection of the vector components specified by the operator can be easily accomplished during the formation of operand streams. Hence it appears desirable and efficient to allow compressed vectors in data streams for pipelines created by STREAM. For instance, consider the APL program:

$a \leftarrow (1,0,1,0)$

$b \leftarrow (0,1,0,0,1)$

$c \leftarrow (1,0,1)$

$z \leftarrow a/w + (b/x * c/y)$.

The program computes $z = (w_1 + x_2 y_1, w_3 + x_5 y_3)$. The program is translated using STREAM as:

$A \leftarrow STREAM(\otimes, \uparrow_1 \uparrow_2; \oplus, \uparrow_3 \downarrow_1)$
.
.
$z \leftarrow A(b/x, c/y, a/w)$

The compression of vectors is done when the input streams are formed. Similar comments apply to the expansion operator. In a tagged architecture, sparse vectors could be recognized by the hardware.

At this point, note that the simple constructs so far introduced are sufficient for vector applications in linear algebra and programming. To enhance the usefulness of the language, parallel computation streams are allowed. The primitive PAR(n)STREAM can be used to create n independent and similar pipelines. For instance the program:

$A \leftarrow PAR(3) STREAM(\oplus, \uparrow_1 \uparrow_2; \otimes, \uparrow_3 \downarrow_1)$
.
.
$x \leftarrow A_1(a, b, c)$

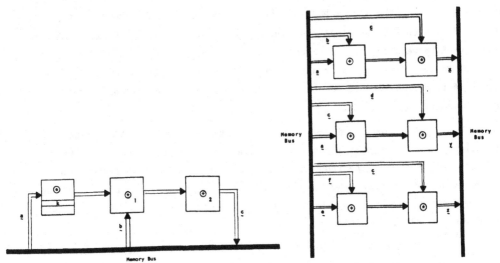

Fig. 3. Pipeline structure set up for executing c←+/(k*a)+b.

Fig. 4. An example of parallel pipeline structure
that can be set up by PAR(.)STREAM.

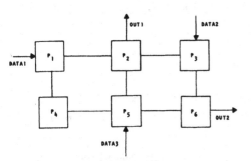

Fig. 5. An array structure set up by ARRAY.

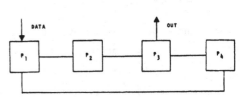

Fig. 6. The RING structure set up by the program:
A←RING(P_1,1;P_2;P_3,1;P_4)

⋮

OUT←A(DATA)

$$\underset{\sim}{y} \leftarrow A_2 * \underset{\sim}{a}, \underset{\sim}{c}, \underset{\sim}{d})$$
$$\underset{\sim}{z} \leftarrow A_3(\underset{\sim}{e}, \underset{\sim}{f}, \underset{\sim}{c})$$

creates the pipelines and computation streams as in Fig. 4.

PARALLEL AND OVERLAP PROCESSING

For applications in these areas of processing, no simple primitive is sufficiently powerful to handle all the structural requirements. Since the ILLIAC IV demonstrated the usefulness of the array structure, the primitive ARRAY is provided. (For simplicity only two-dimensional arrays will be considered.) The primitive can be used as in the following program:

$$A \leftarrow ARRAY(2,3)(P1, \uparrow_1; P2, \downarrow_1;$$
$$P3, \uparrow_2; P4; P5, \uparrow_3; P6, \downarrow_2)$$

.
.

OUT1, OUT2 ← A(DATA1, DATA2, DATA3).

The program creates the resource structure and data paths shown in Fig. 5. One must note that unlike in STREAM there can be more than one output stream. The outputs are matched with the downward arrows just as the inputs with the upward arrows. The input and output streams need not necessarily be simple vector or scalar variables. They can be as complex as program streams, I/O data and system command streams. The arguments of ARRAY are the system resources which may include complex processing entities like the processing elements of the ILLIAC IV, microcomputers, microprocessors, complex I/O equipment or any resource entities defined by the primitive ENTITY (introduced in the next subsection). The links established between the arguments are bidirectional. In general, ARRAY(p,q) establishes a pXq array with each resource of the array having links with its neighbors.

The primitive RING structures the resources as a ring (Fig. 6). This kind of structure may be important in time sharing and multiprocessing applications where programs share the resources in a round robin fashion for a fixed quanta of time. However, if more complex structures than an array or a ring are required, the primitive STRUC can be used.

$$A \leftarrow STRUC(M)(P1, \uparrow_1; P2, \uparrow_2; P3, \downarrow_1; P4)$$

$$M \leftarrow \begin{bmatrix} 0 & 1 & 0 & 1 \\ 0 & 0 & 1 & 0 \\ 1 & 0 & 0 & 0 \\ 0 & 1 & 0 & 0 \end{bmatrix}$$

.
.

OUT1 ← A(DATA1, DATA2) .

The above program creates a structure shown in Fig. 7. The matrix M defines the interconnections between the resources specified by STRUC. There will be a link from Pi to Pj if and only if the $(i,j)^{th}$ element of M is 1. $M_{1,j}$ can also be a Boolean function $f_{1,j}$ of program variables in which case the link will be established only when $f_{1,j}=1$.

CREATION OF RESOURCE ENTITIES

The primitive ENTITY enables us to define processing, storage and I/O entities. For instance the statement

P1←ENTITY($\oplus,\otimes$,M)

creates a processing entity composed of an adder, a multiplier and a memory unit M. Within the entity the resources can control and communicate with each other. Semiconductor manufacturers offer 1K and 4K random access memories at the same cost level as adders and multipliers. By creating resource entities with memory and read only memory units, it is possible to achieve distributed and efficient computing within the system.

Storage entities can be created by a statement like

S1←ENTITY(M1,DISCI,DISC.CONTROL1) .

When the above statement is executed, the system creates a storage entity with a memory unit M1 (assumed to be a fast primary memory), a disc unit and a disc control unit. Similarly I/O entities can be created. An example will show the usefulness of ENTITY. In the following program, M1 and M2 are memory units and ϕ is an input-output unit, say a printer.

P1←ENTITY($\oplus,\otimes$,M1)

ϕ1←ENTITY(ϕ,M2)
P←STREAM(P1,$\uparrow_1$;ϕ1,$\downarrow_1$)
OUT←P(DATA) .

The program creates a structure (Fig. 8) whereby it is possible to overlap the execution and I/O times of several individual programs in a multiprogramming environment. It is assumed that each program requires P1 and the ϕ1. This assumption can be relaxed if RING is used instead of STREAM.

Conditional acquisition of resources by an entity can also be handled by ENTITY. For example if we have

P1←ENTITY(F1,F2,f*F3)

P1 can acquire F3 only when f, a Boolean function of program variables, is 1. This feature coordinates program execution and creation of entities.

329

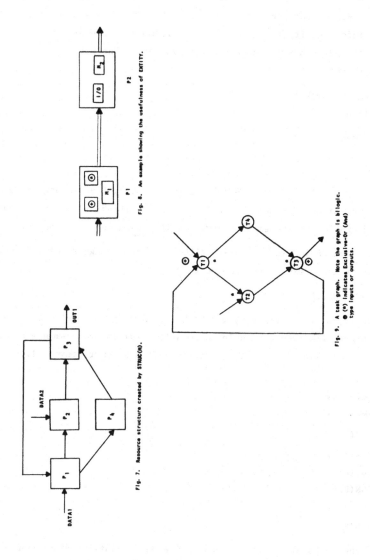

Fig. 7. Resource structure created by STRUC(N).

Fig. 8. An example showing the usefulness of ENTITY.

Fig. 9. A task graph. Note the graph is bilogic. ⊕ (*) indicates Exclusive-Or (And) type inputs or outputs.

ALLOCATION OF RESOURCES AND BUS UNITS

As pointed out in the beginning of this section, resource allocation is an integral part of restructuring. Besides, efficient resource allocation can speed up the system. Hence, the user should be able to assist the system in resource allocation by informing it of his resource requirements. The primitives ALLOC and RELEASE are included in the language for this purpose. The program:

```
ALLOC(A,B,C,D)
    .
    . Program Block 1
RELEASE(B,D)
    .
    . Program Block 2
    .
RELEASE(A,C)
```

conveys to the system that Program Block 1 requires A, B, C and D and releases B and D after its completion. The commands provide a block structure on the resource requirements and enable the system to distribute its resources efficiently.

The primitive ASSIGN is similar to ALLOC. It can assign specific resources to execute a task or a program. The statement

```
T1←ASSIGN(A,B,C,D)
```

assigns resources A,B,...,D to perform a task T1. As can be observed, the system for implementing ASSIGN should be able to identify task and program names. The program given below illustrates the interdependence between resource allocation and structuring.

```
P1←ENTITY(A,B)
P2←ENTITY(A,C)
P3←ENTITY(B,C)
P4←ENTITY(A,D)
T1←ASSIGN(P1)
T2←ASSIGN(P2)
T3←ASSIGN(P3)
T4←ASSIGN(P4)
```

T1,...,T4 are the tasks of a program whose precedence relations are shown in Fig. 9. A suitable resource structure could be the one shown in Fig. 7.

Links play an important part in establishing resource structures. The computer system is assumed to possess bus units BUS1,BUS2,...,BUSm which are used to establish the communication and data links between the resources. The primitive LINK is used for assigning the bus units.

$$A \leftarrow STREAM(F_1, \ldots; \ F_2, \ldots; \ F_3, \ldots; \ F_4 \ldots)$$

$$BUS1 \leftarrow LINK(F_1, F_2; \ F_3, F_4)$$

$$BUS2 \leftarrow LINK(F_2, F_3) \ .$$

The program assigns BUS1 for transferring data streams from F_1 to F_2 and from F_3 to F_4. BUS2 is assigned as a data link between F_2 and F_3. Assignment by the user enables the system to use its bus units more efficiently and avoid congestion. Since the congestion in the bus units is critical in system utilization, the LINK command may prove to be a valuable tool for the user. The design of the bus units is considered in a later section.

SCHEDULING

Scheduling is an important and interesting subject by itself. At first sight, it may appear that scheduling has little in common with restructuring. However, the language provides a primitive (PRIORITY) to facilitate scheduling. The provision can be justified on the basis of two arguments.

1) Scheduling has the same goal as structuring namely efficient resource utilization. Hence the user who resorts to structuring for better resource utilization would prefer to include scheduling as well in his attempts.

2) When the system is allocating tasks to its resources, it has to employ a scheduling discipline (which usually is a First-Come-First-Serve policy). The system and the user, if provided with the scheduling ability, can adopt sophisticated sequencing and overlapping strategies to ensure better resource utilization.

Scheduling a set of tasks can be viewed as associating priorities with the tasks and executing them in descending order of their priorities. The primitive PRIORITY allows the user to specify computation of the priorities. The arguments of PRIORITY are a function and a vector (or a list). The function specifies the computation of the priorities for the tasks represented by the vector components. For instance, let $\underset{\sim}{A}$ be a vector whose components $\underset{\sim}{A}_1, \underset{\sim}{A}_2, \ldots, \underset{\sim}{A}_n$ represent n independent tasks. Assume EXEC.TIME is an attribute function which gives the value of the execution time of its argument. It is required to schedule the tasks in ascending order of their execution times. This achieved by the program:

$$F \leftarrow EXEC.TIME$$

$$\underset{\sim}{B} \leftarrow PRIORITY(F)(\underset{\sim}{A})$$

The components of B give the order of the scheduling. If $\underset{\sim}{A}_7$ has the least execution time (and hence the greatest priority) then $\underset{\sim}{B}_1 = \underset{\sim}{A}_7$. As can be noted PRIORITY(F) associates the greatest (least) priority with the task for which F assumes the least (greatest) value. Furthermore it arranges the tasks in descending order of their priorities.

F can be a complex function. Suppose DUE.TIME and ARRIVAL.TIME are attribute functions that give the due time and arrival time of their arguments respectively. Then F can be as complex as:

F←MAX(EXEC.TIME.DUE.TIME)/(1+ARRIVAL.TIME)

F is interpreted as:

F(T)=MAX(EXEC.TIME(T),DUE.TIME(T))/

(1+ARRIVAL.TIME(T)) .

By a suitable choice of task attributes, PRIORITY can handle most of the existing scheduling strategies. It must be warned that our consideration of scheduling is by no means complete. For instance it may be desirable for the language to incorporate features like defining stacks and waiting spaces and attaching them to the resources, specifying scheduling disciplines for jobs in waiting spaces, etc.

The REALIST language is in its preliminary stage. The language is by no means complete and exhaustive. It is hoped that the basic principles, treated in the development of the language, lay the groundwork for future extensions.

IMPLEMENTATION CONSIDERATIONS

Suitability of Tagged Architecture

The implementation of the restructuring concepts in a computer system will be described in outline. It is proposed that the hardware implementation be done using tagged architecture. There are many factors that justify the use of this architecture. The use of tags allows a compromise between hardware and software control of operand routing in the system. Total hardware control reduces the storage requirements but the user loses flexibility and control over the routing. On the other hand, software control tends to make the system physically large and slow, due to the system dependence on storage. Tags distribute the routing control between hardware and software. By means of a program, the user can specify his operand routes. The system hardware implements them by attaching tags to the operands. Thus the user has flexible and algorithmic control over his operand routing. Note that the capability of algorithmic control helps the user in optimizing his program for the system.

Structuring declarations (e.g., STREAM) results in data which are tagged to make them selfidentifying. Whenever such data are encountered the system traps to a location specified by the tags. The information stored in the location helps the system to set up the required pipelines or structures. (Note that the "escape action" of Iliffe (1968) is employed.) The desirability of making variables and data self-identifying has been indicated during the development of STREAM and ASSIGN.

When STREAM has input operands that contain both vectors and scalars, the system's ability to recognize variable and data types ensures proper input streams and correct execution. In the ASSIGN statement, the system should be able to recognize program and task names. The PRIORITY primitive requires the computer system to store and manipulate the structural information concerning tasks and their attributes. In these instances the use of tagged architecture can significantly facilitate the implementation.

A System with Resource Structuring Capabilities

A system (Fig. 10) is proposed for which resource structuring can be effected with ease and little effort. The system employs distributed computing [12]. The Priority Computing Unit (PCU) performs task scheduling and dispatching. The advantage of having a separate PCU is that it is possible to overlap scheduling overhead, and program execution, thus improving the system performance. The Memory Fetch Unit (MFU provides and routes streams of operands from the Memory to data buses. The MFU also fetches tasks and their resource requirements. The Memory Storage Unit (MSU) stores operands, which are sometimes contained in streams, in proper locations of the Memory. Furthermore, the units MFU and MSU serve as buffers between the storage and execution units of the computer system. $F_1, F_2, \ldots, F_n$ independent functional units. They can be adders, multipliers, shifters, memory units, read only memory units, microcomputers, minicomputers, digital devices and 1/0 equipment. BUS1, BUS2,...,BUSm are the bus units which establish data transfers and set up resource structures. The Structure Descriptor (SD) contains the description of the structures currently present in the system. Note that any resource structure can be established by setting up the appropriate data and control paths between the functional units.

Design of the Bus and Establishing Links

Since the bus units are necessary to organize resource structures, the design of these units is considered. In the course of the design, the establishment of links using the bus units will be indicated. Consider the program:

$$A \leftarrow STREAM(F_1, \ldots; F_2, \ldots; F_3 \ldots)$$

$$BUSi \leftarrow LINK(F_1, F_2; F_2, F_3)$$

BUSi is assigned to transfer data from F_1 to F_2 and F_2 to F_3. The bus units can be made to scan all the functional units to detect any data transfer requests. This is time consuming and inefficient. The proposed bus unit (Fig. 11) scans only the resources assigned to it. In our running example BUSi scans only F_1 and F_2 for requests.

The notation of AHPL is followed [13]. Each functional unit is assigned a unique Device Identification Number (DIN). Let these numbers be 000, 001 and 010

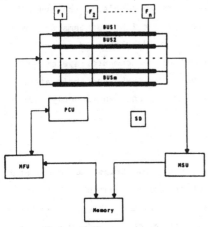

F$_1$: Functional Unit
BUSI: Bus Unit
SD : Structure Descriptor
PCU : Priority Computing Unit
MFU : Memory Fetch Unit
MSU : Memory Store Unit

Fig. 10. Proposed system with restructuring capabilities.

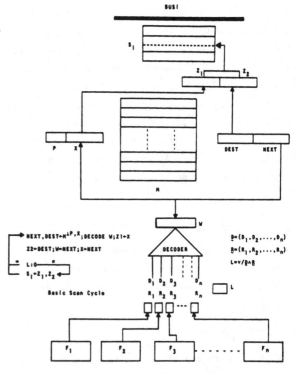

NEXT,DEST←M$^{\triangle P,X}$;DECODE W;Z1←X

Z2←DEST;W←NEXT;X←NEXT

L:0

S$_1$←Z$_1$,Z$_2$

Basic Scan Cycle

$\underline{D}=(D_1,D_2,\ldots,D_n)$

$\underline{R}=(R_1,R_2,\ldots,R_n)$

L=v/$\underline{D}$∧$\underline{R}$

Fig. 11. Proposed bus unit which handles data streams between functional units that are assigned to it.

for F_1, F_2 and F_3 respectively. The random access memory M (Fig. 11) stores details regarding the functional units assigned to the bus unit and structural requirements. The register P contains the structure description whose use will be discussed later on. For the present assume that P contains 00. X and W will initially contain the DIN of the first functional unit to be scanned. The location specified by the contents of P and X registers contains two numbers. These numbers are the DIN's of the next functional unit to be scanned and the destination of the data from the functional unit specified by the X register. In the present example P, S and W will be 00, 000, and 000 initially. The location 00 000 in M contains 001 001 since F_2 is the next unit to be scanned as well as the destination for the data from F_1. Similarly the location 00 001 contains 000 010. NEXT and DEST registers contain the DIN's of the next functional unit to be scanned and the destination of the data from the functional unit specified by X. The basic scan cycle is shown in Fig. 11. R_i is set whenever F_i has a request. If the flip flop L is set, the DIN's of the functional unit presently under the scan and the destination of the data from this functional unit are sent to S_i. S_i is a First-In-First-Out queue for the requests waiting for BUSi. If M and DECODE take one cycle to access and decode respectively, the basic scan cycle takes three cycles. Hence if k functional units are assigned to a bus unit, the bus unit scans at every $3k^{th}$ cycle to see if a particular functional unit has a request. The details of resetting R_i's and terminating the scan cycle are not shown in the figure.

The field P is used to store different structure or pipeline descriptions in M. For instance, suppose a different pipeline is needed consisting of F_1, F_3 and F_4. If BUSi is again assigned to handle the data transfers between the functional units, P is set to 01. The new pipeline description is stored in locations starting with 01. The bus unit considers the requests in S_i on a First-Come-First-Serve basis. If it encounters a request of the form NL N2, it transfers data from the functional unit identified by N1 to the functional unit whose DIN is N2. A semiconductor random access memory, which is fast but inexpensive, can be used for M.

For transferring data between the functional units, a modified version of United States Patent 3,644,901 may be used [14]. In this patent Zingg presents a system which controls transfers between registers and data buses. The system basically contains storage and control registers, and data buses. Each storage register SR_i is paired with a control register CR_i. The contents of CR_i specify (i) the data bus onto which the contents of SR_i should be loaded and (ii) the data bus whose contents should be loaded into SR_i. The circuitry of the system establishes the desired transfers.

The design of other units of the proposed system (Fig. 10) does not present any difficult problems. MFU and MSU should incorporate techniques of operand streaming for efficient pipeline operations. CDC STAR and TI ASC demonstrated the feasibility of such techniques and hence the design of MFU and MSU may not pose any real problems. The functional units should be design to align and interpret data streams properly.

CONCLUSIONS AND FUTURE RESEARCH

This paper presented an attempt to introduce and specify resource structures in computer systems. A language REALIST is developed to assist the user in restructuring for efficient operation. For implementation of structuring, tagged architecture is suggested and shown to be a suitable candidate. A system is considered for which resource structuring can be achieved in a simple manner. The design of bus units necessary for establishing resource structures is given. Future research will extend the primitives and show the usefulness of REALIST in improving system performance for large problem applications. Research should be concentrated on the production of better systems and programs by using the interaction between computation, data and resource structures. Further investigations may reveal simple and effective implementation techniques for restructuring.

ACKNOWLEDGMENTS

Professor J. R. Jump, through his constructive criticisms and suggestions, significantly improved the presentation of the paper. The authors want to acknowledge the influence of the research efforts of Professor G. Estrin and his group on restructurable computer systems, and Professor C. V. Ramamoorthy and his group on program parallelism. The authors are grateful to one of the referees for pointing out Reference [14]. Special appreciation is extended to Mrs. Ruth Collins for her proofreading and typing the manuscript.

REFERENCES

[1] W. J. Watson, The Texas Instruments Advanced Scientific Computer, COMPCON 72, Sixth Annual IEEE Computer Society International Conference, (Sept., 1972, pp. 291-293.

[2] W. K. Bouknight, S. A. Denenberg, D. E. McIntyre, J. M. Randall, A. M. Sameh and D. L. Slotnick, the ILLIAC IV System, Proc. of IEEE, (April, 1972), pp. 369-388.

[3] K. E. Iverson, A Programming Language, John Wiley and Sons, (1962), 286 pp.

[4] J. K. Iliffe, Basic Machine Principles, American Elsevier Publishing Co., (1968), 86 pp.

[5] S. Fernbach, Class V Computers to Challenge Mathematicians, SIAM News, (Dec., 1973), pp. 1-5.

[6] E. A. Feustel, On the Advantages of Tagged Architecture, IEEE Trans. Computers, (July 1973), pp. 644-656.

[7] W. T. Wilner, Design of Burroughs B1700, Proceedings AFIPS Fall Joint Computer Conference, vol. 41, (Dec., 1972), pp. 489-497.

[8] C. G. Bell and A. Newell, Computer Structures: Readings and Examples, McGraw-Hill (1971), 688 pp.

[9] R. M. Holt and M. R. Lemas, Current Microcomputer Architecture, Computer Design, (Feb., 1974), pp. 65-73.

[10] Lockheed Electronics Co., Inc., SUE Computer Handbook, Data Products Div., Lockheed Electronics Co., (1973).

[11] H. W. Cadow, OS/360 Job Control Language, Prentice-Hall, (1970), 301 pp.

[12] P. D. Jones, N. R. Lincoln and J. E. Thornton, Whither Computer Architecture?, Proc. IFIP Congress 71, vol. 1, North Holland Publishing Co., (Aug. 1971), pp. 729-736.

[13] F. J. Hill and G. R. Peterson, Digital Systems: Hardware Organization and Design, John Wiley and Sons, (1973), 481 pp.

[14] R. J. Zingg, U.S. Patent No. 3,644,901, (Feb., 1972).

ON PROGRAMMABLE PARALLEL DATA ROUTING NETWORKS VIA CROSS-BAR SWITCHES FOR MULTIPLE ELEMENT COMPUTER ARCHITECTURES

C. J. CHEN
Norand Corporation, Cedar Rapids, Iowa
and
A. A. FRANK
University of Wisconsin, Madison, Wisconsin

Abstract -- This paper deals with the reduction of the number of cross-bar switches required to form a programmable data routing network [PDRN] for interconnecting multiple computing elements [CE]'s and the programming of such networks. The reduction is done by using triangular PDRN's [TPDRN's] to form a multistage network, conditioned on an a priori knowledge of interconnections. The programmability of the proposed PDRN's is specified by the design and the implementation of a route finding algorithm in a multistage PDRN. It is also found that all existing methods used for finding maximum flow in transport networks or used for finding completely matched sets [CMS] in bipartite graphs can be used to solve the middle block assignment problem in a PDRN. A set-up algorithm for a particular type of memory cell in a TPDRN is developed. The worst case propagation delays in the proposed PDRN's are also analyzed. Note that the proposed PDRN's become more advantageous when the number of CE's is large (more than 100). The applications of the proposed PDRN's may include multiprocessors, single and multiple access memory modules, dynamic allocations of memories, dynamic digital computers, digital differential analyzers, automatic patching of analog/hybrid computers with some modifications etc.

INTRODUCTION

Recent advances in LSI technology have created an increasing interest in multiple element computer architectures. Such computers can be structured with a PDRN for interconnecting the multiple computing elements [CE's]. Several different designs of PDRN have been developed including Illiac IV computers' type PDRN [8], CDC 6600 computers' register-barrel type PDRN [6], and cross-bar switch type PDRN [3,4,9,10]. This paper deals with the design of programmable cross-bar type PDRN's which require fewer cross-bar switches to interconnect N inputs to N outputs for parallel operation of the computing elements. As revealed by earlier studies [3,4,10], the most obvious approaches to design a PDRN for large amounts of data require a large number of switches. In fact, the number of switches must grow faster than linearly with the size of the computer. In the simplest designs, the number of switches increases quadratically with the number of CE's. Several designs [3,4,10] have reduced the growth rate to something less than quadratic. This paper further reduces the switch count by employing TPDRN's to form a multistage PDRN based upon the availability of an a priori knowledge of interconnections. Another difficulty revealed in designing an operating PDRN is the programmability of the PDRN. In other words, a route finding algorithm is necessary to provide the interconnections in the PDRN. A sufficient algorithm to find such routes is also discussed in this paper. To begin the discussion, several definitions are in order.

Definitions

D1. A data routing network [DRN] is a set of switches used to connect a set of terminals called inputs to another set of terminals called outputs. If the DRN is used to interconnect CE's of a computer, the inputs are outputs of CE's and vice versa as illustrated in Figure 1.

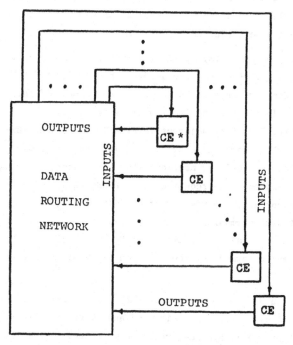

*Computing Element

Figure 1.   Illustration of a data routing network
terminology.

D2. S_K is the number of switches required to interconnect N inputs to N outputs for routing N single-bit words in parallel in a K-stage DRN. A K-stage DRN is a DRN in which each route connecting an input to an output passes K blocks of switches in series. Each block is a group of switches which is a small DRN.

D3. A PDRN is a DRN which operates in the true parallel fashion, i.e. operation of CE's are performed simultaneously. If a PDRN has N inputs and N outputs,
it is called an NxN PDRN.

Now the stage is set for the discussion of a new method used for reducing the
switch count required in a PDRN for interconnecting CE's.

A METHOD FOR REDUCING THE NUMBER OF SWITCHES REQUIRED IN THE
PDRN OF A MULTIPLE ELEMENT COMPUTER

The design of PDRN via cross-bar switches has been well developed in telephone
traffic networks [3,4,10,11]. However in this design, the number of switches required to interconnect N inputs to N outputs has been minimized without a priori
knowledge of connections. In fact, if the connections are known a priori in addition to the ability to use TPDRN's, the number of switches can further be reduced
by a factor of 2 to 10. The reduction factor depends upon the number of inputs,
outputs, and stages (to be explained).

A TPDRN as proposed by Kautz, et al. [5] instead of a conventional rectangular
PDRN [RPDRN] has been selected for this study. This is due to its possibility for
extra-high packing density, ease of fabrication, simplicity of testing and diagnosis,
and programmability, in addition to its low cross-bar switch count (not necessarily
minimum). A TPDRN requires only adjacent intercell connections which make the
fabrication easier, while some other types of PDRN's require fewer switches (cells)
with many nonadjacent intercell connections [5]. For interconnecting N inputs to
N outputs, $(N^2-N)/2$ switches are required in a TPDRN. Contrarily, an RPDRN requires
N^2 switches. The computation of the number of switches (S_K) is between the CE's and
based on single-bit data communication in this paper. It is clear that to route a
w-bit data word in true parallel, requires w x S_K switches. In other words, a "3-
dimensional" PDRN can be formed for routing N multiple-bit data words in the true
parallel fashion.

Figure 2 shows an 8 x 8 TPDRN. A cross-bar switch (cell) realized in terms of
NOR gates as proposed by Kautz, et. al is used and illustrated in Figure 3(A). Although a basic switching cell has been realized with fewer gates [13], the selecced
cell has several different properties. Each cross-bar switch is capable of performing a line switching operation controlled by a memory cell (RS flip-flop). Figure
3(B) gives the Boolean equations of the cell logic. The terminal "MR" in every cell
is connected to a master "Reset" line. "SU" in each cell is connected to a master
"Set-Up" line to control the mode of a PDRN. If "SU" and MR are in logic "0", the
PDRN is in the "set-up" mode. Note that to have S=1 and MR=1 is prohibited due to
the nature of an RS flip-flop. For the other cases, the PDRN is in the "operate"
mode. Each cell has two modes consisting of a "crossing" and "bending" of the pair
of input leads to the pair of output leads. If the memory cell is set at (state

INPUTS

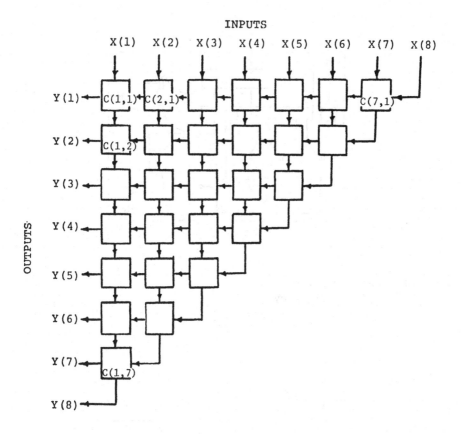

Figure 2. The two dimensional triangular data routing network,
N = 8.

"1"), the switch is in the "bending" mode. Otherwise, it is in the "crossing" mode as depicted in Figure 3(C) and (D), respectively. Each memory cell is set from a coincidence of "0" signals on its horizontal and vertical inputs, simultaneously with a globally applied "set-up" pulse. This can also be done by applying a set of binary digits to the input terminals. More discussions on the set-up algorithm of memory cells is given later.

By using a TPDRN for each block, a 3-stage PDRN consisting of input blocks, and output blocks can be formed. Figure 4 shows a block diagram of an N x N 3-stage PDRN. For simplicity, the following notation is used:

N: Number of inputs and outputs in a PDRN

p: Number of terminals in each input block

q: Number of terminals in each output block

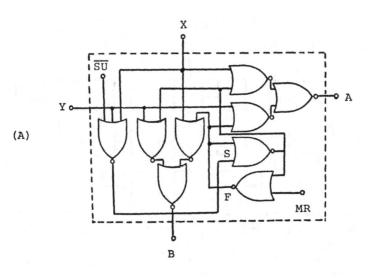

(A)

(B) $A = FX + \overline{F}Y$

$B = \overline{F}X + FY$

$F_{n+1} = SU \cdot \overline{X} \cdot \overline{Y} \cdot \overline{MR} \cdot F_n + \overline{MR} \cdot F_n$

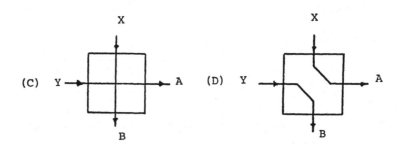

(C)   (D)

Figure 3.   (A)   The NOR gate Realization of a cross-bar switch (cell).
(B)   Boolean equations of the cell.   (C)   The crossing mode
(F=0).   (D)   The bending mode (F-1).

T: Number of input blocks
U: Number of middle blocks
V: Number of output blocks

Several definitions and theorems are next to be given for further discussions.
Readers are referred to Liu [6] for details and proofs of theorems.

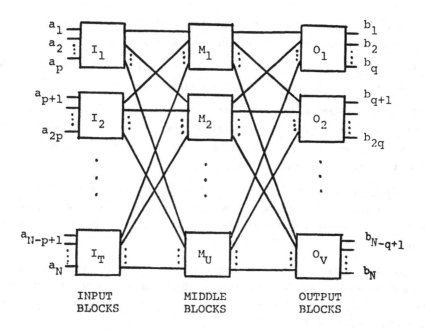

Figure 4.   The two dimensional 3-stage PDRN.

D4. A __bipartite graph__ is a graph in which the vertices can be divided into two disjoint subsets such that no vertex in a subset is adjacent to vertices in the same subset. Figure 5 illustrates a bipartite graph, in which G and H denote the two disjoint subsets.

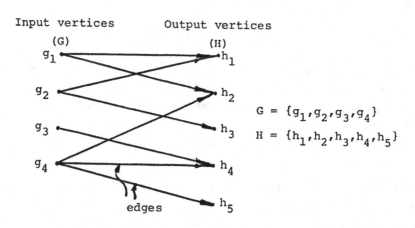

Figure 5.   The bipartite graph.

D5. A matching in a bipartite graph is a selection of edges such that no two edges in the selection are incident with the same vertex in G and H.

D6. A complete matching of G into H in a bipartite graph is a matching such that there is an edge incident with every vertex in G.

Theorem 1. [Given by Liu [2]]   In a bipartite graph, a complete matching G into H exists if and only if $|A| \leq |R(A)|$ for every subset A of G, where R(A) denotes the set of vertices in H that are adjacent to vertices in A and $|\ |$ is defined as the number of members of a set.

Corollary 1. [by Liu [2]] In a bipartite graph, there exists a complete matching of G into H if every vertex in G is adjacent to k or more vertices in H and if every vertex in H is adjacent to k or less vertices in G where k is a positive nonzero integer.

It has been shown that without a priori knowledge of connections, a 3-stage PDRN requires p+q-1 middle blocks for interconnection [3]. However only p=q middle blocks in a 3-stage PDRN are needed if the interconnections are known a priori. This is to be discussed next.

If $N/p \geq N/q$, the number of switches in a 3-stage PDRN (S_3) can be expressed in terms of its parameters as follows:

$$S_3 = \frac{N(U^2-U)}{2p} + \frac{N(U^2-U)}{2q} + \frac{U[(N/p)^2-(N/p)]}{2}$$

$$= U[\frac{N(U-1)}{2p} + \frac{N(U-1)}{2q} + \frac{N^2}{2p^2} - \frac{N}{2p}] \qquad (1)$$

If $\frac{N}{p} < \frac{N}{q}$, the equation becomes

$$S_3 = UN[\frac{U-1}{2p} + \frac{U-1}{2q} + \frac{N}{2p^2} - \frac{1}{2p}] \qquad (2)$$

Given N, S_3 can be minimized by properly choosing U, p and q. Note that S_3 is an increasing function of U and a decreasing function of p and q. It is clear that U must be greater than or equal to p. Otherwise, all interconnections cannot be made if all inputs in an input block are in use. At the optimum point, U must be the same as p. Similarly, it can be shown that U must be equal to q. Thus U=p=q is necessary.

The "sufficiency" of using p (or q) middle blocks to interconnect N inputs to N outputs in a 3-stage PDRN has been proven by converting the interconnections of elements into a bipartite graph and showing the existence of complete matching in the bipartite graph [12]. For p middle blocks, it has been shown that conditions in Liu's theorem (Theorem 1) are satisfied [12]. Thus a completely matched set [CMS] in the graph is guaranteed. After the removal of the CMS, the conditions of Liu's theorem are still satisfied for the remaining graph. By repeating this process p times, p CMS's can be found which implies the sufficiency of using p middle blocks. Thus, by substituting q by p, Equations (1) and (2) lead to the same equation as follows:

$$S_3 = N(p-1) + \frac{N^2}{2p} - \frac{N}{2} .$$

Differentiating S_3 with respect to p, it becomes

$$\frac{dS_3}{dp} = N[1 - \frac{N}{2p^2}] .$$

Letting $\frac{dS_3}{dp} = 0$, the optimum value of p can be found as $p = \sqrt{N/2}$. This gives the optimum value of S_3 as follows:

$$S_3 = N\sqrt{2N} - \frac{3N}{2} .$$

If N is large enough, a 5-stage PDRN can be designed for further reduction in the number of switches by substituting each middle block by a 3-stage PDRN. Similarly, a PDRN with larger number of stages can be designed for very large N. For a K-stage PDRN, the total number of switches (S_K) for the optimum cases has been computed as follows [12]:

$$S_K = (\frac{K+1}{4}) \times 2^{\frac{K-1}{K+1}} N^{\frac{K+3}{K+1}} - \frac{KN}{2} \quad \text{for}$$

$$n = (\frac{N}{2})^{(\frac{K+1}{2})-1}$$

where K = 3, 5, ...

A list of expressions of S_K in terms of N for Benes' method [3] without a priori knowledge of connections and with RPDRN's), Hannauer's method (with a priori knowledge of connections and RPDRN's) [4] and the proposed method for K = 1, 3, 5, 7 is given in Table 1. Figure 6 shows a plot of S_K vs. N for K = 1, 3, 5, 7 and N ranging from 100 to 9000. It is noted that the reduction in S_K in this proposed method is a function of N and K. When K is greater than 7, the reduction in S_K is no longer significant for a given N.

Admittedly, the above analysis ignores the fact that p and q given by the equations are not integers in most of cases. In addition, p and q may not be exactly divisible into N. Therefore, the results are exact for some special cases only. However, the results are usually close enough for practical purposes. This completes the discussion on the reduction of the number of switches. The next section is to focus on the programmability of the proposed PDRN, i.e., the formulation of a route finding algorithm for the proposed PDRN's.

TABLE 1

A LIST OF EXPRESSIONS OF THE NUMBER OF SWITCHES REQUIRED
BY THREE DIFFERENT METHODS FOR N=M CASES

METHODS	EXPRESSIONS OF THE NUMBER OF SWITCHES	
Benes	$S_1^* = N^2$	$S_5 = 16N^{4/3} - 14N + 3N^{2/3}$
	$S_3 = 6N^{3/2} - 3N$	$S_7 = 36N^{5/4} - 46N + 20N^{3/4} - 3N^{1/2}$
Hannauer	$S_1 = N^2$	S_5: not given
	$S_3 = 2^{3/2} N^{3/2}$	S_7: not given
Newly Proposed	$S_1 = (N^2 - N)/2$	$S_5 = 3 \times 2^{-1/3} N^{4/3} - 5N/2$
	$S_3 = 2^{1/2} N^{3/2} - 3N/2$	$S_7 = 2^{7/4} N^{5/4} - 7N/2$

$^*S_i$ means the number of switches required to form an i-stage PDRN.

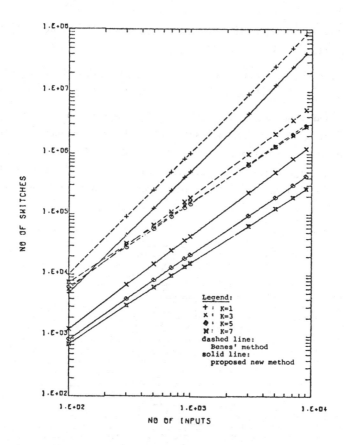

Figure 6. A plot of the number of switches (S_K) vs. the number of inputs
(outputs) in an NxN K-stage PDRN for K = 1, 3, 5, 7.

FORMULATION OF A DIGITAL COMPUTER ALGORITHM FOR FINDING
ROUTES IN THE PROPOSED PDRN's

For interconnecting a large number of CE's, a route finding algorithm becomes
a necessary part of an operating PDRN. The purpose of this section is to formulate
such an algorithm for the proposed multistage PDRN's. The approach taken in the
development of the algorithm has been done mathematically, i.e. in form of theorems
and proofs [12]. However, they are too lengthy to give here. Hence only the flow
charts of the algorithms are given. To begin the description, more definitions are
needed (Refer to Figure 2):

<u>D7</u>. X(1), X(2),...,X(N) are the N inputs to a TPDRN while Y(1), Y(2),...,Y(N)
are the N outputs of the TPDRN.

<u>D8</u>. [XI, YJ] is an interconnection pair connecting the input X(XI) to the output Y(YJ) for XI, YJ = 1, 2, ..., N.

<u>D9</u>. C(r,s) is the cell specified by the horizontal coordinate r and the vertical coordinate s in a TPDRN where r,s = 1, 2, ..., N.

The first algorithm, called Algorithm RFTPDRN, is used to find the state of each memory cell in a TPDRN to perform any specified interconnections. This algorithm is designed based upon the structure of a TPDRN. A flow chart of Algorithm RFTPDRN is shown in Figure 7. The interconnection pairs are ordered in the ascending sequence of the y coordinate. The computation is done in the same sequence one

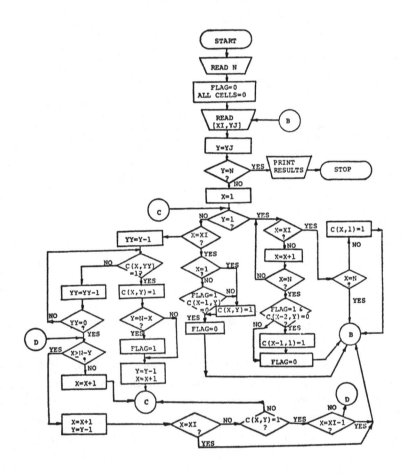

Figure 7. Flow chart for Algorithm RFTPDRN.

pair at a time. However for interconnecting N inputs to N outputs, it has been shown that only the computation for the first (N-1) interconnection pairs is necessary [12]. The validity of the algorithm for any positive integer N has been proven theoretically and has been tested on a digital computer [in FORTRAN] [12].

The second algorithm, called RFPDRN1 is used to compute all local interconnection pairs in each block of a 3-stage PDRN from an *a priori* knowledge of connections. In a 3-stage PDRN, each block always has sufficient routes for their local interconnection pairs. This is due to the fact that each block is a TPDRN. "Local interconnection pairs" is defined as the interconnection pairs in each block of a multistage PDRN. Therefore the problem encountered in developing a multistage route finding algorithm is the assignment of a route in a middle block to each interconnection pair such that no conflict exists for all pairs. Although the "sufficiency" of p (or q) middle blocks has been shown previously, routes are not always guaranteed without carefully assigning middle blocks to all interconnections.

To continue the discussion, more definitions cited from Hu [1] are given below. Readers are referred to [1] for details and Hu's labeling method.

D10. A directed graph that is connected and contains no loops is said to be a transport Network if the following conditions are satisfied:

(1) There is one and only one vertex that has no incoming edges; it is called the source.

(2) There is one and only one vertex that has no outgoing edges; it is called the sink.

(3) There is a nonnegative number associated with each edge; it is called the capacity of the edge. The capacity of edge (g,h) is denoted by $\alpha(g,h)$.

D11. A flow in a transport network, β, is an assignment of a nonnegative number $\beta(g,h)$ to each edge (g,h) such that the following conditions are satisfied:

(a) $\alpha(g,h) \leq \alpha(g,h)$ for each edge (g,h).

(b) $\sum_{\text{all } g} \beta(g,h) = \sum_{\text{all } k} \beta(h,k)$ for each vertex h except the source and the sink.

D12. A maximum flow in a transport network is a flow that achieves the largest possible value.

Algorithm RFPDRN1 has been developed by converting the assignment of the middle block problem into a complete matching problem in a bipartite graph [12]. As mentioned above, there exist p CMS's by using Liu's theorem. It has been shown by Liu [2] that a complete matching problem in a bipartite graph can be changed to a maximum flow problem in a transport network with some modifications. Then the labeling method for getting maximum flow, proposed by Hu [1], has been used to solve the middle block assignment problem. Based upon Hu's labeling method and some special properties of a bipartite graph, Algorithm RFPDRN1 has been developed [12]. This algorithm is to be described by parts first and to be integrated together at the end.

First, the formulation of a connection matrix from given a priori knowledge of interconnections is to be discussed. A connection matrix in which every entry $K(i,j)$ represents the number of interconnections desired between the ith input block (I_i) and the jth output block (O_j) of a 3-stage PDRN. A flow chart of an algorithm used for forming such a connection matrix is shown in Figure 8, where the following notation is used.

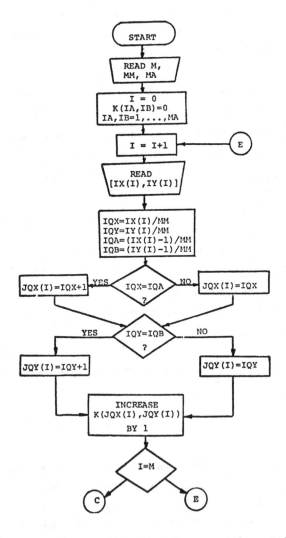

Figure 8. Flow chart of the formulation of a connection matrix from a priori knowledge of interconnections.

M: Number of inputs or outputs in a 3-stage PDRN (M=N).

MM: Number of local interconnection pairs in each input or output block (MM = p = q).

MA: Number of input or output blocks (MA = T = V).

[IX(I),IY(I)]: The Ith interconnection pair.

K[IA, IB]: The entry at the IAth row and the IBth column of a connection matrix.

Initially an MA by MA (or T by T) matrix with all zero entries is formed. Then check one interconnection pair at a time. If IX(I)/MM is equal to [IX(I)-1]/MM, the input terminal IX(I) is in the $(\frac{IX[I]}{MM} + 1)$th input block. Otherwise, it is in $(\frac{IX[I]}{MM})$th input block. Similarly, the output block which contains IY(I) can also be identified. Then increase the corresponding entry in the connection matrix by 1. By repeating this process for each interconnection pair, a connection matrix can be formed.

The following subroutines are necessary for the formulation of Algorithm RFPDRN1:

(A) SUBROUTINE ESCAPE (I,J)

This subroutine is used to determine the possibility of forming an augmenting path starting from the Ith row of a connection matrix or the Ith input vertex of the converted bipartite graph. This is done by checking the existence of a nonzero entry, K(I, J), in the Ith row with the Jth column being unassigned to form an augmenting path. If more than one entry have not been assigned in the Ith row, select the left most one. A column is said to be assigned if the flag 'YFLAG' is raised for the column. If there exists such an entry, specify, its vertical and horizontal coordinates and raise all the following flags:

(1) ESFLAG: If this flag is raised, it indicates that there exists a nonzero entry in the Ith row with an unassigned column.

(2) KFLAG(I,J): If raised, it shows that the entry K(I,J) is committed.

(3) YFLAG(J): If not raised, it means that the Jth column is unassigned. In other words, it is possible to form an augmenting path ending at Jth output vertex of the converted bipartite graph. Figure 9 illustrates a flow chart of this subroutine.

(B) SUBROUTINE YMODFY (I,J)

This subroutine is used to modify the assigned entry in the Jth column. This is to make K(I,J) as the committed entry and to release the previously committed in the Jth columns. This is done by resetting KFLAG(A,J) to zero where A and J are the coordinates of the previously committed entry. In fact, each column and each row of a connection matrix is allowed to have only one committed entry. Figure 10 shows a flow chart of SUBROUTINE YMODFY (I,J).

352

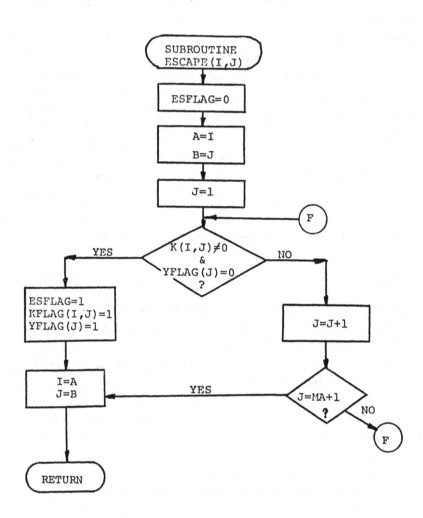

Figure 9. Flow chart of SUBROUTINE ESCAPE.

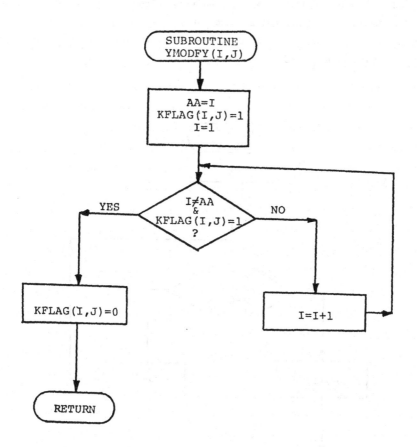

Figure 10. Flow chart of SUBROUTINE YMODFY.

(C) SUBROUTINE XMODFY (I,J)

This subroutine is used to solve any conflict which may be encountered in the Ith row. The left most uncommitted nonzero entry in the Ith row is selected as the committed entry for the row. This is done by raising KFLAG(I,J) for the selected entry K(I,J). This is detailed in Figure 11.

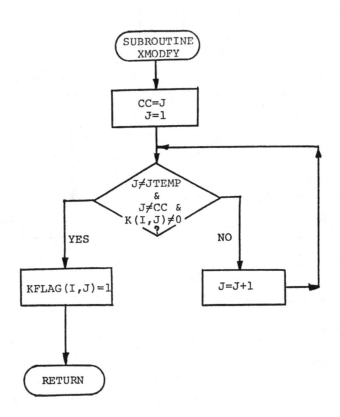

Figure 11. Flow chart of SUBROUTINE XMODFY.

(D) SUBROUTINE ASSIGN (KX,KY)

This subroutine assigns a middle block for the committed entry K(KX,KY). The route is specified by the values JQX(KYY), INA(KYY), MBI(KYY), MBO(KYY), OUTA(KYY), and KYY. Specifically, JQX(KYY) and INA(KYY) identify a local connection pair for the input block which contains JQX(KYY). In addition, MBI(KYY) and MBO(KYY) form a local connection pair in the selected middle block while OUTA(KYY) and KYY form a local connection pair in the output block which contains KYY. After the assignment of a middle block, the value of the entry K(KX,KY) is reduced by 1, and the flag

DONE(KYY) is raised. If DONE(KYY) is 1, it means that a connection pair [JQX(KYY), KYY] has been assigned with a middle block. A flow chart for SUBROUTINE ASSIGN is illustrated in Figure 12.

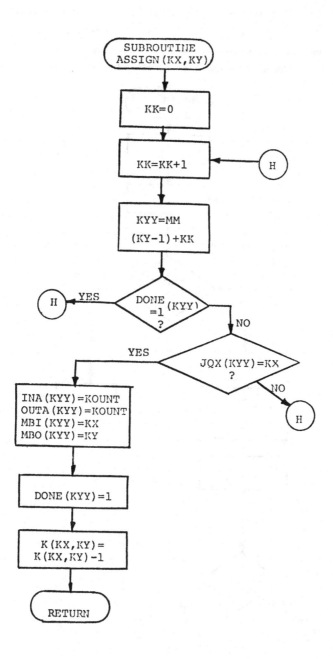

Figure 12. Flow chart of SUBROUTINE ASSIGN.

(E) SUBROUTINE CANDID

This subroutine is called after the search of a CMS is terminated. A CMS is found if and only if each row and each column contain only one committed entry in a connection matrix. This subroutine is to select a candidate (a committed entry) at a time. In addition, it calls SUBROUTINE ASSIGN to assign a middle block to the candidate. (A flow chart of this subroutine is shown in Figure 13. The discussion of the parts of Algorithm RFPDRN1 has been completed.

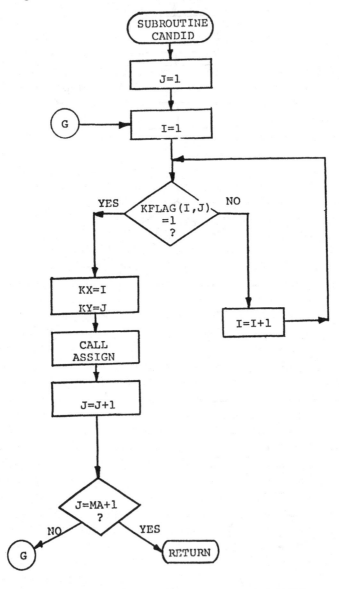

Figure 13. Flow chart of SUBROUTINE CANDID.

357

Algorithm RFPDRN1 is described by the flow chart in Figure 14. This algorithm has also been implemented by writing a FORTRAN program and has been tested on a digital computer for several examples of N = 32 [12]. For a 3-stage PDRN shown in Figure 17 with interconnection pairs shown in Figure 15, Algorithm REPDRN1 computes the four CMS's shown in Figure 16. Table 2 shows the details of interconnections. Figure 17, also depicts all local interconnection pairs by solid lines in each block. This completes the discussion of Algorithm RFPDRN1.

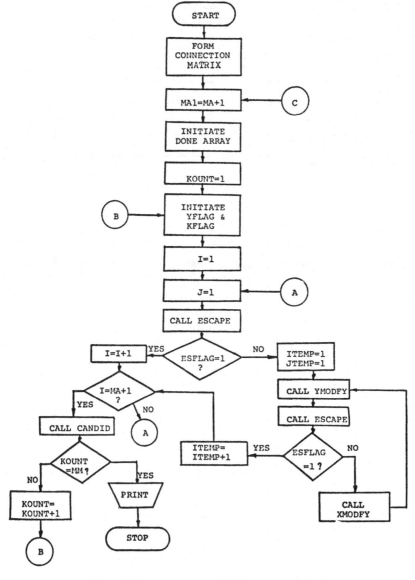

Figure 14. Flow chart of Algorithm RFPDRN1.

Inputs a_i	22	23	24	31	16	17	18	30	19	20	21	29	13	14	15	28
Outputs b_i	1	2	3	4	5	6	7	8	9	10	11	12	13	14	15	16
Inputs a_i	32	1	2	3	10	11	12	27	4	5	6	25	7	8	9	26
Outputs b_i	17	18	19	20	21	22	23	24	25	26	27	28	29	30	31	32

Figure 15. The Desired Interconnection Pairs in a 32x32 3-stage PDRN.

	O_1	O_2	O_3	O_4	O_5	O_6	O_7	O_8
I_1	0	0	0	0	3①	0	1	0
I_2	0	0	0	0	0	0	2①	2
I_3	0	0	0	0	0	3①	0	1
I_4	0	1	0	3①	0	0	0	0
I_5	0	2①	2	0	0	0	0	0
I_6	3	0	1①	0	0	0	0	0
I_7	0	0	0	1	0	1	1	1①
I_8	1①	1	1	0	1	0	0	0

(A)

	O_1	O_2	O_3	O_4	O_5	O_6	O_7	O_8
I_1	0	0	0	0	2②	0	1	0
I_2	0	0	0	0	0	0	1②	2
I_3	0	0	0	0	0	2	0	1②
I_4	0	1	0	2②	0	0	0	0
I_5	0	1	2②	0	0	0	0	0
I_6	3②	0	0	0	0	0	0	0
I_7	0	0	0	1	0	1②	1	0
I_8	0	1②	1	0	1	0	0	0

(B)

Figure 16. (A) The initial connection matrix of Example 4.3 with the first CMS marked by 1 . (B) The reduced connection matrix with the second CMS marked by 2 . (C) The reduced connection matrix with the third CMS marked by 3 . (D) The fourth CMS.

	O_1	O_2	O_3	O_4	O_5	O_6	O_7	O_8
I_1	0	0	0	0	1③	0	1	0
I_2	0	0	0	0	0	0	0	2③
I_3	0	0	0	0	0	2③	0	0
I_4	0	1	0	1③	0	0	0	0
I_5	0	1③	1	0	0	0	0	0
I_6	2③	0	0	0	0	0	0	0
I_7	0	0	0	1	0	0	1③	0
I_8	0	0	1③	0	1	0	0	0

(C)

	O_1	O_2	O_3	O_4	O_5	O_6	O_7	O_8
I_1	0	0	0	0	0	0	1④	0
I_2	0	0	0	0	0	0	0	1④
I_3	0	0	0	0	0	1④	0	0
I_4	0	1④	0	0	0	0	0	0
I_5	0	0	1④	0	0	0	0	0
I_6	1④	0	0	0	0	0	0	0
I_7	0	0	0	1④	0	0	0	0
I_8	0	0	0	0	1④	0	0	0

(D)

Figure 16. (continued)

TABLE 2

DETAILS OF INTERCONNECTIONS FOR EXAMPLE 1

	Entries	IN	INA	MBI	MBO	OUTA	OUT
	{K 1,5}	1	1	1	5	1	18
	{K 2,7}	5	1	2	7	1	26
	{K 3,6}	10	1	3	6	1	21
1st	{K 4,4}	13	1	4	4	1	13
CMS	{K 5,2}	17	1	5	2	1	6
	{K 6,3}	21	1	6	3	1	11
	{K 7,8}	26	1	7	8	1	32
	{K 8,1}	31	1	8	1	1	4
	{K 1,5}	2	2	1	5	2	19
	{K 2,7}	6	2	2	7	2	27
	{K 3,8}	9	2	3	8	2	31
2nd	{K 4,4}	14	2	4	4	2	14
CMS	{K 5,3}	19	2	5	3	2	9
	{K 6,1}	22	2	6	1	2	1
	{K 8,2}	30	2	8	2	2	8
	{K 1,5}	3	3	1	5	3	20
	{K 2,8}	7	3	2	8	3	29
	{K 3,6}	11	3	3	6	3	22
3rd	{K 4,4}	15	3	4	4	3	15
CMS	{K 5,2}	18	3	5	2	3	7
	{K 6,1}	23	3	6	1	3	2
	{K 7,7}	25	3	7	7	3	28
	{K 8,3}	29	3	8	3	3	12
	{K 1,7}	4	4	1	7	3	25
	{K 2,8}	8	4	2	8	3	30
	{K 3,6}	12	4	3	6	3	23
4th	{K 4,2}	16	4	4	2	3	5
CMS	{K 5,3}	20	4	5	3	3	10
	{K 6,1}	24	4	6	1	3	3
	{K 7,4}	28	4	7	4	3	16
	{K 8,5}	32	4	8	5	3	17

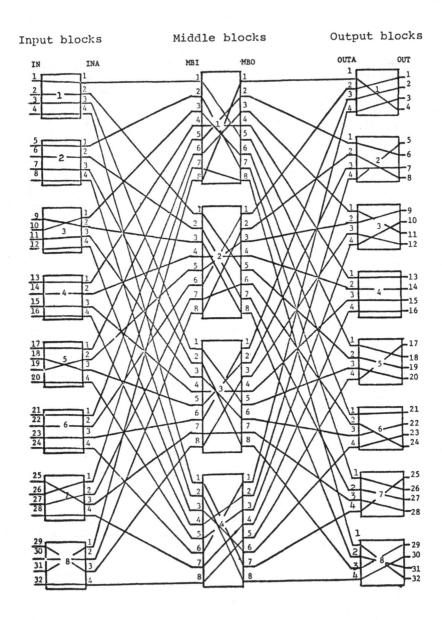

Figure 17. The computed local interconnection pairs of Example 1. A solid line in each block represents such a pair.

Therefore, first, Algorithm RFPDRN1 can be used to compute all local interconnection pairs in each block of a 3-stage PDRN from a priori knowledge of connections. Then Algorithm RFPDRN can determine the state of each memory cell in each block of the PDRN. This completely specifies the programmability of the PDRN. Obviously, these two algorithms can also be used for finding routes in any K-stage PDRN for K=5,7,--, because a 3-stage PDRN has been used as a basic unit to form a higher order PDRN. It is also clear that all existing methods used for finding a CMS in a bipartite graph or used for finding maximum flow in a transport network are possible to use to solve the middle block assignment problem.

ADDITIONAL DESIGN CONSIDERATIONS

The worst case propagation delays in the proposed PDRN's and an algorithm to compute a sequence of sets of binary digits, which is required to set up memory cells in a TPDRN to the desired states are next to be discussed.

In a proposed PDRN, an input is connected to an output through at least one cell. In other words, a data signal applied at an input terminal must propagate through at least one cell before reaching any output terminal in a PDRN. However, only the worst case propagation delay is of interest. A propagation delay is expressed in terms of the number of cells which a signal must propagate between an input and an output. In fact, each cell consists of 2 levels of logic. Let T_k be the worst case propagation delay in a K-stage PDRN. In an NxN TPDRN, T_1 is 2N-3 while T_1 is 2N-1 in a square RPDRN as shown in Figure 18. Consequently, the total delay at the worst case in a 3-stage PDRN (T_3) can be computed as follows:

$$T_3 = (2p-3) + 2 \ (\sqrt{2N}) - 3 + (2p-3)$$

$$= 2^{5/2} \ N^{1/2} - 3^2$$

Similarly, the worst case propagation delay for other higher order PDRN's can also be found. For k = 3, 5, 9, ..., t_K can be generalized and expressed in the following form:

$$t_K = \frac{K + 1}{2} \times 2^{\frac{2K}{K+1}} N^{\frac{2}{K+1}} - 3K$$

Figure 19 shows the relationship between the worst case propagation delay and the number of inputs (outputs) in an NxN K-stage PDRN for K = 1, 3, 5, 7, 9. Also N ranges from 300 to 9×10^5. It is noted that the relationship between the worst case propagation delay and the value of N is linear for a given K if, log-log scales are used. In addition, it is observed that the worse case propagation delay is a decreasing function of the number of stages when N is a constant.

As described by Kautz, et. al. [54], each memory cell of a TPDRN can be set

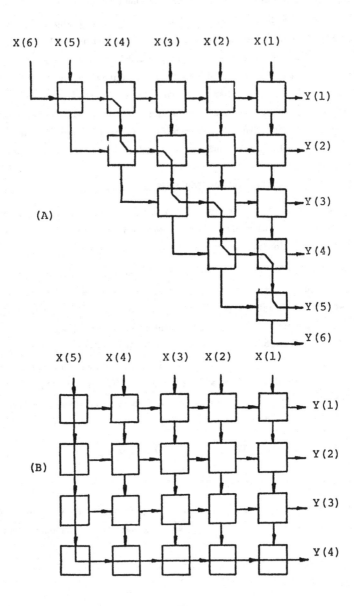

Figure 18. (A) The worst case propagation delay in a 6x6 TPDRN.
(B) The worst case propagation delay in a 5x4 RPDRN.

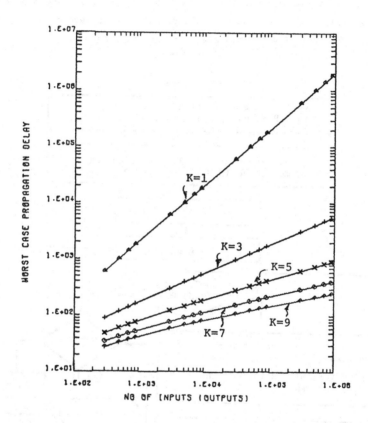

Figure 19. The plot of the worst case propagation delay (t_K) vs. the number of inputs (outputs) in an NxN K stage PDRN.

from a coincidence of '0' signals on its horizontal and vertical inputs, simultaneously with a globally applied "set-up" pulse (or clock). This can also be done by applying a set of binary digits to the input terminals in addition to applying a logic '0' to the terminal, $\overline{SU}$, in the cell of a TPDRN. Therefore, it requires a sequence of sets of binary digits to set up a TPDRN if more than one cell must be set to the 'bending' mode (F=1). An algorithm to compute such a sequence of sets of binary digits becomes essential when the number of cells, which must be set to the 'bending' mode, is large. Such an algorithm has been developed [12] and shown in Figure 20. The validity of this algorithm has also been proved by a theorem [12].

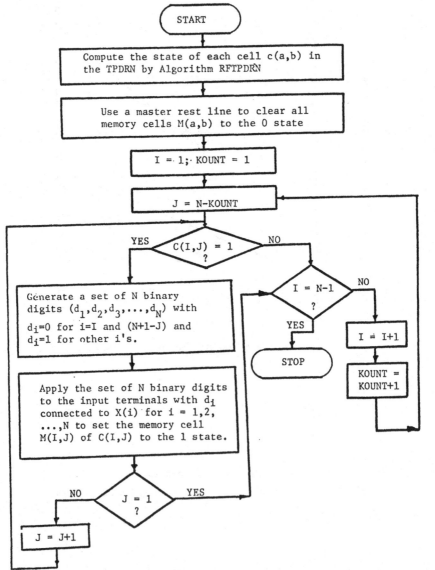

Figure 20. Flow chart of the set-up algorithm of a TPDRN.

Figure 21 shows an example to illustrate the set-up procedure. c(2,3) is the cell being set up. Using the above set up algorithm, a set of binary digits has been computed as 101011. The two dark lines in Figure 21 show the connections from the two zeros applied at the input terminals of the TPDRN to the two inputs of the cell, c(2,3). This completes the discussion on the set up algorithm for a TPDRN.

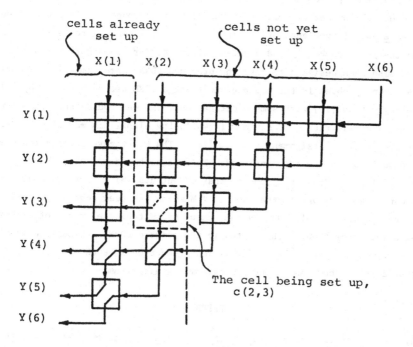

Figure 21. Set up of c(2,3) of the 6x6 TPDRN.

APPLICATIONS OF THE PROPOSED PDRN'S

The proposed PDRN's may be used in any digital system which is required to route data between its elements, conditioned on the availability of a priori knowledge of interconnections. Specifically, the possible applications include multiprocessors, single access and multiple access memory modules, dynamic allocation of memories in a hierarchy, dynamic digital computers [12], digital differential analyzers and automatic patching systems of analog computers with some modifications. Note that the proposed PDRN's become more advantageous when the system is large (over 100 computing elements)

CONCLUSIONS

This paper has presented the ideas of using TPDRN's to form a programmable PDRN to reduce the number of switches required to interconnect N inputs to N outputs, provided an a priori knowledge of interconnections is known. A route finding algorithm for the proposed PDRN's and a set-up algorithm for the memory cells in a TPDRN have also been designed to make the proposed PDRN's programmable. The middle block assignment problem in the proposed multistage PDRN has been solved by using Hu's labeling method [12] with some modifications. It was found that all existing complete matching algorithms or maximum flow finding algorithms may also be used to solve the middle block assignment problem [12]. The worst case propagation delays in the proposed PDRN's has been analyzed. This paper has dealt with the case that the number of inputs (N) is the same as that of outputs (M). In fact, a similar analysis can be easily done to the cases N $\neq$ M which has been covered in [12]. Thus the paper covers one way of reducing the number of switching elements of a PDRN and providing a method of finding the routes in the reduced PDRN. It must be mentioned that there may exist other schemes for element reduction in such systems but each scheme must also be accompanied by a programmable algorithm.

REFERENCES

[1]   Hu, T. C., Integer Programming and Network Flows, Addison-Wesley Publishing Company, Menlo Park, California, 1969.

[2]   Liu, C. L., Introduction to Combinational Mathematics, McGraw-Hill Book Company, New York, 1968.

[3]   Benes, V. E., Mathematical Theory of Connecting Networks and Telephone Traffic, Academic Press, New York, 1965.

[4]   Hannauer, G., "Automatic Patching for Analog and Hybrid Computers," Simulation, 12, May 1969.

[5] Kautz, W. H., et. al., "A Cellular Interconnection Array," IEEE Trans. Compt., vol. C-17, No. 5, May 1968.

[6] Thornton, J. E., "Parallel Operation in the Control Data 6600," Proc. Spring Joint Computer Conference, 1964.

[7] Larson, A. L., "Theory and Design of Precision Digital Integrators Using Linear Multistep Integration Methods," Ph.D. dissertation, University of Wisconsin, Madison, 1973.

[8] Barnes, G. H., et. al., "The ILLIAC IV Computer," IEEE Trans. Compt., vol. C-17, August 1968.

[9] Bell, G. C. and Newell, A., Computer Structures: Readings and Examples, McGraw-Hill, New York, 1971.

[10] Clos, C., "A Study of Non-blocking Switching Networks," BSTJ, No. 32, March 1953.

[11] Higgins, W. H., "A Survey of Bell System Progress in Electronic Switching," BSTJ, No. 6, July-August 1965.

[12] Chen, C. J., "Design of Programmable Data Routing Networks for a Dynamic Digital Computer," Ph.D. dissertation, University of Wisconsin, Madison, 1974.

[13] T. Y. Feng, "Data Manipulating Functions in Parallel Processors and Their Implementations," IEEE Trans. Compt., vol. C-23, No. 3, March 1974.

A RECONFIGURABLE PARALLEL ARITHMETIC UNIT [a]

C. P. HSU and TSE-YUN FENG
Department of Electrical and Computer Engineering
Syracuse University
Syracuse, New York 13210

SUMMARY

For a large-scale purpose parallel processor with a large number of processing elements, the problem of how to fully utilize the facilities for different sizes of applications has yet to be solved. Among the various hardware components constituting the processor, arithmetic unit is frequently one of the most costly and useful circuit components. Thus, the full utilization of the arithmetic unit often means a significant cost saving and higher execution speed. With this in mind, this paper proposes a reconfigurable arithmetic unit design and provides analysis on its performance.

Iterative array logic is employed in this design for its regularity in structure and low cost when realized by large scale integrating circuit. The basic array used is a four-by-four array consisting of 16 basic cells, coupling with four connecting cells for reconfiguration and control. The basic cell itself is a one-bit adder/subtractor. One connecting cell is assigned to each row of the array, which is responsible for controlling the function (addition, subtraction or no operation) to be performed at that row, and for connecting its neighboring arrays. This is the basic building block, called arithmetic element, of the parallel arithmetic unit.

The basic array has a structure similar to that of the improved Hoffmann's array [1], but it is characterized by being able to perform multiplications as well as divisions. This is achieved by reversing the bit order of the operands of division, and modifying the circuit of the basic cell to allow carry/borrow signals to travel in both directions (from right to left and from left to right). The reason is that reversing the bit order of operands also reverses the propagation direction of the carry/borrow signals. The same AE also performs additions and subtractions.

Several assumptions are made on the hardware facilities available in the parallel processor. Among them is that hardware is provided to manipulate the data words and bit slices in several ways, such as subset-shifting the data up or down any distance with end off or end around, flipping the data end-for-end, replicating the data several times, etc. Detail of the data manipulating functions and one of the possible realizations are available in [2]. The memory is assumed that data can be accessed by word, a bit from every word, or a number of bits from a number

---

[a]The work reported here was performed at Syracuse University and was supported by the Air Force Rome Air Development Center under Contract F30602-72-C-0281.

of bits from a number of words. The Multi-Dimensional Access memory of Goodyear's STARAN is such an example.

Flow charts and illustractions are developed [3] to show the possible implementation of the full-width parallel and four-bit parallel arithmetic operations.

Increasing the number of bits which can be processed parallelly decreases the total number of problem elements[*] that can be processed simultaneously, but it reduces the execution time required for processing each problem element proportionally. Hence, by changing the number of bits processed parallelly in accordance with the change of the amount of data (total number of problem elements to be processed), an optimal execution speed can be reached. Comparison studies are made for various operand widths with a 256 × 256 main memory. Some observations are drawn from the studies concerning the different parallelisms that are best for different amounts of data [3].

REFERENCES

[1] J. C. Hoffmann, B. Lacaze, P. Csillag, "Multiplieur Parallels or Circuits Logiques Iteratiffs", Electronic Letters, vol. 4, No. 9, pp. 178, April 1968.

[2] T. Feng, "Data Manipulating Functions in Parallel Processors and Their Implementation", IEEE Transactions on Computers, vol. C-23, No. 3, pp. 309-318, March 1974.

[3] T. Feng, C. P. Hsu, "Design and Analysis of A Parallel Arithmetic Unit", Technical Report, TR-73-13, Dept. of Electrical and Computer Engineering, Syracuse University, (December 1973).

---

[*] A problem element is one of a number of problem segments that can be processed simultaneously in a parallel processor.

ARCHITECTURAL CONSIDERATIONS IN INTERFACING A PARALLEL PROCESSOR TO THE AIR TRAFFIC CONTROL SYSTEM

W.L. HEIMERDINGER, G.F. MUETHING, S.J. NUSPL AND L.B. WING
Honeywell Systems & Research Center
Minneapolis, Minnesota 55413

Abstract -- Interfacing of parallel processors and other special purpose computers to a general purpose host is a very important consideration in effectively using these processors. This paper describes how a parallel processor configuration
is connected to a host machine, in this case an ARTS III[a] multiprocessor system.
The constraints leading to the configuration are first presented. Then we give descriptions of the matched hardware and software interfaces which ensure that the full
capabilities of the processors can be utilized and that the cost and risk of developing the system is minimized. This paper presents only one experience in designing
a parallel processor to host computer interface, but some of the considerations encountered in this experience will be applicable to other such interface attempts.

INTRODUCTION

Parallel processors, because of their high ratio of data transformation and
transfer logic to control sequencing logic, provide a cost-effective facility to
solve highly structured problems with heavy computational demands. Furthermore,
large arrays of processing elements can provide massive redundancy in the data manipulation portion of the computer system. Parallel processors are highly structured,
however, and this structure requires careful design to match the parallel processor
to the problem. The tracking and conflict prediction calculations required to real-
ize the potential of the ARTS III system are repetitively performed on a large data
base. As air traffic processing requirements grow more demanding, parallel processors emerge as attractive candidates for augmentation of the ARTS system.

The parallel processor was postulated as an augmentation to an existing computer based system. The Honeywell design team, therefore, had to provide both hardware and software interfaces with the existing ARTS III host computer complex. Furthermore, the ARTS III system concept included stringent requirements for system reliability and fault recovery.

This paper describes the architectural and system design developed by Honeywell
to configure the PEPE (Parallel Element Processing Ensemble) design [2,3] to effectively augment the ARTS III air traffic control system. The effort was one of three
such parallel processor design tasks carried out for the Department of Transportation

---

[a]ARTS -- Automated Radar Terminal System -- a multiprocessor configuration for
Real-Time Control of terminal area air traffic.

Transportation Systems Center, during 1973. A companion paper describes the implementation of the conflict prediction function on the parallel processor (PP) [1].

The PP had to be configured to use the processing elements to provide high computational capacity through parallelism as well as increased reliability via redundant processing elements. The augmented parallel processor-ARTS system had to provide failsafe/failsoft fault detection and recovery facilities comparable to the extensive facilities being implemented in the new ARTS III systems [4]. These include provisions to interrupt normal system processing on the occurrence of a fault, procedures to provide systematic system diagnosis and effective measures to isolate failed units and to restore system functions, possibly at a reduced level, with the remaining good units.

The algorithms for structuring the application software and for configuration analyses were constrained to be essentially identical to the ARTS III algorithms. Some of these are discussed briefly in the paper by Schmitz and Huang [1].

The design goal for production ARTS/PP systems was to provide full ATC support with a mean up time of 4000 hours and a mean down time of 0.5 hours. The following represents a summary of Honeywell's key results with regard to the PP design developed in the study:

°   The architecture of the parallel processor consists of a control unit and relatively few (9-36) processing elements, each with relatively powerful (.5 MIPS) arithmetic units with parallel arithmetic. This degree of parallelism fits the parallelism of the ATC problem.

°   The fault tolerance/reliability needed to satisfy failsafe/soft constraints requires only a small number of redundant processing elements and redundant control units. The PP failsafe/soft operation is fully compatible with the ARTS III concept.

°   The interface with the ARTS III System provides for a true off-loading capability because the overhead imposed on the ARTS III processor by the parallel processor is negligible. There is a minimum hardware and software impact. The parallel processor connects only to the standard IOP[b] channels and to the well-defined port into the central memory. No executive changes to ARTS III are required; the PP software lives within the constraints of the ARTS III multiprocessor executive.

°   An ARTS III compatible support software approach can be used.

°   The system has growth potential for expanded traffic and expanded ATC function sets.

---

[b] IOP -- Input-Output Processor (ARTS mainframe).

SYSTEM CONFIGURATION

The system design is such that the ARTS III multiprocessor subsystem is the master in the ARTS/PP processing system. What has changed as far as the ARTS system is concerned is that functions which are suited to parallel computation have been moved to the parallel processor subsystem for more efficient implementation, while the sequential and I/O processing remains in the ARTS multiprocessor subsystem. The PP works entirely under direct control of the ARTS III executive. A companion paper in this proceedings discusses this question more deeply with specific emphasis on airspace sectorization to utilize maximum parallelism [1].

The PP control unit is modular in design, and was partitioned to provide two independent control centers, each capable of driving all operable processing elements and of interfacing them with an ARTS III multiprocessor system through a special port in the ARTS III multiprocessor memory matrix and through one of two separate ARTS III processors. This redundancy was provided for failsafe reconfiguration. The configurations of the PP control unit and the interface units is shown in Figure 1. The structure of the processing element is described elsewhere [2]. The discussion below concentrates on the control unit and interfaces. First the control unit components are briefly described.

SCL   Sequential Control Logic -- Fetches and executes instructions involving only control unit operations and passes parallel instructions to the PICU for execution.

ICL   Interrupt Control Logic -- Handles all the special conditions associated with starting and stopping execution in the SCL; also contains a timer file for accumulating measurement data.

PIQ   Parallel Instruction Queue -- Holds instructions issued by the SCL but not yet executed by the parallel elements.

PICU   Parallel Instruction Control Unit -- Receives parallel instructions and generates the detailed control signal sequences.

Data Memory -- Holds temporary variables used by SCL programs. By keeping data in this memory separate from instructions in the program memory, more efficient SCL execution results.

Radar Data Memory -- Used as a buffer for holding incoming radar data until it can be processed.

The above collection of units form a control unit. Both the A and the B control unit can be executing programs at the same time, but only one may be the active controller of the parallel elements. The configuration control unit (CCU) is used to control which control unit is active.

The program memories which are shown between the control units are connectable

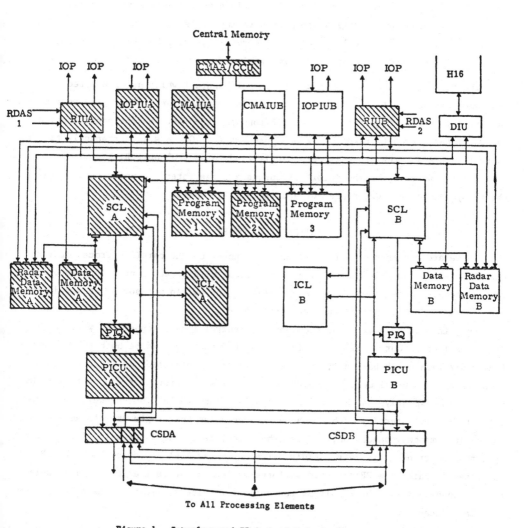

Figure 1. Interface and PP Control Unit Configuration

to either control unit. Switches are provided so that each of the modules can be independently connected to each of the control units. The modules connected to a control unit will contain the programs for that unit.

CSD   Central Signal Distributor — A switch that controls which of the two control units will be connected to the processing elements and which set of global control and element output lines will be used. Note that the CSD's are not connected permanently to one control unit.

The two sets of busses shown at the top of Figure 1 which are connected to all the memories and all interface units are the interface busses. They play an important role in the configuration, since all communication between the control units and the interface units takes place on these busses. One bus is permanently tied to control unit A and the other is permanently tied to oontrol unit B.

All the units above the interface busses are the interface units which connect the PP system to the host processor and the outside world.

INTERFACE HARDWARE

There are a number of alternatives for connecting the parallel processor into the ARTS III system: via channels, as a processor with direct connections into the central memory ports, as a memory accessible by the multiprocessor or as a modification to the ARTS III Input/Output Processor (IOP).

Only the IOP channel connection and the central memory connection were considered practical. Our final conclusions were that there should be both an IOP interface connection which basically controls the parallel processor as if it were a peripheral and a central memory connection. The parallel processor can be treated by the ARTS III executive as one of its peripherals through the IOP channel. All the capabilities for starting such a channel and handling interrupts are already provided. The central memory connection, on the other hand, is intended for situations in which data must be transmitted very rapidly between the parallel processor and the IOP and for cases in which the PP must access large tables in the central memory in a relatively random order. The resulting connections provide sufficiently capable and low risk interfaces.

For reliability and failsafe reasons, the connections between the ARTS III multiprocessor and the PP are made dual redundant. These are switchable under program control so that a faulty unit can be removed without degrading the system.

Each interface unit is functionally independent. This allows for flexible configuration control and for ease in performing diagnosis. The interface unit can be connected to either interface bus A or interface bus B. This connection is controlled with the configuration control switches. At any one time, a particular interface unit is connected to only one interface bus. This ensures that there is no access conflict problem. The interface bus address space allows for the addressing of all the interface units. Therefore, all units can be connected onto one interface bus (during off-line diagnostics, for example). Except for the CMA Adapter[c], there are two copies of each type of interface unit in the PP system.

A feature of the interface system is that it includes hardware format conversion for communicating data between the 30-bit one's complement multiprocessor system and the 32-bit two's complement parallel processor system. This conversion hardware is very simple and adds no overhead to data transmission between the multiprocessor and parallel processor. No software conversion is needed.

The interface units are briefly described below:

IOPIU IOP Interface Unit -- Allows the IOP to control the operation of the parallel processor system, both at a low level of control and during normal operations. During system initialization or recovery the IOPIU is used by the ARTS III multiprocessor system to diagnose the PP control unit components, to load programs and preset data into the PP control unit memories, and to initiate independent PP functional operations.

   During normal operation the IOPIU is used to start function executions, to interrupt PP function execution for higher priority functions, and finally to transfer data between the multiprocessor and the PP system.

CMAIU Central Memory Access Interface Unit -- Provides the PP a high speed random access port into the ARTS III central memory. With this interface the PP control unit can perform read and write functions to the central memory as well as perform test and set operations for communicating with asynchronous tasks running in the IOP's.

   The hardware for the CMAIU essentially consists of two buffer registers, an address register, conversion mode registers, and a set of registers and logic which duplicate the ARTS III IOP address translation and memory lockout hardware.

   The CMAIU can only be controlled from the PP side and only through the interface unit to which it is connected. An address space for addressing 12 16K central memory modules through the CMAIU is provided.

CMAA CMA Adapter -- Provides the single point through which either of the CMAIU's communicate with one port in the ARTS III central memory.

RIU Radar Interface Unit -- Allows radar input data from the radar unit to be buffered into the PP Radar Data Memory while the PP is processing other functions.

   There are two RIU's in a dual sensor system, each connected to a separate radar data acquisition unit. Both units must be active in a fully operational system. Both units can be connected to interface bus A or B. The RIU's also contain switches to allow the radar data to be

_____

[c] CMA -- Central Memory Access

sent directly to IOP's.

DIU   <u>Diagnostic Interface Unit</u> -- Connects an H716 support minicomputer and a maintenance and control panel to a control unit. Off-line diagnostics can be performed through this interface.

CCU   <u>Configuration Control Unit</u> -- Controls the interconnection of the redundant control unit components, interface units and signal distribution systems. The states of the switches which provide this control are normally set by the ARTS III multiprocessor. The CCU is designed to be very reliable since it represents a single point failure area.

INTERFACE SOFTWARE

The design of the interface software is directed at extending and making available the full capabilities of the hardware interfaces, thereby allowing the full operational, debug and initialization modes of operation. Sufficient flexibility is provided for data transmission in a call-by-value mode over the IOP interface units and in a call-by-reference mode over the CMA interface unit.

Our approach to interfacing with existing ARTS III software is to minimize changes in the design of the IOP software. The design relies strictly on the use of the existing multiprocessor executive and depends on the executive service requests to exercise control over the parallel processor.

The software on the parallel processor side of the interface operates in a slave mode. There is no executive in the normal sense of the word. PP tasks and functions are controlled and initiated by the multiprocessor executive.

IOP Resident Interface Functions

The interfaces to the PP tasks and functions are made simple for the IOP programmer. There are only a few major subroutine entry points into the interface software which provide all the required PP control capability.

The most frequently used entry is a routine "PCALL", which calls PP resident functions from the IOP. This entry is a closed subroutine and has as arguments the name of the PP function, a function input parameter address and an output buffer address. The optional parameters are passed in a call-by-value mode. For short PP functions, the calling program can elect to wait until the function is completed or can continue other IOP operations and let the PP work on the function concurrently.

Another interface software entry from the IOP sets up a PP task initiation request and is similar to scheduling other "POPUP" multiprocessor tasks. No parameters are passed.

The CMAIU allows the PP to access central memory with addresses generated in the PP. To prevent illegal accesses, memory lockout is provided and must be set for the CMAIU in the same way as for tasks running in the IOPs. There is a special software interface routine defined to allow the setting of the memory lockout registers in the CMAIU during initialization and reconfiguration.

One low level interface routine entry also available to the IOP programmer is a Channel Start entry. This routine has as parameters the input channel and output channel starting control word addresses. Both channels are started and control is returned immediately to the calling routine. This entry is used primarily during recovery and initialization.

The main PP control function is implemented to provide for multiple simultaneous calls for PP functions. These calls may come from different tasks executing concurrently on different IOPs in the ARTS multiprocessor subsystem. The call requests are entered in a queue and executed in a first-in-first-out order. Some IOPs which made requests may be waiting and some may have continued processing as soon as the function was recorded in the queue. For the waiting IOPs, a return is allowed when an interrupt from the PP indicates that the function has been completed. Only one function request is sent to the PP at a time.

PP Resident Interface Functions

The PP side of the software interface has been kept very simple. There are essentially no executive tables or routines in the PP control unit memories. The execution of the PP programs are strictly in a slave mode. The program performs its function, reports back and the PP returns to what it was doing or remains idle until another program is started.

The execution control of the PP programs is interrupt driven. Interrupt priorities are primarily controlled through the hardware interrupt masks, which are set through software. When a routine of a specified interrupt level is entered, lower level interrupts are inhibited by resetting the mask bits.

There are no specific system tables associated with this interrupt handling. The program associated with each level of the interrupt provides its own storage area for holding the interrupted status.

If some of the operational programs call subroutines from several interrupt levels, these subroutines may be interrupted while they are executing. They must therefore be coded such that they are re-entrant. The PP control unit has all the instructional capability to allow the PP programmer to code subroutines re-entrantly.

RELIABILITY CONSIDERATIONS

A key factor in assessing the usefulness of the ARTS/PP system is its reliability. There are four operating states for the system that are important for reliability purposes:

° Fully operational

° Failsafe

° Failsoft

° Inoperative

In the fully operational state, all ATC functions are fully supported and all system components are fully operational. In the failsafe state, all ATC functions are still fully supported, although some system components may be inoperative. The fully operational and failsafe states should be indistinguishable to the ATC controller. A system in the failsoft state provides only selected ATC functions because of failed system components. There may be several levels of functional degradation in this state. The system provides no ATC support in the inoperative state. The ARTS/PP is designed to provide failsafe operation in the face of single failures in major units and failsoft operation if multiple failures occur.

Two options were available for increasing the reliability of the ARTS/PP system design; replication of units and the use of high reliability components. Both options were explored in detail. The configuration selected relies mainly on replication but also uses high reliability parts in the critical CMAA/CCU section.

As in the present ARTS system, ARTS/PP achieves a high level of system reliability by strongly partitioning the system into major functional units separated by well-defined interfaces. Major units are replicated and hardware and software are provided to detect faulty units, effectively isolate the faulty units, reconfigure the system to restore functional capability, and to restart the system with uncontaminated data -- all within a time span on the order of seconds, so that ATC functions are effectively uninterrupted. The major replicated units are processing elements, Control Units, ARTS/PP Interface Units, and sections of the Central Signal Distribution System. To provide the necessary time response, all units are electrically active and are isolated and connected under program control. Units that are not part of the operational ATC system are available for diagnosis and repair.

The resulting ARTS/PP system was analyzed for reliability using the classical spare inventory calculations based on the Einhorn method [5]. The ARTS/PP system was modeled as a number of series/parallel subsystems which can be repaired or replaced when failures are detected.

The reliability estimates for each of the proposed ARTS/PP configurations exceed the production system minimum Mean Up Time design goal by a factor of ten or more and the maximum Mean Down Time goal by a factor of two or more.

The figures were calculated for a SSI implementation of the production systems. Based on a conceptual evaluation of impact of implementation techniques on a sample digital system, an LSI implementation would result in failure rates 3.5 times smaller [6].

Fault Detection and Isolation

On-line spares provide increased system reliability only if faults are detected before data contamination sufficient to prevent a correct restart occurs. Such a system also requires effective means for promptly locating failed components so that mean times to repair are substantially lower than mean times between failures. The PP system includes extensive hardware and software facilities for prompt fault detection. Additional fault location and diagnosis hardware and software are provided to minimize repair time.

Operational fault detection software intercepts faulty data at major system boundaries. The main boundary of interest is the interface between the PP and ARTS system.

Failsafe/Failsoft Fault Recovery Techniques

System reliability depends upon an effective fault recovery procedure to respond to failure alarms, determine the largest system that can be assembled from fault-free components (either by removal of known faulty resources from the list of available resources or by complete diagnosis of all major system elements) and to configure and restart the fault-free system with uncomtaminated data.

Recovery procedures must be tailored to the fault encountered. The primary concern is the spread of data contamination. Peripheral devices have a limited opportunity to contaminate ARTS/PP data or programs because of the limitations imposed on their access to central memory by IOP channel control hardware, memory lockout registers, etc. Faulty central resources such as IOPs and main memory modules have much greater potential for mischief because of their access to virtually all system resources. The present ARTS processor system units react to faults with a scatter interrupt followed by a complete diagnosis of all major units, while errors in peripheral devices, such as Beacon Data Acquisition Systems, are relegated to ARTS functional tasks for disposition.

The isolation and fault detection features of the ARTS/PP system partition the system into three areas, each corresponding to a different level of system integrity. The most protected area is the central area, which includes the ARTS multiprocessor units and the CMAIU and CMAA units. The central area extension includes the remainder of ARTS/PP interface and the active PP control unit. The area of least concern is the peripheral area, which includes the normal ARTS peripherals and the array of processing elements. The recovery procedure considers only two fault recovery levels. Peripheral or PE faults are handled by individual IOP popup tasks that merely reassign the peripheral or PEs involved. All other faults require some form of system reconfiguration and are thus considered critical faults.

All critical fault conditions ultimately generate a system-wide interrupt. Once this interrupt occurs, the standard critical fault recovery procedure is invoked in all cases. This procedure, an extension of the current ARTS failsafe/failsoft recovery process, includes complete system diagnosis, reconfiguration, and restart.

REFERENCES

[1] H.G. Schmitz, and C. Huang, "An Efficient Implementation of Conflict Prediction in a Parallel Processor", Proc. 1974 Sagamore Computer Conference on Parallel Processing.

[2] R.O. Berg, S.J. Nuspl, and H.G. Schmitz, "PEPE - An Overview of Architecture, Operation and Implementation", National Electronics Conf. Proceedings (Sept. 1972).

[3] J.A. Githens, "A Fully Parallel Computer for Radar Data Processing," NAECON (May 1970).

[4] W. Walther, "Multiprocessor Self Diagnosis, Surgery and Recovery in Air Traffic Control," ACM Operating Systems Review, 7, No. 4, (October 1973).

[5] S.J. Einhorn, "Reliability Prediction for Repairable Redundant Systems," Proceedings of the IEEE (February 1963).

[6] R.O. Berg, et al, "Approaches to Custom LSI," U.S. Air Force Systems Development Command, Air Force Avionics Laboratory Technical Report, AFAL-TR-73-16, (April 1973), pp. 191.

AN EFFICIENT IMPLEMENTATION OF CONFLICT PREDICTION IN A PARALLEL PROCESSOR

H. GREGORY SCHMITZ and CHENG-CHI HUANG
Honeywell Systems & Research Center
Minneapolis, Minnesota 55413

Abstract -- Two widely different parallel processor approaches to the terminal Air Traffic Control (ATC) problem are considered, and an efficient implementation of the Conflict Prediction (CP) function in a parallel processor whose elements are capable of handling multiple tracks is described. An airspace sectorization scheme which facilitates such an implementation and is compatible with other terminal ATC functions is introduced. Also, considerations which determine the optimal sector size are examined. Finally, an example is presented which shows how the conflict prediction function can be implemented on the parallel processor.

INTRODUCTION

The inherently parallel nature of Air Traffic Control (ATC) functions like tracking, report-track correlation, and conflict prediction make them potentially good candidates for possible implementation in a Parallel Processor (PP). However, to only implement a particular function or set of functions in a parallel processor is not particularly noteworthy as there is no question that some sort of a mechanization is always possible for a given function. What _is_ important is whether the implementation can be such that very efficient use is made of the parallel processor hardware. Otherwise, it will never be economically feasible to use parallel processors, either in a stand-alone configuration or as an augmentation to a conventional sequential machine.

This paper examines different parallel processor implementations of some of the terminal ATC functions and considers some of the factors that are important for an efficient implementation of those functions. Also, some airspace sectorization concepts are discussed as they apply to a particular type of parallel processor. Here, an attempt is made to determine the optimum number of sectors as far as conflict prediction processing efficiency is concerned. Finally, an example is presented which shows how the conflict prediction function can be implemented in a parallel processor using the sectorization ideas developed in the paper.

SINGLE-TRACK/PE VS. MULTI-TRACK/PE PARALLEL PROCESSORS FOR ATC

There are really two basic parallel processor hardware approaches that can be used to implement the conflict prediction function and other traffic control functions in the terminal ATC environment. One is to utilize a parallel processor that

associates a unique Processing Element (PE) with each "aircraft track" and contains
a number of PE's sufficient to cover the entire airspace. That is, n total aircraft
would require at least n PE's, whether n was equal to 50 or 500. The other approach
is to have a parallel processor with a smaller number of processing elements but
have each PE capable of handling multiple "aircraft tracks". In this situation, the
number of PE's required would be approximately n/m, where m is the number of "aircraft tracks" stored in each PE. (Here an "aircraft track" refers to the collection
of data necessary to represent a particular aircraft in the airspace. The data includes such things as aircraft ID, range, altitude, beacon code, etc.)

Of the two approaches, the multiple track/PE solution is preferred because it
lends itself to the most efficient utilization of parallel processor hardware. The
reasoning behind this statement is as follows: The ATC problem is not a totally
parallel one because of the physical operation of the radar and beacon. The entire
airspace is not illuminated simultaneously but rather only small slices are sequentially interrogated as to the presence or absence of objects. Only in the immediate
area of the radar and beacon sweeps is there any "parallel" activity possible, and
real-time display constraints prevent the "saving up" and subsequent processing of a
complete scan (4 seconds) of radar and beacon data. Therefore, the very nature of
the ATC problem forces it to be somewhat less than totally parallel.

The implications of these physical constraints on the two parallel processor
approaches for the ATC input processing and tracking functions are significant. For
the single track/PE parallel processor it means that a given processing element will
be active; i.e., doing useful computations, only when the radar and beacon sweeps
are in the immediate vicinity of the aircraft assigned to the PE in question. During
the remainder of the four-second scan, which is by far the largest timewise, the PE
in question will be inactive.

A similar situation is also true in the case of the conflict prediction function for the single track/PE parallel processor. That is, in conflict prediction,
it is not necessary to compare aircraft that are many miles further apart than the
conflict region of interest. A "gross filtering" operation can be done initially
which reduces the total number of aircraft that have to be checked against the aircraft in question. For the single track/PE parallel processor, this implies that
PE's which are assigned to aircraft that are far from the aircraft of interest will
remain inactive; i.e., not doing useful computations.

On the other hand, in the multi-track/PE approach, where many tracks are
stored in each processing element, a much better utilization of hardware is possible.
Here, if the aircraft tracks are distributed across the PE's such that each processing element is used over and over again as the radar sweeps around the airspace, a
high level of hardware efficiency can be maintained. Because a given PE "represents" many different aircraft tracks, the amount of time a PE remains inactive over

a 4-second scan can be made very small.

Clearly, the multi-track/PE approach potentially has a much better chance of using less hardware to solve a particular ATC problem than one which dedicates an entire processing element to a single aircraft. However, in order for the multi-track/PE approach to work as described above, a track management function must be maintained that ensures that all the aircraft contained in the airspace are properly distributed across the available processing elements. Otherwise, the parallel processing efficiency can rapidly approach zero. For example, if an aircraft is going to be checked against, say, ten other aircraft for possible conflict, the ten other aircraft should ideally be located in ten different PE's. Under these conditions, the conflict prediction calculation need only be computed once. However, if instead of being located in separate PE's, the ten aircraft were clustered in a single PE, ten separate conflict prediction computations would be required and no parallel processing advantage could be obtained.

Proper implementation of the track management function requires that certain aircraft tracks be moved from PE to PE as aircraft physically move from one region to another. It will be shown in a later section of this paper that the overhead incurred by such track movement is very small.

In the next section, possible ways of dividing up or sectorizing the terminal airspace are considered that not only facilitate the distribution of aircraft across the PE's in a multi-track/PE parallel processor but will also handle multiple functions like tracking and conflict prediction. The emphasis is on an effective sectorization scheme for the conflict prediction function, since it is the one that has the most stringent requirements. In addition, some of the considerations involved in determining the most efficient sector size are presented.

AIRSPACE SECTORIZATION

In order to manage Conflict Prediction (CP) and other ATC functions in a multi-track/PE parallel processor, the terminal airspace must be sub-divided in some fashion into a number of smaller regions called sectors. The ATC algorithms can then be applied sequentially to each of the sectors until the entire airspace has been covered.

In this section, the derivation of a sectorization scheme that can be used for the CP function and still be compatible with the other ATC functions of interest will be described. It will also be shown that an optimal or near-optimal number of sectors can be determined for a given combination of processing elements and aircraft.

Since much of the aircraft data that is used for the conflict prediction function is also used by other ATC functions, it would be very desirable to have the same sectorization scheme used by all ATC functions. If a single scheme can be used, then redundant storage of aircraft tracks is not required, and a considerable amount of PE memory can be saved. Therefore, it makes sense to consider the sectorization requirements of some of the other ATC functions.

The airspace sectorization scheme used to perform the target correlation and tracking functions in today's Automated Radar Terminal System III (ARTS III) is shown in Figure 1. The airspace is divided into thirty-two 11-1/4° pie-shaped sectors. Each sector corresponds to 125 ms. of real time and the sectors are used to keep track of the age of radar and beacon reports. Sectors are processed sequentially with some type of processing activity going on in up to 8 consecutive sectors at any one time (i.e., track correlation in one sector, turning correlation in another, track prediction in a different one, and so on). The airspace sectorization scheme shown in Figure 1 can be used for the target detection and tracking functions regardless of whether these functions are implemented in a sequential or parallel processor. While this sectorization scheme is suitable for most of the ATC functions, it will be seen below that the same sectorization scheme cannot easily be used for the CP function. (Note the sectors in Figure 1 will be referred to as "tracking sectors" in the discussion that follows.)

In any sectorization scheme used for conflict prediction, special consideration must be given to boundary conditions. Care must be taken to insure that a conflict pair straddling a sector boundary is detected. Assuming a one-minute lookahead time and a maximum aircraft speed of 240 knots, then any pair of aircraft with distance less than 8 nm have to be tested for possible conflict. (The 8 nm is obtained by (240/60)x2, which is the maximum distance that two aircraft can travel in one minute's time.) Refer to Figure 2 for a possible conflict pair from Sector A and Sector B.

To guarantee that all sector-boundary straddling pairs like the one shown in Figure 2 are tested for possible conflict requires that all aircraft in Sector A that are within 4 nm of the sector boundary be tested for conflict against the aircraft in Sector B and all aircraft in Sector B which are within 4 nm of the sector boundary be tested for conflict against the aircraft in Sector A.

One way of doing this is to extend the sector boundary 4 nm on both sides of the boundary. Then, as the particular sector is processed, the potential conflict will be tested because all aircraft which were within 4 nm of the sector boundary also "belong" to the sector in question. This implies that the near-boundary aircraft have to be stored twice, once for each sector. Unfortunately, this is unacceptable because of the extra amount of memory that would be required and the possible confusion that could arise from having multiple copies of the same aircraft track.

An alternate approach, which trades off a small amount of processing time for

extra memory, requires that the aircraft data be stored only once. Instead of
storing a track in an adjacent sector if it is within 4 nm of the adjacent sector,
the track is simply tested with all the aircraft in the adjacent sector if it is
within the 4 nm region. In this way, a minimum of extra processing is done and the
memory requirements are still kept as small as possible. (A later example will
illustrate this scheme.)

Note, however, if the above scheme is applied to the sectors of Figure 1, then
any aircraft that is close to the origin will need to be tested against all other
sectors. This is obviously undesirable, as too much unnecessary processing would
have to be done. Therefore, the sectorization scheme used for the tracking function
cannot be used in any practical way without some modification.

In order to effectively accommodate the 4 nm boundary problem, it becomes
apparent that any useful sectorization scheme for the CP function will have to avoid
having its sector boundaries cluster together, as is the case in Figure 1.

There are a number of alternate sectorization approaches that would avoid this
clustering effect. One would be to use an X-Y (or rectangular) sectorization scheme
and lay out the airspace in a simple grid fashion. Unfortunately, this type of a coordinate system is not consistent with the (r,θ) system used in the tracking and correlation functions, so that if it were adopted, separate data bases would have to be
kept for the tracking and conflict prediction functions. As mentioned before, this
would require multiple storage of the same track data or much PE to PE data transfer,
and should be avoided if at all possible.

Another sectorization scheme would be to use the tracking sectorization where
possible but make modifications to it where it cannot be used for conflict prediction. Note that in Figure 1, the only place the tracking sectorization scheme gets
into trouble for conflict prediction is near the origin. In order to eliminate the
crowded sectors near the origin, it would be reasonable to have fewer sectors nearer
the center. To eliminate the problem at the center itself, a small circle centered
on the origin could comprise a single sector. Under these considerations, a possible
sectorization scheme for conflict prediction might be as shown in Figure 3.

The scheme shown in Figure 3 is identical to the tracking sectorization scheme
when the range is greater than 21 nm. For ranges of less than 21 nm, a few of the
"spokes" have been removed, thus eliminating the crowding that occurs near the center.
The range boundaries shown, 6 nm and 21 nm, have been selected so that any one aircraft will have to be compared with no more than four neighboring sectors. The criteria is that the boundary line between any two sectors must be 4 nm or greater. The
size of each sector type is given below:

Sector 1: (Same as Sectors 2 through 32)
$$= 98.7\pi \text{ nm}^2$$

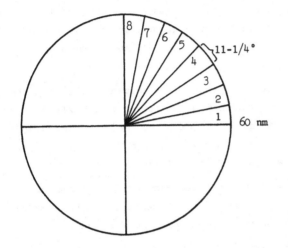

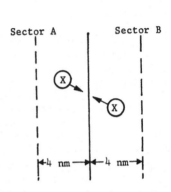

Figure 1. ARTS III Sectorization Scheme

Figure 2. Possible Conflict Pair

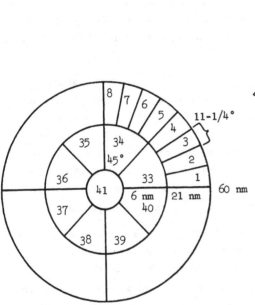

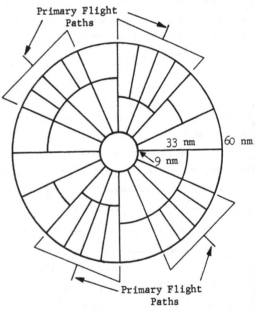

Figure 3. A Sectorization Scheme for
Conflict Prediction

Figure 4. A More Realistic Sectorization
Scheme for Conflict Prediction

Sector 33: (Same as Sectors 34 through 40)

$$= 50.6\pi \ nm^2$$

Sector 41: $= 36\pi \ nm^2$

Note that Sector 41 has the smallest sector size, and the Sector 1 type the largest sector size. If a sectorization scheme with more even sector sizes is desired, the two radius values can be increased accordingly.

The sectorization scheme shown in Figure 3 would tend to imply a relatively even distribution of aircraft throughout the terminal airspace. However, such is not likely to be the case in actual practice. Because of runaway orientations, traffic densities will always tend to be higher in certain portions of the airspace. The sectorization shown in Figure 3 can easily be modified to take this into account because the sector boundaries indicated do not have to remain fixed. Since they exist only as entries in a table, the boundaries can be modified to fit the expected traffic patterns at a particular site. A more realistic sectorization scheme is shown in Figure 4. The organization of sectors in Figure 4 indicates the primary routes of traffic flow.

The general philosophy that would be followed in laying out a sectorization pattern for a particular site would be to size the sectors so that each would roughly contain the same number of aircraft. In this way, the parallel processor efficiency would tend to be maximized. If it is not realistic to divide the airspace so that all sectors contain the same number of aircraft (some sectors may get too small), then a processing efficiency tradeoff can be made. On one hand, a sufficient number of PE's would be provided to efficiently process the most populated sector. Here, although the processing throughput would be maximized, the parallel processor would be under-utilized in some of the lesser populated sectors.

On the other hand, if the number of PE's is chosen such that the processing efficiency of the "average" sector is maximized, then more processing time would be required in the heavily populated sectors but the PP would be used more efficiently in the remaining sectors. Clearly, there are tradeoffs that can be made and the result will depend on such factors as the total amount of processing time available and the maximum time delays permitted in the system.

Because the size (indirectly the number of aircraft) of the sectors and the total number of PE's available will determine the number of times the CP algorithm will be repeated in a given sector, it is possible to establish an optimal number of sectors for a given combination of processing elements and aircraft. Figure 5 shows four possible airspace sectorization schemes. They are all sectorized in r, θ coordinates but each has a different total number of sectors. The numbers of sectors for subfigures (a), (b), (c), and (d) in Figure 5 are 25, 33, 41 and 57, respectively. (In the analysis that follows, an even distribution of aircraft is

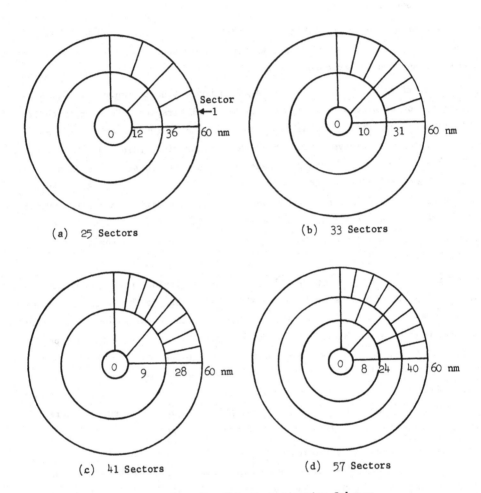

(a) 25 Sectors

(b) 33 Sectors

(c) 41 Sectors

(d) 57 Sectors

Figure 5. Four Possible Sectorization Schemes
for the Conflict Prediction Function

assumed. Although it has already been pointed out that an even distribution is not likely, the results of the analysis are still generally valid.)

As discussed earlier, an aircraft within 4 nm of a boundary has to be tested for conflict against the aircraft in the neighboring sector sharing that boundary. For each case shown in Figure 5, the percentage of area that is repeated due to the 4 nm requirement is computed and shown in Table 1. To show how these numbers are computed, consider Sector 1 of Figure 5(a). A magnified version of this sector is shown in Figure 6. In this figure, the aircraft in the diagonally slashed area have to be tested for possible conflict against some neighboring sector or sectors (the cross-hatched area). The size of the slashed area is computed with the cross-hatched area counted twice or three times (for some sectors). The same procedure applies to each of the other 24 sectors in Figure 5(a).

All of the repeated area is then summed up and the total is 73% of the total airspace as shown in Table 1, row 1. The numbers for the cases of (b), (c) and (d) are obtained similarly. It is obvious that the smaller the number of sectors, the smaller the percentage overlap is. It should be noted that the shape of a sector also has a significant effect on the percentage because of the 4 nm requirement. This can be seen by comparing the schemes (c) and (d) of Table 1. There are 16 more sectors in scheme (d) than in scheme (c), but the percentage of area repeated in (d) is only 7% higher than in (c). This is due to the fact that the majority of the sectors in scheme (c) are long narrow strips which requires much of the area to be repeated.

For a certain combination of processing elements and total aircraft, the optimal or near-optimal number of sectors can be determined as shown in the following example.

Assume that there are 500 aircraft, evenly distributed in the airspace, and that a parallel processor containing 16 PE's is used to implement the ATC functions. The four sectorization schemes shown in Figure 5 are considered for the CP function execution. The number of CP computations for each of the four schemes can be derived based on the percentage of repeated area and the number of aircraft contained in each sector. The result is shown in the last column of Table 2 and plotted in Figure 7.

Briefly, the number of CP algorithm computations were obtained in the following way. For schemes (b), (c), and (d), where the number of aircraft per sector is less than the number of PE's, consider a sector with n aircraft and having x percent of the sector to be repeated because of the 4 nm requirement. This sector requires $(n-1)$ CP computations to identify conflicts among the n aircraft and $(x \cdot n)$ CP computations between them and the aircraft in the neighboring sectors. For scheme (a), there are 20 aircraft in each sector. With only 16 PE's available, the 20 aircraft have to be stored in two levels, one level with 16 aircraft and the other with

4 aircraft. Because only the aircraft in one level can participate in a CP computation at any given time, this two-level storage requires a greater number of CP computations, as indicated in Table 2, row 1.

Figure 7 shows that the sectorization scheme (b) in Figure 5, which has 33 sectors, requires the smallest number of CP computations among the four schemes. Note that the number of aircraft in each sector of scheme (b) is 15.1, which is very close to the total number of processing elements, 16. Once the number of aircraft in a sector is greater than 16, a two-level storage will be required for that sector and, as disucssed before, the number of CP computations will then increase substantially. Hence, the sectorization scheme (b) is an optimal or a near-optimal sectorization for the given example case.

The amount of processing time spent by a multi-track/PE parallel processor to redistribute the aircraft tracks which move from one sector to another is an overhead penalty that must be incurred to keep the processing efficiency high. The number of aircraft which move from one sector to a neighboring sector in a 4-second scan can be computed as follows.

Consider a tracking sector, as shown in Figure 8. In 4 seconds, an aircraft with a speed of 240 knots can travel $(240/60) \times (4/60) = 0.27$ nm. Therefore, only those aircraft which are in the shaded area of Figure 8 can possibly move to a different sector in one 4-second scan time. The size of the shaded area is $(0.27 \times 2 \times 60) = 32.4$ nm^2. The size of the whole sector is $(60 \times 12/2) = 3600$ nm^2. Hence the shaded area is about 32.4/3600 or 9% of the total sector area. Assuming that the direction of the aircraft is randomly distributed, then only half of the total aircraft are moving out of the sector. Thus, the percentage of aircraft which moves across the sector boundaries is only about 5% of the total number of aircraft.

The actual processing required to relocate an aircraft track from one PE to another is very small. To locate a processing element that can accept a particular track, either a new one or one from another sector, all PE's are associatively queried as to whether they already contain a track from the sector in question. (Each PE would contain a set of status words indicating the number of tracks from each sector stored in it.) Those PE's not already containing a track from the sector, or containing the least number of tracks from the sector, would be identified and the first available one would be used to store the relocated track. The pieces of data that characterize the track would then be transferred via the PP Control Unit to the selected PE.

Because the percentage of aircraft that must be moved each scan is small (only about 5%) and the amount of parallel processing required to identify and move track data to a new PE is likewise small, the computational load imposed by the track management function in a multi-track/PE parallel processor is very minimal.

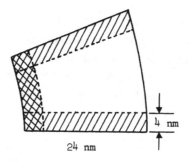

Figure 6. Computation of Repeated Area

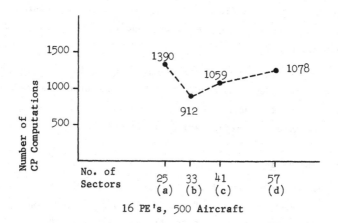

Figure 7. Optimal Number of Sectors

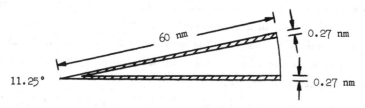

Figure 8. A Tracking Sector and Area for
Possible Crossing Tracks

EXAMPLE OF CONFLICT PREDICTION IN A "PEPE TYPE" PARALLEL PROCESSOR

In this section, an example of how the ATC conflict prediction function could be implemented in a multi-track/PE parallel processor is given. The emphasis in the example will not be in the exact mathematical computations required to detect whether any pair of aircraft are in possible conflict but rather in the mechanics of how the function can be efficiently implemented in the parallel processor. Use is made of the sectorization ideas presented in the previous section.

Conflict Prediction Function

Conflict prediction is not currently implemented in today's ARTS III system. However, the nature of the computation typically envisioned is fairly straight-forward, at least in concept. Normally, an aircraft pair is said to be in a conflict state when the projection (usually straight line) of the aircraft positions over a certain lookahead interval (30 or 60 sec.) results in the separation of the aircraft pair over the interval being less than a specified distance in each of the horizontal and vertical planes.

To determine whether the above conditions have been satisfied, the appropriate distances are computed for the given aircraft with all the other aircraft in its vicinity. If any aircraft is found to be within the specified distance of the aircraft under test, some type of remedial action is in order.

Parallel Processor Description

The type of parallel processor of interest in this example is best character-ized by the Parallel Element Processing Ensemble (PEPE) [1]. The segment of the PEPE architecture that is most applicable to the ATC problem is shown in Figure 9. As evidenced in the figure, the processing requirements of the ATC problem are such that the PEPE Correlation and Associative Output Units [1] are not required.

The parallel processor control unit shown in Figure 9 contains its own program and data memories plus a sequential processing capability to enable the parallel processor to operate either in a stand-alone mode or as an augmentation to a sequential host device requiring very low overhead. The sequential logic of the control unit can be used to execute the serial portions of an algorithm being im-plemented in the parallel processor.

Besides removing the Correlation and Associative Output subunits, the proces-sing element shown in Figure 9 has been modified to make it more applicable to the ATC application in two ways. First, a local indexing capability has been added to the PE. The local indexing capability is required because many ATC computations are table dependent. Without local indexing, these table dependent computations

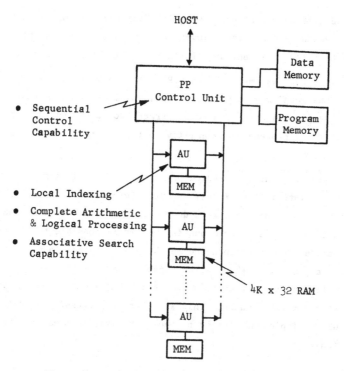

Figure 9.   ATC Parallel Processor Architecture

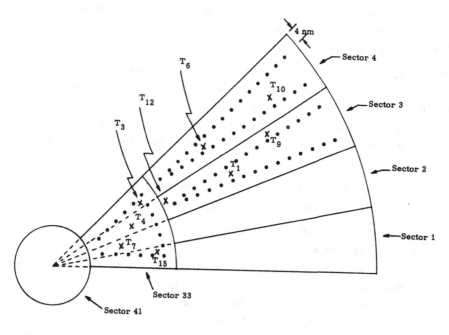

Figure 10.   Example

result in a considerable amount of processing inefficiency. Also, because multiple tracks are stored in each PE, local indexing is needed for a flexible memory addressing scheme to allow efficient use of the available PE memory.

The second change that was made to the PEPE PE shown in Figure 9 was to increase the size of the local data memory to a maximum of 4K 32-bit words. The larger data memory simply allows more aircraft tracks to be stored in each PE and permits a better match of processing capability to the requirements of the ATC problem.

Before going into the conflict prediction example, there is a special processing capability that exists in the processing ensemble shown in Figure 9 that should be mentioned. It is the ability to do associative searches over the ensemble of PE accumulators. What this means is that it is possible to select processing elements for further computation based on the value of their accumulator. Equality, greater-than, and less-than search capabilities are available. It is also possible to select from a set of PE's the PE (or PE's) which contain the largest or smallest accumulator value. This associative processing capability is particularly useful for implementing some of the sectorization ideas presented in the previous section.

Example

In this example, we shall try to demonstrate the mechanics involved in handling the conflict prediction function in a multi-track/PE parallel processor using the sectorization ideas developed earlier.

For the purposes of this example, the sectorization scheme shown in Figure 3 will be used. A portion (Sectors 1,2,3,4,33, and 41) of Figure 3 has been repeated in Figure 10, and the presence of 9 aircraft are indicated. Also, the aforementioned 4 nm test boundaries are shown as dotted lines in sectors 3, 4 and 33 and the extensions of sectors 1,2,3 and 4 for tracking purposes are indicated by the dashed lines.

For this example, it will be assumed that the parallel processor contains only four PE's, each capable of handling multiple aircraft tracks.

Initially, it will be necessary to distribute the tracks shown in Figure 10 across the four available PE's. Recall from the earlier discussion on sectorization that the key idea in the distribution of aircraft is to keep tracks within a given sector spread across as many different PE's as possible. For the tracks shown in Figure 10, T_1, T_9 and T_{12} should be in separate PE's as well as T_3, T_4, T_7 and T_{15}. In sector 4, T_6 and T_{10} should be in different PE's. If these conditions are met, then the conflict prediction function will be executed as efficiently as possible under the problem assumptions.

If, in addition to conflict prediction, tracking will also be executed in the parallel processor, then some additional constraints must be put on the allocation of tracks to processing elements if the same data base is to be shared by both functions. If the sectors shown in Figure 1 are used for the implementation of the tracking function, then tracks T_1, T_4, T_9, T_{12} all lie within the same tracking sector. Therefore, in order to maximize the parallel processor efficiency for tracking, T_1, T_4, T_9, and T_{12} should all reside in different PE's. For the same reason, T_3, T_6, and T_{10} should also be located in separate PE's.

An allocation of tracks to processing elements which satisfies both the conflict prediction and tracking constraints is indicated in Figure 11.

The execution of the conflict prediction function would then take place as follows: in Sector 3, the T_1 track data is transferred from PE 1 to the PP control unit. Then, the PE's which contain other tracks from Sector 3 are activated (PE 2 and PE 3), and the conflict prediction computation is completed. If a conflict situation is detected, an operator is alerted or some similar action is taken. Since T_1 does not lie within 4 nm of any adjacent sector, no additional computations are required for T_1. Next, T_9 would be transferred from PE 2 to the control unit, and the conflict prediction test would be repeated for T_9 and T_{12}. (Note that T_9 was checked against T_1 in the previous test.) Because T_9 lies within 4 nm of an adjacent sector (a fact that is easily determined using the ensemble's associative capability), it must be checked against all the aircraft in sector 4. Therefore, PE 1 and PE 2 would be activated and a check for a possible conflict between T_9 and (T_6, T_{10}) would be made. The last aircraft in sector 3, T_{12}, would then be read out to the control unit. Since T_{12} was already checked against T_1 and T_9 during earlier computations, no check would have to be made with other aircraft in sector 3. However, T_{12} lies within 4 nm of 2 adjacent sectors so two conflict prediction computations would have to be done. One would test T_{12} against (T_6, T_{10}) while the other would test against (T_3, T_4, T_7, T_{15}).

The processing required in sector 4 is minimal. One of the tracks must be transferred to the control unit and a check made against the remaining track. Since neither aircraft in sector 4 is within the 4nm boundary, no additional tests are required.

In sector 33, there are four aircraft but none are within 4 nm of other sectors. Therefore, all that is required is three iterations of the conflict prediction algorithm.

The complete sequence of conflict prediction computations is shown in Table 3.

In examining the example just completed, a few things should be pointed out. First, note how important it is that all the tracks in sector 33 be in different PE's. If this were not the case, then additional computations would be required to

test for all the possible conflicts with T_{12}. Also, more computations would be
required to test for possible conflicts within sector 33 as well. In the above
example, there was a sufficient number of processing elements to meet the maximum
number of tracks in any one sector. If there were more tracks in a sector than

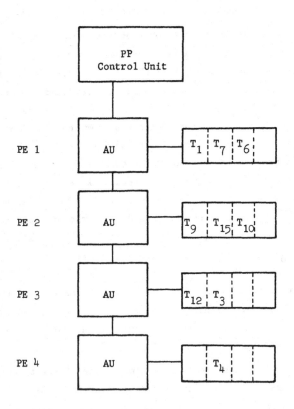

Figure 11. Track/PE Allocation

PE's, then more computation time would be required to allow for additional iterations of the conflict prediction algorithm. As discussed earlier, there is obviously a tradeoff that can be made here between processing time and the number of
processing elements.

REFERENCES

[1] R. O. Berg, S. J. Nuspl, and H. G. Schmitz, "PEPE--An Overview of Architec-
     ture, Operation, and Implementation, Proceedings, National Electronics
     Conference (October, 1972).

Table 1

Percentage of Airspace Repeated

Sectorization Scheme	Number of Sectors	Area Repeated
(a)	25	73%
(b)	33	89%
(c)	41	120%
(d)	57	127%

Table 2

Determination of Optimal Number of Sectors

Sectorization Scheme	Number of Sectors	No. of Aircraft /Sector	No. of Levels of Storage per Sector	No. of CP Algorithm Computations
(a)	25	20	2	1390
(b)	33	15.1	1	912
(c)	41	12.2	1	1059
(d)	57	8.8	1	1078

Total number of aircraft = 500   Total number of processing elements = 16.

Table 3

Conflict Prediction Comparison Sequence

Sector 3
$$\begin{cases} T_1 \to T_9, \ T_{12} \\ T_9 \to T_{12} \\ T_9 \to T_6, \ T_{10} \\ T_{12} \to T_6, \ T_{10} \\ T_{12} \to T_3, \ T_4, \ T_7, \ T_{15} \end{cases}$$

Sector 4 $T_6 \to T_{10}$

Sector 33
$$\begin{cases} T_7 \to T_{15}, \ T_3, \ T_4 \\ T_{15} \to T_3, \ T_4 \\ T_3 \to T_4 \end{cases}$$

AN ASSOCIATIVE PROCESSOR ARCHITECTURE FOR AIR TRAFFIC CONTROL

H. N. BOYD
Goodyear Aerospace Corporation
Akron, Ohio 44315

Abstract -- Hardware architecture is described for an associative processor (AP) designed to augment an existing automated air traffic control system (ATC). Basically, this AP is tailored to the ATC environment from the general purpose associative processor, STARAN[a]. The ACT/AP consists of two identical AP modules to be integrated into an existing ATC system with minimal impact other than to increase the system's capabilities. System availability is a primary consideration in the ATC/AP architecture and in the method of integration into the remainder of the system. The hardware of the ATC/AP is described with particular emphasis on the differences from the more general AP - STARAN - and the method of interfacing to acquire high availability.

INTRODUCTION

The parallel processor, or associative processor, is well suited to many of the automated air traffic control tasks. A companion paper presented at this conference describes the use of the associative processor in the tracking of aircraft [1]. The architecture of such an AP is different from that of the general purpose AP - STARAN.

An AP operating in an automated ATC system must demonstrate a high availability. The architecture of the ATC/AP is tailored to the ATC tasks at hand to increase the efficiency of the operation and reliability. The AP design contains both hardware and software methods of on-line error detection. The ATC/AP system is completely redundant both in the hardware and the method of interface to the remainder of the ATC system.

The architecture[b] of an AP system for use in the ATC environment (ATC/AP) is described with particular emphasis on the differences from the general AP and the use of the redundancy to attain high availability and failsafe operation.

ATC FACILITY ARCHITECTURE

The associative processor described in this paper is designed to augment an existing automated ATC system. The system to be augmented contains multiple input-

---

[a]Trademark, Goodyear Aerospace Corporation, Akron, Ohio 44315.

[b]The ATC/AP architecture development was partially funded by the Transportation System Center of the Department of Transportation under Contract DOT-TSC-624 (Vivian Hobbs, TSC project monitor).

output processors (IOP's) connected to a shared memory system of several 16K word modules. The IOP's receive digitized radar and beacon inputs, provide data required for a bank of display systems, and connect to standard peripherals including disc and magnetic tape used for backup storage. The system is constructed so that if an element of the system malfunctions, the integrity of the system is not lost. The like elements are connected to allow the functions of one to be handled by one of the others, if the first should fault. The system memory capacity allows for sufficient storage should a memory module fault. If an element of the system faults, the system is reconfigured with minimal loss of data. The faulted element is isolated from the operational configuration to be repaired.

The AP augmentation of the system must not hinder the reconfiguration in the event of a malfunction. The augmented system configuration is shown in Figure 1. To maintain operational availability, two identical associative processors are used to augment the system. Either AP is capable of performing any and all associative functions. The chosen method of integrating the AP into the system is to connect the AP as a peripheral to the IOP's. This integration allows the main program executing in the IOP's to assign appropriate functions to the AP with very little impact upon existing software.

To provide for system reconfiguration, connection is made so that either of two IOP's may be in control of either AP. The AP is connected directly to the memory system, which allows for the transfer of data to or from the AP without loading of the IOP's channel. The AP has full access to the memory system which allows for use of data from system data tables and the creation of tables containing the processed data from the AP. Each of the AP's connects to a separate port of the memory system, maintaining the isolation of the AP's.

The resulting AP augmented ATC system is one that exploits the interface hardware and software existing in the original ATC system. There are many functions that can be carried on in parallel (functions the AP performs best). These functions do not require I/O capability and are completely internal to the system. Other functions involving input and output tend to be sequential (better suited to the IOP). The overall functional scheduling and executive control of the system is also a sequential task left to the IOP. From the controller's point of view, the augmented system appears unchanged, although the system is now capable of handling higher traffic density. The use of an AP to perform the parallel type of functions provides for considerable increase in capability without addition of IOP's.

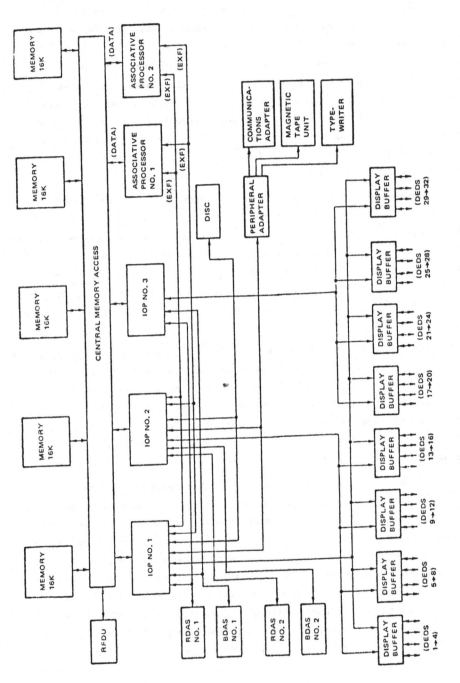

Figure 1 – System Configuration with AP

ATC/AP ARCHITECTURE

Description

The associative processor designed to augment the automated air traffic control system (ATC/AP) is based upon the general purpose AP - STARAN. An AP performing in the air traffic control environment is application oriented. Many of the general functions provided for within the STARAN architecture are not needed in the ATC/AP. Portions of the general AP are not adapted to the function or data encountered by the ATC/AP. By tailoring the architecture of the AP, a less expensive and more reliable system is obtained.

Each of the two ATC/AP's interfaced with the ATC system is identical and contains all control memory, control logic, and associative arrays required of the particular installation. The number of associative arrays required for an installation is dependent upon the number of aircraft to be controlled by that installation and the ATC functions to be performed by the ATC/AP. Each AP with all required interface logic, cooling, and power is contained within its own cabinet completely isolated from the other. The following discussion of the ATC/AP hardware architecture refers to either one of the AP's.

The functional capabilities of the ATC/AP are identical to most of the STARAN functions. The associative type operations are the same as those of STARAN, while the input-output and sequential functions are reduced to the level required for the task at hand.

The basic architecture of the AP is shown in Figure 2. The control memory portion of the AP contains the assembled AP instructions and can also be used for data storage. The program control logic is responsible for maintaining correct program execution. Data transfer to and from control memory and the shared external memory (considered an extension of the control memory addressing) is also controlled by this logic. The associative array control logic is directly responsible for data transfer to and from the arrays and the manipulation of data for an associative operation. The associative arrays (the heart of the AP) may be controlled separately or in parallel by the array control. Each array contains a multidimensional access storage section, permutation network, and a processing element for each word. The external function (EXF) logic enables the program control logic and/or an external processor to control AP operations. The IOP is interfaced to the AP via the EXF logic allowing for control of the AP program flow through EXF code issued by an IOP. The EXF logic also is used to issue an interrupt to an IOP.

Control Memory

The primary function of the control memory is to store the assembled AP instructions. The speed of the control memory directly affects the operating speed

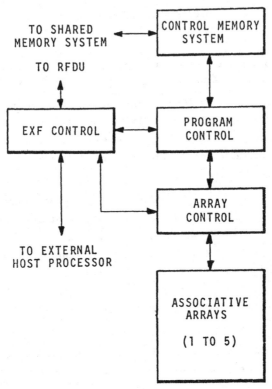

TO SHARED MEMORY SYSTEM

TO RFDU

TO EXTERNAL HOST PROCESSOR

Figure 2 - ATC/AP Block Diagram

of the AP. The control memory system of the STARAN consists of a core memory shared by both the AP control and the sequential processor portion. A system of three high-speed, solid-state pages and pager logic are used in STARAN to provide AP instructions at the required rate. The control memory of the ATC/AP is all solid state. The control memory is divided into two portions; the larger, 32K words, referred to as bulk storage; and the smaller nonvolatile, 2K words, referred to as read only memory (ROM).

The bulk storage portion of control memory is implemented using N-channel MOS random access memory and the interleaving technique. The effective access and cycle time of the bulk storage memory is about 0.2 microsecond. For some 80 percent of the AP instructions, the bulk store is faster than the execution time. Only 20 percent of the instructions are limited by the control memory cycle time. The instructions with execution times less than 0.2 microsecond are all of the associative subroutines. An optional small-fast cache memory module is used, if required by the installation (aircraft load), to decrease the effective bulk storage cycle time. The cache contains 16 words of very fast solid-state storage. The access time of the cache is less than 0.1 microsecond, which exceeds the execution time of all AP instructions. The small instruction loops that make up the associative subroutines and contain most of the "fast" AP instructions fit the constraints of the small cache nicely. The cache is transparent to the software and the remainder of the hardware.

The solid-state bulk storage memory with the cache allows operating speed comparable to the STARAN with its page memory system. The physical size of the solid-state bulk store is comparable to that of the page memories, pager, and memory bus system that it replaces. The page memories, as well as the pager, are deleted for the ATC/AP control memory. The memory bus system is reduced by deletion of buses that provide for pager, sequential control and external device access of the bulk core memory. Advances in solid-stage technologies (the number of bits of storage per chip) allow for the full 32K words of bulk store with the simplified bus system and cache to be implemented without physical size increase over the STARAN control memory system. The core memory system used in STARAN is deleted resulting in additional space savings. The use of solid-state for the control memory increases the reliability.

The nonvolatile portion of control memory is used to store programs that must be permanently available. This portion is implemented using solid-state read-only memory, (ROM). The 2K words of ROM contain the initialization (bootstrap) program that the AP uses to load the AP's main program into control memory. The ROM portion of control memory also contains an AP verification program that is executed by the AP as a self check in the event of a system failure. If one of the AP's should fail the verification check, the system is notified and that AP is excluded from the operational system until repaired. Other AP error checking and diagnostic programs are executed from the bulk store portion of control memory.

The control memory stores 32 bit words with an additional bit for parity. Each word is checked for correct parity at the time it is read. If parity is incorrect, the access is retried before posting of a parity error to the system. An instruction from control memory with incorrect parity is not executed.

Program Control Logic

The program control logic controls the AP program flow. The instructions are fetched from the control memory and loaded into the 32-bit instruction register. The address for the instruction fetch is contained in the program counter. The program counter and a four-bit interrupt mask make up the program status word. When one of the fifteen AP control interrupts occurs, it is checked against the interrupt mask. If the interrupt level is higher than the mask level, the interrupt is accepted and the next instruction, a swap program status word, is fetched from the appropriate interrupt vector location. The program control also contains a data bus used to move data to and from the control memory and between internal registers. A data pointer and a block length counter may be used to transfer blocks of data to or from control memory or external memory. A portion of the program control executes certain types of AP instruction held in the instruction register. The execution of AP instructions is performed in an asynchronous manner. The required phases or operations are done in the correct order, each following the other with no time lost awaiting clock controlled phases. The completion of the last required operation releases the program control to load the next instruction for execution into the instruction register. The four instruction types executed by this logic are: 1) register, 2) branch, 3) loop, and 4) EXF.

The register type of instruction is used to effect moving of data from control memory or external memory to a register and vice versa. Data may also be moved from internal register to register. Indexing of the memory address is also provided using the data pointer. The data bus used to move the data allows for left end around shifts by 0-, 8-, 16-, or 24-bit positions.

The branch instruction is used to modify the program counter as a function of certain internal conditions such as a register equal to zero. The branch instruction has address indexing using either the data pointer or one of either return jump registers. The return jump registers are loaded by a branch and link instruction to allow for returns to the main program.

The loop instruction makes use of a set of hardware markers used to implement a first-level program loop. The start and end instruction addresses of the loop are stored in markers. The number of times the loop is to be repeated is loaded into a counter and decremented each time the loop is executed. When the counter equals zero, normal program flow is resumed.

The EXF instruction issues a 19-bit code to the EXF control logic. The EXF logic is discussed later.

Associative Array Control Logic

The function of the associative array control is to control data manipulation within the arrays. The array control provides addresses, control parameters, and timing pulses required to operate the array. The arrays are controlled in parallel or separately as a function of the array control. A system of field pointers are used to select the area of the array involved in the operation. The resolution of the responses from the array and conversion to usable data is also performed by array control. A common register, 32 bits, is used to contain the argument for a common search operation, the input data to be stored into an array, or the output data from an array. The array output data is loaded through a mask, which allows formatting of an output word from noncontiguous data in the array. Field pointers generally contain bit slice or word addresses in the associative array operation. The field length counters control the number of bits to be operated on in sequence. There are three field pointers and two field length counters. The array control logic executes the associative type of instruction. The control lines required by the processing element (PE), response store, are generated directly from the instruction. The precise timing of control signals to the array is controlled by the array control logic. The selection of which array or arrays are involved in an operation is also made by the array control.

Associative Array

The associative array is the key element of the AP. The ATC/AP may have from one to six identical arrays. The array used for the ATC/AP differs from the array used in STARAN. Figure 3 shows a block diagram of the associative array. The array contains only 64 words and PE's as compared to 256 for the STARAN array. The storage portion of the array is extended in the bit direction to either 1024 or 2048 bits per word unlike the 256 bits per word of the STARAN array. The resulting array is more tailored to the type of data to be processed in the ATC/AP. Due to the permutation network and the PE's of an array, the cost and physical size of an array is much more dependent upon the number of words than the number of bits. The reduction from 256 to 64 words results in a considerable array cost savings while increasing reliability. The increase in bits per word has little effect upon the amount of hardware due to the advancing state-of-the-art in the size of standard solid-state RAM integrated circuits.

The reduction in the number of PE's reduces the parallel capabilities of the array hardware from that of STARAN. The use of the extended array word as multiple track files tends to increase the processing time. The busy time of the AP is increased by the sharing of PE's by more than one track file yet the overall maximum percent of time the AP is active is less than 70 percent. The increase in processing efficiency is a result of reducing the parallelism of the arrays to that required by the system.

The ATC/AP array module contains a multi-dimensional-access (MDA) memory communicating with three 64-bit registers (M, X, and Y) through a flip (permutation) network. In effect, the array has 64 small processing elements (PE's). Each PE contains one bit of each of the three registers. The M register holds the mask used when performing a mask write into the MDA memory. Unmask writes are also allowed. The M register may be loaded from any of the other components of the array. The X and Y registers are the working registers of the PE's. The logic associated with the X and Y registers of the PE can perform any of the 16 Boolean functions of two variables. The X and Y may be operated together or separately. Selective operation of X using Y as a mask is also allowed. The Y may also be operated on while being used to mask X operation; Y is changed after the X operation.

The array module differs from the one used in STARAN [2] only in that the number of words and PE's is 64 instead of 256 and that the MDA memory is extended in the bit direction. The MDA memory is considered as either 16 or 32 folds, 64 bits by 64 words, sharing the 64 PE's.

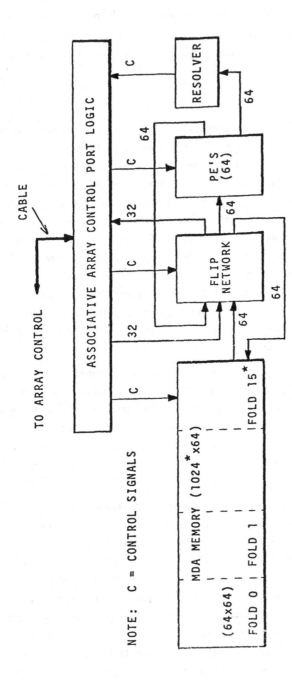

Figure 3. Associative Array Module

The MDA memory contains either 65,536 (2^{16}) or 131,082(2^{17}) bits of storage organized in 64 words. An address map of the array storage is shown in Figure 4. The 1024 or 2048 bits per word is a function of the installation requirement (aircraft load). To accommodate both bit-slice accesses for associative processing and word-slice accessess for data input/output, the data are stored in a multi-dimensional-access (MDA) memory. It has wide read and write buses for parallel access to a large number (64) of memory bits. Memory accesses (both read and write) are controlled by the address and access mode control inputs. The bit slices are selected by an eleven-bit address. Access in the word direction is made using the

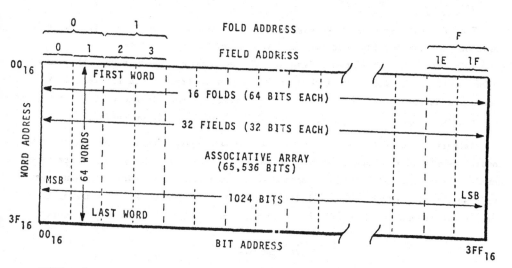

NOTE: FOR 2048 BIT BY 64 WORD ARRAY ALL HORIZONTAL LENGTHS ARE DOUBLED EXCEPT THAT THE BITS PER FIELD AND FOLD REMAIN 32 AND 64, RESPECTIVELY.

Figure 4. Associative Array Address Map.

most significant five bits to select one of the 16 or 32 folds. The word within
that fold is addressed by the least significant six bits. The multi-dimensional-
access technique used for each fold (64 by 64) is the same as that used in STARAN's
256 x 256 array. The extension of the array from the 256 bits per word to 1024 bits
per word is accomplished by use of a standard 1024 bit random access memory chip
instead of the 256 bit chip used in the STARAN array. To provide 2048 bits per word
(where required), two chips are installed in the array for each word.

External Function Logic

The external function (EXF) logic is used to control numerous functions within
the AP. These include AP and IOP interrupt, AP activity control, resets, and clears.
Control and status sensing of these functions are accomplished by issuing a 19-bit
EXF command to the EXF logic and receiving a one-bit sense signal in return.

The EXF logic allows for receipt of EXF commands from the AP program control
logic or from the IOP interface logic. A resolver in the EXF logic resolves any
conflicts among the two elements issuing EXF codes and allows only one EXF command
to be treated at a time. The interrogation and/or control called for in the EXF
command is performed and then any other EXF command present is accepted. A function
code can interrogate for status and control an element in one operation.

As part of the EXF logic, a set of flip-flops is provided for posting of error
conditions should they occur or for benchmarks as the on-line diagnostics are executed. These error stores can be sensed or set using EXF commands. Certain ones
are also set by hardware signals indicating hardware malfunction. The use of the
error store speeds the detection and verification of a malfunction if it occurs.

ATC/AP INTERFACES

Each ATC/AP has its own interface logic, level translators, and line driver/
receiver circuits for all required interfaces. The AP is directly interfaced to two
IOP input/output channels, one requester port to the shared memory system, and a
common interrupt line used by all processors to indicate processor malfunction. The
input/output channel to the IOP is used to transfer EXF commands to the AP and to
send interrupt commands to the IOP. Data are transferred by the AP to and from the
shared memory using its direct memory access port. The scatter interrupt connection,
used to start the system reconfiguration process if a fault occurs, is both driven
and sensed by each processor (IOP or AP) in the installation.

Interface to the IOP's

The IOP interface connection allows the IOP to control the operation of the AP
via EXF commands. This interface takes the place of the sequential control portion
of a STARAN. The STARAN, because of its general purpose and stand-alone features,

requires a dedicated closely integrated sequential processor. The sequential processor provides for such general functions as 1) peripheral control for input and output of data, 2) a communication link to the operator, 3) off-line capabilities for assembling and debugging STARAN programs, and 4) control for diagnostic and test programs. Because of the more defined tasks required of the ATC/AP, most general and I/O functions are removed from the ATC/AP. The sequential functions required of the ATC/AP are most efficiently done by one of the IOP's. By providing for direct control via EXF's of the AP by the IOP, the sequential control hardware is not required. The deletion of the sequential control hardware both lowers the cost and raises the reliability of the AP.

The IOP to AP connection is only used to pass control commands and interrupts. Data are transferred between the AP and IOP by using "mailbox" locations in the memory system shared by the IOP's and AP's.

Each AP is connected to the input/output channels of two IOP's. This connection allows the AP to be treated as a peripheral of either IOP in the event that the other IOP is down. The interface logic is such that only one IOP may control the AP at a time. The IOP requesting control of the AP must first issue a predefined EXF command. If the AP is not under the control of the other IOP, the connection will be made, placing the AP under direct control of that IOP. Once the connection has been made, the controlling IOP issues EXF commands to the AP and receiver sense information in return. The IOP may issue any of the EXF commands that the AP control issues, in addition to the special commands used to connect to or disconnect from the AP. An IOP connected to the AP may receive interrupts from the AP.

EXF commands from an IOP are handled in the same manner as those issued by AP control. Since most EXF codes issued by the AP control allow for the sensing of single bit information, the same capability is given the IOP issued command. The sense information is returned to the IOP on its data input channel. If the answer to the EXF code is true, Bit 4 is set; if false, Bit 0 is set in the input channel data buffer. The IOP must set up the input buffer for sense information. The format used to issue an EXF command from the IOP is as shown in Figure 5. EXF commands issued by the IOP differ in one respect in that if it is not desired to have

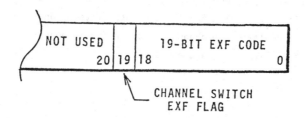

Figure 5. External Function Control Word Format

a sense return loaded into the input buffer, the two least significant bits in the EFCW should be cleared.

Once the connection between IOP and AP is made, interrupts can be sent to the IOP via the IOP input channel. The interrupt is issued by the AP via the EXF logic. A five-bit vector code is placed on the data input channel (least significant five bits) as the interrupt is generated.

Error detection is also performed in the interface logic. EXF commands from the IOP are checked for correct parity. An attempt to connect the AP to more than one IOP, or to control an AP that is not connected, causes errors to be indicated.

Interface to Memory

The interface connection to the shared memory system allows for data transfer between the AP and any other processor in the system. Transfer of data at this interface is under the AP's control. The shared memory is accessed directly by the AP using an extension of its control memory addresses. The shared memory system is made up of from one to fifteen modules each containing 16K words and a reconfiguration-fault detection unit (RFDU), which is addressable as a memory module.

The AP uses a sliding window approach to accessing the possible 256K locations of the shared memory. The AP uses address 4000_{16} to $7FFF_{16}$ to access the memory module. In this region of address, only the least significant 14 bits of AP address are passed on to the memory module along with a memory module enable signal as decoded from four bits of the memory module register contained in the interface logic. Figure 6 shows an address map of AP control memory and the shared memory modules.

A lockout register, located in the least significant 16 bits of the module register, provides protection against the AP reading or writing protected areas of the memory module. The protection is applied over 2K word segments of the selected memory module. The format of the module register is shown in Figure 7. Bits 16 through 23 determine the read-protected areas, and Bits 24 through 31 determine the write-protected areas. Should an access be attempted by the AP that violates the protection portion of the register, an error store in the interface is set and the AP notified.

The module register of the memory interface logic is assigned a dedicated control memory address (1000_{16}). Altering the contents of the module register to access different memory modules or to change lockout codes is done by the AP writing the least significant 20 bits of AP address 1000_{16}.

413

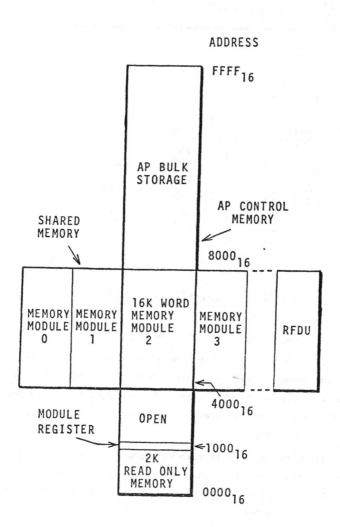

Figure 6. Control Memory Map

```
┌─────────────────────────────────────────────────────┐
│ 12   15│16 READ   23│24    WRITE      31│
│        │   PROTECT  │     PROTECT        │
└─────────────────────────────────────────────────────┘
  ↑
  └ MODULE
    ADDRESS
```

BIT POSITION		ABSOLUTE AP MEMORY
		ADDRESSES AFFECTED
READ	WRITE	(HEX)
23	31	4000 TO 47FF
22	30	4800 4FFF
21	29	5000 57FF
20	28	5800 5FFF
19	27	6000 67FF
18	26	6800 6FFF
17	25	7000 77FF
16	24	7800 7FFF

Figure 7. Module Register Format

Interface to the Reconfiguration-Fault Detection Unit(RFDU)

The AP, like the other processors of the system, communicates primarily with
the RFDU in the same manner as with a memory module. The RFDU is loaded with status
information about each element in the system. These data are used to configure the
active system. The modules not required to be active are configured so that testing
and maintenance may be performed.

Direct interface with the RFDU is also required. Each processor sends a signal
to the RFDU to indicate an airflow failure should one occur. The RFDU distributes
scatter interrupt inhibit signals to each inactive processor to ensure complete
isolation from the active system.

FAILSAFE OPERATION

Failsafe operation of the ATC facility augmented by the AP is dependent upon
the ability of the AP, as well as other processors, to detect a malfunction as soon
as it occurs. Once a malfunction is detected in the AP and the scatter interrupt
issued, the system must reconfigure with the faulty AP no longer part of the active
system. The faulted AP must then be repaired and made available to the system as
soon as possible.

The AP contains both hardware and software methods for on-line error detection. When a hardware fault condition is detected by either the hardware or software in the AP system, an internal error indicator is set and an interrupt is scattered to the entire system. The scatter interrupt forces all processors to their respective self verification routines.

The AP raises the scatter interrupt line when any internal error store (flip-flop) is set and the interrupt inhibit from the RFDU is not present. These error stores are set by hardware error-detected faults and software error-detection routines. Hardware detected faults include:

1. Parity errors on internal memory buses
2. Internal memory bus timeouts
3. Airflow failure
4. Overtemperature
5. Partial loss of power (one power supply malfunction)

Software error detection routines include both on-line diagnostic executed during idle time and ATC functional checks such as test tracks flying precomputed flight plans. If any error is found by the software routines, an error store is set.

The AP responds to a scatter interrupt in much the same manner that the other processors do. When a scatter interrupt is received, the AP is forced to execute the verification program stored in the read only portion of AP control memory. If the AP is inactive, it is forced to start executing the self-check routine. If the AP is active, it is halted, cleared, and restarted at the self-check routine.

The verification routine is designed to work with the systems multiprocessor execution (MPE) program. The routine contains all necessary software to test the AP, boot load, and cooperate with the MPE recovery module. The heart of the routine is the self-diagnosis programs contained in the verify module. These are a subset of the off-line diagnostics and will detect failures and isolate them to particular areas of hardware for further diagnosing and isolation off-line. The steps executed in the verify module are:

1. An instruction test including EXF, branch, register, and associative operations
2. An internal memory test
3. A main memory test to attempt access to all memory modules

The AP halts if an error occurs in the verify tests. The AP must also be able to access at least two of the memory modules. Upon completion of the verify tests, the AP will store its status into all memory modules as does the other processors. From this point the recovery procedure is left to the IOP's recovery program, which configures an operation system via the RFDU. The faulted modules are excluded from the system and then are repaired. The off-line diagnostic routines used to isolate the fault and verify the repairs are structured so that the mean time to repair (MTTR) is 30 minutes. The use of redundancy of the AP modules provides the high availability required for ATC operation. The availability is expected to be 0.9^7360 based upon the MTTR of 0.5 hour.

REFERENCES

[1] E. E. Eddey and W. C. Meilander, <u>Application of an Associative Processor to Aircraft Tracking</u>, GER-16128, Goodyear Aerospace Corporation (20 August 1974).

[2] K. E. Batcher, <u>STARAN/RADCAP Hardware Architecture</u>, GER-15947, Goodyear Aerospace Corporation, 22 August 1973. Paper published in <u>Proceedings of the 1973 Sagamore Computer Conference on Parallel Processing</u>. Syracuse University in cooperation with IEEE and ACM, Syracuse, New York, 22-24 August 1973, pp. 147-154.

APPLICATION OF AN ASSOCIATIVE PROCESSOR TO AIRCRAFT TRACKING

E. E. EDDEY and W. C. MEILANDER
Goodyear Aerospace Corporation
1210 Massillon Road
Akron, Ohio 44315

Abstract -- Aircraft tracking is the process in which successive scans of radar target returns are used to derive the estimated position and velocity of an aircraft. The process consists of sensor report to track correlation as well as smoothing and prediction of track position. With an associative processor the tracking algorithms are changed from those used with a sequential processor. These changes exploit the parallel processing capabilities of the associative processor. Lower track drop and track swap as well as improved track performance should result. The functional operation of the associative processor based system is described and timing data are presented. Approximately 6.7 percent of the associative processor capacity is utilized for the radar tracking function in a 1000-aircraft two-sensor environment.

INTRODUCTION

Aircraft tracking is the process in which successive scans of radar target returns are used to derive the estimated position and velocity of an aircraft. By making use of information from previous scans, the tracking operation reduces the scan-to-scan uncertainty of the sensor systems. The process consists of three functions: correlation of sensor reports with the tracks, smoothing of the data in accordance with some criteria, and prediction of the track positions for use in further tracking.

In an air traffic control (ATC) application, the tracking process is the key operation in providing greater assistance to the air traffic controller through increased automation. Since tracking provides velocity information, this operation is required for the automation of such ATC functions as conflict detection and resolution, terrain avoidance, automatic hand-off, and flight plan performance checking. Tracking permits automatic identification of primary radar-only targets and non-discrete beacon targets and supports more useful display outputs. Finally tracking provides the controller with the best possible estimate of aircraft position and velocity.

The tracking accuracy requirements vary for the functions mentioned above. The conflict detection, resolution, and terrain avoidance operations require more accuracy than the display and automatic handoff functions.

To provide good tracking performance, the computer to be used for the tracking operation should have sufficient capacity to provide for three-dimensional tracking of all aircraft in the environment. This capacity is necessary to minimize the probability that tracks are dropped and that crossing tracks will swap identity. Tracking should make use of the full set of information available from the sensors. For example, information about report signal strength, and the information from overlapping sensors provide for better track performance.

Optimal tracker performance should minimize: track drop, track swap, position error, speed error, and heading error. This performance is dependent on: sensor error, number of sensors, track-to-report correlation techniques, and non-linear adaptability of the smoothing function.

Currently, the aircraft tracking functions are being performed by sequential processors. This paper will discuss the application of a parallel processor, the associative processor, to these functions. In this application the parallel search capabilities of the associative processor are used in the correlation functions while the parallel arithmetic capabilities of the associative processor are used in the track smoothing and prediction operations.

With an associative processor the relation between the tracking operation as described in this paper and some of the other operations in the ATC system are as indicated in Figure 1. The sensor data that will establish target reports are delivered to an input buffer for sensor within beam (sweep-to-sweep) correlation, report generation, and radar/beacon correlation. These operations may be performed at least in part in special-purpose sensor processors. The target reports are sent to a buffer that is part of the associative processor. This buffer is provided so that the tracking operation may take place in parallel over a sizable segment (usually 45 to 90 deg.) of the sensor coverage.

The smooth flow of data through the ATC system is indicated in Figure 1. There need be no feedback of data from one processing block to another or transfer of partial results between processing blocks. Since all the track processing is performed internal to the associative processor, the input requirements on the associative processor are low and utilize a fraction of one percent of the associative processor capacity. The track information is then available for the other operations that require it.

The remainder of this paper will first describe the way in which the tracking algorithms are influenced by the availability of the associative processor. Then functional operations with an associative processor-based system are discussed.

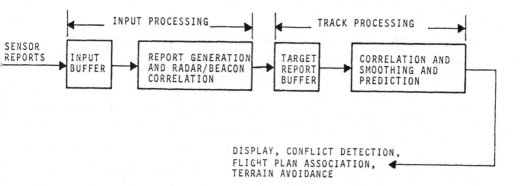

Figure 1 - Relation of Tracking to Other ATC Functions

CORRELATION

Correlation is the process by which target reports are received from the sensor and are correlated with past track data to form new information about each aircraft track. For correlation, the report must be tested and compared in some fashion with each aircraft track that the new data might support. In a sequential processor this usually involves ordering the track data into azimuth sectors. As the antenna scans, the reports from each azimuth sector are buffered. Then, each of the reports is compared with each of the tracks in that sector and if necessary, adjacent sectors. Thus in a sequential processor, the worst case amount of time spent is roughly proportional to the product of the number of reports and the number of tracks in a sector. In the associative processor, since each report can be compared with the entire track set in one operation, the processing time is proportional to the number of reports. Although techniques can be applied to sequential algorithms to reduce the N square figure, it is not necessary to concern one's self with the problem when using an AP. This demonstrates one of the advantages of parallelism in tracking.

SMOOTHING AND PREDICTION

A second function in tracking is smoothing of the data in a tracker. Smoothing involves the evaluation of the quality of correlation of a report with a track, the determination of the smoothing coefficients to be used, and the smoothing of the data. The use of dynamic coefficients is a change in the algorithm that is possible due to the availability of processing times introduced by the presence of an AP in the system.

Dynamic smoothing is the process of selecting weighting functions so that optimum tracking is achieved. The weighting is a function of: (1) distance between track predicted position and report position, (2) hit/miss/ambiguity criteria, and (3) expected aircraft acceleration. In a conventional computer because of the selection processing time, the smoothing may be only bivalued and a function of only Items 1 or 2 above. The process is executed once for each track. In an associative processor the process is executed in parallel for all tracks.

Prediction involves the use of the developed track rates to determine an estimate of the position that the aircraft will occupy at the next observation. This function can also be carried out in parallel over the set of tracks being predicted at any given time.

Compromises are sometimes made in a sequential processor because of processor, or memory limitations, when tracking large numbers of aircraft. Some of these compromises are: tracking only certain classes of aircraft, using only two correlation boxes, limiting weighting functions to a small set, abandoning useful data in sensor overlap regions, ignoring altitude tracking, using less adequate coordinate transforms in changing datum coordinates, and updating tracks less frequently.

DATA ORGANIZATION

Differences also exist between the sequential and parallel processing approach to tracking in the way which the data are organized. Three approaches to organization are considered.

The first organization of the data might be one in which data about one track is gathered in one contiguous set of memory locations. Consider that data within the set is unformatted and the sets of data are unordered. Processing time to organize the data is minimized, but association of related items and data access often will involve searching through the entire data base. Since data within the set is unformatted, storage is increased because each data item in each set must include identification of its specific track attribute.

A second organization would reduce storage by formatting data within the set. In this organization a specific number of contiguous words is allocated to a track. Each of the track attributes is located at a specific position or field in the set of words describing a track. In this second organization, association or access of data is achieved by interrogating given fields of all tracks. Data received about a particular track are entered into the specific attribute fields of that track. Tracks exiting the area are abandoned for lack of data and their space made available for new tracks. Since the tracks are unordered, each new track is merely entered into an available area of storage.

In a sequential computer the many accesses to specific data leads to a third organization to minimize search processing time. Data in storage can be accessed most readily if a specific address for the data is known. Or, failing a specific address, a small number of addresses can be examined for the data. A realistic approach involves developing an ordered list for each of the attributes to be accessed frequently, and then searching the desired attribute list. A specific item in this ordered list can be located in t trials where $t = 1 + \log_2 n$ and n = number of items in the list.

However, the development of an ordered list for each attribute to be used in accessing the data base requires: (1) considerable processing time to maintain the list, and (2) additional storage to provide for linking the associated attributes of a given aircraft track.

In contrast the AP can effectively use the second organization for data without incurring the search overhead necessary in a sequential processor. The highly dynamic data about a given track are stored in a contiguous space within one word in the associative array. Other sets of data to be used in updating the track information can also be stored in other fields of the same word to take advantage of the parallelism of the AP. Searching and processing can take place on all words in parallel. Table I shows a data arrangement that can be used to optimize machine throughput.

In Table I, 512 bits in the array word are designated as processing scratch pad. For the tracking operation, these bits are arranged as shown. The same array space can be used, at other times, for radar target detection, display processing, and conflict evaluation and resolution.

The contents of each field is shown in Tables II through V. Each symbol is described. The subfield bit length is shown and the least significant bit (LSB) value is given if definable.

Table I - Array Data Organization

	A	B	C	D	E, etc.
			Field		
Bit location	0 191	192 319	320 447	448 511	512
Array words (64n n≠0)	Permanent Track Data (192 bits)	Temporary Track Data (128 bits)	Current Report Data (128 bits)	Tentative Track Store (64 bits)	Permanent Track Store

Scratch pad area

Table II – Permanent Track Data

Symbol	Bits	LSB	Description
BEAC	12	–	Beacon code
LDC	12	–	Last different beacon code
XS	13	1/32 nm	Smoothed X position
YS	13	1/32 nm	Smoothed Y position
XDOT	9	2^{-10} nm/sec	X velocity
YDOT	9	2^{-10} nm/sec	Y velocity
HR	12	100 ft	Reported mode C altitude
HP	13	12-1/2 ft	Predicted altitude
HDOT	9	3-1/8 ft/sec	Altitude rate
ACID LOC	16	–	ACID location in control memory
Q	1	Weak/strong	Quality of last report
CST	1	Yes/no	Coast state
TRKFRM	4	1 of 16	Track quality state
MODC	1	Yes/no	Altitude reporting track
SPI	1	Yes/no	Identification squawk
ALTCT	2	Yes/no	Altitude firmness count
ALTVAL	1	Yes/no	Altitude report valid
CODVAL	1	Yes/no	Beacon code report valid
LDCCT	2	–	Last different code repeat counter
UPDAT	1	Yes/no	Track ready for smoothing
RADAR	1	Yes/no	Radar report correlated
BEACR	1	Yes/no	Beacon report correlated
BOX	2	–	Small, medium or large correlation box
ALTCOR	1	Yes/no	Altitude correlated
LDCCOR	1	Yes/no	Last different code correlated
CODCOR	1	Yes/no	Beacon code correlated
BB	1	Yes/no	Track location active
CONF	5	–	Conflict status
CONT	1	Yes/no	Controlled track
CONT ID	6	1 of 64	Controller identity
HAND	1	Yes/no	Handoff in process
RCV ID	6	1 of 64	Receiver identity
TDS ADD	16	–	Address of permanent track data in array
TOTAL	176		

Table III - Temporary Track Data

Symbol	Bits	LSB	Description
XP	13	1/32 nm	Predicted X position
YP	13	1/32 nm	Predicted Y position
θP	12	0.088 deg	Predicted azimuth
RP	13	1/32 nm	Predicted range
RTL	13	1/32 nm	Track correlation box, lower range
RTU	13	1/32 nm	Track correlation box, upper range
θTL	12	0.088 deg	Track correlation box, lower azimuth
θTU	12	0.088 deg	Track correlation box, upper azimuth
RR or XR	13	1/32 nm	Correlated report range or X value
θR or YR	12	0.088 deg	Correlated report azimuth or Y value
TOTAL	126		

Table IV - Current Report Data

Symbol	Bits	LSB	Description
RR	13	1/32 nm	Report range
θR	12	0.088 deg	Report azimuth
HR	12	100 ft	Report altitude
HVAL	1	Yes/no	Report altitude valid
BEAC	12	–	Report beacon code
BEACVAL	1	Yes/no	Report beacon code valid
Q	1	Strong/Weak	Report quality
RADR	1	Yes/no	Report is radar
BEACR	1	Yes/no	Report is beacon
RRL	13	1/32 nm	Report range, lower box limit
RRU	13	1/32 nm	Report range, upper box limit
θRL	12	0.088 deg	Report azimuth, lower box limit
θRU	12	0.088 deg	Report azimuth, upper box limit
HRL	12	100 ft	Report altitude, lower box limit
HRU	12	100 ft	Report altitude, upper box limit
TOTAL	126		

Table V - Tentative Track Store

Parameter	Bits	LSB	Description
RTT1	12	1/16 nm	First report range
RTT2	12	1/16 nm	Last report range
HIT	1	Yes/no	Correlation occurred
HITCT	3	1	Hit count
θTT1	12	0.088 deg	First report azimuth
θTT2	12	0.088 deg	Last report azimuth
TIMS1	3	1/scan	Time since first hit
LAST	3	1/scan	Last hit time
TOTAL	58		

FUNCTIONAL OPERATION

Figure 2 shows the functional flow in tracking (boxes with double lines indicate parallel processes). Both primary (radar) and secondary (beacon) returns are received from the sensor system. The individual returns from each interrogation pulse are evaluated to determine the existence of a target and to determine a best estimate of target position. The primary and secondary reports then are correlated to yield a combined report - if such a combination can be found. Both combined and uncombined reports from the primary/secondary process are accumulated in a buffer (Table IV items to and including BEACR) for a predetermined time period. When the time period is up, the ATC executive calls the tracking function. Tracking then selects (via a parallel search) those aircraft tracks, from the permanent track file, that may correlate with the buffered reports. These selected tracks are moved from permanent space to temporary space of Field A (Table I).

Track correlation is carried out by setting up positional limits about each primary, secondary, or combined report. The limits are a function of the sensor error, report range, and report quality. Separate limits are also set up about each track. The limits are the track level and a function of the track quality. The limits describe enclosed areas called "boxes".

The separate limits about the sensor report position and track position are a departure from conventional processing and effectively reduce the total correlation box size. The increased computing operations are difficult in a sequential processor, but are carried out easily in the associative processor. The report limits are merely added (in parallel) to the report positions before the other correlation operations take place. The operations are somewhat more complex in a

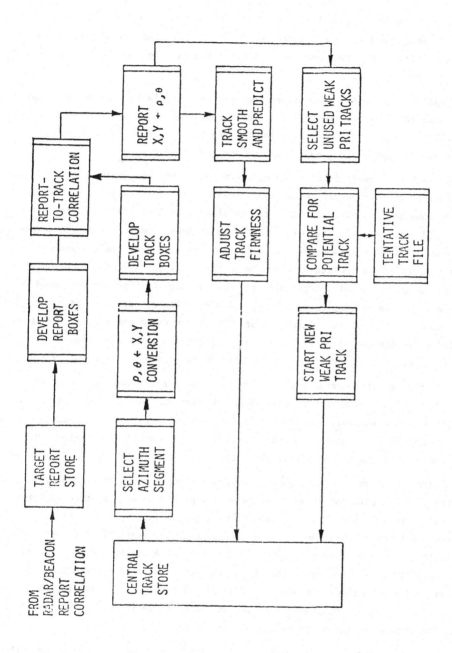

Figure 2 – Correlation and Tracking Functional Flow

sequential processor, especially if special correlation algorithms have been used to reduce the overall correlation processing time. Therefore sequential processor correlation algorithms have employed positional limits only about the track position to save processing time.

To minimize correlation box sizes further, the correlation operation is carried out in radar coordinates. Box sizes in radar coordinates are one-half or less of those in X,Y coordinates. The box sizes for the best report and track quality can be quite small, representing approximately one sigma radar error.

Correlation proceeds by determining the intersection of report boxes. This determination is made by passing each report sequentially against all the tracks in parallel, thus the algorithm is both sequential and parallel. Reports that correlate in the small box are associated with correlating tracks. Medium boxes are developed about those tracks that did not correlate in the small box correlation process. Those reports that did not correlate with tracks in the small box are passed against the medium box developed about uncorrelated tracks. A large box is then developed about uncorrelated tracks and any remaining reports are tested against the large box. Reports that do not satisfy the large box are used to initiate new tracks. New tracks are retained in the system until track history indicates them to be either valid aircraft or noise. Noise tracks when so identified are eliminated from the system.

After the set of reports are correlated with the tracks and new tracks are initiated, the track firmness for each track is updated. This process, unlike correlation, proceeds entirely in parallel for all tracks that have been updated during the last sector. As a function of the track quality, smoothing coefficients are established in the track and smoothing is performed.

The state diagram for track quality determination is shown in Figure 3. In this diagram track firmness is increased when the predicted and reported positions match well. Track firmness is decreased when larger deviations exist between the predicted and reported positions, or when a report is not available for correlation with the track. States 8 through 10 are coast states. A coast condition occurs when an anticipated correlation is missed or ambiguous. Missed correlations decrease track firmness through state 3 to states 8, 9 and 10. At state 10, the history in the track is considered useless and the track is dropped. Four to eight consecutive misses are necessary before a track is dropped.

Following smoothing, the predicted positions of the tracks are developed. The operations of smoothing and prediction are performed on all of the tracks in parallel. The data then are ready for other uses of the track file such as display outputting, conflict detection and resolution, terrain avoidance, automatic handoff, and flight plan association.

The associative processor discussed in this paper is described in greater

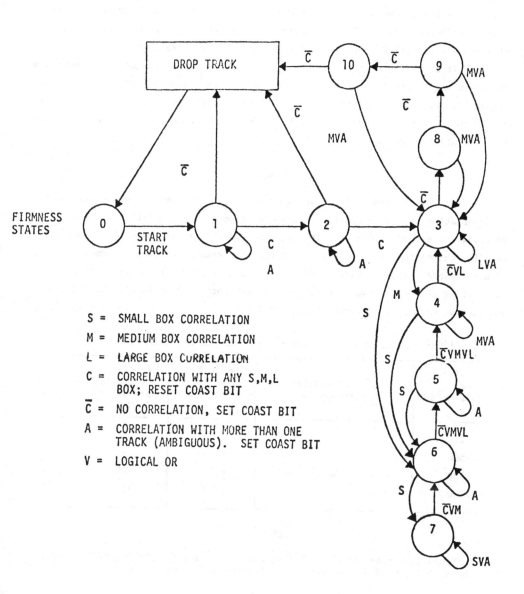

S = SMALL BOX CORRELATION

M = MEDIUM BOX CORRELATION

L = LARGE BOX CORRELATION

C = CORRELATION WITH ANY S,M,L BOX; RESET COAST BIT

$\overline{C}$ = NO CORRELATION, SET COAST BIT

A = CORRELATION WITH MORE THAN ONE TRACK (AMBIGUOUS). SET COAST BIT

V = LOGICAL OR

Figure 3 – Track Firmness State Diagram

detail in a companion paper [1] presented at this conference. The percent time for the associative processor to perform the tracking functions in a two-sensor environment at different traffic loads is shown in Table VI. The percent time for a sequential processor (with 0.6 MIPS capacity) to perform the same function is also included. It should be noted, however that the timing comparison is quite rough since the basic algorithms that are compared differ in some respects. For example, the sequential processor develops turning trial tracks; the associative algorithm need not do this. Also altitude tracking is performed in the AP, but is not required in the sequential algorithm.

SUMMARY

A data organization and set of algorithms have been described for efficient implementation of the aircraft tracking operation on an associative processor[a]. By using the methods discussed, it should be possible to automate this important air traffic control function effectively in the most dense traffic environments currently anticipated. The programming flexibility and computing capacity provided by the associative processor result in algorithms that should lower track drop and swap and improve tracing performance in general.

Table VI - Percent Processor Utilization-Two-Sensor Environment

Traffic Load (aircraft)	Associative arrays	Percent associative processor	Percent sequential processor (0.6 MIPS)
250	1	4.0	80
500	2	6.6	160
750	4	6.6	260
1000	5	6.7	350

REFERENCE

[1] H. N. Boyd. An Associative Processor Architecture for Air Traffic Control. Akron, Ohio, Goodyear Aerospace Corporation. 20 August 1974.

[a] The work reported in this paper was performed partially under Contract TSC-624 from the Transportation Systems Center, Department of Transportation. The authors wish to thank the contract monitor Vivian Hobbs for the many helpful suggestions made during the preparation of this paper.

ANALYSIS OF PARALLEL PROCESSING FOR AIR DEFENSE AND AIR TRAFFIC CONTROL FOR THAILAND

CHULIT MESSAJJEE and W. RICHARDS ADRION
Department of Electrical Engineering
Oregon State University
Corvallis, Oregon

SUMMARY

Thailand occupies a stragegic position within Southeast Asia. Bangkok Inter-national Airport has played the main role as both Commercial Air Traffic center and Military Air Traffic center for Thailand. To ensure her security and economic development, Thailand needs a high efficiency Air Defense and Air Traffic Control System.

The efficiency of a real time air traffic control system depends on the effici-ency of the command and control computer at its heart. A command and control com-puting system requires more functional capabilities than a conventional commercial or scientific system. Requirements include <u>Availability</u>: a function of hardware reliability and maintainability; <u>Adaptability</u>: the ability to be dynamically and automatically restructured to a working configuration responsive to the problem-mix enviornment; <u>Expandibility</u>: expansion without incurring the cost of providing more capability than as needed at one time.

One possible way to provide the functional requirements of a command and con-trol computing system is through parallel processing. This paper will emphasize three main areas. The first will include a brief survey of parallel processing re-search as it applies to the design of a command and control system. The second area will include the design and specification of a two level parallel architecture.

A multiprocessor architecture provides parallelism at the program or task level. Due to the advance of LSI technology, the cost consideration for further parallel-ism is attractive. A two level parallel processing system with an overall multi-processor architecture and with appropriate functional units within each processor to achieve parallelism at the instruction level, is proposed. A modular multi-processor system architecture can be expanded from an adequate basic configuration to meet increasing needs for computational power. The second level of parallelism within each processor consists of modular functional units and also satisfies the expandability criteria. At both levels the modularity provides the ability for reconfiguration yielding high system reliability and adaptability. The increased speed obtained through the second level of parallelism should meet the needs of a modern command and control system.

The final area discussed includes a simulation study and a cost benefit analysis of the proposed two level parallel system. The simulation study provides data to aid in various design decisions. The proposed system is then compared with existing systems and is shown to best meet the established criteria within the long range budget of the Royal Thai Air Force.

AUTHOR INDEX

REVIEWERS

Prof. J. L. Baer	University of Washington
Dr. Kenneth E. Batcher	Goodyear Aerospace Corp.
Prof. K. M. Chandy	University of Texas at Austin
Prof. I-Ngo Chen	University of Alberta
Dr. Wei-tih Cheng	International Business Machines
Mr. John A. Cornell	System Development Corp.
Dr. George R. Couranz	Raytheon Company
Dr. Robert Downs	Systems Control Inc.
Lt. Col. Philip H. Enslow, Jr.	European Research Office, U. S. Army
Prof. Domenico Ferrari	University of California, Berkeley
Prof. Caxton C. Foster	University of Massachusetts
Prof. Garth H. Foster	Syracuse University
Prof. Bernard Galler	University of Michigan
Prof. Oscar N. Garcia	University of South Florida
Prof. Mario J. Gonzalez	Northwestern University
Mr. Dale C. Gunderson	Honeywell, Inc.
Prof. Bill R. Hays	Brigham Young University
Mrs. Vivian J. Hobbs	Department of Transportation
Mr. C. P. Hsieh	Syracuse University
Mr. C. P. Hsu	Syracuse University
Prof. M. K. Hu	Syracuse University
Prof. Keki B. Irani	University of Michigan
Capt. Robert W. Johnson	Rome Air Development Center
Prof. Robert M. Keller	Princeton University
Capt. Alan R. Klayton	Rome Air Development Center
Prof. David Kuck	University of Illinois
Mr. Leslie Lamport	Massachusetts Computer Associates Inc.
Prof. Duncan H. Lawrie	University of Illinois
Prof. Gerald J. Lipovski	University of Florida
Prof. C. L. Liu	University of Illinois
Prof. John Marzolf	Syracuse University
Mr. David E. McIntyre	University of Illinois
Mr. W. C. Meilander	Goodyear Aerospace Corp.

Mr. James L. Previte	Rome Air Development Center
Prof. C. V. Ramamoorthy	University of California, Berkeley
Mr. Oskar A. Reimann	Rome Air Development Center
Dr. H. Gregory Schmitz	Honeywell, Inc.
Prof. Edward P. Stabler	Syracuse University
Mr. Armand Vito	Rome Air Development Center
Dr. R. Wishner	Systems Control Inc.
Mr. S. M. Yang	Syracuse University
Prof. Stephen S. Yau	Northwestern University
Prof. R. J. Zingg	Iowa State University